Title-page and Verso from the Dye Copy of Wayland's Edition of Lydgate

The
Mirror for Magistrates

EDITED *from* ORIGINAL TEXTS
in the
HUNTINGTON LIBRARY
by
LILY B. CAMPBELL

BARNES & NOBLE, INC. • NEW YORK
PUBLISHERS • BOOKSELLERS • SINCE 1873

Published in 1938 by the
Cambridge University Press

Reprinted by Barnes & Noble, Inc.
by Special Arrangement with the Cambridge University Press

First printing, 1960

PRINTED IN THE UNITED STATES OF AMERICA

Contents

v

CONTENTS

Illustrations

IN COLLOTYPE

LINE BLOCKS IN THE TEXT

vii

THE
MIRROR *for* MAGISTRATES

INTRODUCTION

INTRODUCTION

SINCE the publication of Warton's *History of English Poetry*,[1] some account of the *Mirror for Magistrates* has been included in almost every history of English literature.[2] Bibliographers have recognized as intriguing the complex history of its printing.[3] Sackville's induction has been decreed the best poem in English between Chaucer and Spenser and is duly incorporated in anthologies of the period. Historians of the drama have from time to time noted that the work contains tragedies which in the reign of Elizabeth were remade in dramatic form.[4] Yet the *Mirror* itself remains practically unknown and unread, its tragedies are classed as medieval, and literary criticism has dealt scarcely at all with its experiments in verse, its critical theory, its poetic vocabulary, its embodiment of a new conception of tragedy, and similar matters where darkness should be turned into day. The reason for the neglect of a work so generally recognized as important is not far to seek, however, for the early editions are extremely rare, and the only modern edition, that by Joseph Haslewood, was published in 1815 in an edition of one hundred and fifty copies.[5]

A number of years ago, while working in the Huntington Library on a study of Shakespearean tragedy, I discovered that the then unexplored library had, through the interest of its former librarian, Mr G. W.

[1] Thomas Warton, *A History of English Poetry*, III (London, 1781), 209–82. It should be noted, however, that Mrs Cooper's *Muses Library* (1737) and Capell's *Prolusions* (1760) had preceded Warton's interest in the work.

[2] See, for instance, W. J. Courthope, *A History of English Poetry* (London, 1897), II, 110–26, and J. W. Cunliffe, "*A Mirror for Magistrates*," in *The Cambridge History of English Poetry* (Cambridge, 1930), III, 192–200.

[3] For a recent study, see H. J. Byrom, "John Wayland—Printer, Scrivener, and Litigant," *The Library*, 4th Ser., XI, 312–49, esp. pp. 346–49.

[4] F. B. Fleay, "Excursus on *The Mirror for Magistrates*," in *A Biographical Chronicle of the English Drama, 1559–1642* (London, 1891), I, 17–20, and F. E. Schelling, *The English Chronicle Play* (New York, 1902), pp. 34–36 *et passim*.

[5] *Mirror for Magistrates*, ed. Joseph Haslewood (London, 1815). Sir Egerton Brydges was originally associated with the plan to publish the *Mirror*. For evidence, see *The British Bibliographer*, IV (London, 1814), Appendix, p. 260, and Haslewood, *Mirror*, I, xxxii.

Cole, built up a collection of the first editions of the various parts of the *Mirror* which was unique in its completeness. Proposing to complement my study of Shakespearean tragedy by a study of the history plays, I found that I could not get far without knowing the *Mirror for Magistrates*. The combination of circumstances resulted in a decision on the part of the Huntington Library authorities to publish from their copies a new edition of the *Mirror*, and I postponed my study of Shakespeare.

It was, of course, obvious that the first objective of a new edition of the *Mirror* must be to make available an accurate text. Since the publication of the *Mirror* was progressive and cumulative, it was decided to use as basic texts for this edition the first extant printed text of every part of the work, and to collate later editions of these parts with the original texts.

The second objective has been to bring together all available records concerning the publication of the *Mirror*, so that students may have easy access to the documents which must serve as evidence upon which to base any conclusions whatsoever as to its history and significance.

The third objective has been to suggest the approach which is necessary if the *Mirror* is to be comprehended at all, though the limitations of space render it, of course, impracticable to do more than make suggestions in the introduction.

The text which is here reproduced, then, is arranged in the way in which it was published. From the abortive first attempt to print the *Mirror* there remain only two variant title-pages and one leaf of text. These are reproduced in photographic facsimile. The text of the first edition, that of 1559, is printed in full. Following that is the text of the additions to the original *Mirror*, made in 1563, in 1578, and in 1587, with facsimiles of the title-pages of these and of intervening editions. Thus, the history of the various editions and the cumulative nature of the text should be apparent at once to the eye of anyone who consults this edition.[1]

[1] Haslewood used the 1587 edition as a basic text, collating earlier copies with it. The spelling of the variant readings makes it clear that he did not always collate from the edition indicated.

INTRODUCTION

What we know concerning the history of the printing of the *Mirror*
for Magistrates is for the most part gathered from the evidence offered
by the texts of the work itself, but, fortunately, both printer and editor
were explicit in their statements in the early editions.

In the Dyce Collection in the Victoria and Albert Museum in South
Kensington there is an unique title-page affixed to a copy of Wayland's
undated edition of Lydgate's translation of the old work of Boccaccio
on the fall of princes, though it was evidently not originally a part of
the volume with which it is now bound.[1] This title-page reads:

The fall of / Prynces. / Gathered by Iohn Bochas, / frõ the begynnyng
of the world / vntyll his time, translated / into English by Iohn / Lidgate
Monke / of Burye.

⟮Wherunto is added the / fall of al such as since that time / were
notable in Englande: / diligently collected out / of the Chronicles. / (?) /
¶LONDINI / In ædibus Johannis Waylandi. / Cum priuilegio per Sep= /
tennium.

On the reverse of the title leaf appears the address of "The Prynter
to the Reader," which I here transcribe in full:

WHile I attended the quenes highnes plesure in setting fourth an vni-
forme Primer to be vsed of her Subiectes, for the Printynge wherof it
pleased her highnes (which I besech god long to preserue) to geue me
a Priuilege vnder her letters Patentes, I thought it good to employ and
occupy my Print & seruauntes for that purpose prouided, about sum
necessary & profitable worke. And because that sundry gentlemen very
wel lerned, commended much the workes of Lydgate, chefely the fall
of Prynces, which he drew out of Bochas, whereof none were to be
got, after that I knew the Counsayles pleasure & aduice therein, I
determined to print it, & for that purpose caused the copy to be red
ouer & amended in dyuers places wher it was before eyther through the
wryters or Prynters fault corrupted: for verye fewe names were true
besydes muche matter dysplaced as to the conferrers may appere. Yet
is it not so throughly well corrected as I would haue wyshed it, by
meanes of lacke of certayne copies and authours which I could not get
by any meane⸴ And yet I doubt not (Gentle reader) but thou shalt
fynde it as clere as any other heretofore set fourth. To which I haue

---

[1] For an account of the discovery of this title-page, see W. A. Jackson, "Wayland's
Edition of *The Mirror for Magistrates*," *The Library*, 4th Ser., XIII, 155–7.

added a continuacion of that Argument, concernynge the chefe Prynces of thys Iland, penned by the best clearkes in such kinde of matters that be thys day lyuing, not vnworthy to be matched with maister Lydgate. Whose doynges do prayse theymselues, as to the indifferente reader shall appere. Wherefore I beseche the (good reader) to take in worthe these my endeuoures, and to iudge and reporte of them as they do deserue. And as I shall be encouraged herein, so wyll I procede to cause other notable woorkes to be penned and translated, whiche I trust shalbe to the weale of the whole countrey and to the singuler profit of euerye subiecte: And so Imprynte the Quenes hyghnes Primer, whan I shall get the copy, as shall content her and all the Realme.

The *Primer* was off the presses on June 4, 1555, and this title-page must, therefore, have been printed some time before that date, since clearly it was printed before the copy for the *Primer* had been received.

Wayland's edition of Lydgate's work, in a copy of which this title-page is inserted, has in all other copies a title-page which reads:

The trage= / dies, gathered by Ihon / Bochas, of all such Princes as / fell from theyr estates throughe / the mutability of Fortune since / the creacion of Adam, vntil his / time: wherin may be seen what / vices bring menne to destrucci= / on, wyth notable warninges / howe the like may be auoyded. / Translated into Englysh by / Iohn Lidgate, Monke / of Burye. / ¶ Imprinted at London, by / Iohn Wayland, at the signe / of the Sunne ouer against / the Conduite in Flete= / strete. / Cum priuilegio per Sep= / tennium.

Sometimes bound at the end of this volume is a second title-page, which reads:

A memorial / of suche Princes, as since / the tyme of King Richard / the seconde, haue been / vnfortunate in the / Realme of / England. / (?) / ¶ LONDINI / In ædibus Johannis Waylandi. / cum priuilegio per Sep= / tennium.

On the reverse of this additional title-page, Wayland's letters patent granted him by Queen Mary on October 24, 1553, for the printing of the *Primer* are printed in full. The letters patent begin in the usual fashion, "MAry by the grace of God, Quene of Englande Fraunce and Ireland, defendour of the faith, and in earth of the Churche of

Title-page from the Undated Wayland Edition of Lydgate

To entre the church þ shalt not com in sight:
Reason shal hold so iust the balaunce,
Tyl thou haue fully accomplished thy penaunce.

what I haue said take therof good hede,
For this time thou gettest no more of me,
withdraw thy hád innocentes blode to shede,
For any rancour or hasty cruelte:
Than beholde the great humilitie
Of the Emperour, and consydre wele
For it wolde haue perced a hert of stele.

With heed enclyned no word he spake again,
Syll in wepinge, wᵗ sobbyng vnstaunchable,
His purple wede bedewed as with rayne,
Returning home withchere most lamétable:
So continued in his purpose stable,
with al the tokens of faithfull repentaunce,
In lowly wyse accomplished hys penaunce.

He gaue ensample to princes euery chone
In case semblable that worke of wylfulnes
To execution to procede anon:
Sertain their errour & froward cursednes,
Desid their trespas meintein their wodnes,
Farre out of ioint if it shalbe declared,
To Theodosy for to be compared.

To the earth he mekely did obey,
Goddes knight did lowly his penaunce:
Where there be some that wronglyit warrei,
Holde ther again by froward maintenance,
Touching this mater set here in remébrāce,
As men deserue let euery wight take hede,
He that seeth al, quiteth them their mede.

Theodosius list nothyng abredge
To short the yard of his correction,
For loke the platte of rigour toke the edge,
Mekely to suffre his castygacion:
To bowe his chine was no rebellion,
By meke confession knowing his trespace,
By saynt Ambrose restored agayne to grace.

Uertuous princes may ensample take
Of Theodosy how they the lord shal queme,
He nat froward amendes for to make
His septre, his swerde, and his diademe
Subiect to Ambrose what him list deme,
Obeied al thing, and for his great offence
To holy churche to make recompence.

He knew that God was his souerayn Lorde,
To holy church how greatly he was bound:

Grutched neuer in wyll, thought nor word
Holy on Christ his empyre for to found,
where vertu reigneth vertu will ay rebound,
And for this prince obeyed to al vertue,
Hath now his mede aboue with Christ Iesu.

The.xviii.Chapter.

¶ Howe knightes and gentilmen, chase Ile
rike king: and the comnons chase Radagasus whyche ended in myschefe.

It is remembred of antiquite
In the Byble, after Noes floud
Howe by discent of his sonnes thre
Of their lineage plainly and theyr bloud,
All kinreddes dylated ben abrode,
And myne authour as it is made mynde,
Of Japhet seuen nacions he did finde.

The people fyrste of Gaule and Galathe,
Of Magoth, Gothes, and folke of Itayle,
Tyre, Cithia, with many a great countre,
Standing in Asia, as by thers ayle:
But in Europe stant Trace it is no fayle:
Gothes & Cithiens, of purpose did ordaine,
Among them selfe gouernours twayne.

Knyghtes and gentelmen chase Alericus,
To be their prince and haue the souerayntie,
Where the commons chase Radagasus,
The Gothes fyrst for greate suerte
With king Alerike entring the cyte,
Into Rome to finde there socour,
That time Honorius being their emperour

By graunt of whome al the hole countre
Gaue to Alerike, Gaule Spayn and Fraunce,
There to abide and thereto holde his fee,
Gothes spaynolses vnder his obeisaunce,
Takyng on hym al the gouernaunce:
Tyl Stillicon out of the Occident,
To mete with him was from Rome sent.

That time Honorius beyng Emperoure
Stillicon gan Alerike enchace,
With many a sturdy proud soudioure,
For to fight they chose haue their place:
But Aleryke stode so in the grace
Of fortune that by very might
Stillicon he put vnto the flyght.

Radagasus and Alerike of assent
Haue concluded, and full accorded be,
Thrugh Itaile for to make their went

To:

A memorial
of suche Princes, as since
the tyme of King Richard
the seconde, haue been
vnfortunate in the
Realme of
England.

¶LONDINI
In ædibus Johannis waylandi,
cum priuilegio per septennium.

ARISE,FOR
IT IS DAY

Additional Title-page sometimes bound with Wayland's Edition of Lydgate

The copy of the quenes Maiesties letters Patentes.

MAry by the grace of God, Quene of Englande Fraunce and Ireland, defendour of the faith, and in earth of the Churche of Englande, and also of Ireland, the supreme head. To al Printers of bookes, and bookesellers, and to al other our Officers, Minysters, and Subiectes these our letters patentes hearing or seeing, gretyng. Knowe ye that we of oure especial grace and meare mocion: haue geuen and graunted, and by these presentes doo geue and graunte full power, licence, auctoritie, and Priuilege vnto our welbeloued Subiect Jhon Wayland, Citezeyn and Seruenour of London. That he & his Assignes only, and none other person or persons shal fromhensfoorth haue auctoritie, & lybertie to prynt al and euery such vsual Primers or Manual of prayers by whatsoeuer other title ye same shal or may be called, which by vs our heyres, successours, or by our clergy by our assent shalbe auctorised, set furth, and deuysed for to be vsed of all our louing Subiectes thoroughout all our Realmes, and dompnyons, duringe the full tyme and terme of seuen yeares next ensuing the date of these our letters Patentes. And farther that it shal not be lawful for any maner of other person or persones of out said Subiectes, to Prynt or to procure to be imprinted, anye Prymers or Manuall of prayers by whatsoeuer title the same shall or may be called, or set furth, during the said tearme, nor any booke, or bookes, which the saide John Waylande or his Assignes at his or theyr costes and charges shall first Prynte, or set furth during the said terme of seuen yeares next ensuing the printing of the same booke or bookes, vpon payne of forfature, and confiscacion of thesame Prymers, Manuall of prayers, and bookes, to thuse of vs and oure successours. Wherfore we woll and commaunde all you our Printers, and other our Subiectes that ye nor any of you, do presume, procure, or attempt to print or setfurth any maner Prymers, Manuall of prayers, booke or bookes, which the said Jhon Wayland or his assignes shal first Print during the tyme of thys our Priuilege, and licence, vpon payne of forfature and confiscacion of the same Prymers, Manual of prayers, and bookes, as aforesaide. And as ye tendre oure pleasure, and wyl auoyde the contrarie. In witnes wherof we haue caused these our letters to be made patentes. Wytues our selfe at Westminster the foure and twentith daye of Octobre, in the fyrst yeare of our reigne.

Per bre̅ de priuato sigillo
et de data predicta.

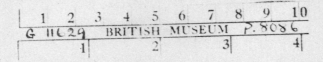

Verso of Additional Title-page sometimes bound with Wayland's Edition of Lydgate

Englande, and also of Ireland, the supreme head. To al Prynters of bookes, . . ."[1]

There are in the British Museum duplicates of a single leaf which by its format seems clearly to have belonged to this continuation of Wayland's Lydgate. This leaf bears the prose link occurring in the *Mirror* between the tragedies of Richard II and Owen Glendower, together with eighteen stanzas of the latter tragedy. Its running title is *A briefe memorial of | Vnfortunate Englysh princes.*[2]

[1] The first study of the history of the printing of the *Mirror* was made by Professor W. F. Trench, in *A Mirror for Magistrates: Its origin and influence* (privately printed, 1898). Upon this study all succeeding writers have based their accounts of the *Mirror*. Professor Trench did not know the Dyce title-page. He argued for 1554 as the date of the suppressed edition, on the ground that the letters patent here printed use the title of "supreme head," which would have been dropped after 1554. In accordance with his assumption that the *Mirror* editors were Protestants, he determined that the printer who instigated the work was Edward Whitchurch. For a further development of these ideas, see E. I. Feasey, "The Licensing of *The Mirror for Magistrates*," *The Library*, 4th Ser., III, 177–93. In an article on "The Suppressed Edition of *A Mirror for Magistrates*," published in *The Huntington Library Bulletin*, No. 6, pp. 1–16, I argued: (1) that the Dyce title-page gives new evidence for Wayland as the printer at whose instigation the work was undertaken, and that we are without evidence of any previous plans; (2) that Baldwin's own statement in the 1563 edition as to the date of the suppressed edition fixes it as four years before the first year of Elizabeth's reign—which would be 1555; (3) that the Dyce title-page and that on the verso of which the letters patent appeared were probably separated by a period of time; and (4) that the authors were more conspicuous as opportunists than as Protestants. Furthermore, I argued that the edict of June 13, 1555, suppressing Halle's chronicle was probably related to the suppression of the *Mirror* which was based upon it, and that the act of Parliament instanced by Professor Trench as evidence for the disuse of the title of "supreme head" did not forbid the use of the title, but specifically made legal all letters patent in which it had been used. There would, in any case, have been no reason for dropping the title of "defendour of the faith." (Acts of the Parliament held at Westminster, November 12–January 15, *Anno primo & secundo Phillipi and Mariae*, fol. xxii.) In the London *Times Literary Supplement* "Bibliographical Notes" for December 28, 1935, Mr Fitzroy Pyle objected to my conclusions. My answer was published under the same heading on February 29, 1936.

[2] In the London *Standard* for June 25, 1836, was printed an account of the rescue of these duplicates of the single leaf of the suppressed edition of the *Mirror* from a copy of Wayland's 1557 edition of *The Dyall of Princes*.

7

In the *Stationers' Register* is an entry for the year July 10, 1558, to July 10, 1559, which gives us our next bit of evidence in the history of the *Mirror*:[1]

Thomas marshe hathe lycense to prynte *The myrroure of maies-trates* . . . . vj^d

In accordance with this permission there appeared, bearing the date 1559, *A MYRROVRE For Magistrates* printed by Thomas Marshe. A four-page address "To the nobilitye and all other in office," signed by William Baldwin, explains the purpose of the book and also relates something of its early misadventures, for Baldwin says:

> The wurke was begun, & part of it printed .iiii. yeare agoe, but hyndred by the lord Chauncellour that then was, nevertheles, through the meanes of my lord Stafford, lately perused & licenced. Whan I first tooke it in hand, I had the helpe of many graunted, & offred of sum, but of few perfourmed, skarce of any: So that wher I entended to have continued it to Quene Maries time, I have ben faine to end it much sooner: yet so, that it may stande for a patarne, till the rest be ready: which with Gods grace (if I may have anye helpe) shall be shortly.[2]

Following this address, which is printed on leaves bearing the signatures ❡ .ii. and ❡ .iii., begins what is apparently the original work, for a new title heads the address of "William Baldwin to the Reader," and the regular signatures commence, the first leaf signed A.i., the second A.ii., etc. The title as here given is *A Briefe Memorial of sundrye Vnfortunate Englishe men*, a title that clearly recalls the running title found on the single leaf remaining from the early edition, *A briefe memorial of | Vnfortunate Englysh princes*. The address to the reader supplies information complementary to that on the reverse of the title-page of the Dyce copy:

> WHan the Printer had purposed with hym selfe to printe Lidgates booke of the fall of Princes, and had made priuye thereto, many both honourable and worshipfull, he was counsailed by dyuers of theim, to procure to haue the storye contynewed from where as Bochas lefte,

---

[1] Edward Arber, *A Transcript of the Registers of the Company of Stationers of London; 1554–1640 A.D.*, I (London, 1875), 97.

[2] See below, p. 11, for the 1563 version of this statement.

Unfortunate Englysh prynces.

Han master Chaloner had ended thys so eloquent a tragedy, and to al Prynces a right notable and wurthy instructiō, we paused having passed through a miserable time ful of piteous tragedies And seing the reyne of Henry the fourth ensued, a man more prosperous although not untrobled with warres both of outforth and inward enemies, we began to serch what Prynces were fallen therin, wherof the number was not small: and yet because theyr examples wer not muche to be noted for our purpose, we passed ouer all the Maskers (of whome King Richardes brother was chiefe) whiche wer all slaine and put to death for their traiterous attempt. And finding Owen Glendour next, one of fortunes owne whelpes, & the Percies his cōfederates, J thought them vnmete to be ouer passed, and therfore sayde thus to the silent cōpany: what my masters is euery man at once in a browne studye, hathe no man affeccion to any of these stories? you minde so much some other belike, that these do not moue you: And to say troth there is no speciall cause why they should. Howbeit Owen Glendour because he is a man of that countrey whence (as the welchmen beare me in hand) my Petigre is discended, althoughe he be but a slender prynce, yet rather then he should be forgotten, J wyll tell his tale for him vnder the priuilege of Martin Hundred: which Owen comming naked out of the wilde moūtaynes, like the Image of death in all poyntes (his dart onely excepted) so sore hath famine and hunger consumed him, lamenteth his infortune after this maner.

¶ Howe Owen Glendour seduced by false prophecies toke vpon hym to be prince of Wales, and was by Henry then prince thereof chased to the Mountaynes, where he miserably dyed for lacke of foode.

J pray the Baldwyn sith thou doest entend
To shewe the falles of suche as clymbe to hie,
Remember me, whose miserable ende
May teach a man hys vicious life to flie:
Oh fortune, fortune, out on her J crie,
My body and fame she hathe made leane & slender
For J poore wretch am sterued Owen Glendour.

A Welch man borne, and of a gentle blud,
But ill brought vp, wherby full well J fynd,
That neither byrth nor lynage make men good
Though it be true that Cat will after kynde:
Fleshe gendreth fleshe, so doth not soule or mynde,
They gender not, but fowly do degender
Whan men to vice from vertue them doo render.

Eche thing by nature tendeth to the same
Wherof it came, and is disposed lyke:

Down sinkes y mould, vp moūtes the fiery flam
With borne the hart, with hofe y horse doth stri
The Wolf doth spoyle, the suttle Fox doth prae,
And generally no fish, flesh, fowle, or plant
Doth any property that their dame had want.

But as for men, sith seuerally they haue
A mynd whose maners are by lerning made,
Good bringing vp alonly doth them saue
In vertuous dedes, which w their parentes fai
So that true gentry standeth in the trade
Of vertuous life, not in the fleshly line:
For blud is Brute, but Gentry is diuine.

Experience doth cause me thus to saye
And that the rather for my contreymen,
Which vaunt and boast them selues aboue the b
If they may strayne their stocke for worthy m
D.v.

The Recto and Verso of the Single Leaf extant from the Suppressed Edition of the Mirror for Magistrates

hic.: let be true, are they the better then,
nay rather the wurse if so they be not good,
for w if they stayne the bewty of their blood.

Howe would we mock the burdenbearing mule
If he would brag he wer an horses sunne,
To presse his pride (might nothing els him rule)
his boast to proue, no more but byd him runne:
The horse for swiftnes hath his glory wuthine,
so which the mule could neuer the more aspyre
Though he should proue that Pegas wer his sire.

Eche man may crake of that which is his own,
Our parentes vertues theirs are and not oures:
Who therfore will of noble kinde be knowen
Ought shine in vertue like hys auncestors,
Gentry consisteth not in Landes and Towers,
he is a Churle though all the world be his
he is Arthurs heyre, if that he liue a mys.

For vertuous life doth make a gentilman
Other possessour, all be he poore as Job,
yea though no name of Elders shew he can:
for profe take Merlin whose father was an hob,
But who so settes his mind to spoyle and rob,
Although he cum by due discent fro Brute,
It is a Chorle, vngentle, vile and brute.

Well thus dyd I for want of better wyt,
Because my parentes noughtly brought me vp:
forgettle men they sayd, was nought so fyt
is to at taste by bolde attemptes the cup
A Conquestes wyne, wherof I thought to sup:
and therfore bent my selfe to rob and ryue,
And whome I could of land and goodes depryue.

For Henry the fourth did the vsurpe the crowne,
Despoyled the king, with Mortymer the heyre:
For which his subiertes sought to put him downe.
And I while Fortune offered me so fayre,
Did what I might his honour to appeyre:
And toke on me to be the Prince of Wales,
Entisde therto by many of Merlyns tales.

For which, such Idle as wayte vpon the spoyle
from euery parte of Wales vnto me drew:
For liuyng youth vntaught in any toyle
Set to wage ill mischefe to ensue.
Through help of these so great my glory grew,
that I defyed my king through lofty hart,
And made sty warre on all that toke his part.

See I toke lord Reinold Grey of Rythen,
And him enforst my daughter to espouse:

And so vnraunsomed held him still, and I her
In Wygmore land through battayle rygorous
I caught the right heyre of the crowned house:
The Erle of march syr Edmond Mortymer,
And in a dongeon kept him prysoner.

Than all the marches longing vnto Wales
By Syberne west, I did inuade and burne:
Destroyed the townes in mountaynes & in vales
And with rich spoyles did homward safe returne
Was none so bold durst once agaynst me spurne.
Thus prosperously doth fortune forward call
Those whome the mindes to geue the sorest fall

Whan fame had brought these tidinges to the kin
(Although the Skoffes that vexed him right sore)
A mighty army agaynst me he did bring:
Wherof the French king being warned afore,
Who mortal hate agaynst king Henry bore,
To geue our foe, he quicklye to me sent
Twelue thousand Frenchmen armed to war & b

A part of them led by the Erle of Marche
Lord James of Burbon a valiaunt tried knigh
Withheld by winds to wales ward furth to marc
Toke land at Plymmouth priuelye on a night:
And whan he had doen all he durst or might
After that a magny of his men wer slayne
He stole to shyp and sayled home agayne.

Twelue thousand other in Mylford did ariue,
And came to me, than lying at Denbigh
With armed welche men thousandes double fiue:
With whome we went to Wurcester wel nigh,
And there encampte vs on a mounte on high,
To abyde the king, who shortly after came
And pitched his field on a hill hard by the same.

Ther eyght dayes long or hostes lay face to face
And neyther durst the others power assayle.
But they so stopt the passages the space
That vitayles coulde not come to our abayle,
Wher through costrained our hartes begō to fayle
So that the Frenchmen shrancke awey by night
And I with mine to the moūtaines toke our flight

The king pursued vs, greatly to his cost,
From Hilles to wuds, fro wuds to valey & playne
And by the way his men and stuf he lost.
And whan he see he gayned nought saue payne
He blewe retreat, and got him home agayne:
Then with my power I boldly came abrode
Taken in my cuntrey for a very God.

vnto this presente time, chiefly of suche as Fortune had dalyed with
here in this ylande: whiche might be as a myrrour for al men as well
noble as others, to shewe the slyppery deceytes of the waueryng lady,
and the due rewarde of all kinde of vices. Whiche aduyse lyked him
so well, that he required me to take paynes therin: but because it was
a matter passyng my wyt and skyll, and more thankles than gaineful
to meddle in, I refused vtterly to vndertake it, excepte I might haue
the helpe of suche, as in wyt were apte, in learning allowed, and in
iudgemente and estymacion able to wield and furnysh so weighty an
enterpryse, thinkyng euen so to shift my handes. But he earnest and
diligent in his affayres, procured Athlas to set vnder his shoulder: for
shortly after, dyuers learned men whose many giftes nede fewe praises,
consented to take vpon theym parte of the trauayle. And whan certayne
of theym to the numbre of seuen, were throughe a generall assent at
an apoynted time and place gathered together to deuyse therupon, I
resorted vnto them, bering with me the booke of Bochas, translated by
Dan Lidgate, for the better obseruacion of his order: whiche although
we lyked well, yet woulde it not cumlily serue, seynge that both Bochas
and Lidgate were dead, neyther were there any alyue that meddled
with lyke argument, to whom the vnfortunat might make their mone.

To make therfore a state mete for the matter, they al agreed that I
shoulde vsurpe Bochas rowme, and the wretched princes complayne
vnto me: and tooke vpon themselues euery man for his parte to be
sundrye personages, and in theyr behalfes to bewayle vnto me theyr
greuous chaunces, heuy destinies, & wofull misfortunes.

This doen, we opened suche bookes of Cronicles as we had there
present, and maister Ferrers, after he had founde where Bochas left,
whiche was about the ende of king Edwarde the thirdes raigne, to begin
the matter, sayde thus.

To these prefatory statements we owe our knowledge of the main facts
concerning the history of the *Mirror*. They show that Wayland proposed
to print a continuation of the work of Lydgate, that he went to Baldwin
in the matter but that Baldwin refused to undertake so thankless a job
without the help of able men, that the printer secured the promise of co-
operation from a group of gifted men, seven in number, who met to consider the enterprise. Baldwin was to become the interlocutor to whom
the unfortunate English princes might make their complaints, but the

9

prospective authors took upon themselves each to write "sundrye" complaints. That it was decided to begin at the reign of Richard II and to base the work upon the available English chronicles, we know also on Baldwin's authority. The words of Baldwin which I have already quoted from the preface dedicating the work to the nobility and all others in office, are those of the disillusioned editor who found the promised co-operation more generous in promise than in fulfilment.

Of the group[1] assembled at the planning of the *Mirror*, only William Baldwin and George Ferrers are identified in the 1559 text. However, the prose link found on the single extant leaf of the suppressed edition names "master Chaloner" as the author of the preceding tragedy of Richard II, and in the edition of 1578 the authorship of the tragedy of Owen Glendower is attributed to Thomas Phaer.

The prose links state explicitly that the work was based upon the histories compiled by Fabyan, Halle, and Sir Thomas More. Wherever the chronicles disagreed, the authors accepted the authority of Halle.[2]

The 1559 edition of the *Mirror* contained nineteen tragedies, but two last-minute omissions are indicated. The first is that of the tragedy which is indexed in *The Contentes and Table of the booke* as that of

⁋ Good duke Humfrey murdered, and   fol. xl.
    Elianor Cobham his wife banished.

The tragedy here indexed is not included in any of the known copies of this edition, and the prose link on Folio xxxix indicates a sudden change of plan, for Ferrers suggests that they leave affairs with which they have been concerned in the tragedy of James I, and return to their own story. He proposes, then:

How the cardinal Bewford maligneth the estate of good duke Humfrey the kinges vncle & protector of the realme, & by what driftes he first banisheth his wife from him. And lastly howe the good duke is murderously made away through conspiracy of Quene Margaret and other: both whose tragedies I entend at leasure to declare, for they be notable.

[1] For a discussion of the number and identity of those so assembled see Haslewood, I, xx, and Trench, pp. 66-70.
[2] See Prose Links 4 and 24, and Tragedy 15, ll. 15-35.

INTRODUCTION

In the usual fashion one of the group bids him, "Do so I pray you," but, instead of the tragedy's being inserted at this point, the speaker continues:

And I to be occupied the meane time, will shewe what I haue noted in the duke of Suffolkes doinges, one of the chiefest of duke Humfreyes destroyers, . . .

Likewise, Ferrers leads up to the introduction of the Duke of Somerset's tragedy on Folio xlviii, saying:

. . . let sum man els take the Booke, for I mynde to say sumwhat of this duke of Somerset.

But the tragedy is not printed, and, immediately after these words of Ferrers, a paragraph beginning "Whyle he was deuisyng thereon" is added to introduce the tragedy of Richard Plantagenet, Duke of York. A hand is used by the printer to call attention to this added paragraph.

Sometime within the year between July 22, 1562, and July 22, 1563, The Edition of 1563 Thomas Marshe was granted a new licence. The *Stationers' Register*[1] again records:

Recevyd of Thomas marshe of his lycense for pryntinge of *the ij*^{de} *parte of [the] myrror of magestrates* . . . . iiij^d

This new licence was undoubtedly necessary because Marshe was printing, in addition to the prose and verse of the original edition, *The seconde PARTE OF THE Mirrour for Magistrates*, containing a new preface by Baldwin, eight new tragedies, and the usual prose links.

This edition of 1563 reprinted the edition of 1559, with only such minor variations as are indicated in the collations of the text. It should be noted, however, that Baldwin made clearer his prefatory statement as to the date of the suppressed edition, when he revised his dedication to read:

The wurke was begun and parte of it prynted in Queene Maries tyme, but hyndred by the Lorde Chauncellour that then was, nevertheles, through the meanes of my lord Stafford, the fyrst parte was licenced, and imprynted the fyrst yeare of the raygne of this our most noble and vertuous Queene, and dedicate then to your honours wyth this Preface.

[1] Arber, I, 208.

11

Certain later statements of Baldwin in the revised preface are also of importance. First, there is an incidental allusion to the fact that, since he had published the first edition of the *Mirror*, he had been called "to an other trade of lyfe," which seems clearly, in the light of other evidence, to refer to his having become a minister. Second, Lord Stafford's continued interest in the project is indicated, and Baldwin, indeed, says that, "through his Lordshyppes earnest meanes," he has been brought to set forth another part of the *Mirror*. Third, Baldwin states that this new part contains as little of his own work as the first part did of other men's; and on the basis of this evidence many of the tragedies of the 1559 edition not specifically assigned therein to other writers are generally attributed to Baldwin.

The new part of the *Mirror* is linked by the prose narrative to the first part. Toward the close of the 1559 edition[1] Baldwin says:

. . . nyghte was so nere cum that we could not conveniently tary to-gether any longer: and therfore sayd mayster *Ferrers*: It is best my masters to staye here. For we be cum now to the ende of Edwarde the fowerth his raygne. For the last whom we finde vnfortunate therein, was this Duke of Clarens: In whose behalfe I commende much that which hath be noted. Let vs therfore for this time leave with him. And this daye seuen nightes hence, if your busines will so suffer, let vs all mete here together agayne. And you shal se that in the mean season I will not only deuise vppon this my selfe, but cause divers other of my acquayntauns, which can do very well, to helpe vs forwarde with the rest.

After the recital of Skelton's tragedy of Edward IV, therefore, Baldwin concludes the first edition with these words:

WHan this was sayde, every man tooke his leave of other and departed: And I the better to acquyte my charge, recorded and noted all such matters as they had wylled me.

The second part, added in the 1563 edition, opens with the account of the meeting so arranged:

THe tyme beynge cum, whan (according to our former appoynt-ment) we shuld meete together agayne to deuyse vpon the tragicall

[1] Prose 18.

affayres of our English Rulers, I with suche storyes as I had procured & prepared, went to the place wherein we had debated the former parte. There founde I the prynter and all the rest of our frendes and furderers assembled & tarying for vs, Save Maister Ferrers, . . .

When Ferrers did arrive, Baldwin tells us, he brought with him certain tragedies: that of the Duke of Somerset, which he had written himself, that of Jane Shore by Churchyard, and others which he left without recommendation. The printer gave to Baldwin the tragedy of Hastings by Dolman, and that of Richard III by Seager. Baldwin announced that he had himself secured Sackville's tragedy of the Duke of Buckingham and Cavyl's tragedy of the blacksmith. These six tragedies, together with that of Lord Rivers and Scales, and that of the poet Collingbourne, constitute the additions made in this second part and bring the total number of tragedies printed to twenty-seven. As Baldwin himself noted, Ferrers' tragedy of Somerset should have been printed in the first part. The tragedy of the blacksmith, added to the second part temporarily, belonged, he also advised, to the proposed third part of the *Mirror*, which was intended to bring the record down to the time of Queen Mary.

Certain indications in the prose links between the tragedies of this second part of the *Mirror* point to the conclusion that, like the part printed in 1559, it must have been ready for printing during the reign of Mary. In the first place, Baldwin says that "Lord Vaulx" was to have prepared the tragedy of the two young princes slain by Richard III, "but what he hath done therein I am not certayne, & therfore I let it passe til I knowe farder."[1] Since Lord Vaux died in 1556, this statement must have preceded that event unless Baldwin was speaking of a dead man, which does not seem likely. In the next place, the prose passage which closes the edition could obviously have been written only during the reign of Mary and Philip, for it was confessedly written to answer those who objected to the rule of the Queen because she was a woman and of the King because he was a foreigner. Churchyard's tragedy, the author records in his *Challenge*, was written during the reign of Edward VI.

[1] Prose 21.

The problem of dating the tragedies of this edition is, therefore, a very complicated one.[1]

It must be noted, too, that the first tragedy of the second part, that of Sir Anthony Woodville, clearly represents his ghost as speaking after the first part of the *Mirror* had been finished. Indeed, the opening stanzas are given over to a discussion of his complaint's not having been included in the first edition. He compares himself to the suitors who sit all year waiting for the prince, only to be told at last that he will hear no more suits:

> My case was such not many dayes agoe.
> For after brute had blased all abrode
> That Baldwyn through the ayd of other moe,
> Of fame or shame fallen prynces would vnloade
> Out from our graves we got without abode,
> And preaced forward with the rufull rout,
> That sought to have theyr doynges bulted out.

But after long waiting, just as he thought at last he was to have his say,

> The hearers paused, arose and went theyr way.

His first idea was that it was political exigency which had determined their action,

> But after I knew it only was a pause,
> Made purposely, most for the readers ease,
> Assure thée Baldwyn, highly it dyd me please.

He recognized the fact that readers easily grow weary, but he noted:

> And syth the playntes alredy by the pende,
> Are briefe ynough, the number also small,
> The tediousnes I thynk doeth none offend,
> Save such as have no lust to learne at all, . . .

The tragedy thus seems to corroborate Baldwin's statement that the second installment of tragedies was gathered a week later than the first, but it would take a better theologian than I am to decide whether the seven days are to be conceived as existing in time or eternity. At any rate, this first complaint of the second part must have been either written or revised after the first edition was finished.

[1] See also Trench, pp. 63–66, "Summary of Date-Indications."

The tragedy of Lord Hastings, the second of those added, is irregular in that the author, "maister Dolman," continues the complaint in his own person, in nine stanzas of description and moralizing.

Moreover, three tragedies which from a literary point of view are unmistakably superior to the rest make this edition of the *Mirror* notable: the tragedy of Collingbourne (probably Baldwin's), Churchyard's tragedy of Jane Shore, and Sackville's tragedy of Buckingham, with its great poetic induction. The eight tragedies added in this edition are, indeed, generally much longer than those of the first part and are definitely more literary in the amplification and adornment of their material.

The third edition, that of 1571, is indicated on the title-page as "Newly corrected and augmented."[1] The title is amended to read: The Edition of 1571

A MYRROVR for Magistrates, Wherein may be seene by examples passed in this realme, with howe greueous plagues, vyces are punished in great princes and magistrates, and how frayle and vnstable worldly prosperity is founde, where Fortune seemeth moste highly to fauour.

There is no new material in this edition, but the long preface to the second part (added in 1563) is omitted, the tragedies are rearranged (as will be seen in the table in Appendix B), Ferrers' tragedy of the Duke of Somerset being inserted between that of Jack Cade and that of Richard Plantagenet, Duke of York, and the tragedy of the blacksmith being placed before that of Jane Shore, so that the complaint of Jane Shore is now the concluding one of the volume. Signatures are affixed to certain tragedies.[2]

---

[1] Titles of such editions as are described in Appendix A, and titles of works other than the *Mirror*, are transcribed without any indication of their arrangement on the page. In footnotes and in casual references to books, I have ignored title-page eccentricities in type and capitalization, when no bibliographical purpose is served by retaining them.

[2] Signatures are affixed as follows: 1 G.F.; 2 Ca. (T.Ch., in 1578); 3 G.F.; 4 T.Ch.; 5 G.F.; 11 W.B.; 21 Maister D; 22 T.S.; 24 F.Seg.; 25 Tho.Churchyarde (Th.Churchyarde, in 1574, 1575, and 1578); 26 G.F.; 27 Maister Cauyll (Maister Cauille, in 1578). In the 1578 text, 6 is signed Th.Ph., and 28 and 29 are signed G.F. In the 1587 text, 30 is signed Iohn Higins; 32 is signed Frauncis Dingley (the name of the scribe in the Scots MS.); 33 is signed Tho.Churchyard. The signatures remain the same throughout subsequent texts (with variants noted), save in the case of 6, which appears in one edition only.

There are 168 folios in this edition, the colophon occurring on the verso of folio 168. Yet the preliminary "Table of the contents of this booke" indexes at the very end two additional tragedies:

28. The vnworthy death of ẙ worthy Duke Hũfrey of Glocester, protectour of England, contriued by false practises. Fol. 199.

29. The penance & exile of ẙ Lady Elyanor Cobham Duches of Glocester, for witchcraft and sorcery.

It will be remembered that the tragedy of "Good duke Humfrey murdered, and Elianor Cobham his wife banished" was indexed but did not appear in the 1559 edition, nor did the two tragedies here indexed in 1571 appear in the text. Apparently the "augmentation" referred to on the title-page related to the proposed addition of these tragedies. The collation of the text proves that the edition was, however, definitely "corrected." This correction seems to have been concerned, first, with bettering the poetry of the tragedies, and, secondly, with the revision of the historical mirror to adapt it to new situations.

The Editions of 1574 and 1575

With only minor variations in the text, and with no mention of the additional tragedies indexed in the edition of 1571, another edition of the original *Mirror* was published in 1574, under the title of *THE LAST parte of the Mirour for Magistrates.* The reason for the change of title was that Thomas Marshe in 1574 was also publishing a new work by John Higgins. To this new work Higgins gave the title:

THE FIRST / parte of the Mirour for / Magistrates, contai- / ning the falles of the first / infortunate Princes of / this lande: / From the comming of Brute / to the incarnation of our / sauiour and redemer / Iesu Christe.

Higgins adopted not only the title but also, with slight changes, the dedicatory heading used by Baldwin:

Loue and liue, / TO THE NOBILITIE / and all other in office, God graunt / the increase of wysedome, with all thinges / necessarie for preseruacion of their / estates, Amen.

He referred to Baldwin's "Epistle of the other volume of this booke," and in his address to the reader explained that he was induced to undertake his task by reading Baldwin's words:

INTRODUCTION

It were (sayth hee) a goodly and a notable matter to search and discourse our whole story from the beginninge of the inhabiting of this Isle.

While deferential in his attitude toward the writers of the older *Mirror*, Higgins clearly regarded his contribution as an additional volume of the same work. It should be noted that, whereas the 1574 edition of Baldwin's *Mirror* ends with a colophon, Higgins' work ends merely with his signature after a *Finis*. It is probable that the two volumes were to be sold either separately or bound as one.

In 1575 Thomas Marshe printed a new edition of Higgins' own *FIRST parte of the Mirour for Magistrates*, with which was sometimes bound a reissue of the 1574 edition of Baldwin's work, with a new setting of leaves ★ 1–4, and with the colophon deleted from X8r.

In 1578 there appeared another edition, "Newly corrected and en- The Edition larged," of *THE LAST part of the Mirour for Magistrates*, the most of 1578 interesting feature of which was the introduction of the long-promised tragedy, which now appeared in the index under the following entry:

11. Humphrey Plantagenet Duke of Glocester Protector of England by practyse of Enemies was broughte to confusion.   Fol. 40.

That this tragedy, announced in 1559 and again in 1571, should at last be published as it was originally intended, and that it should even begin on folio 40, as it was originally indexed to begin, indicates the surprising pertinacity with which the original plans for the *Mirror* were carried out some twenty years later. The prose link preceding this tragedy of Duke Humphrey was essentially the same as that which had appeared in the edition of 1559, save that the last sentence did not have to be distorted to permit the substitution of the tragedy of Somerset.

The edition of 1578, however, appeared also with a cancel,[1] folio 39 being cancelled and a new unfoliated gathering being substituted for the cancelled leaf (sig. F¶.), F¶.1. falling on folio 39. This gathering con-

---

[1] Full details concerning this cancel were given in my letter published in the London *Times Literary Supplement*, June 30, 1932, p. 480. According to W. C. Hazlitt (*Handbook to the . . . Literature of Great Britain* [London, 1867], p. 378), there was also an edition of the first part of the *Mirror* in 1578, but I have found no other record of a copy. The cancelled pages are reproduced on pages 429–30.

tained a new prose link, a new tragedy (not indexed), and a rewritten prose link to introduce the tragedy of Humfrey, Duke of Glocester. The new tragedy bore the title:

HOW DAME ELIANOR Cobham Duchesse of Glocester, for practising of witchcraft and Sorcery, suffred open penance, and after was banished the realme into the yle of Man.

The story of Elianor Cobham is, of course, part of the tragedy rehearsed by her husband, but, curiously, she and her husband in their two tragedies disagree not only in the lessons which they draw from their falls but also in matters of fact. The inference seems to be that these tragedies were not written to mirror the same contemporary situation, and that they may have been, and probably were, written at different times.[1] The 1559 edition had indexed one tragedy, the 1571 edition had indexed two separate tragedies, the edition of 1578 indexed and printed only one tragedy, but the second tragedy was nevertheless introduced in a cancel. Such is the problem which has puzzled every student of the *Mirror for Magistrates*. It was a problem considerably complicated by the fact that, until the discovery of a copy of the uncancelled edition of 1578 in the Huntington Library, the cancelled volume was the only one recorded by bibliographers.

It will be evident from the collation that the 1578 edition, besides being enlarged by new material, was also "newly corrected" with an enthusiasm for change which it is hard to explain. Very often neither rhyme nor reason is improved by the corrections introduced. It seems very doubtful whether the text was derived from the immediately preceding texts.

In 1578 there was also published another supplementary work, THE | *Seconde part of the* | *Mirrour for Ma-* | *gistrates, conteining the falles*| *of the infortunate Princes* | *of this Lande.* | *From the Conquest of* |*Caesar,* | *vnto the com-* | *myng of Duke Wil-* | *liam the Con-* | *querour.* | The twelve tragedies of this volume were all written by Thomas Blenerhasset.

---

[1] See my article, "Humphrey Duke of Gloucester and Elianor Cobham His Wife in the *Mirror for Magistrates*," *The Huntington Library Bulletin*, No. 5, pp. 119–55.

It was published, not by Marshe, but by Richard Webster, and it seems to have been less well known than either the original work or the volume added by Higgins.

In 1587 appeared an edition which fused the work of Higgins with the original *Mirror*, but disregarded that of Blenerhasset, the tragedies of the first and the last parts being numbered continuously and the foliation being likewise continuous. The original section of the *Mirror* was introduced by Baldwin's original preface to the reader. To this section, however, four new poems were added: a tragedy of Sir Nicholas Burdet, Churchyard's tragedy of Wolsey, and two poems taken from an old Scots manuscript rehearsing the tragedy of James IV of Scotland and the story of Flodden Field. A new prose link was substituted to introduce the tragedy of Jane Shore—a prose link that, like the one which introduces the tragedy of Wolsey, was designed to fight Churchyard's battle against Baldwin.

The introduction of these old Scots tragedies raises new problems concerning the date at which the additions were proposed. In the first place, the prose link introduced between them says that the manuscript "was pende aboue fifty yeares agone, or euen shortly after the death of the sayd King," which, since "the death of the sayd King" took place in 1513, would indicate not long after 1563 as the date of this conversation in the *Mirror*. Further, Holinshed printed in 1577 the letters exchanged between King James and King Henry which are here described in terms that would be inappropriate if they were already available in a printed text.[1] These Scots tragedies are still to be seen in Harleian MS. 2252 in the British Museum, amended frequently to the reading of the *Mirror* text in marginal notes presumably written by the one who revised the text for the *Mirror*.[2]

As I have said, this manuscript must have been in Holinshed's

---

[1] *The First volume of the Chronicles of England, Scotlande, and Irelande* (London, 1577), pp. 417–20 (misprinted 430). It should be noted that the history of Scotland is written "vnto the yeare, 1571," which may have been the date of compilation.

[2] For further details and a collation of the manuscript with the *Mirror* text, see Appendix D.

possession at some time, for he printed from it in his *Chronicles* in 1577. Moreover, the possible participation of Holinshed as a writer for the *Mirror* is further suggested by the continuation of the old prose link which had terminated the 1563 *Mirror*, added by way of introducing the new tragedy of Sir Nicholas Burdet:

> This talke thus being ended: I was willed my maisters (quoth I) by Maister Holinshed, to bring Sir *Nicholas Burdet* vnto you. Were you? (quoth they.) On his word we will heare what he sayes. Read it I pray you (quod one.)

If Holinshed sent the Burdet tragedy, and if the *Mirror* writers printed the Scots tragedies from the manuscript from which Holinshed printed the letters between King James of Scotland and King Henry of England, the question of date has again to be considered, for Holinshed is supposed to have died in 1580. It is quite possible that Higgins, deciding to print a *Mirror* which should include both the first and the last parts, incorporated a section, or sections, written earlier but never printed.

The 1587 edition was the last of the editions of the *Mirror* to follow the original plan. The edition of 1609–10, arranged by Richard Niccols, cannot be integrated in the tradition. Niccols played Colley Cibber to the *Mirror*.

The Authors of the *Mirror for Magistrates*

Baldwin wrote of the contributors to the *Mirror for Magistrates* as "dyuers learned men whose many giftes nede fewe praises." If we are to see the *Mirror* in true perspective, it is necessary to understand that it was written, not by literary hacks nor by minor writers of the day, but by learned men who were accepted as important figures in their own time. I have neither space nor inclination to recount here lives and adventures which can be read in the *Dictionary of National Biography* and in similar works.[1] But it is necessary to recapitulate the evidence in regard to three points.

[1] I have often included minor biographical details because they are unknown or significant, and I have often excluded major biographical facts because they are well known or are without special significance for the purposes of this study. I have, in general, paid scant heed to events which occurred in the life of the author after the date of his relation to the *Mirror*.

INTRODUCTION

First, the men who wrote the *Mirror* were adroit enough not to suffer from a change of rulers. So far as we know their history, most of them might have written their autobiographies as favourites under four reigns. Second, they were accepted as distinguished men of letters. Third, they had ample opportunity to know the affairs of the court and the nation. In other words, they had the necessary qualifications for writing a political *Mirror* which should take its place in literature: they kept their heads on their shoulders, which required a good deal of political wisdom; they had more skill in their craft of writing than did any other group to be listed during the reign of Mary; and they had intimate and first-hand acquaintance with the happenings they wrote about. Furthermore, so far as the authors of the various tragedies have been identified, they seem to have written about affairs which were, so to speak, in their own line.

With the object, therefore, of making the position of these writers clear, I shall attempt to point out, for each one, only the evidences of his political adroitness, his literary reputation, and his particular contribution to the *Mirror*.

It is inevitable that I begin with William Baldwin,[1] the man who was chosen by the printer to assume primary responsibility for the whole undertaking. He seems to have been best known for *A treatise of Moral Philosophy*, first published by Edward Whitchurch in 1547, and dedicated to Edward, Earl of Hertford, whose father, the Duke of Somerset, had just risen to be Protector. The *Short Title Catalogue* records eighteen editions of this work before 1640, and, to John Bale, Baldwin was an English Cato.[2]

William Baldwin

---

[1] The fullest surveys of Baldwin's life and work are W. F. Trench, "William Baldwin," *Modern Quarterly of Language and Literature*, I, 259 ff., and E. I. Feasey, "William Baldwin," *Modern Language Review*, xx, 407–18. Miss Feasey does not seem to have known of Professor Trench's earlier study.

[2] John Bale (*Scriptorum illustrium maioris Brytannie, . . . Catalogus* [Basle, 1557–59]) writes: "GUILHELMUS Baldevuyn, homo multarum, ut ex scriptis apparet, literarum & sapientae, qualis in ipso Catone relucebat, plurimarum rerum usu camparatae." Listing the four divisions of the *Moral Philosophy* as separate works, he adds: "*Comoedias etiam aliquot.*" (Pt. 2, p. 108.)

In 1549 was published *The Canticles or Balades of Salomon, phraselyke declared in Englysh Metres*, the colophon of which stated that it was "Imprinted at London by William Baldwin, seruaunt with Edwarde Whitchurche." This work was dedicated to the young King Edward VI, and the dedication serves to establish Baldwin as on the side of Calvin against Castellio in the bitter fight over the interpretation of The Song of Solomon. The work itself shows dexterity, and the variety of meters here attempted is astonishing when it is remembered that Tottel's *Songes and sonettes* was not to be published till eight years later.[1]

At the end of Edward's reign, we find Baldwin working upon plays and pastimes at court at the Christmas season of 1552–3 when George Ferrers was serving as Master of the King's Pastimes. Of a night's conversation after Ferrers, the King's divine, the King's astronomer, and Baldwin had gone to bed in the same chamber (Ferrers and Baldwin in bed and the other two on pallets on the floor), Baldwin has left an account in the preface to *Beware the Cat*, a work the significance of which is still an unsolved mystery, published during the reign of Elizabeth but apparently written in 1553.[2]

To Baldwin is also attributed *The Funeralles of King Edward the sixt*, which he says, in a preface to the 1560 edition, he could not succeed in

---

[1] The only appreciative consideration of Baldwin as poet is that of W. F. Trench in the article on Baldwin previously noted. It should be remembered that, on the verso of the title-page of Christopher Langton's *A very brefe treatise, ordrely declaring the pricipel partes of phisick*, which was published by Whitchurch in 1547, there was printed a poem by Baldwin, which is said to be the first sonnet printed in England. I have not seen the book.

[2] For an account of the entertainments prepared during this season, see: A. Feuillerat, *Documents Relating to the Revels at Court in the Time of King Edward VI and Queen Mary* (Louvain, 1914), pp. 89–114, 134–43 and notes; E. K. Chambers, *Mediaeval Stage* (Oxford, 1903), I, 405–7; F. Brie, "William Baldwin's 'Beware the Cat,'" *Anglia*, XIII, 303–50; F. Brie, "William Baldwin als Dramatiker," *Anglia*, XXXVIII, 157–72; the articles by Professor Trench and Miss Feasey, on William Baldwin, previously mentioned; and my note, "The Lost Play of *Aesop's Crow*," *Modern Language Notes*, XLIX, 454–57.

having published before that time. If it is his, he was much more than a poet-by-conviction.[1]

The choice of Baldwin—philosopher, poet, printer, playwright—as keystone for the undertaking can easily be accounted for. He had evidently worked with Whitchurch, the Protestant printer, but his revised edition of the *Moral Philosophy*, as well as the *Mirror*, was printed in the Catholic Wayland's shop during Mary's reign. Further, his play, *Love and Lyve*, was produced at court in the time of Mary, in 1556.[2] In 1556 Baldwin was also listed among the members of the "community" of the Stationers' Company, in the charter granted by Mary and Philip. It is

[1] This work, found among the papers of Sir John Cheke, was published in 1610 as his work, under the title *A Royall Elegie*. Further to confound confusion, Sir John Harington, in a statement hitherto unnoticed, attributed the poem to "Mr. Ferres" (*A Tract on the Succession to the Crown*, ed. C. R. Markham for the Roxburghe Club [1880], pp. 99–100). The *Funeralles* was edited for the Roxburghe Club in 1817; the *Royall Elegie* was reprinted as an appendix to W. Trollope's *History of the Royal Foundation of Christes Hospital* (London, 1834).

[2] Feuillerat, *op. cit.*, pp. 215–17, and *Historical MSS. Commission, Seventh Report* (London, 1879), p. 613. Baldwin's letter to Sir Thomas Cawarden speaks of the desire of the Inns of Court to put on his play. His popularity in the Inns of Court is also evidenced by the Preface of Jasper Heywood to his translation of *The Seconde Tragedie of Seneca entituled Thyestes*, printed in 1560. Deprecating himself as unworthy of the task which Seneca lays upon him, the author suggests:

> goe where Mineruaes men,
> And finest witts doe swarme: whome she
>   hath taught to passe with pen.
> In Lyncolnes Inne and Temples twayne,
>   Grayes Inne and other mo,
>
> . . . .
>
> . . . suche yong men three,
>   as weene thou mightst agayne,
> To be begotte as Pallas was,
>   of myghtie Ioue his brayne.
> There heare thou shalt a great reporte,
>   of Baldwyns worthie name,
> Whose Myrrour dothe of Magistrates,
>   proclayme eternall fame.

reasonable to suppose that he was working with Wayland. In 1559 Elizabeth confirmed the grant to the Stationers' Company, and exactly the same names of the members of the community were listed, so that Baldwin was still numbered among the printers.[1] The first edition of the *Mirror* was printed in 1559, and *The Funeralles of King Edward the sixt* in 1560, by Thomas Marshe. I therefore suspect Baldwin to have been associated with Marshe at this period. From Whitchurch to Wayland to Marshe, the changing political scene shifted favours. We know from his own statement that, by 1563, Baldwin had been called to another way of life, though he was still responsible for the *Mirror*. On the authority of the ghost of Jane Shore, we know he was "a Minister and a Preacher."[2]

Baldwin's contributions among the *Mirror* tragedies are not clearly identified. In the revised dedication of the 1563 edition he said:

I have nowe also set furth an other parte, conteynyng as litle of myne owne, as the fyrst part doth of other mens.

On the evidence of this assertion it has been easy to assign to him all tragedies not claimed by others, but only the tragedies of Richard, Earl of Cambridge (8), Richard, Duke of York (13), and George,

---

[1] Arber, I, xxvii–xxxiii.

[2] According to Anthony à Wood (*Athenae Oxonienses* [London, 1813], I, col. 341), a William Baldwin supplicated for a degree in 1532. There was a William Baldwin among those ordained deacon on January 14, 1559/60, in pursuance of Bishop Grindal's plan "to furnish the Church with men of learning, honesty, and good religion." (John Strype, *The Life and Acts of . . . Edmund Grindal* [Oxford, 1821], p. 53.) Miss Feasey further identifies our author as the William Baldwin who became Vicar of Tortington in Sussex and in 1561, Rector of St Michael le Quern in Cheapside. She thinks he died in 1563. In view of Heywood's linking of Baldwin's name with the Inns of Court, it should be noted also that there was at the time of his writing a William Baldwin resident in the Middle Temple, to which he was admitted May 20, 1557, being then described as "son and heir of John Baldwin, deceased, of Byfelde, Northants." Lord Stafford was also a member of the Middle Temple at this time. William Baldwin still maintained his chambers in the Temple in 1577, and the records show him to have had a continuous legal career to that date. (C. H. Hopwood, *Middle Temple Records: Minutes of Parliament* [London, 1904], I, 110 *et passim*.)

Duke of Clarence (18), are consistently attributed to him in the *Mirror* texts.[1]

Among the "dyuers learned men," George Ferrers was certainly the one who gave most assistance to Baldwin.[2] A man of good family, he seems to have been in turn at Oxford and at Lincoln's Inn, and in 1534 he saw his first work published, a translation of *Magna Carta* into English. He rose to place through Cromwell, according to Leland,[3] and in 1538 "young Ferys" was listed, along with Thomas Chaloner and others, "Among the Gentlemen most mete to be daily waiters upon my said lord and allowed in his house." In 1539 his name occurs among "The names of the spears" in "The New Body Guard," and in 1539 and 1540 he was listed among the "Squires" appointed to receive Anne of Cleves.[4]

Thus, George Ferrers rose with Cromwell, but he was adroit enough not to fall with him, for he remained after Cromwell's fall as page of the chamber in the King's Household. In 1542 Ferrers, a member of

(margin note: George Ferrers)

[1] See: Haslewood's ed., I, xix, xxii; Trench, *A Mirror for Magistrates*, pp. 66–70; and Henrietta C. Bartlett, "The Mirror for Magistrates," *The Library*, 3rd Ser., III, 22–32.

[2] The best account of the life of George Ferrers is that in *The Victoria History of the Counties of England: Hertfordshire*, II (London, 1908), 189–90. Since no adequate biography is available to students of literature, I have tried to indicate new sources of information.

[3] John Leland ("Ad Georgium Ferrarium," in *Principium, Ac illustrium aliquot & eruditiorum in Anglia virorum, Encomia, Trophaea, Genethliaca, & Epithalamia* [London, 1589], p. 99) hails Ferrers as one who is bringing glory again to the ancient city of Verulam (St Albans). He speaks of Ferrers' work on the laws of his country, of his bringing back the ancient pleading at the bar, of the shrewd Cromwell's claiming him as his own, of his life at court after Cromwell's fall, of his prowess against the Scotch and French. He urges him to go on as he has begun and "nostro carmine maior eris." Ferrers' presence in Lincoln's Inn is attested by an amusing entry in the *Records of the Society of Lincoln's Inn* (*Black Books*, I [n.p., 1897], 240) for November 13, 1534, which orders Messrs Norwood, Ferrers, and others to put away their lackeys or else to be put out of commons.

[4] For references to Ferrers (whose name is variously spelled), see *Letters and Papers of Henry VIII* (London), XIII, Pt. 2 (1893), p. 497; XIV, Pt. 2 (1895), pp. 202, 345; XV (1896), 6.

Parliament and also a member of the King's Household, was the unwitting occasion of a dispute between king and Parliament when he was arrested for debt, thereby winning prominent mention in English legal history.[1] Probably his marriage in 1541 to Elizabeth, widow and executrix of the estate of Humphrey Bourchier, illegitimate son of Lord Berners and cousin to Sir Francis Bryan, furthered his fortunes.[2] Her will was probated in 1547,[3] but she must have died some time before, since a licence for the marriage of George Ferrers "of the King's household" and "Jane Sowthtrote" of St Albans is recorded as of March 5, 1545/6.[4]

At the death of Henry VIII, Ferrers was heir to 100 marks under his will, but afterwards Ferrers served the new Protector, Edward, Duke of Somerset, as is evidenced by Patten's account of him as "a gentleman of my lord Protectors & one of the commissioners of the cariages in this army," in his description of the English punitive

[1] *Letters and Papers of Henry VIII*, XVII (1900), 107; K. Pickthorn, *Early Tudor Government: Henry VIII* (Cambridge, 1934), pp. 465–72; and the chronicles of Halle, Grafton, and Holinshed.

[2] Legal action by George Ferrers and his wife Elizabeth, "executrix of Humphrey Bourgchier, esquire," is recorded in *Public Record Office Lists and Indexes, No. 51: List of Early Chancery Proceedings*, VIII (London, 1929), 82 (File 983, No. 15). Ferrers alone appeared to pay Humphrey's debt to the King, June 24, 1546. (See *Letters and Papers of Henry VIII*, XXI, Pt. 1 [London, 1908], p. 631.) That Ferrers continued in the King's service is attested by his inclusion, in the lists "For the invasion of France," among those of "The Privy Chamber," where he is entered "Ferres 2 billmen." (*Ibid.*, XIX, Pt. 1 [London, 1903], p. 164.)

[3] J. C. C. Smith, comp., *Index of Wills Proved in the Prerogative Court of Canterbury*, I (British Record Society; London, 1893), 199: "1547 Ferrers *formerly* Burgchier, Elizabeth, High Offeley, etc., Stafford 45 Alen."

[4] J. L. Chester and G. J. Armytage, *Allegations for Marriage Licences Issued from the Faculty Office of the Archbishop of Canterbury at London, 1543 to 1869* (London, 1886), p. 7. This is the marriage noted in Metcalfe's *Visitations of Hertfordshire* (Harleian Society Publications, XXII [1886], 142), where the bride's name is given as "Jane, da. of John Southcote." Of this marriage (according to Metcalfe) was born Julius, heir to his father's estates; and probably also Richard, for the *Middle Temple Records* (I [London, 1907], 186) lists among the admissions for April 29, 1572: "Richard Ferrers, late of Davids Inne, gent., second son of George Ferrers of Markate, Herts. Esq., generally; fine .30s. Bound with his father."

expedition into Scotland in the first year of the young King's reign.[1] On July 29, 1548, Ferrers seems to have reaped his reward for having been the servant of Henry VIII and the husband of Elizabeth Bourchier, for he was given the extensive properties formerly held under lease by Humphrey Bourchier,[2] the grants being made

for good service by the king's servant George Ferrers *alias* George *de Ferrariis*, esquire, to the king's father and himself; and for 325*l*. 8*s*. 4*d*.; and in fulfilment of the will of the king's father and a tripartite indenture between the king of the first part, the Protector and the other executors (named) of Henry VIII.'s will of the second part and the said George Ferrers of the third part, dated 14 Oct. 1 Edward VI.[3]

When the Protector's star in its turn had set, and the fallen Duke was in prison at the Christmastide of 1551–2 awaiting execution, Ferrers was again on the side of the angels, as a passage from Grafton's *Chronicle at Large* testifies:

The Duke beyng condempned as is aforesayd, the people spake diuersly and murmored against the Duke of Northumberlande, and against some other of the Lordes for the condempnation of the sayd Duke, and also as the common fame went, the kinges maiestie tooke it not in good part: wherfore aswell to remooue fond talke out of mennes mouthes, as also to recreate and refreshe the troubled spirites of the yong king, it was deuised that the feast of Christes Natiuitie, commonly called Christmas then at hand, should be solemply kept at Greenewiche with open houshold, and franke resorte to the Court,

---

[1] *The Expedicion into Scotlãde of the most woorthely fortunate prince Edward, Duke of Soomerset, vncle vnto our most noble souereign lord ỹ kĩges Maiestie Edward the .VI. Goouernour of hys hyghnes persone, and Protectour of hys graces Realmes, dominions & and subiectes: made in the first yere of his Maiesties most prosperous reign, and set out by way of diarie, by W. Patten Londoner* (London, 1548), sig. D.v., recto.

[2] A clear and concise account of the grants to Humphrey Bourchier, and of his financial difficulties due to Sir Francis Bryan, is given in the *Victoria History: Hertfordshire*, II, 189. The complete list of his holdings is recorded in the *Calendar of the Patent Rolls, Edward VI, Vol. 1, 1547–1548* (London, 1924), p. 314.

[3] The complete record of the estates transferred to Ferrers in 1548 is given in *ibid.*, pp. 314–16. It is interesting to note that Croxley Manor was given, at the Dissolution in 1538, to William Baldwin, under a lease for forty-four years. There is no indication which William is meant. (*Victoria History: Hertfordshire*, II, 378.)

(which is called keping of the Hall,) what time of olde ordinarye course, there is always one appoynted to make sporte in the Courte, called commonly Lorde of Misrule, whose office is not vnknowne to such as haue bene brought vp in Noblemens houses, and among great house keepers, which vse liberall feasting in that season. There was therefore by order of the counsaile a Gentleman both wise and learned, whose name was George Ferrers appoynted to that office for this yere: who beyng of better calling then commonly his predecessors had bene before, receyued all his commissions and warrauntes by the name of the Maister of the kinges pastimes. Which Gentleman so well supplyed his office, both in shew of sundry sightes and deuises of rare inuention, and in act of diuers enterludes and matters of pastime, played by persons, as not onely satisfied the common sorte, but also were very well liked and allowed by the counsayle and other of skill in the like pastimes: But best of al by the yong king himselfe, as appered by his princely liberalitie in rewarding that seruice.

This Christmas being thus passed and spent with much mirth and pastime, wherewith the mindes and eares of murmorers were meetely well appeased, according to a former determination as the sequele shewed, it was thought now good to proceede to the execution of the iudgement geuen against the Duke of Somerset touching his conuiction and attaynder of the felony afore mencioned.[1]

So well had Ferrers performed his office, that he was recalled for the next Christmas season, and further reward came in a new grant:

For war services both in France under Henry VIII. and in Scotland under the king, and for offices performed at home in the king's Court meriting a perpetual testimony of the royal munificence.

Grant to the king's servant George Ferrers *alias* George de Ferrariis, esquire, of the lordship and manor of Flampsted, Herts, parcel of the lands called Warwickes Londes.[2]

For this new grant Ferrers was to pay a yearly fee of a fortieth part of a knight's fee, 20 marks. That he won favour with the boy King is also evidenced by a manuscript account of the expedition into Scotland,

[1] Richard Grafton, *A Chronicle at Large*, II (London, 1568), 1317. For the account of Ferrers' activities at court during the Christmas seasons of 1551/2 and 1552/3, see also Feuillerat, *op. cit.*, pp. 56–63, 89–114, 134–43, and the notes thereon.

[2] *Calendar of the Patent Rolls, Edward VI, Vol. IV, 1550–1553* (London, 1926), p. 378.

addressed by the author, J. Berteville, to the King, whereon is an inscription which reads, "LIBER GEORGII FERRERS EX DONO REGIS EDOUARDI."[1]

When Edward VI was dead, when the nine-day reign of Jane Grey was over, and the ambitious Duke of Northumberland had gone to his death, cringing for his life, Ferrers was again aiding the winning side by assisting to put down Wyatt's Rebellion. Underhill recorded:

When I came to the courte gate, ther I mett with mr. Clement Throngemartone, and George Feris, tindynge ther lynges to go to London. Mr. Throngemartone was cume post frome Coventry, and hadde byne with the quene to declare unto her the takynge off the duke off Suffoke. Mr. Feris was sentt from the councelle unto the lorde William Hawwarde, who hadde the charge off the whache att London bryge. As we wentt, for thatt they weare bothe my frendes, and protestanes, I tolde them my goode happe, . . .

Trying to enter the city at Ludgate, the trio were challenged, and Ferrers answered:

"I am Ferris, that was lorde off misrule with kynge Edwarde, and am sentt from the councelle unto my lorde William, . . . uppon weyghtie affayres; . . ."[2]

In 1555 Ferrers was loyally acting as informant to the Privy Council concerning the machinations of the young Princess Elizabeth, who was said to have been engaged with Dr John Dee and others in casting the nativity of King Philip, Queen Mary, and Elizabeth herself. It was suspected that Elizabeth was using Dr Dee to destroy the King and Queen by means of enchantments, and all concerned suffered long detention and severe questioning. In a letter to Edward Courtenay, Thomas Martyn wrote that Dee evidently had a familiar spirit, since "Ferys, one of their accusers, had, immediately upon the accusation,

---

[1] *Recit de l'expedition en Ecosse l'an. M.D.XLVI. et de la battayle de Muscleburgh par le sieur Berteville au Roy Edouard VI* (Bannatyne Club; 1825).

[2] "Autobiographical Anecdotes of Edward Underhill, One of the Band of Gentlemen Pensioners," in *Narratives of the Days of the Reformation*, ed. J. G. Nichols (Camden Society; 1859), pp. 163–65.

both his children strucken, the one with present death, the other with blindness."[1] According to the *Return of Members of Parliament*, Ferrers was elected in 1544/5, 1552/3, 1554, and 1555.

Of Ferrers' activities after Elizabeth's accession we know little. He was again married,[2] he held the office of escheator for the counties of Essex and Hertford in 1567, he was concerned in 1571 in the attempt to secure the English throne to Mary Stuart.[3] But he contributed to the entertainment of Queen Elizabeth at Kenilworth Castle in 1575.[4] And, of most significance, he was, according to Stow, the author of the section of Grafton's chronicle which recorded the events of Queen Mary's reign.[5]

According to Sir Sidney Lee, the "administration of his effects was granted by the prerogative court of Canterbury 18 May 1579," but I can find no evidence in the published records of the court.

It is a curious fact that Ferrers' first name seems not to have been familiar to those about him. He is referred to as "young Ferys" in

[1] For a full account of this incident and its possible mirroring in the tragedy of Elianor Cobham, see my article on "Humphrey Duke of Gloucester and Elianor Cobham His Wife in the *Mirror for Magistrates*," *loc. cit.* Professor Kittredge apparently misunderstood the incident, thinking that Dee was called before the Privy Council on an accusation, by "George Ferrys," of having blinded one child by magic and killed another. (G. L. Kittredge, *Witchcraft in Old and New England* [Cambridge, Mass., 1928], pp. 69, 254.)

[2] The licence is recorded as of November 26, 1569, for his marriage to "Margaret Prestone, Widow, of St Albans, Herts." See J. L. Chester and G. J. Armytage, *Allegations for Marriage Licences Issued by the Bishop of London, 1520–1610* (London, 1887), I, 44. This wife, his third, survived him, married a Thomas Hall after his death, and continued to hold the manor of St Agnels settled upon her by Ferrers in 1577. (*Victoria History: Hertfordshire*, II, 366.)

[3] William Murdin, *A Collection of State Papers relating to Affairs in the Reign of Queen Elizabeth* ("Burghley Papers"; London, 1759), pp. 20, 30, 43, 51.

[4] J. Nichols, *The Progresses and Public Processions of Queen Elizabeth* (London, 1788), I, 702–3. Robert Withington, *English Pageantry* (Cambridge, Mass., 1920), I, 218, n. 6, refers to further accounts of Ferrers' later work of this sort, but I have not been able to locate the reference.

[5] John Stow, *Annales, or, A Generall Chronicle of England. . . . Continued . . . By Edmund Howes* (London, 1631), p. 632.

Cromwell's records, King Henry's will bequeaths a sum to "——Ferrys," and Puttenham and Meres both praise the work of "Edward Ferrys" (or "Ferris"), though the person indicated is clearly George Ferrers.[1]

The evidence of the text makes Ferrers the author of the tragedies of Tresilian (1) and Thomas of Woodstock (3), together with the three tragedies which for one reason or another were "stayed": Edmund, Duke of Somerset (26), Elianor Cobham (28), and Humphrey, Duke of Gloucester (29).

Thomas Chaloner, whose authorship of the tragedy of Richard II is Thomas attested by the text of the only remaining leaf of the 1555 edition of the Chaloner *Mirror*, was, like Ferrers, a not inconspicuous servant of four rulers of England, of which service the records of the State Papers give ample proof.[2] In 1538, as I have said before, he was, with Ferrers, listed among the gentlemen favoured by Cromwell. He accompanied Sir Henry Knevet as ambassador to Charles V and went with the Emperor on his African expedition, was made Clerk of the Privy Council on his return, and wrote a great Latin poem, *In Laudem Henrici Octavi*.[3] He was returned to Parliament in 1544/5 and 1547. Like Ferrers, furthermore, he was of service to the Protector during the reign of Edward VI, and was knighted by the Duke himself after the battle of Musselborough in 1547. At the Christmas season of 1551-2, he was working with Ferrers, apparently as his assistant, in making the young King forget the plight of his uncle, the Duke of Somerset.[4] Under Mary, however, he continued to serve England in negotiations with Scotland over the borderland and similar questions. When Elizabeth came to the throne,

[1] The 1813 edition of the *Athenae Oxonienses* (1, cols. 340, 443–46) corrects the mistake of identification in regard to Edward and George Ferrers. Sir Sidney Lee gave considerable attention to the subject in his article on Ferrers in the *Dictionary of National Biography*.

[2] The authoritative source for our knowledge of Chaloner's life is the biographical account, by William Malim, prefixed to the posthumous edition of his great work, *De Rep. Anglorum Instauranda Libri Decem* (London, 1579). In general, accounts of his life are fairly accurate, except that his son's activities are sometimes attributed to him.

[3] Published in the ed. of his work by William Malim, noted above.

[4] Feuillerat, *op. cit.*, pp. 60, 61.

he went, in turn, to Emperor Ferdinand to draw him from the French alliance, to Philip II in Brussels to conciliate him, and to Spain as ambassador. When he died, William Cecil was chief mourner, and to Cecil, William Malim dedicated the posthumous edition of Chaloner's works published in 1579.

When, in 1553, John Whitals (or Withals) dedicated to Chaloner *A short Dictionarie for Yonge Beginners*, he described him as "beyng worthily esteemed of all men, to be as well learned wyse and vertuous, as any gentleman in this realme."[1] Peacham held him up as a model of the ideal of nobility set forth in *The Compleat Gentleman*.[2] Indeed, so numerous are the tributes to his many excellences that it is impossible to record them here. But it must be noted that, in 1543, he had published a translation of *A Book of the Office of Servants*, in 1544 a translation of Sir John Cheke's translation of *An Homilie of Saint John Chrysostome*, and, in 1549, a translation of Erasmus' *Praise of Folie*. He must be ranked, therefore, in 1555, as a man of importance in the service of both Mars and the Muses (to use Camden's phrase), even though his great Latin poem, *De Republica Instauranda*, was not published until after his death, which occurred in 1565. And it should be mentioned that, among his works published with this Latin poem, was an epitaph on Thomas Phaer.

Thomas Phaer

Thomas Phaer, the last of the four whose names have been associated definitely with the tragedies of the first edition of the *Mirror*, made a will in 1558, which included a legacy of friendship:

my body to be bured in the p'ishe churche of Kilgerran, wth a stone vpon my grave, in man' of a marble stone, with suche Scripture thereupon, graven in brasse, as shalbe devised by my frynd Mr. George fferers.[3]

The evidence of this "Scripture" still speaks of the interlocking friendships of the *Mirror*, as does the epitaph written for Phaer by Thomas

[1] Quoted from the edition of 1556.

[2] Henry Peacham, *The Compleat Gentleman* (London, 1622), pp. 93–94.

[3] Peter Cunningham, "The Will of Thomas Phaer, the poet and translator from Virgil," *The Shakespeare Society's Papers*, IV (London, 1849), 1–5. Cunningham also quotes an interesting epitaph written by Barnabe Googe on Phaer, comparing him with earlier translators of Virgil.

Chaloner, of which I have spoken. Furthermore, Phaer must already have been known to Baldwin through Whitchurch, for by 1555 Whitchurch had published five editions of Phaer's translation of Goeurot's great medical work, *The Regiment of Lyfe* (to which he had added a treatise on the plague and *A Boke of Children*), as well as the original edition of *The boke of Precedentes, in maner of a Register* (the later editions of which were published by other printers), with a preface by Phaer and probably altogether of his writing. These two popular and important works had given prominence to Phaer as physician and as lawyer.

However, the work by which Phaer is generally known today is his translation of the *Aeneid*, the first seven books of which were published in 1558. The work was dedicated to Queen Mary in humble words of adulation, and Phaer described himself as "sollicitour to the king and quenes maiesties, attending their honorable counsaile in the Marchies of Wales." He calls Mary "moste famous and excellent princesse," his "moste souerain good Ladie, and onely redoughted maistresse," and avows, "I shall praie almightie god for your pre-eminente estate, to encreas in all vertue, honor, prosperitie, and quiet." Moreover, Phaer says that he was preferred to Mary's service by William, Marquis of Winchester, whom he calls "my firste brynger vp and patrone."

Since Phaer professed himself desirous of rendering an account to the Queen of how he spent his vacations, he has added at the end of each book of Virgil a statement of the time spent in its translation. The first book is subscribed:

Per Thomam Phaer .xxv. Maij finitum. Inchoatum .ix. eiusdem .1555. in foresta Kilgerran Southwallie. Opus vndecim dierum.

The second is subscribed:

Per Thomam Phaer in foresta Kilgerran mense Iulij. Anno .1555. Opus viginti dierum.

The third, dated October 10, 1555, is recorded as the work of twenty days; the fourth, dated April 9, 1556, as the work of fifteen days; etc. It is well to note, too, that Phaer was returned to Parliament from Cardigan County, Wales, in 1555, 1557/8, and 1558/9.

The evidence of these facts concerning Phaer's residence in Wales is of importance in considering the problem of his authorship of the tragedy of Owen Glendower in the *Mirror*, concerning which various editions give apparently inconsistent accounts. The prose link which introduces this tragedy in the 1555 edition represents Baldwin as saying:

Howbeit Owen Glendour because he is a man of that countrey whence (as the welchmen beare me in hand) my Petigre is discended, althoughe he be but a slender prince, yet rather then he should be forgotten, I wyll tell his tale for him vnder the priuilege of Martin Hundred:

In the 1559 edition, this passage reads:

Howbeit Owen Glendour because he was one of fortunes darlinges, rather than he should be forgotten, I wil tel his tale for him vnder the priuilege of Martine Hundred:

Reference to the Welsh descent of the author is omitted, as Professor Trench long ago pointed out, and Baldwin seems to claim the authorship. But in the edition of 1578 the last phrase of the text, as quoted from the 1559 edition, becomes:

I wil pray Maister Phaer who of late hath placed hymselfe in that country, & haply hath met with his ghost in the forest of Kylgarran that he wil say somwhat in his person:

The signature in this edition is "Th. Ph."[1] The appropriateness of Baldwin's addressing Phaer, in 1555, as one who had lately placed himself in the country of Wales and who might, therefore, have met the ghost of Owen Glendower in the Forest of Kilgerran is so apparent that the reliability of the 1578 text in establishing both text and authorship seems pretty well proved.

William Baldwin, George Ferrers, Thomas Chaloner, and Thomas Phaer are the only contributors whose names are associated with the first

---

[1] Professor Trench (*A Mirror for Magistrates*, pp. 44–45) argues that George Ferrers probably edited this edition of the *Mirror* and in friendly fashion assigned the tragedy to the dead Phaer. Professor Trench had evidently not seen Phaer's translation of Virgil, for he says of Phaer's authorship of the Owen Glendower tragedy: "If he wrote the Glendour tragedy, it was before undertaking the Æneid, for this was not begun until 1557."

edition of the *Mirror* on the authority of the extant texts. The preface to the 1563 edition, however, adds four names of writers responsible for additional tragedies. Most famous of these four is Thomas Sackville.

When Richard Niccols in 1609-10 published his edited and enlarged version of the *Mirror*, he wrote of Sackville that

Thomas
Sackville

by how much he did surpasse the rest in the eminence of his noble condition, by so much he hath exceeded them all in the excellencie of his heroicall stile, which with a golden pen he hath limmed out to posteritie in that worthy obiect of his minde, the Tragedie of the Duke of *Buckingham*, and in his preface then intituled Master *Sackuils* induction.[1]

With this judgment posterity has been in complete accord.

Sir Richard Sackville, Sackville's father, was a first cousin of Anne Boleyn, but the record of his services to the Crown during the reigns of Henry, Edward, Mary, and Elizabeth proves that he was master of his fate. He seems to have justified his nickname of "Fillsack." Among his many remunerative appointments was that of Chancellor of the Court of Augmentation, an office to which he was appointed by Edward VI but in which he was continued by Mary, who made him a member of her Privy Council.[2] Thomas Sackville was, therefore, certainly of surpassing eminence among the group with whom he was associated in the *Mirror*.[3] Of his life we have an account written by no less a person than Queen Elizabeth, according to Dr Abbot, who included this account in the sermon which he preached at Sackville's

[1] A separate title-page introduces the original *Mirror*, bearing the title, "THE VARIABLE FORTUNE AND VNHAPPIE FALLES OF SUCH PRINCES AS hath happened since the Conquest," with the date 1609. The account of Sackville is from Niccols' address "To the Reader," p. 253.

[2] See the article by W. A. J. Archbold in the *Dictionary of National Biography*.

[3] Sackville's biography is still to be written, though it has been attempted many times. Little has been added to the account in Arthur Collins, *Peerage of England; . . . Greatly Augmented, and Continued to the Present Time, by Sir Egerton Brydges* (London, 1812), II, 110–46. A standard account is that prefixed to the edition of his works by R. W. Sackville-West, in 1859.

funeral.[1] Elizabeth, it is said, thus described the first of Sackville's seven ages, the age which concerns us here:

The first was his yoonger daies, the time of his scholarship, when first in that famous Vniuersitie of Oxford, and afterward in the Temple,[2] (where he tooke the degree of Barrister) *he gaue tokens of such pregnancie, such studiousnesse and iudgement, that he was held no way inferiour to any of his time or standing.*

Dr Abbot added to this testimony from the Queen:

And of this there remaine good tokens both in English and in Latine published vnto the world.

A marginal note on "good tokens" instanced:

The life of *Tresilian* in the Mirrour of Magistr. *Epist. prefix. Aulic, Barth. Clerke.*[3]

This is the only evidence that Sackville was responsible for any part of the *Mirror* other than his "Induction" and the tragedy of the Duke of Buckingham, which contributions are not mentioned. Since the *Mirror*

---

[1] *A Sermon Preached at Westminster May 26. 1608. At the Funerall Solemnities of the Right Honorable Thomas Earle of Dorset, late L. High Treasurer of England. By George Abbot Doctor of Diuinitie and Deane of Winchester, one of his Lordships Chapleines* (London, 1608). See especially p. 13.

[2] Miss Hearsey (see below, p. 38, n. 1) and a recent contributor of a leading article on Sackville in the London *Times Literary Supplement* (Jan. 25, 1936) insist there is no evidence for Sackville's having been a member of the Inner Temple. Yet F. A. Inderwick, *The Inner Temple* (London, 1896), p. 180, records Thomas Sackville's admission on July 1, 1555. He is also listed in *Students Admitted to the Inner Temple, 1547–1660* (London, 1877), p. 20, though here he is said to have been admitted in November, 1554. The admissions in this list seem, however, to include all those of the year between November, 1554, and November, 1555. It should be noted that, on p. 113, when his sons' admission to the Inner Temple is recorded, it is again stated that their father is a member of this Inn. In regard to his university training, see Wood, *op. cit.*, cols. 30–43, and C. H. and T. Cooper, *Athenae Cantabrigienses* (Cambridge, 1861), II, 484–91, the latter containing a very full bibliography.

[3] Bartholomew Clerke's translation of Castiglione's *Courtier* into Latin (*De Curiali siue Aulico*) was published in 1571, with a prefatory epistle written by Sackville to Clerke. It should be noted that a sonnet, "Thomas Sackevylle in commendation of the worke. to the reader," was prefixed to Thomas Hoby's translation of the same work into English in 1561.

text specifically reports the tragedy of Tresilian as the contribution of Ferrers, and since the poem itself shows no resemblance to Sackville's other work, it seems probable that Dr Abbot remembered only vaguely the nature of Sackville's contribution to the *Mirror*.

Far more seriously misleading was Richard Niccols' story of the origin of the *Mirror* prefixed to his 1609-10 edition,[1] where he attributed to Sackville the original design:

This worthie President of learning, intending to perfect all this storie himselfe from the Conquest, being called to a more serious expence of his time in the great State-affaires of his most royall Ladie and Soueraigne, left the dispose thereof to M. *Baldwine*, M. *Ferrers* and others, the composers of these Tragedies, who continuing their methode which was by way of dialogue or interlocution betwixt euery Tragedie, gaue it onely place before the Duke of *Buckinghams* complaint, which order I since hauing altered, haue placed the Induction in the beginning, with euery Tragedie following according to succession and the iust computation of time, which before was not obserued.

His account has proved so intriguing that, in spite of the evidence of the 1563 edition, and in spite of the correction made by Haslewood and later scholars, it has persisted through Warton to Sidney Lee and the *Dictionary of National Biography*.

In the preface to the second part of the *Mirror*, added in 1563, Baldwin announced to the group that he had procured from Sackville the Duke of Buckingham's tragedy. Later, when he came to read the tragedy into the *Mirror*, he proposed first to read the "preface or Induction":

Hath he made a preface (quoth one) what meaneth he thereby, seeing none other hath vsed the like order? I wyl tell you the cause thereof (quoth I) which is thys: After that he vnderstoode that some of the counsayle would not suffer the booke to be printed in suche order as we had agreed and determined, he purposed with him selfe to haue gotten at my handes, al the tragedies that were before the duke of Buckinghams, Which he would haue preserued in one volume. And from that time backeward euen to the time of William the conquerour, he determined to continue and perfect all the story him selfe, in such order as Lydgate (folowing Bocchas) had already vsed. And therfore

[1] See above, p. 20.

37

to make a meete induction into the matter, he deuised this poesye: which in my iudgement is so wel penned, that I woulde not haue any verse therof left out of our volume.

Sackville must, therefore, have been cognizant of events connected with the suppressed edition, and he may well have been one of the group who undertook to write the account of the unfortunate English princes, but that he was the "primary inventor" of the design, as Warton calls him, there is certainly not the faintest suggestion.

The manuscript recently discovered by Miss Marguerite Hearsey in St John's College, Cambridge,[1] adds new complications when considered in conjunction with this explanation offered by Baldwin, for here the induction and the tragedy are written continuously. The title of the whole work is given as "*The Complaint of Henrie Duke of Buckinghame.*" Even as it is printed in the *Mirror*, the induction introduces the character of the Duke of Buckingham in preparation for his complaint, and neither in manuscript nor in printed form does the work bear any evidence of having been written to introduce tragedies from William the Conqueror to the Duke of Buckingham.

Of Sackville's other literary work, we know only the tragedy of *Gorboduc*, written in collaboration with Thomas Norton and presented at the Temple on Twelfth Night, 1560/61, and before the Queen on January 18, 1561/62, by the gentlemen of the Inner Temple, of which Sackville's father was governor.[2] *Gorboduc* applies the methods of the *Mirror for Magistrates* in its dramatic treatment of historical material, again using history as a mirror to the present and making tragedy rehearse the disastrous ends of political error. Since this tragedy has been generally accepted as the first English tragedy and the precursor

[1] Thomas Sackville, *The Complaint of Henry Duke of Buckingham: Edited, from the Author's manuscript . . . by Marguerite Hearsey* (New Haven, 1936). Another, and later, manuscript, which contains most of Sackville's "Induction" and four stanzas of the tragedy of the blacksmith, is recorded by E. A. Strathmann, in "A Manuscript Copy of Spenser's *Hymns*," *Modern Language Notes*, XLVIII, 217–21.

[2] Miss Hearsey gives two different accounts of the dates of these performances, both inaccurate (pp. 26, 27). See J. W. Cunliffe, *Early English Classical Tragedies* (Oxford, 1912), p. lxxxi, and Inderwick, *op. cit.*, pp. lxx–lxxi.

of the great Elizabethan tragedies, it is of special significance that it adapted to dramatic writing the purpose and the method of the *Mirror*.

That Sackville did write other poems, however, is indicated by Jasper Heywood's reference, in 1560, to the work of the Inns of Court men:

> There Sackuyldes Sonetts sweetely sauste
> and featly fyned bee.

Only one sonnet has been identified as his,[1] but praise of Sackville as a poet was common to all pens of the sixteenth century. Even Spenser wrote to him:

> In vain I thinke right honourable Lord,
>   By this rude rime to memorize thy name;
>   Whose learned Muse hath writ her owne record,
>   In golden verse, worthy immortal fame:
> Thou much more fit (were leasure to the same)
>   Thy gracious Soverains praises to compile
>   And her imperiall Maiestie to frame,
>   In loftie numbres and heroike stile.[2]

Far removed in his fortunes from the man who was to be Lord Buckhurst, Earl of Dorset, and Lord Treasurer of England, was the other well-known contributor to the 1563 *Mirror*, the poor but prolific soldier-poet, Thomas Churchyard,[3] who wrote and rewrote, published and republished his work, and continually proclaimed his worth and his woes to an inattentive world.

Thomas Churchyard

That he was early attached to the household of the Earl of Surrey, he testified when he dedicated to the Earl's grandson, in 1580, *A light Bondell of liuly discourses called Churchyardes Charge*, protesting that he

---

[1] See above, p. 36, n. 3.

[2] The octave of the sonnet which was among those added in the second issue of the 1590 edition of the *Faerie Queene* to the group of complimentary sonnets. See Francis R. Johnson, *A Critical Bibliography of the Works of Edmund Spenser* (Baltimore, 1933), pp. 15–16. I have quoted from the Oxford edition (1916), p. 412.

[3] Henry W. Adnitt, "Thomas Churchyard," in *Transactions of the Shropshire Archeological and Natural History Society* (Shrewsbury [and] Oswestry, 1880), III, 1–68. This is still the most complete account of Churchyard's life; the *Short-Title Catalogue* is the best authority on his works.

must show that he had lost no time in the service of him whom he honored in his heart, "your Lordshipps graundfather; & my master (who was a noble warrior, an eloquent Oratour; and a second Petrarke)." It is quite possible, then, that he may have been, as he testified in 1593 in *Churchyards Challenge* that he was, the author of "many things in the booke of songs and Sonets," most of which were written in the days of Henry VIII though not printed till the reign of Mary, in the work now known familiarly as *Tottel's Miscellany*. That he was indebted, during the reign of Edward VI, to Protector Somerset is likewise attested by his dedication to the son of the Protector of *The Fortunate Farewell to the . . . Earle of Essex*, printed in 1599, where he explains that "your most honorable father the Duke of Sommerset (vncle to the renowmed impe of grace noble *King Edward* the sixt) fauoured me when I was troubled before the Lords of the Counsell, for writing some of my first verses." *An Epitaph vpon the deth of kyng Edward* proved his resiliency in sorrow, however, for after bewailing,

> The Lorde hath taken him
> And for his peoples sinne
> A iust plage for our iniquitie,

he was able to conclude:

> But his soule we do commende,
> Vnto the Lordes hande,
> Who preserue our noble Quene Mary.
> Longe with vs to endure,
> With myrth ioy and pleasure,
> To rule her realme a right:
> All her enemies to withstande
> By sea and by lande,
> Lorde preserue her both day and nighte.
> God saue the Kinge and the Queene.

It is not my purpose here to rehearse the wanderings of Churchyard in his varied adventures as soldier-at-large. He tells us that he served four English princes loyally in war and three foreign kings for wage. At the time of the publication of the 1559 *Mirror*, he was the forgotten man in a French prison whom no one remembered to rescue. He was probably serving the Emperor when publication of the *Mirror* was first attempted.

His literary work was as varied, and received, it would seem, as little recognition, as his soldiering. With his always diffuse and often dull writings, I am not concerned here except to note the possible extent of his contribution to the *Mirror* and to point out what seems to have remained unnoticed—his particular antipathy toward William Baldwin.

In the list of his works which he prefixed to *Churchyards Challenge* by way of daring an apparently doubting world to dispute their authorship, Churchyard wrote:

First in King Edwards daies, a book named *Dauie Dicars dreame*, which one *Camell* wrote against, whome I openly confuted. *Shores wife* I penned at that season.

Yet it was not until the 1563 edition of the *Mirror* that the tragedy of Jane Shore appeared. In the preface to the second part of the *Mirror*, Baldwin lists, among the works brought by Master Ferrers, the tragedy of Shore's wife as penned by Churchyard, and at the close of the reading of the tragedy he records the favourable comment of the group upon the poem, together with their desire to have more of Churchyard's work. He adds that he promised to do his diligence therein.

In 1575, in *The Firste parte of Churchyardes Chippes*, . . . *Deuised and published, only by Thomas Churchyard Gentilman*, and published by Thomas Marshe (the same printer who was reprinting the *Mirror* at intervals), there was printed "Syr Symon Burleis Tragedie," which began:

> AM I of blud, or yet of byrth so base,
> O *Baldwin* now, that thou forgetst my name
> Or doth thy pen, want cunning for that case.
> Or is thy skill, or sensis fawllen lame,
> Or dost thou feare, to blase abrode my fame.

Five nine-line stanzas of reproach to Baldwin are climaxed with the taunt:

> And so I leaue, the Baldwin in thy bower.
> Of lawrell leaues, where thou maist sit and sée,
> At open vew, what Churchyard writes of mée.

41

The first poem in this collection is addressed "To the dispisers of other mens workes that shoes nothing of their owne," but I do not know whether this was aimed at Baldwin.

In *Churchyards Challenge* of 1593 was also published "The Earle of Murtons Tragedie," which was written in the usual seven-line stanza, and which appealed "to some true writers pen: / That doth the life, and death of Princes touch." It bears every mark, down to the "qd. T.C." at its close, of having been prepared for the *Mirror*.

The 1587 edition of the *Mirror* contained two tragedies of Churchyard's authorship, for, in addition to "Shores wife," the tragedy of Cardinal Wolsey was set forth. Curiously, both tragedies were here introduced by prose links which eliminated Baldwin as interlocutor and as narrator. Jane Shore and Cardinal Wolsey speak their own prose links instead of waiting for an introduction, and they take this opportunity to tell us what Churchyard thought of Baldwin. Jane Shore says:

And making more haste then good speede, I appeared fyrst to one *Baldwine* a Minister and a Preacher: whose function and calling disdaynes to looke so lowe, as to searche the secrets of wanton women, (though commonly a Preacher with sufferaunce may rebuke vice.) Wherefore I haue better bethought mee, and so doe sodaynly appeale and appeare to some martiall man, who hath more experience both in defending of womens honour, and knowes somwhat more of theyr conditions and qualityes: and the rather, because my tragedy was in question among some that would not spare due commendation to the autor therof. I now appeare to him that fyrst set mee forth, . . . whose name is *Churchyard*: hee shall not only haue the fame of his owne worke (which no man can deny) but shall likewise haue all the glory I can gieue him, if hee lend mee the hearing of my woefull tale, . . .

The same tone distinguishes Wolsey's introduction of his own tragedy:

As *Baldwine* indeede being a Minister, had bene most fit to set forth the life of a Cardinall and Byshop . . . so to encourage a writer now aliue to play the part of a Pasquill, and rather make his pen his plough, than in a hard season, liue like a labourer, that doth seruice to many, and litle good to him selfe, I thought it necessary . . . to bestow some credit on that person that not only hath preferred my tragedy to the Printer, (being of his owne deuice and penning) but also hath enlarged, by playne and familier verse, the matter the world desires to heare or read, and made things common among a multitude, that were secret and held priuat among a fewe.

A reuyuing of the deade, in 1591, showed Churchyard still tilting at his favourite windmill:

The Tragedies in my next book called my Challenge) shal make manifest . . . the effect of those passages: . . . that therby the world shall see what wrong I haue suffred to endure a deniall (by busie tunges) of mine owne workes: Shores wife shall speake in her kinde, to defend me and such as waites on her . . . shall tell the world I haue beene abused, and not iustly and rightly vnderstood.

In 1592 even Thomas Nashe had come to terms with Churchyard and was assuring him that "Shores wife is yong, though you be stept in yeares; in her shall you liue when you are dead."[1] Yet in 1593, in *Churchyards Challenge*, not only is there printed a list of the author's works, but the tragedies of Sir Simon Burley and Jane Shore are reprinted, the latter with a letter of dedication to "the Lady Mount Eagle and Compton, wife to the right honourable the Lord of Buckhursts son and heire," making an interesting new connection with Sackville and the *Mirror*.[2] Again Churchyard vilifies those who have doubted his authorship of this tragedy, professing before God that he wrote it, and in proof of his continued ability beautifying it with additional verses. I do not know the explanation of the difficulties between Baldwin and Churchyard, but this is the story so far as I have been able to recreate it.

In 1592 Churchyard wrote *The vnhappye mans deere adewe*, in which he summed up his disappointment with life:

> Youth first beguilde, in Court with hope forlorne,
> Than middle age, all wearied with sharp war:
> And nowe olde eld, to liue in lack and scorne,
> Whose wounded limbs, showes many a wofull skar;

[1] R. B. McKerrow, ed., *Works of Thomas Nashe* (London, 1914), I, 309, in *Strange Names, of the intercepting of certaine Letters* (1592).

[2] The poem had stanzas added to prove not only that Churchyard did do it but that he could do it. *Censura Literaria* (1806) printed the original tragedy (II, 97–114), and the additional stanzas (II, 309–17), the last account being signed T. P.

> And sundry waies, consum'd with trauaile far.
> These open plagues, and inward griefes of mind:
> Cryes out and saith, my Country is vnkinde.
>
> I seru'd in field, foure Princes of greate fame,
> Borne vnder those, an humble subiect true:
> Three other Kings, of great renowne and name,
> In faithfull sort, I seru'd for wages due;
> But heere liege Lords, I doe appeale from you,
> That neuer did, aduaunce my loyall hart,
> For treble toile, for paines, nor iust desart.[1]

But in the following year he could rejoice, for he then could write:

> The booke I calld, of late *My deere adiew*,
> Is now become, my welcome home most kinde:[2]

by way of celebrating his peace with God and prince, since Queen Elizabeth had given him a pension. He died in 1604, but, as the ill-natured would have it, his works had preceded him in death.

Churchyard was buried in St Margaret's Church, near the poet Skelton, for whom his admiration is attested by his verses, prefixed to the works of that writer, published by Thomas Marshe in 1568, and it is an admissible conjecture that he was "an other" of the original group who suggested closing the first part of the *Mirror* with Skelton's complaint of Edward IV.

John Dolman

"Maister Dolman," the author of the tragedy of Hastings, which was brought to Baldwin by the printer, is generally identified as John Dolman, and the identification seems reasonable because Thomas Marshe was the printer who in 1561 published *Those fyue Questions, which Mark Tullye Cicero, disputed in his Manor of Tusculum . . . translated, & englished, by Iohn Dolman, Studente and felowe of the Inner Temple.* The work was dedicated to Bishop Jewell. In the dedication Dolman explained that he had left the university to apply himself to the study of the common law, but that memories of his earlier studies came between him and the

---

[1] *A feast full of sad cheere* (London, 1592), p. 10.

[2] *A Pleasant conceite penned in verse. Collourably sette out, and humblie presented on New-yeeres day last, to the Queenes Maiestie at Hampton Courte* (London, 1593), sig. B 2, verso.

law, so that he was forced to experiment with translation. To the reader, he justified his temerity in undertaking the task in spite of his lack of years and eloquence.

John Dolman was the grandson of William Dolman, manager to "Jack of Newbury" made famous by the novel of Thomas Deloney.[1] His father was Thomas Dolman, the rich Newbury clothier who in 1554 acquired the manor of Shaw and began to build Shaw House, thereby securing to himself the gibes of which the most famous has come down to us:

Lord have mercy on us miserable sinners!
Thomas Dolman has built a new house, and has turned away all his
    spinners.

John Dolman was admitted to the Inner Temple in 1560, when he was twenty years old. He was admitted to the bar in 1570 and was called to the bench in 1586. In 1587 he was Autumn Reader and in 1598 Treasurer for the Temple, and the records show him to have been a man of importance in the law.[2] As eldest son he was his father's heir, but he sold his one-third interest in the manor of Shaw to his brother Thomas, probably because he had had Frethornes, in Berkshire, settled upon him at his marriage. Dolman was, therefore, a very rich young man who found in the law his opportunity to satisfy the family ambition. He was a member of the Inner Temple when Sackville and Norton produced *Gorboduc*. To have a tragedy published in the *Mirror for Magistrates*, along with that of the aristocratic Sackville, whose father was governor of the Temple, must have been as incense to the nostrils of the ambitious family of Dolman.

The tragedy which was the young lawyer's contribution is remarkable in several respects. It is probably the worst poetry in the *Mirror*, and, when Baldwin read it to the assembled group, it was noted as difficult

[1] For an account of the Dolman family, see *Victoria History: Berkshire*, IV (London, 1924), 87–89, 274; I (London, 1906), 389–90. See also J. Nichols, *Progresses of King James I* (London, 1828), I, 266, n., and my "John Dolman," *ELH*, IV, 192–200.

[2] *Students Admitted to the Inner Temple, 1547–1560*, p. 39; *Masters of the Bench of the Hon. Society of the Inner Temple, 1450–1883, and Masters of the Temple, 1540–1883* (1883; "not published"), p. 15; and Inderwick, *op. cit.*, Index, for later record.

to be understood. Its language is often curious, and the frequent use of *hit* for *it* distinguishes it from the other tragedies. But, in learning and in thoughtful philosophizing on the rewards of evil-doing, it is second only to Sackville's tragedy. Dolman's tragedy is particularly noteworthy, however, for containing a passage discussing Chaucer's *Nuns Priests Tale*, more extensive and detailed than any other of its date—a fact which is interesting because Shaw was only a few miles from Donnington and its Chaucer's Oak, under which, tradition said, Chaucer wrote his great poems.[1]

Francis
Seager
    The other tragedy brought to Baldwin by the printer was that of Richard III, "compiled by Frauncis Segars." Of Seagers, or Seager, very little is known, save that he made his contribution to the courtesy books of the sixteenth century.[2] His first work was in this tradition, being a translation (or an edition of Caxton's translation) of a book written by Alain Chartier and published in 1549 under the title of *A brefe declaration of the great myseries ĩ courtes ryal.* Only two leaves remain of this book, and its printer is not known, but Francis Seager's verses to the reader are in the extant portion. In 1553 Seager dedicated to Lord Russell (later the second Earl of Bedford) his translation of *Certayne Psalmes select out of the Psalter of Dauid*, which was published by William Seres. In 1557 the work by which he is best known was published—*The schoole of vertue and booke of good nourture for chyldren a. youth to learne theyr dutie by.* Robert Crowley was joint author with Seager and seems to have contributed the second section of the book. Republished in 1582, 1593, and 1626, this work became one of the better known of the courtesy books. The article on Seager in the *Dictionary of National Biography* suggests that he may have been the Francis Nycholson, "alias Seager," who was made free of the Stationers' Company on September 24, 1557.

Cavyl
    Of the "Master Cavyl" who "aptly ordered" the tragedy of the blacksmith, Michael Joseph, there is nothing known.[3] The most likely

---

[1] Henry Godwin, "On Donnington Castle, Berkshire," *Archaeologia*, XLIV, 459–79.

[2] See J. E. Mason, *Gentlefolk in the Making* (Philadelphia, 1935), pp. 41, 256.

[3] Tragedy 2 (of the Mortimers) was, it will be remembered, signed "Ca." in the 1571 and subsequent editions, save in the 1578 edition, where it was signed "T. Ch."

person seems to be Humphrey Cavell, who was a member of the Middle Temple, and who was returned to Parliament in 1552/3, 1554, and 1555, but there is no evidence to link him to the business of authorship.

There are no new contributors to the later *Mirrors*, except the author of the tragedy of Sir Nicholas Burdet, which was introduced in 1587, along with the two Scots tragedies from an old manuscript. Since Holinshed's interest in the *Mirror* has never been considered, it will be necessary to review the evidence which associates him with its history. Raphael Holinshed

In the 1587 edition, the tragedy of Sir Nicholas Burdet is introduced by a continuation of the prose which had closed the 1563 edition. No change of narrator being indicated, Baldwin apparently continued to serve in that capacity, though it seemingly was Higgins who wrote:

I was willed my maisters (quoth I) by Maister Holinshed, to bring Sir *Nicholas Burdet* vnto you. Were you? (quoth they.) On his word we will heare what he sayes. Read it I pray you (quod one.) You must thinke then (quoth I) that you see him. . . .

Sir Nicholas addressed the closing stanza of his complaint to Higgins:

So *Higins* yf thou write, how this my fall befell;
Place it in *Baldwines Miroir* with the reste.

The tragedy is signed "Iohn Higins." In the ensuing prose link, Ferrers is represented as discussing the poem, though Ferrers is supposed to have died in 1579, as I have elsewhere noted. Also "M.H." is represented as commenting on the poem, the usual interpretation of the initials being that they represent Higgins' own respectful allusion to himself as Master Higgins. The interlocutor then proceeds to announce other poems in his possession:

. . . I haue King *Iames* the fourth here, which was slayne at the batayle of *Brampton*, or *Floddon fielde*, but hee is very rude.

At the close of King James' complaint, there is comment on the character of the Scots King:

Than (quod M.H.) he is still one and the same man: for in life he was neither well liked, beleeued, nor trusted. Why than (quoth one) if hee speake as hee was, let him passe as hee is; and if not, let him bee mended.

Mended (quoth hee?) Nay hee is paste mending, hee is to olde: for it seemes by the copy, that it was pende aboue fifty yeares agone, or euen shortly after the death of the sayd King: for I found therewith, in an olde hand, the copyes of the sayd King *Iames* letters sent vnto King *Henry* at *Turwin*, and the Kings aunsweres & letters sent to him againe, with this lamentation ensuing them: and lastly the sayd batayle of *Floddon fielde*, in such verse described, with the order of the same, and the names of the noble men, Knights, and gentlemen, which serued at the same fielde.

Then follows the comment of the group on the desirability of rescuing these details for history, with the added hope that knowledge of their ancestors' worthiness may encourage men of the day in like virtues.

Certainly Holinshed was responsible, therefore, for the tragedy of Sir Nicholas Burdet. Whether the tragedy was actually written by him, or at his request by Higgins, is not clear, but it should be remembered that Holinshed was steward to Thomas Burdet, Esq., of Bramcote in Warwickshire. His will, dated October 1, 1578, and probated April 24, 1581, gave all his property to his master.[1] Since Sir Nicholas Burdet was an ancestor of Thomas Burdet,[2] it is at least romantically possible that Holinshed chose this manner of memorializing the family. But it is also much more natural, in the light of other facts, to read the comments of "M.H." on the Scots tragedies as those of Holinshed, for in 1577 he printed from the manuscript which he here described as penned "aboue fifty yeares agone," "the copyes of the sayd King *Iames* letters sent vnto King *Henry* at *Turwin*, and the Kings aunsweres & letters sent to him againe," as may be seen by anyone who will take the trouble to compare them.

The Conception of History as a Mirror

The authors of the *Mirror for Magistrates* were clearly, their biographies show, men who could adjust their sails to the prevailing winds. The *Mirror*, as might be expected, was written in complete accord with

[1] Leslie Hotson, "Shakespeares of Stratford: A Holinshed Link," London *Times*, July 6, 1935, pp. 13–14, offers evidence to correct inaccuracies in the article by Sir Sidney Lee in the *Dictionary of National Biography*, based on the account of Cooper, *op. cit.*, I, 430–31. There is, of course, a possibility that Ottiwell Holinshed may have been referred to in the *Mirror*. He is mentioned among the writers listed by Holinshed in 1577.

[2] Sir William Dugdale, *The Antiquities of Warwickshire* (2nd ed., by William Thomas; London, 1730), pp. 846–49.

Tudor ideas. The very title indicates as much, for every apology for history in the period affirmed that history was a glass wherein the present might see and learn the patterns of conduct which had brought happiness or unhappiness to nations and to men in the past. A typical expression of this conception of history is that of Peter Ashton, who wrote in the dedication of his translation of *A shorte treatise vpon the Turkes Chronicles*[1] to Sir Ralph Sadler:

The great lerned philosopher and wise man Plato, . . . saith, That a man . . . ought often tymes to behowlde hym selfe in a glasse: . . . This glasse that Plato speketh on . . . maye be taken not without a cause . . . espetially for Chronicles & histories. . . .

So . . . shal ye see in hystories, euen from the first monarchie vnto this day, the forme & figure of all Empires & common welthes, . . . But now to see the course of the world, . . . how kingdomes haue chaunged & altered, what fasshion hathe bene vsed emonge men, how & by whom kingdomes haue bene gouerned, how vertue hath bene rewarded, & vices ponisshed, . . . To read and know al these thinges . . . Is not that glasse worthy to be often tymes loked in . . . ?

More striking than the pleas of the professional historian, however, were the utterances of those who urged their countrymen to learn vicariously, in history, what they would otherwise have to learn by hard experience. Among the most dramatic of such warnings was that uttered by Sir Thomas Wyatt from the scaffold, when he was about to be executed for his part in the rebellion of 1554. Given permission to speak what he would, he began:

I muste confesse my selfe giltie, as in the end the truth of my case must enforce me, I must acknowlege this to be a iust plague for my synnes, which most grieuously I therfore haue committed against God, who suffred me thus brutely & beastly to fall into this horrible offence of the law. Wherfore all you Lords & Gentlemen with other here present, note well my words. Lo here & se in me the same end which all other commonly had, which haue attempted like enterprice from the begynning. For peruse the Cronicles through, and you shall see that neuer rebellion attempted by subiectes against their prince and countrye from

---

[1] A work by Paolo Giovio (Paulus Jovius), the translation of which was published by Whitchurch in 1546.

the begynning did euer prosper or had better successe, except the case
of king Henry the fourth, who although he became a Prynce: yet in
his act was but a Rebell, for so must I call him. And though he preuayled
for a time, yet was it not long, but that his heires were depriued and
those that had right againe restored to the kingdome and crowne, and
the vsurpation so sharply reuenged afterward in his bloud, as it well
appered that the long delaye of Gods vengeaunce was supplyed with
more grieuous plague in the third and fourth generation. For the loue
of God all you Gentlemen that be here present, remember and be taught
as well by examples past as also by this my present infelicity and most
wretched case.[1]

In the original preface to the *Mirror*, Baldwin wrote, therefore (in
line with this tradition), that the purpose of the printer was to have
Boccaccio's work continued,

chiefly of suche as Fortune had dalyed with here in this ylande: whiche
might be as a myrrour for al men as well noble as others, to shewe the
slyppery deceytes of the waueryng lady, and the due rewarde of all
kinde of vices.

In his dedication of the *Mirror* "To the nobilitye and all other in office,"
he stated even more definitely the motivating purpose of the book:

For here as in a loking glas, you shall see (if any vice be in you) howe
the like hath bene punished in other heretofore, whereby admonished,
I trust it will be a good occasion to move you to the soner amendment.
This is the chiefest ende, whye it is set furth, which God graunt it may
attayne.

Those who have written about the history of history have been
accustomed to proclaim the work of Jean Bodin as initiating a new
conception of history when he asserted that, "En effet, la première
utilitie de l'histoire est de servir à la politique."[2] Yet it must be apparent
to anyone who has read the English chronicles of such men as Lanquet

---

[1] Grafton, *op. cit.*, pp. 1339–40.

[2] For a brief summary of Jean Bodin's *Methodus ad facilem historiarum cognitionem*,
first published in 1566, see J. W. Allen, *A History of Political Thought in the Sixteenth
Century* (London, 1928), pp. 405–7. See also W. A. Dunning, *A History of Political
Theories: from Luther to Montesquieu* (New York, 1905), p. 83.

and Halle[1] that, long before Bodin, history was serving in England the purpose of political teaching.

The *Mirror for Magistrates* was an important pioneer work in literature, because it transferred to the poet the accepted task of the historian— a task which, if the defenders of poetry are to be believed, he could perform more delightfully, more directly, and hence more effectively, than could the historian. Of this superiority of the poet over the historian, Sidney was later to write:

. . . the best of the Historian is subiect to the Poet; for whatsoeuer action, or faction, whatsoeuer counsell, pollicy, or warre stratagem the Historian is bound to recite, that may the Poet (if he list) with his imitation make his own, beautifying it both for further teaching, and more delighting, as it pleaseth him, hauing all, from *Dante* his heauen to hys hell, vnder the authoritie of his penne.[2]

The importance of this transfer of the function of political teaching from the historian to the poet[3] can, however, be fully realized only when consideration is given to the long line of historical plays and poems popular during the reign of Elizabeth.

[1] The work begun by Lanquet, and dedicated by him to Protector Somerset, contains in its preface a complete exposition of the contemporary theory of history. It was printed in 1559 by Thomas Marshe, as was the *Mirror*, and the continuator who brought it down to date was Robert Crowley, who, as has been noted, was coauthor with Francis Seager of *The schoole of vertue*. The full title of the chronicle is interesting: *An Epitome of Cronicles. Conteyninge the whole discourse of the histories as well of this realme of England as al other coūtreys, with the succesion of their kinges, the time of their reigne, and what notable actes they did: much profitable to be redde, namelye of Magistrates, and such as haue aūctoritee in commō weales, gathered out of most probable auctours. Firste by Thomas Lanquet, from the beginning of the worlde to the incarnacion of Christe, Secondely to the reigne of our soueraigne lord king Edward the sixt by Thomas Cooper, and thirdly to the reigne of our soueraigne Ladye Quene Elizabeth, by Robert Crowley.* Edward Halle's work was first published in 1542, but was again published in 1548 (two editions), 1550, and 1552 (?). The title was *The Vnion of the two noble and illustre famelies of Lancastre & Yorke, beeyng long in continual discension for the croune of this noble realme, ...* (I quote from a copy of the 1548 edition.)

[2] *Sidney's Apologie for Poetrie*, ed. J. Churton Collins (Oxford, 1907), p. 22.

[3] I have discussed this whole matter in a lecture printed as *Tudor Conceptions of History and Tragedy in "A Mirror for Magistrates"* (Berkeley, 1936).

The political doctrine which it was the acknowledged purpose of the *Mirror* to teach was the orthodox Tudor doctrine. That it often bore the stamp of Calvinism in its phraseology was not inconsistent with its orthodoxy, for, as political historians have pointed out, England and the Reformation were forced by circumstances to adopt much the same attitude toward the secular ruler, and the theory which came to be known as that of the divine right of kings was accepted as the result of both ecclesiastical and political necessity. The *Mirror*, then, teaches in its tragedies, and in the prose expositions of these tragedies, the lessons that were inculcated alike in the *Institutes* of Calvin,[1] and in certain homilies appointed by the Tudor rulers to be read in all the churches,[2] as well as in the addresses of the Tudor sovereigns to their people.

The use of the term *magistrate* is the key to this teaching. Calvin wrote, in the words of Norton's translation:

Wheras whosoeuer be in place of magistrates are named gods, let no man thynke that in that naming is smal importance: For therby is signified that they haue commaundement from God, that they are furnished with the authoritie of God, & do altogether beare the person of God, whoes stede they do after a certaine maner supplie.[3]

Baldwin, dedicating to the magistrates their mirror, wrote likewise:

For as Iustice is the chief vertue, so is the ministracion therof, the chiefest office: & therfore hath God established it with the chiefest name, honoring & calling Kinges, & all officers vnder them by his owne name, Gods. Ye be all Gods, as many as have in your charge any ministracion of Iustice.

The whole of the theory of the divine right of kings is implicit in this definition: The King is vicegerent to God. He is responsible to God

---

[1] *The Institution of Christian Religion* was published in the translation of Thomas Norton in 1561. Book IV, chapter XX, discussed civil government. Norton worked with Sackville on *Gorboduc*, which was produced in the same year.

[2] "An exhortacion, concernyng good ordre and obedience, to rulers and magistrates" was published in 1547 among *Certayne Sermons, or Homelies*. *An Homelie against disobedience and wylfull rebellion*, published in 1571, reiterated the same doctrines.

[3] Calvin, *op. cit.* (ed. 1561), fol. 161. See also Allen, pp. 126–7, and A. A. Dudley, "The Attitude of the State in Anglican Literature from 1525–1550," *Economica*, IX, 42.

alone. Subjects may, therefore, under no circumstances rebel against the ruler, for he represents God, and to resist him is to resist God. If God is pleased, he will send a good ruler; if he wishes to try or to punish the people, he may give them a tyrant for their king.[1]

The authors of the *Mirror*, however, realizing that the doctrine was a two-edged sword, did not stop with the exemplification of the part of the doctrine so often expounded by the Tudors. Their tragedies taught, not only the duties of subjects to their king, but also the accountability of kings to the King of Kings—a part of the theory of the divine right less popular with the reigning monarchs. Against the tyrant, God permits the rebel to rage and war to threaten, conscience torments him, his kingdom may be taken from him, and by God's doom an ignominious death awaits him. These writers in the *Mirror* would, to use Sidney's words, make kings fear to be tyrants.

The history of the printing of the *Mirror* indicates that the poet Collingbourne was speaking as Baldwin might have spoken in his own person, when he warned:

> BEware, take heede, take heede, beware, beware
> You Poetes you, that purpose to rehearce
> By any arte what Tyrantes doynges are, . . .

Collingbourne's description of the poet's office concludes, too, with a timely account of the final requisite for a poet:

> He must be swyft when touched tyrants chafe,
> To gallop thence to kepe his carkas safe.

It sounds like the work of one who had "felt the whip," as Sir John Tiptoft anachronistically explains that the chronicler Halle had felt it.[2]

The method by which the lessons of history were to be taught was indicated in Baldwin's own dedicatory words previously quoted:

For here as in a loking glas, you shall see (if any vice be in you) howe the like hath bene punished in other heretofore, whereby admonished, I trust it will be a good occasion to move you to the soner amendment.

[1] See, especially, Allen, *op. cit.*, and J. N. Figgis, *The Divine Right of Kings* (Cambridge, 1922). Note, however, Calvin's discussion (*loc. cit.*) of the duties of parliaments.
[2] See Tragedy 15, ll. 22–42.

The very titles of the tragedies emphasize the relation of sin to punishment, by way of offering a deterrent to sin, as the following, selected
at random, will show:

The fall of Robert Tresilian chiefe Iustice of Englande, and other his
felowes, for misconstruyng the lawes, and expounding them to serue
the Princes affections.

Howe kyng Richarde the seconde was for his euyll gouernaunce deposed
from his seat, and miserably murdred in prison.

How Richard erle of Cambridge entending the kinges destruction was
put to death at Southhampton.

How king Iames the first for breaking his othes and bondes, was by
gods suffrauns miserably murdred of his owne subiectes.

That the tragedies of the *Mirror* were chosen for their usefulness in
teaching political truth, rather than for their historical importance, is
implicit in the acknowledged purpose. And cutting the cloth of history
to fit a political pattern led, in the *Mirror* (as it must always lead), to a
high degree of selectiveness in the choice of historical incidents and, in
certain cases, to a clear modification of historical fact. It is not within
the province of an introduction to consider these problems of selection
and modification, requiring as they do the most exhaustive and detailed
comparison of sources and poetical manipulation of sources. But it may
be well to note, on Baldwin's own authority, that he proposed to divide
the *Mirror* into three sections, the first to extend from Richard II to
Richard III, the second to cover the period of Richard III, the third to
include the Tudor period up to the reign of Mary. Of the third division,
there is no tragedy to give evidence save that of the blacksmith (except,
of course, the tragedy of Wolsey added in 1587), and how serious were
Baldwin's efforts to collect tragedies for this division there is no way of
gauging. But, in the first section, the reigns of Henry IV and Henry V
are represented only by the tragedies of Owen Glendower; Henry
Percy, Earl of Northumberland; and Richard, Earl of Cambridge. It is
evident that the tragedies of those omitted "because their examples
were not much to be noted for our purpose" are often of far more
importance from the historical point of view than are those which

are included. The tragedies of the first section are, indeed, preponderantly those dealing with situations which arose during the periods when England was ruled by minor kings. The tragedies of the second part picture England in the days of a tyrant, Richard III, and the political lessons are definitely concerned with tyranny. Whether or not the first part was intended to mirror the days of Edward VI, and the second part those of Mary, I am not prepared to say, but it is at least probable.

That identifying the persons and situations reflected in the *Mirror for Magistrates* was a favourite indoor sport, even as late as 1614, is indicated in *Bartholomew Fair*, where hearers and spectators are made to agree that none "will pretend to affirme (on his owne *inspired ignorance*) what *Mirror of Magistrates* is meant by the *Iustice*, what *great Lady* by the *Pigge-woman*, what *conceal'd States-man*, by the *Seller of Mouse-trappes*, and so of the rest."[1] But into that gossip I do not propose to go in this introduction. When such identifications are made, however, they should be made with due consideration of the method which Baldwin said repeatedly was the method of the *Mirror*. And it must be borne in mind that the usefulness of the *Mirror* as a vehicle for political doctrine depended upon the assumption that God's justice was eternally the same, so that history did repeat itself in discernible patterns of sin and divine vengeance for sin.

To a certain extent, the literary form of the *Mirror for Magistrates* was conditioned by its having been conceived as a continuation of the *Fall of Princes*.[2] Like the *Fall of Princes* it showed the influences of two older literary genres: tragedy and vision literature. Its tragic complaints, however, were not alone those of princes but included any which might teach useful political lessons. Nor did its ghosts merely bewail the deeds of fortune "that with unwar strook overturneth the realme of great

The Influence of Older Literary Types

---

[1] From the Induction to the play.

[2] See Willard Farnham, *The Medieval Heritage of Elizabethan Tragedy* (Berkeley, 1936), especially chap. 7, for a discussion which summarizes much of Professor Farnham's long and fruitful study of the *Mirror* in relation to the development of the ideas of tragedy in England.

nobleye";[1] rather, they used their lives as examples to expound the current political philosophy, and substituted an analysis of divine justice for the older philosophizing on the uncertainty of fortune.

The vision of the fallen princes that appeared to Boccaccio "as hym thought in his inwarde syght,"[2] was given much more elaborate treatment by Baldwin, who made of the prefaces and prose links of the *Mirror* a connected narrative which rationalized the appearance of the ghosts and, at the same time, offered an excellent vehicle for critical comment by the assembled group of writers who were the *dramatis personae* of the prose sections. Into this prose narrative are fitted the poetic tragedies which it was the primary objective of the *Mirror* to relate. But, curiously, some of the tragedies so set in the prose narrative are in themselves representatives of vision literature.[3] In point of time of composition, the earliest of these tragedies is that of King James IV of Scotland. The interlocutor, in introducing James's tragedy into the *Mirror*, says of him:

Thinke then . . . that you see him standing all wounded, with a shafte in his body, and emongst other woundes, one geuen by a byll, both deadly, to say in his rude and faithlesse maner as followeth. . . .

But, when the poem begins, it is not King James but the author who speaks:

As I lay musing, my selfe alone,
In minde not stable, but wauering here & there,

---

[1] See Chaucer's translation of Boethius, *De consolacione philosophie* (*The Works of Geoffrey Chaucer* [Globe Edition; London, 1907], p. 366).

[2] See Wayland's edition of *The tragedies, gathered by Ihon Bochas*, the companion volume to the suppressed edition of the *Mirror*, "Leaf. 1" [A iv], recto.

[3] For a very suggestive treatment of vision types see A. B. Van Os, *Religious Visions* (Amsterdam, 1932). The most interesting political tragedy, in a vision setting, which preceded the *Mirror* is Sir David Lindsay's *The Tragedie of the Umquhyle Maist Reverend Father Dauid, be the Mercy of God, Cardinale and Archibyschope of Sanctandrous. And of the haill Realme of Scotlande Primate, Legate, and Chancelare, and Administrator of the Byschoprik of Merapoys in France* (1547). (*The Works of Sir David Lindsay of the Mount*, ed. Douglas Hamer [Scottish Text Society, 1931], I, 129–43.) Courthope long ago suggested this poem as a model for the *Mirror*.

INTRODUCTION

Morpheus my frend espyed mee anone,
And as hee was wont, whistered in mine eare.
Shortly conuyede I was, I wist not where:
Mine eyes were closed fast, I could not see.

It is not, indeed, until the third stanza that the complaint which was introduced by the interlocutor really begins.

The tragedy of Richard, Duke of York, which was composed later than this Scots tragedy but found its way into the *Mirror* much earlier, is also introduced by a variant type of vision. Baldwin recounts his own experience thus:

. . . I was so wearye that I waxed drowsye, and began in dede to slumber: but my imaginacion styll prosecutyng this [t]ragicall matter, brought me suche a fantasy me thought there stode before vs, a tall mans body full of fresshe woundes, but lackyng a head, holdyng by the hande a goodlye childe, . . . And whan through the gastfulnes of this pyteous spectacle, I waxed afeard, and turned awaye my face, me thought there came a shrekyng voyce out of the weasande pipe of the headles bodye, saying as foloweth.

When Richard had finished his complaint, Baldwin continues:

WIth this, mayster *Ferrers* shooke me by the sleve, saying: why how now man, do you forget your selfe? belike you mind our matters very much: So I do in dede (quoth I) For I dreame of them. And whan I had rehearced my dreame, we had long talke concerning the natures of dreames, which to stint and to bring vs to our matter againe, thus sayde one of them: . . .

Here is the dream vision in its regular setting.

Of the greatest interest, however, is Sackville's induction to the tragedy of the Duke of Buckingham, which represents a totally different type of vision literature—that of the descent into hell. Introducing an alien type, which derived from Virgil and Dante, it did not fit into the *Mirror*. Had Sackville followed out the plan for a new and revised *Mirror* with which Baldwin credited him, he must, perforce, have discarded the Boccaccio type of vision altogether.

In regard to verse form, too, it will be noted that not all the writers for the *Mirror* adhered to the seven-line stanza which Lydgate had adopted from Chaucer. The metrical experiments in the *Mirror* demand, however, more exhaustive study than is possible here.

This edition of the *Mirror for Magistrates* is being published, not with the hope of settling the problems of its printing history, or its literary or political significance, but only with the hope that the accessibility of the rare and scattered material here assembled may make possible further research in the comparatively unexplored period of Edward and Mary. When the *Mirror for Magistrates* is seriously studied, it will, I believe, be recognized as a pioneer work of the great English Renaissance and of first-rate importance in the study of the Elizabethan historical poems, historical plays, and tragedies.

The Procedure Followed in Collating the Text

There has been no attempt to establish a text of the *Mirror for Magistrates* in the following pages. Instead, the earliest printed text of each part of the *Mirror* has been reprinted and later texts collated with this earliest surviving text. The single leaf of text extant from the suppressed edition is referred to as *X* and is collated with the corresponding portion of the 1559 text. The 1559 text is referred to as *A*, the two copies of the 1563 text as *B* and *B²*; the two copies of the 1571 edition as *C* and *C²*; the 1574 text as *D* and the 1575 issue of the 1574 text as *E*; the uncancelled copy of the 1578 edition as *F* and the cancelled copy as *F²*; the 1587 edition as *G*. There are no liberties taken with the text as it appeared. I have made the changes indicated in the lists of faults escaped in the printing in the 1559 and 1563 texts, referring to the lists as *Ae* and *Be*, but all such authorized changes are noted in the collation. I have ventured few corrections, even where they might be termed obvious, for I believe that more harm has come through rationalizing and amending texts than through neglecting to do so, as the 1578 edition of the *Mirror* amply proves. I have, therefore, made no corrections save where the letters did not form a word, and in every case where any change whatsoever has been introduced into the text I have indicated in the collation what has been done, save that turned letters have been silently corrected.

I have, however, transcribed long *s* as *s*, and *vv* and *VV* as *w* and *W*, and I have expanded the conventional printer's contractions, except the ampersand, which I have retained.

The collation is purely a verbal one. To indicate changes in spelling and punctuation from edition to edition would have necessitated practically reproducing the texts of all editions. This limitation made inevitable the omission of much that is of philological interest, but I was able to devise no half-way system that did not result in confusion. I have not indicated as a variant reading an elision of an article or preposition with the initial vowel sound of a succeeding word, save in rare instances where such elision forms a transition to a later reading. The manner of collation will easily be seen to be that of quoting the inclosing words with which the variant begins and ends, except in cases where the change is an internal change in a single word. I have disregarded the variations of type in the titles of texts and tragedies, and I have reproduced the original black-letter texts in roman type, indicating variations from the original black letter by italics. Finally, I have indented the first line of prose paragraphs and the first line of stanzas of poetry, in accordance with modern usage.

The editing of the *Mirror for Magistrates* has been possible only through the generous co-operation of the Huntington Library, the Cambridge University Press, and the university which I serve, the University of California at Los Angeles. To each of them I acknowledge my very great debt of gratitude. The Huntington Library not only gave me access to its own rare collections but secured from other libraries in England and the United States supplementary information and reproductions of necessary documents. From every department in the library I have had technical help without which I should often have gone astray, but to the bibliographical knowledge of Mr C. K. Edmonds and the experience of Mr H. C. Schulz in reading sixteenth-century manuscripts, I owe some special debts of honor. Mr M. H. Crissey, who has prepared the manuscript for the press, and Mr DeWitt Bodeen and Mrs Marion Tinling, who have assisted in transcribing the text, have given patient and careful help in a tedious task. My special gratitude, however, is due to Mr Godfrey Davies, of the research staff of the Library, whose generous co-operation has been far too helpful to be adequately acknowledged.

To Mr W. A. Jackson, librarian of the Pforzheimer collection in New York, I am indebted for many suggestions and for copies of the photostatic reproductions of the unique title leaf now in South Kensington; to the authorities of the Victoria and Albert Museum for permission to reproduce the recto and the verso of the title leaf bound with the Dyce copy of the *Fall of Princes*; to St John's College, Cambridge, for permission to collate the manuscript of Sackville's contribution to the *Mirror* with the *Mirror* text; to the British Museum for permission to reprint copies of the supplementary title-page and the leaf remaining from the suppressed edition of the *Mirror*; and, finally, to Professor R. W. Chambers I am indebted for wise counsel in regard to the collating of the texts.

I am grateful to Mr Vincent F. Bonelli, of the New York University Library, and to Dr F. B. Adams, Jr, of the Pierpont Morgan Library, New York City, whose kindness in loaning copies of the text made it possible for Barnes & Noble, Inc. to issue this printing.

It is needless to say that I realize that all of the help so generously given will not have prevented me from making mistakes, which critics will discover, alas, too late to be remedied here.

LILY B. CAMPBELL

UNIVERSITY OF CALIFORNIA AT LOS ANGELES

TRAGEDIES
OF THE
1559 EDITION

A MYRROVRE

For Magiſtrates.

Wherein may be ſeen by

example of other, with howe gre
uous plages vices are puniſhed: and,
howe frayle and vnſtable worldly
proſperitie is founde, euen of
thoſe, whom Fortune ſee
meth moſt highly
to fauour.

*

Foelix quem faciunt aliena pericula cautum.

Anno .1559.

LONDINI,

In ædibus Thomæ Marſhe.

Love and Lyve.

[Preface 1]

҈ To the nobilitye and all other in office,
God graunt wisedome and all thinges
nedeful for the preseruacion
of theyr Estates.
Amen.

PLATO Among many other of his notable sentences concerning the government of a common weale, hath this: Well is ,,
that realme governed, in which the ambicious desyer not to ,,
beare office. Wherby you may perceive (right honorable)
what offices are, where they be duely executed: not gaynful spoyles [5]
for the gredy to hunt for, but payneful toyles for the heedy to be
charged with. You may perceyve also by this sentence, that there is
nothing more necessary in a common weale, than that officers be diligent
and trusty in their charges. And sure in whatsoever realme such pro-
vision is made, that officers be forced to do their duties, there is it as [10]
harde a matter to get an officer, as it is in other places to shift of, and put
by those, that with flattery, bribes, and other shiftes, sue and preace for
offices. For the ambicious (that is to say prollers for power or gayne)

[Title] TO AL THE C–F. *The preface is omitted in G, but the dedicatory title, with
slight changes, was adopted by Higgins in 1574 to serve his preface to* The First
parte of the Mirour for Magistrates, *and was retained in later editions of his
work. See above, p. 16.*
[1]   *amonge many of C–F.*
[7]   *sentence, there C–F.*
[8]   *that magistrates be C–F.*
[11–12] *to repulse & shift of, those C–F.*
[12]   *brykes C.*

seeke not for offices to helpe other, for whiche cause offices are ordayned,
[15] but with the vndoing of other, to pranke vp them selves. And therfore
bar them once of this bayte, and force them to do their duties, & they
will geve more to be rid fro their charges, than they did at the first to
bye them: For they seke only their commodity and ease. And therfore,
where the ambicious seeke no office, there no doubt, offices are duly
[20] ministred: and where offices are duly ministred, it can not be chosen, but
the people are good, whereof must nedes folow a good common weale.
For if the officers be good, the people can not be yll. Thus the goodnes or
badnes of any realme lyeth in the goodnes or badnes of the rulers. And
therfore not without great cause do the holy Apostels so earnestly
[25] charge vs to pray for the magistrates: For in dede the welth and quiet of
everye common weale, the disorder also and miseries of the same, cum
specially through them. I nede not go eyther to the Romans or Grekes
for proofe hereof, neyther yet to the Iewes, or other nacions: whose
common weales have alway florished while their officers were good, and
[30] decayed and ranne to ruyne, whan noughty men had the regiment, Our
owne countrey stories (if we reade & marke them) will shewe vs
examples ynow, would God we had not seen moe then ynowe. I purpose not to stand here vppon the particulers, because they be in part set
furth in the tragedyes. Yet by the waye this I note (wishing all other
[35] to do the like) namely, that as good governers have never lacked their

[14]   cause officers are C–F.
[15]   to enrich themselues. C–F.
[16–17] dueties, then will they geeue C–F.
[17]   from C–F.
[17–18] to come by them: C–F.
[18]   their priuate profite. And C–F.
[22]   the magistrates be C–F.
[27]   specially *is misprinted* specicially *in the text.*
[28]   for the proofe B–F.
[29]   their Magistrates were C–F.
[30]   when vicious men had the gouernment. C–F.
[30–31] Our countrey C–F.
[34]   tragedies folowing. C–F.

deserved renowme, so have not the bad escaped infamy, besides such plages as are horrible to hear of

For God (the ordeyner of Offices) although he suffer them for punishment of the people to be often occupied of such, as are rather spoilers and Iudasses, than toylers or Iustices (whom the scripture therfore [40] calleth Hipocrites) yet suffreth he them not to skape vnpunished, because they dishonour him. For it is Gods owne office, yea his chiefe office, whych they beare & abuse. For as Iustice is the chief vertue, so is the ministracion therof, the chiefest office: & therfore hath God established it with the chiefest name, honoring & calling Kinges, & all [45] officers vnder them by his owne name, Gods. Ye be all Gods, as many as have in your charge any ministracion of Iustice. What a fowle shame wer it for any now to take vpon them the name and office of God, and in their doinges to shew them selves divyls? God can not of Iustice, but plage such shameles presumption and hipocrisy, and that with shamefull [50] death, diseases, or infamy. Howe he hath plaged euill rulers from time to time, in other nacions, you may see gathered in Boccas booke intituled the fall of Princes, translated into Englishe by Lydgate: Howe he hath delt with sum of our countreymen your auncestors for sundrye vices not yet left, this booke named *A Myrrour for Magistrates*, can shewe: [55] which therfore I humbly offre vnto your honors, beseching you to accept it fauorably. For here as in a loking glas, you shall see (if any vice be in you) howe the like hath bene punished in other heretofore, whereby admonished, I trust it will be a good occasion to move you to the

[36]   deserued prayses: so *C–F.*
[38]   for *is blurred in the HN copy of the text.*
[40–41] the scriptures call Hypocrites) *C–F.*
[53]   *Lydgate* a Monke of the Abbey of Bury in Suff. *C–F.*
[55–56] *Magistrates,* shall in parte plainlye [*misprinted* plalinye] set forth before your
          eyes which boke I *F.*
[57]   in a mirror or looking glasse, *C–F.*
[57–58] se if any vice be found how *C–F.*
[59]   moue men to *C–F.*

[60] soner amendment. This is the chiefest ende, whye it is set furth, which
God graunt it may attayne.

The wurke was begun, & part of it printed .iiii. yeare agoe, but
hyndred by the lord Chauncellour that then was, nevertheles, through
the meanes of my lord Stafford, lately perused & licenced. Whan I first
[65] tooke it in hand, I had the helpe of many graunted, & offred of sum, but
of few perfourmed, skarce of any: So that wher I entended to have continued it to Quene Maries time, I have ben faine to end it much sooner:
yet so, that it may stande for a patarne, till the rest be ready: which with
Gods grace (if I may have anye helpe) shall be shortly. In the meane

[60]   the chief end why thys booke is C–F.
[61]   may talke according to the maner of the makers. F.
[62]   printed *is blurred in the HN copy of the text.* [Captain R. B. Haselden, of the
        Huntington Library, says acid has been used deliberately to eradicate the
        word. Other known copies are, however, unmarred.] prynted in Queene
        Maries tyme, but B–F.
[62–63] but staid by such as then were chiefe in office, neuertheles, C–F.
[64]   of the right honorable Henry Lord Stafford, C–F.
[64–69] Stafford, the fyrst parte was licenced, and imprynted the fyrst yeare of the
        raygne of this our most noble and vertuous Queene, and dedicate then to
        your honours wyth this Preface.
        Since whych time, although I have bene called to an other trade of lyfe,
   5   yet my good Lorde Stafforde hath not ceassed to call vpon me, to publyshe
        so much as I had gotten at other mens hands, so that through his Lord-
        shyppes earnest meanes, I have nowe also set furth an other parte, conteynyng
        as litle of myne owne, as the fyrst part doth of other mens. Which in the
        name of all the authors, I humbly dedicate vnto your honours, instantly
   10   wishyng, that it may so like and delyte your myndes, that your chearefull
        receyuing thereof, maye encourage wurthy wittes to enterpryse and per-
        fourme the rest. Which as soone as I maye procure, I entende through Gods
        leave, and your favourable allowaunce, to publyshe with al expedicion. In
        B–F. [*In l. 2 above read* dedicated to *for* dedicate then to *In l. 4 read* I wanted
        such helpe as before, *for* I have bene called to an other trade of lyfe, *In l. 5
        read* the sayde *for* my *In l. 6 insert* thereof *after* so much *In l. 8 read* as much
        as I coulde obteyne at the handes of my frendes. *for* as litle of myne owne,
        as the fyrst part doth of other mens. C–F.]

while my lords and gods (for so I may call you) I most humbly beseche [70]
you, fauourably to accepte this rude myrrour, and diligently to read and
consider it. And although you shall finde in it, that sum haue for their
vertue been enuied and murdered, yet cease not you to be vertuous, but
do your offices to the vttermost: punish sinne boldly, both in your
selues and other, so shall God (whose lieutenauntes you are) eyther so [75]
mayntayne you, that no malice shall preuayle, or if it do, it shal be for
your good, and to your eternall glory both here and in heaven, which I
beseche God you may covet and attayne. Amen.

Yours most humble,

William Baldwin. [80]

[70–71] beseche your honours favourablye *B–F.*
[71]   rude worke, and *C–F.*
[73]   and brought vnto miserie: yet *C–F.*
[74]   vttermoste: suppres sinne *B.* your office to the vttermost. Embrace vertue
        and suppresse the contrary, both *C–F.*
[75]   (whose officers you are) *B–F.*
[78]   maye both covet *B–F* [*read* seke *for* covet *C–F*].
[80]   *W. B. C–F.*

❧ A Briefe Memorial of sundrye Vnfortunate Englishe men.

William Baldwin to
the *Reader*.

Han the Printer had purposed with hym selfe to printe
Lidgates booke of the fall of Princes, and had made priuye
thereto, many both honourable and worshipfull, he was
counsailed by dyuers of theim, to procure to haue the storye contynewed
[5] from where as Bochas lefte, vnto this presente time, chiefly of suche as
Fortune had dalyed with here in this ylande: whiche might be as a
myrrour for al men as well noble as others, to shewe the slyppery
deceytes of the waueryng lady, and the due rewarde of all kinde of vices.
Whiche aduyse lyked him so well, that he required me to take paynes
[10] therin: but because it was a matter passyng my wyt and skyll, and more
thankles than gaineful to meddle in, I refused vtterly to vndertake it,
excepte I might haue the helpe of suche, as in wyt were apte, in learning
allowed, and in iudgemente and estymacion able to wield and furnysh so
weighty an enterpryse, thinkyng euen so to shift my handes. But he

[2]   Lidgates translation of Bochas, of the *C–G*. Princes, hauinge made priuy *F*.
[4–5] procure a continuance of the Storye from *F*.
[6]   had abused here *F*.
[7]   nobles *B*. Myrrour for men of all estates & degres as well Nobles as other to
             behold the slippery *C–G*. [*Read* others *for* other *G*.]
[11]   gaynefull to enterprise I *F*. vtterly alone to *F*.
[12]   without the helpe *F*.
[13–14] and discharge the weight of sutch a burden, *F*.
[14]   thinkinge so to *C–G*.

earnest and diligent in his affayres, procured Athlas to set vnder his [15]
shoulder: for shortly after, dyuers learned men whose many giftes nede
fewe praises, consented to take vpon theym parte of the trauayle. And
whan certayne of theym to the numbre of seuen, were throughe a
generall assent at an apoynted time and place gathered together to
deuyse therupon, I resorted vnto them, bering with me the booke of [20]
Bochas, translated by Dan Lidgate, for the better obseruacion of his
order: whiche although we lyked well, yet woulde it not cumlily serue,
seynge that both Bochas and Lidgate were dead, neyther were there any
alyue that meddled with lyke argument, to whom the vnfortunat might
make their mone. [25]

  To make therfore a state mete for the matter, they al agreed that I
shoulde vsurpe Bochas rowme, and the wretched princes complayne
vnto me: and tooke vpon themselues euery man for his parte to be
sundrye personages, and in theyr behalfes to bewayle vnto me theyr
greuous chaunces, heuy destinies, & wofull misfortunes. [30]

  This doen, we opened suche bookes of Cronicles as we had there
present, and maister Ferrers, after he had founde where Bochas left,
whiche was about the ende of king Edwarde the thirdes raigne, to begin
the matter, sayde thus.

  I meruaile what Bochas meaneth to forget among his myserable [35]
princes, such as wer of our nacion, whose numbre is as great, as their
aduentures wunderful: For to let passe all, both Britons, Danes, and
Saxons, and to cum to the last Conquest, what a sorte are they, and sum

---

[15–16] procure me an Athlas to laye the burden vppon my shoulders, which I would
        not haue vndertaken, but that shortly F.
[19]   at one apoynted G.
[22]   wee did not mislyke, yet F. cumly serue, B. conueniently serue, C–G.
[24]   that had medled F.
[30]   sundry chaunces, F.
[35]   maruayle (quoth hee) what F.
[36]   our owne nation, G.

euen in his owne tyme? As for example, king Rycharde the fyrste,
[40] slayne with a quarlle in his chiefe prosperitie, also king Iohn his brother
as sum saye, poysoned: are not their histories rufull and of rare example?
But as it shoulde appeare, he beynge an *Italien*, mynded most the *Roman*
and *Italike* story, or els perhaps he wanted our countrey chronicles. It
were therfore a goodlye and a notable matter to searche & dyscourse
[45] oure whole storye from the fyrst beginning of the inhabitynge of the
yle. But seinge the printers mynde is to haue vs followe where *Lidgate*
left, we wyll leaue that great laboure to other that maye intende it, and
(as blinde bayarde is alway boldest) I wyll begin at the tyme of Rycharde

[39]   euen in his own time or not much before. As for Example William Rufus
       the second King of England after the Conquest, eyther by malice or mis-
       aduenture slaine in the new Forest, as he was in hunting there, by Walter
       Tirrell with the shotte of an Arrow. Robert Duke of Normandy eldest
5   sonne to William Conqueror depriued of his inheritance of Englande, by
       the sayed William Rufus his second brother, and after by Henry his yongest
       brother hauing both his eyes put oute, miserablye imprisoned in Cardiffe
       Castel, where as hee dyed. Lykewise the moste lamentable case of William,
       Richard, & Mary, children of the said Henry: drowned vpon the sea. And
10   King Richard *C–G*. [*In l.* 1 *above read* also in the time of Bochas himselfe,
       for euen in his own time *In l.* 3 *read* slayne hunting in the new Forest, *for*
       slaine in the new Forest, as he was in hunting there, *In ll.* 5–6 *omit* by the
       sayed William Rufus his second brother, and after *In l.* 7 *insert* and after,
       after oute, *In l.* 8 *omit* Lykewise *In l.* 9 *insert* the first called Beauclerke,
       after Henry, *and insert* by the negligence of drunken Mariners *after* sea *F*.
       In ll. 2–3 *omit* eyther by malice or misaduenture *In l.* 3 *omit* in *G*.]
[40–41] prosperity. The most vnnaturall murther of Artur Duke of *Britayne* right
       Heyre of Englande, by king Ihon his vncle, with the death of Isabell his
       Sister by Famyne. The myserable ende of the sayd king Ihon their vncle by
       Surfet, or as some write poysoned by a Monke of the Abbey of *Swinsted*
       in Lyncolneshrye. Are not *F*.
[42]   apeare, Bochas being *C–G*.
[43]   wanted the knowledge of ours. *C–G*.
[44]   and notable *C–G*.
[46]   vs supply where *F*.
[48]   (as one being bold first to breake the yse) *C–G*. at the reigne of *F*.

the second, a tyme as vnfortunate as the ruler therein. And forasmuche
frende *Baldwin*, as it shalbe your charge to note, and pen orderly the [50]
whole proces, I wyll so far as my memorie and iudgement serueth, sumwhat further you in the truth of the story. And therefore omytting the
ruffle made by Iacke Strawe and his meyny, and the mourder of many
notable men which therby happened, for Iacke (as ye knowe) was but a
poore prince: I will begin with a notable example whiche within a [55]
whyle after ensued. And althoughe he be no great prince, yet sythens
he had a princelye offyce, I wyll take vpon me the miserable person of
syr Robert Tresilian chiefe Iustice of Englande, and of other which
suffred with him: thereby to warne all of his authorytie and profession,
to take heed of wrong Iudgementes, mysconstruyng of lawes, or [60]
wrestyng the same to serue the princes turnes, whiche ryghtfullye
brought theym to a myserable ende, whiche they may iustly lament in
maner ensuyng.

[49]   time as troublesome to the people, as vnlucky to the Prince. *F.*
[50]   charge to penne *F.*
[53]   meiney, with the *C–G.* [*Read* Lewd meiney, *F.*]
[56]   although the person at whom I begin, was no king nor prince: *C–G.*
[58–59] other his fellowes learned in the Law that were plagued with *F.*
[59–60] of theyr callinge & profession, to beware of *F.*
[61]   Prynces turne, *F.*

The fall of Robert Tresilian chiefe Iustice of Englande, and other his felowes, for mis-construyng the lawes, and expoun-ding them to serue the Princes affections.

IN the rufull Register of mischief and mishap,
Baldwin we beseche thee with our names to begin,
Whom vnfrendly Fortune did trayne vnto a trap,
When we thought our state most stable to haue bin,
So lightly leese they all which all do ween to wyn: [5]
Learne by vs ye Lawyers and Iudges of the lande
Vncorrupt and vpryght in doome alway to stande.

And print it for a president to remayne for euer,
Enroll and recorde it in tables made of brasse,
Engraue it in marble that may be razed neuer,   [10]
Where Iudges and Iusticers may see, as in a glasse,
What fee is for falshode, and what our wages was
Who for our princes pleasure corrupt with meed and awe
wittyngly and wretchedly did wrest the sence of lawe.

[Title]	affections. Anno. 1388. C–G.
[6]	this Land, G.
[7]	Vpright and vncorrupt C–G.
[8]	printe ye this presydent C–G.
[11]	Where Iudges of the Lawe may see, C–G. [*Read* the Iudges G.]
[12]	What guerdon is for guyle, C–G.
[13]	Who for filthy lucre, corrupt F.

[15]   A chaunge more newe or straunge seldome hath be seen
Then from the benche aboue to cum downe to the bar:
was neuer state so turned in no tyme as I ween,
As they to becum clyentes that counsaylours erst were,
But such is Fortunes playe, which featly can prefer
[20]   The iudge that sate aboue, full lowe beneth to stand,
At the bar a prisoner holdynge vp his hand.

Whiche in others cause coulde stoutly speake and plead,
Both in court and countrey, careles of the tryall,
Stande muet lyke mummers without aduyse or read,
[25]   Vnable to vtter a true plea of denyall:
Whiche haue seen the daye when that for halfe a ryall,
We coulde by very arte haue made the blacke seme white,
And matters of most wrong, to haue appered most right.

[15]   be *is printed* he *but is corrected in* Ae.
[15–21]   A chaunge more new or straunge, when was there euer seene
Then Iudges from the Bench, to come doune to the Barre
And counsaylours that were, most nigh to King and Quene
Exiled their countrey, from Court and counsaile farre,
5   But such is Fortunes play, which can both make and marre,
Exaltinge to most highe, that was before moste Lowe
And turning tayle agayne, the lofty doune to throwe. *C–G.*
[*In l.* 19 *read* that *for* which *D–F.*]
[22]   And such as late afore, could *C–G.*
[24]   muet as *C–G.*
[25]   All to seke of shifting, by trauerse or deniall *C–G.*
[26]   when for a golden Riall, *C–G.*
[27–28]   By finesse and conning, could haue made black seme white
And moste extorted wronge, to haue appered righte. *C–G.*
[*In l.* 27 *read* finenesse *for* finesse *G.*]
Insert between 28 *and* 29:
    Whilst thus on bench aboue, we had the highest place,
Our reasons were to strong, for any to confute,
But when at barre beneth, we came to pleade our case
Our wits were in the wane, our pleading very brute,
5   Hard it is for prisoners, with Iudges to dispute
When all men against one, and none for one shall speake
Who wenes himselfe moste wise, shall happely be to weake.

Beholde me vnfortunate forman of this flocke,
Tresilian sumtime chief Iustice of this lande, [30]
By discent a gentleman, no staine was in my stocke,
Loketon, Holt, and Belknap, with other of my bande
Whiche the lawe and iustice had wholy in our hande
Vnder the seconde Richarde a prince of great estate,
To whom frowarde fortune gaue a foule checkmate. [35]

In the common lawes our skill was so profounde,
Our credite and aucthoritie suche and so estemed,
That what so we concluded was taken for a grounde,
Allowed was for lawe, what so to vs best semed:
Lyfe, death, landes, goodes, and all by vs was demed, [40]
Whereby with easye paine, so great gaine we did get,
That euery thing was fishe that came vnto our net.

At sessions and at syses we bare the stroke and swey,
In patentes and commissions of *Quorum*, alway chiefe:
So that to whether syde so euer we did wey, [45]
Were it right or wrong it past without repriefe,

> To you therefore that sit, these few wordes will I say,
> That no man syts so sure, but he may haply stand,
> Wherfore whilst you haue place, and beare the swinge & sway 10
> By fauour without rygor, let pointes of Lawe be skand:
> Pitty the poore prisoner that holdeth vp his hand,
> Ne lade him not with lawe, who least of law hath knowen,
> Remember ere ye dye, the case may be your owne *C–G*.
> [*In l. 6 above read* many *for* all men *F. In l. 9 read* may be brought
>   to *for* he may haply *F.*]

[31] A Gentleman by byrth, *C–G.*
[34] great estates *F.*
[35] To whome and vs also, blinde Fortune gaue the mate. *C–G.*
[38] That what we *C–EG.* That what that we *F.*
[41] paine, greate gaine we did in fet, *C–G.*
[42] And euery *C–G.*
[43] and Sises *F.*
[44] commission, *C–G.*
[46] Were it by right *C–G.*

We let hang the true man sumwhiles to saue a thiefe
Of golde and of syluer our handes were neuer emptye,
Offices, fermes, and fees, fell to vs in great plentye.

[50]   But what thing maye suffyse vnto the gredye man?
The more he hath in holde, the more he doeth desyre,
Happy and twise happy is he that wisely can
Content him selfe with that whiche reason doth requyre,
And moyleth for no more then for his needfull hyre:
[55]   But gredynes of mynde doth neuer kepe the syse,
Whiche though it haue enough yet doth it not suffyse.

For lyke as dropsye pacientes drinke, and styll be dry,
Whose vnstaunched thyrst no lyquor can allaye.
And drinke they neuer so muche yet styll for more they cry:
[60]   So couetous catchers toyle both nyght and day,
Gredy and euer nedy prollyng for theyr praye.
O endles thyrst of golde corrupter of all lawes,
What mischiefe is on molde whereof thou art not cause?

Thou madest vs forget the fayth of our profession,
[65]   When sergeantes we were sworne to serue the common lawe.
Whiche was that in no poynte we should make digression
From approued principles in sentens nor in sawe:
But we vnhappy wretches without all drede and awe

[47]   The true man we let hang somewhiles *C–G.*
[55]   doth seeldome *C–G.*
[56]   To whome ynough and more doth neuer well suffise. *C–G.* [*Read* at no time doth *for* doth neuer well *F.*]
[59]   they nere so mutch *FG.* yet thirst they by and by *C–G.*
[60]   So catchers and snatchers toyle *C–G.*
[61]   Not needy but greedy, styll prolling *C–G.*
[64]   the fayth we did professe, *F.*
[66]   Makyng a solempne oth in no poynt to dygresse. *F.*
[68]   vnhappy wyghtes *C–G.*

Of the Iudge eternall, for worldes vayne promocion,
More to man than God dyd beare our hole deuocion. [70]

    The lawes we interpreted and statutes of the lande,
Not trulye by the texte, but nuly by a glose:
And wurds that wer most plaine whan thei by vs wer skande
We turned by construction lyke a welchmans hose,
Wherby many one both lyfe and lande dyd lose: [75]
Yet this we made a mean to mount aloft on mules.
To serue kings in al pointes men must sumwhile breke rules.

    Thus clymyng and contendyng alway to the top
From hye vnto hygher, and than to be moste hye,
The hunny dewe of Fortune so fast on vs dyd drop [80]
That of kinge Richards counsayle we came to be full nye:
To crepe into whose fauour we were full fyne and slye
Alway to his profite where any wurde myght sounde
That way (all were it wrong) the sens we dyd expounnde.

    So wurkyng lawe lyke waxe, the subiecte was not sure [85]
Of lyfe, lande, nor goods, but at the princes wyll:
Which caused his kingdome the shorter tyme to dure,
For clayming power absolute both to saue and spyll,
The prince therby presumed his people for to pyll:
And set his lustes for lawe, and will had reasons place, [90]
No more but hang and drawe, there was no better grace.

[69–70]	eternall, more high to be promoted.
	To Mammon more then God, all wholly were deuoted. *F.*
[71]	we did interprete and *C–G.*
[74]	construction to a *C–EG.*
[75]	many a one *C–G.*
[76]	made our meane *C–G.*
[77]	And seruing times and turnes, peruerted Lawes and rules. *C–G.*
[81]	be most nye: *C–G.*
[82]	Whose fauour to attaine we were full fine and slye *C–G.*
[83]	Alway to his auayle, where any sense might *F.* where any thinge might *C–EG.*
[84]	the Laws *C–G.*

The king thus transcending the lymittes of his lawe,
Not raygning but raging by youthfull insolence,
Wyse and wurthy persons, dyd fro the courte withdrawe,
[95]   There was no grace ne place for auncient prudence,
Presumcion and pryde with excesse of expence
Possessed the palays, and pillage the countrye:
Thus all went to wracke, vnlyke of remedie.

The Baronye of Englande not bearyng this abuse,
[100] Conspyring with the commons assembled by assent,
And seynge neyther reason, nor treaty, coulde induce
The king in any thing his Rygor to relent,
Mawgree all his might they called a parlyament
Francke and free for all men without checke to debate
[105] As well for weale publyke, as for the princes state.

In whiche parlyament muche thinges was proponed
Concerning the regaly and ryghtes of the crowne,
By reason kynge Richarde, whiche was to be moned,
Full lytell regardynge his honour and renowne,

[92]   Thus the King outleaping, *C–EG.* The King thus outleaping, *F.*
[93]   raginge, as youth did him entise, *C–EG.* as wyll did him entice, *F.*
[94]   persons from Court did dayly drawe, *C–G.*
[95–98] Sage counsaile set at naught, proud vauntours were in price,
        And roysters bare the rule, which wasted all in vice,
        Of ryot and excesse, grewe scarsitye and lacke,
        Of lacking came taxinge, and so went welth to wracke. *C–G.*
[99]   The Barons of the Lande not *C–G.*
[101]   no reason *F.*
[103]   Maugre his mighte *B–EG.* Maugre his princely mynde: *F.*
[104]   men, vnchecked to *F.*
[106–10] In this high assembly, great thynges were proponed
        Touching the Princes state, his regaly and Crowne,
        By reason that the King, which much was to be moned,
        Without regarde at all of honour or renowne.
        Mysledde by yll aduise, had tournd all vpsydowne. *C–G.*
        [*In l.* 106 *read* which *for* this *F. In l.* 107 *read* regalty *for* regaly *G.*
        In l. 108 *read* Richard *for* the King *F.*]

By synister aduyse, had tourned all vpsodowne.   [110]
For suerty of whose state, them thought it dyd behooue
His corrupt counsaylours, from him to remooue.

Among whom, Robert Vere, called duke of Irelande
with Myghell Delapole of Suffolke newe made erle,
Of Yorke also the Archebysshop, dyspatcht wer out of hande, [115]
with Brembre of London Mayor, a full vncurteous churle,
Sum learned in the lawe in exyle they dyd hurle:
But I poore Tresilian because I was the chiefe
was dampned to the gallowes most vyly as a thiefe.

Loe the fyne of falshode, the stypende of corruption,   [120]
Fye on stynkyng lucre, of all vnryght the lure:
Ye Iudges and ye Iusticers let my most iust punycion,
Teache you to shake of bribes and kepe your handes pure.
Ryches and promocion be vaine thynges and vnsure,
The fauour of a prince is an vntrusty staye,   [125]
But Iustyce hath a fee that shall remayne alwaye.

what glory can be greater before god or man,
Then by the pathes of equitie in iudgement to procede,

[111]   whose estate, B.
[112]   His counsaylours corrupt, by reason to remoue. C–G. [*Read* order
              for reason F.]
[115]   Tharchbyshop of Yorke was also of our band: F.
[116]   of London a full C–G. [*Read* at *for* of DE.]
[118]   I iudge Tresilian, F.
[119]   Gallowes to dye there as F.
[121]   The fee of dowble fraude, the fruites it doth procure C–G. [*Read*
              fickle fee of *for* fee of dowble F.]
[122]   Iudges vpon earth, let our iuste C–G. [*Read* now liuing *for* vpon
              earth F.]
[123]   handes al pure. F.
[127]   What glory is more greater in sight of God F.
[128]   by pathes of Iustice C–G.

So dulye and so trulye the lawes alwayes to skan.
[130] That ryght may take his place without rewarde or mede,
Set aparte all flattery and vaine worldly drede:
Take god before your eyes the iust iudge supreme,
Remembre well your reckening at the daye extreme.

Abandon all affray, be soothfast in your sawes,
[135] Be constant and careles of mortall mens dyspleasure,
With eyes shut & hands close you should pronounce the lawes
Esteme not worldly hyre, thynke ther is a treasure
More worth then golde or stone a thousande tymes in valure,
Reposed for all suche as righteousnes ensue,
[140] Whereof you cannot fayle, the promys made is true.

If sum in latter dayes, had called vnto mynde
The fatall fall of vs for wrestyng of the ryght,
The statutes of this lande they should not haue defynde
So wylfully and wyttingly agaynst the sentence quyte:
[145] But though they skaped paine, the falte was nothing lyght:
Let them that cum hereafter both that and this compare,
And waying well the ende, they wyll I trust beware.

[129]   So duelye and truely *F.* alway to *C–G.*
[130]   That Iustice may take place without *F.* without regarde or *G.*
[132]   Set God before *C–G.* the righteous Iudge *F.*
[136]   hands closde *F.*
[137]   worldly goods, *C–EG.* Way not this worldly mucke, *F.*
[141]   If Iudges in our dayes, would ponder well in minde, *C–G.*
[142]   wresting Lawe and right, *C–G.*
[143–46] Such statutes as touch life should not be thus definde
        By sences constrained, against true meaning quite,
        As well they might affirme the blacke for to be white,
        Wherefore we wish they would, our act and end compare, *C–G.*
[147]   well the case, *C–G.* we trust *C–G.*

Han maister *Ferrers* had finished this tragedye, whiche [Prose 1]
semed not vnfyt for the persons touched in the same. An
other whiche in the mean tyme had stayed vpon syr Roger
Mortimer, whose miserable ende as it should appeare, was sumwhat
before the others, sayd as foloweth. Althoughe it be not greatly apper- [5]
tinent to our purpose, yet in my iudgement I thynke it woulde do wel
to obserue the times of men, and as they be more aunciente, so to place
theym: for I fynde that before these, of whom maister *Ferrers* here hath
spoken, there were two Mortimers, the one hanged in Edwarde the
thirdes tyme out of oure date, another slayne in Irelande in Richarde the [10]
secondes tyme, a yere before the fall of these Iustices: whose historye
syth it is notable and the example fruitfull, it were pitie to ouerpasse it.
And therfor by your lycence and agrement, I will take vpon me the
personage of the last, who full of woundes, miserably mangled, with a
pale countenaunce, and grisly looke, may make his mone to *Baldwin* as [15]
foloweth.

[1]   WHen finished was this *F.* his Tragedy, *G.*
[4]   Mortimer Earle of March, and heyre apparaunt of Englande, whose *F.*
[6]   our purposed matter, *F.*
[7]   tymes of these great infortunes, *F.*
[7–8]   auncient in tyme, so to place their seuerall plaintes: *F.*
[9]   the one in *C–EG.*
[9–11] two earles of the name of Mortimer, the one in the tyme of king Edward the
        third out of our date: another in Richard the secondes time, slayne in Ireland,
        a *F.*
[12]   were not good to *C–G.*
[13]   and fauours, *F.*
[14]   of woundes mangled, *C–EG.* the earle Mortimer called Roger, who full of
        bloudye woundes mangled, *F.*
[15–16] Baldwin, in this wise. *F.*

Howe the two Rogers, surnamed Morti-
mers, for theyr sundry vices ended
theyr lyues vnfortu-
natelye.

ᚷMong the ryders of the rollyng wheele,
That lost theyr holdes, Baldwin forget not me,
whose fatall threede false Fortune nedes would reele,
Ere it were twysted by the systers three.
[5] All folke be frayle, theyr blysses brittle bee:
For proofe whereof although none other wer,
Suffyse may I, syr Roger Mortimer.

Not he that was in Edwardes dayes the thyrde,
Whom Fortune brought to boote and efte to bale,
[10] With loue of whom the kyng so muche she sturde,
That none but he was heard in any tale:
And whyles she smooth, blewe on this merye gale,
He was created earle of Marche, alas,
Whence envy sprang whiche his destruction was.

[Title]   vnfortunately the one. An. 1329. the other. 1387. C–G. [*Read*
          Anno 1387. *D–F.*]
[1]   on the *F.*
[2]   Which lost *F.*
[3]   thred, vntimely death dyd reele *F.*
[9]   brought from boote to extreme bale, *F.*
[10–14]   With loue of whom, the Queene so much was stird,
          As for his sake from honour she did scale,
          And whilest Fortune, blew on this pleasaunt gale,
          Heauing him high on her triumphall Arch,
          By meane of her hee was made Earle of March. *F.*
[12]   this pleasant gale *C–E.*

For welth bredeth wrath, in suche as welth do want,   [15]
And pryde with folly in suche as it possesse,
Among a thousande shall you fynde hym skant,
That can in welth his loftye harte represse,
Whiche in this Erle due proofe did playne expresse,
For where he sumwhat hauty was before,   [20]
His hygh degree hath made hym nowe muche more.

For nowe alone he ruleth as him lust,
Ne recketh for rede, save of kyng Edwardes mother:
Whiche forced envy foulder out the rust,
That in mens hartes before dyd lye and smother.   [25]
The Piers, the people, as well the one as the other,
Agaynst hym made so haynous a complaynt,
That for a traytour he was taken and attaynt.

Then all suche faultes as were forgot before,
The skower afresh, and sumwhat to them ad: [30]
For cruell envy hath eloquence in store,
whan Fortune byds, to warsse thinges meanely bad.

[15–21]   Whence pryde out sprang, as doth appeare by manye,
        Whom soden hap, aduaunceth in excesse,
        Among thousandes, scarse shal you fynde anye,
        Which in high wealth that humor can suppresse,
        As in this earle, playne proofe did wel expresse:
        For whereas hee too loftye was before,
        His new degree hath made him now much more. *F.*
[15]   breedes *G.*
[17]   fynde one skant, *C–EG.*
[20]   For where as he was somewhat haut before, *C–EG.*
[23]   Respecting none saue only the Queene mother, *F.*
[24]   Which moued malice to foulder *F.*
[25]   Which deepe in hate, before *F.*
[26]   one as other, *C–G.*
[28]   traytour, they did the Earle attaynt. *F.*
[29]   forgot afore, *C–EG.* such crimes as hidden lay before, *F.*
[30]   They skower *C–G.*
[31]   For hydden hate hath *F.*
[32]   biddes small faultes to make more bad, *F.*

Fyue haynous crymes agaynst hym soone were had,
Fyrst, that he causde the kyng to yelde the Skot,
[35]   To make a peace, townes that were from him got:

And therewithall the charter called Ragman.
That of the Skots he bribed pryuy gayne,
That through his meanes syr Edward of Carnaruan
In Barkley castell trayterously was slayne:
[40]   That with his princes mother he had layne.
And fynally with pollyng at his pleasure,
Had robde the kyng and commons of theyr treasure.

For these thynges loe whiche erst were out of minde
He was condemned, and hanged at the last,
[45]   In whom dame Fortune fully shewed her kynde,
For whom she heaues, she hurleth downe as fast:
If men to cum would learne by other past,
This cosen of myne myght cause them set asyde,
High clymyng, brybyng, murdring, lust, and pryde.

[50]   The fynall cause why I this processe tell,
Is that I may be knowen from this other,
My lyke in name, vnlyke me though he fell,
Whiche was I thinke my graund sier or his brother:

[34-35]   Causing the king to yeld vnto the Scot,
           Townes that his father, but late afore had got. *F.*
[37]   he had bribed priuy gayne, *C-EG.* Yeuen to the Scots for brybes
           and priuie gayne, *F.*
[38]   That by his *F.*
[39]   Castell most traiterously *C-EG.* Castel, most cruelly was slayne: *F*
[41]   And last of all by pyllage at *F.*
[42]   Had spoyld the *F.*
[44]   Dampned he was, *F.*
[48]   My coosins fall might *F.*
[49]   brybing, adultery and pryde, *F.*
[53]   I wene *F.*

To counte my kyn, dame Philip was my mother,
Deare doughter and heyre of douty Lyonell,   [55]
The seconde sonne of a kyng that dyd excell.

My father hyght syr Edmunde Mortimer,
True erle of Marche, whence I was after erle
By iust discent, these two my parentes wer,
Of whiche the one of knighthoode bare the ferle,   [60]
Of womanhoode the other was the perle:
Throughe theyr deserte so called of euery wight,
Tyll death them tooke, and left in me theyr ryght.

For why the attaynder of my elder Roger,
(whose shamefull death I tolde you but of late)   [65]
was founde to be vniust, and passed ouer
Agaynst the lawe, by those that bare hym hate.
For where by lawe the lowest of free estate
Should personally be heard ere iudgement passe,
They barred hym this, where through distroyed he was. [70]

[55–56] Eldest daughter and heire of Lyonell,
         Of King Edward the third the second sequele. *F.*
[56]   kyng who dyd *B–EG.*
[58]   Cald Earle *F.*
[59]   By true discent *F.*
[60]   bare ferll *D–F.*
[61]   Of Ladies all, the *F.*
[62–63] After whose Death I onely stoode in plight,
         To be next heyre vnto the crowne by right. *F.*
[63]   left me in their right. *C–EG.*
[64]   For the attainder *DE.*
[64–66]   Touching the case of my cousin Roger,
         (Whose ruful end euen now I did relate)
         Was found in tyme an vndue atteindre *F.*
[68]   lawe ech man of *F.*
[69–70] Should be heard speake before his iudgement passe,
         That common grace to him denyed was. *F.*

wherfore by doome of courte in parlyament,
whan we had proued our cosen ordred thus,
The Kyng, the Lordes, the Commens of assent,
His lawles death vnlawfull dyd discus:
[75] And both to blood and good restored vs.
A Presydent most worthy, shewed, and left
Lordes lyues to saue that lawles might be reft.

whyle Fortune thus dyd furder me amayne
Kyng Rychardes grace the seconde of the name
[80] (whose dissolute lyfe dyd soone abridge his rayne)
Made me his mate in earnest and in game:
The Lordes them selues so well allowed the same,
That throwe my tytles duely cummyng downe,
I was made heyre apparaunt to the crowne.

[85] who then but I was euery where estemed?
well was the man that myght with me acquaynte,
whom I allowed, as Lordes the people demed.
To what so euer folly had me bente,
To lyke it well the people dyd assente:
[90] To me as prince, attended great and small,
In hope a daye would cum to paye for all.

[71]   doome in Court of Parliament, *F*.
[72]   His atteindre appering erroneous, *F*.
[76]   A president worthy, in record left, *F*.
[77]   Lordes lygnes saue, by lawles meanes bereft. *F*.
[78]   did frendly me reteyne, *F*.
[79]   of that name, *C–EG*.
[79–80] Rychard the king, that second was by name,
         Hauing none heire after him to reigne: *F*.
[86]   that vnderstoode my bent, *F*.
[88–89] And me to serue was euery mannes entent,
         With all that wyt or cunning could inuent: *F*.
[91]   I hoopt a day *C–EG*.

But seldome ioye continueth trouble voyde,
In greatest charge cares greatest do ensue,
The most possest are ever most anoyed,
In largest seas sore tempestes lyghtly brue, [95]
The fresshest colours soonest fade the hue,
In thyckest place is made the depest wounde,
True proofe wherof my selfe to soone haue founde.

For whyles that Fortune lulde me in her lap,
And gaue me gyftes mo than I dyd requyre, [100]
The subtyll quean behynde me set a trap,
whereby to dashe and laye all in the myre:
The Iryshe men against me dyd conspyre,
My landes of Vlster fro me to haue reft,
whiche herytage my mother had me left. [105]

And whyles I there, to set all thinges in stay,
(Omyt my toyles and troubles thitherwarde)
Among myne owne with my retinue lay,
The wylder men whom lytell I dyd regarde,
And had therefore the recheles mans rewarde: [110]
When least I thought set on me in suche number,
That fro my corps my lyfe they rent a sunder.

[96]   soonest chaunge their hue, *F.*
[99]   whyles fayr Fortune *B–E.* [*Read* whilst *for* whyles *G.*]
            whiles Fortune so luld *F.*
[101]   The double Dame *F.*
[102]   To dash me downe and *F.*
[103]   Irish Kernes *F.*
[104]   Vlster vniustly to bereaue, *F.*
[105]   Which my mother for heritage did me leaue. *F.*
[107]   troble *C–E.*
[109]   wylder sort, whom I did least regard, *F.*
[110]   And therfore the *F.*
[112]   the lyfe they set asunder. *F.*

Nought myght auayle my courage nor my force,
Nor strength of men whiche were alas to fewe:

[115] The cruell folke assaulted so my horse,
That all my helpes in pieces they to hewe,
Our blood distayned the grounde as drops of dewe,
Nought myght preuayle to flee nor yet to yelde,
For whom they take they murdre in the fyelde.

[120] They know no lawe of armes nor none wil lerne:
They make not warre (as other do) a playe,
The lorde, the boye, the Galloglas, the kerne,
Yelde or not yelde, whom so they take they slay,
They save no prysoners, for raunsom nor for pay:

[125] Theyr chiefest boote they counte theyr bodohs heade,
Theyr ende of warre to see theyr enmye deade.

Amongest these men or rather savage beastes,
I lost my lyfe, by cruell murder slaine.
And therfore Baldwin note thou well my geastes,

[130] And warne all princes rashnes to refraine:
Bid them beware their enmies when they faine,
Nor yet presume vnequally to strive,
Had I thus done, I had ben man alive.

[114] Nor helpe of frendes, which F.
[117] distaynes G.
[118] flye or yet F.
[120] No law of Armes they know, F.
[125] their bodyes head, DE. Their booty chiefe, they coumpt
a deadmans heade F.
[126] of warre's to see F.
[132] presume to make their match amisse, F.
[133] Had I not so done, I had not come to this, F.

But I dispysed the naked Iryshmen,
And for they flewe, I feared them the lesse: [135]
I thought one man ynough to matche with ten,
And through this careles vnadvisednesse,
I was destroyed, and all my men I gesse,
At vnawares assaulted by our foen,
Whiche were in numbre fourty to vs one.   [140]

Se here the staye of fortunate estate,
The vayne assuraunce of this britell lyfe,
For I but yong, proclaymed prince of late,
Right fortunate in children and in wife,
Lost all at once by stroke of bloody knife: [145]
Wherby assurde let men them selues assure,
That welth and lyfe are doubtfull to endure.

[134–38]   At naught I set a sort of naked men,
                And much the lesse, seeming to flye away,
                One man me thought was good ynough for ten,
                Making small account of number more or lesse,
                Madnesse it is, in warre to goo by gesse, *F.*
[139]   vnwares *B–F.*
[141]   of pompe and highe estate, *F.*
[142]   The feeble hold of this vncerteyn lyfe, *F.*
[143]   Prince but late, *F.*
[144]   Hauing fayre fruict by my belooued wyfe: *F.*

Fter that this Tragedy was ended, mayster *Ferrers* sayde: seyng [Prose 2]
it is best to place eche person in his ordre, *Baldwin* take you the
Chronicles and marke them as they cum: for there are many
wurthy to be noted, though not to be treated of. First the lord Morif a
Scotishman, who tooke his deathes wounde through a stroke lent him by [5]
the erle of Notingham whom he chalenged at the tilte. But to omit him,
& also the fatte Prior of Tiptre, preaced to death with throng of people
vpon London bridge at the Quenes entry, I wil cum to the duke of
Glocestre the kinges vncle, a man muche mynding the common weale,
& yet at length miserably made away, In whose person yf ye wyll gyue [10]
eare, ye shall heare what I thinke mete to be sayd.

[1] After this *C–G*. Tragedye ended, *F*.
[4] not treated *C–G*. Lord Murrey *C–G*.
[9] man myndynge *C–G*. common welth, *C–G*.

Howe syr Thomas of Wudstocke Duke [Tragedy 3]
of Glocester, vncle to king Richarde
the seconde, was vnlawfully
murdred.

Hose state is stablisht in semyng most sure,
And so far from daunger of Fortunes blast,
As by the compas of mans coniecture,
No brasen pyller maye be fyxte more fast:
Yet wantyng the staye of prudent forecast, [5]
Whan frowarde Fortune lyst for to frowne,
Maye in a moment tourne vpsyde downe.

[Title] murdered. Anno. 1397. *C–G*.
[1]   stablisht *is printed* stalysht *but is corrected in Ae.* state stablisht is, *C–EG*.
        Who stablisht is in State, seeming *F*.
[2]   blastes, *C–EG*.

In proofe whereof, O Baldwin, take payne
To hearken awhyle to Thomas of Wudstocke,
[10] Addrest in presence his fate to complayne,
In the forlorne hope of the Englysh flocke:
Extracte by discent from the royall stocke,
Sonne to kyng Edward third of that name,
And seconde to none in glory and fame.

[15] This noble father to maynteyne my state,
With Buckyngham Erldom dyd me indowe,
Both Nature and Fortune to me were grate,
Denyeng nothing which they myght allowe:
Theyr sundry graces in me did so flowe,
[20] As bewty, strength, high fauour and fame.
Who may of God more wysh than the same?

Brothers we were to the numbre of seuen,
I beyng the syxt, and yongest but one:
A more royall race was not vnder heauen,
[25] More stowte or more stately of stomacke and person,
Princes all pereles in eche condicion:
Namely syr Edwarde called the blacke prince,
Whan had Englande the lyke before eyther since?

But what of all this, any man to assure,
[30] In state vncarefull of Fortunes varyaunce?
Syth dayly and hourely we see it in vre,
That where most cause is of affyaunce,
Euen there is founde moste weake assuraunce,
Let none trust Fortune, but folowe Reason:
[35] For often we see in trust is treason.

[9]   Turne thine eare to *F*.
[10] Prest in presence on Fortune to *F*.
[11] of English flocke: *C–G*.
[12] Who by discent was of the royall *F*.
[18] Denyeng me nothyng *B–G*.
[28] before or euer since? *C–G*.

This prouerbe in proofe ouer true I tryed,
Finding high treason in place of high trust.
And most faulte of fayth where I most affyed:
Beyng by them, that should haue been iust,
Trayterously entrapt, ere I coulde mystrust.   [40]
Ah wretched worlde what it is to trust thee,
Let them that wyll learne nowe hearken to mee.

After king Edwarde the thyrdes decease,
Succeded my Nephewe Rycharde to reyne,
Who for his glory and honors encrease,   [45]
With princely wagies dyd me enterteyne,
Agaynst the Frenchmen to be his Chyefteyne:
So passyng the seas with royall puissaunce,
With God and S. George I inuaded Fraunce.

Wasting the countrey with swurde and with fyer,   [50]
Ouerturning townes, high castels and towers,
Lyke Mars God of warre enflamed with yre,
I forced the Frenchmen to abandon theyr bowers:
Where euer we matcht I wan at all howers,
In suche wyse visyting both Cytie and village,   [55]
That alway my soldiers were laden with pillage.

With honoure and triumph was my retourne,
Was none more ioyous than yong king Richarde:
Who minding more highly my state to adourne,
with Glocester Dukedome dyd me rewarde: [60]
And after in mariage I was prefarde,
To a daughter of Bohan an earle honorable,
By whome I was of Englande high Constable.

[38]   And most false of fayth *DE*. And most false fayth *F*.
[42]   to *is printed* vnto *but is corrected in Ae.*
[53]   to abandon *is printed* tabaddon *but is corrected in Ae.*

93

Thus hoysted so high on Fortunes wheele,
[65] As one on a stage attendyng a playe,
Seeth not on whiche syde the scaffolde doth reele,
Tyll tymber and poales, and all flee awaye:
So fared it by mee, for day by daye,
As honour encreased I loked styll hyer,
[70] Not seyng the daunger of my fonde desyer.

For whan Fortunes flud ran with full streame,
I beyng a Duke descended of Kinges,
Constable of Englande, chiefe officer in the realme,
Abused with esperaunce in these vaine thinges,
[75] I went without feete, and flewe without winges:
Presumyng so far vpon my high state
That dread set aparte, my prince I would mate.

For where as al kings haue counsel of their choyse
To whom they refer the rule of theyr lande,
[80] With certayne famyliers in whom to reioyce,
For pleasure or profyt, as the case shall stande,
I not bearyng this, would nedes take in hande,
Maulgree his wyll those persons to dysgrace,
And such as I thought fyt to appoynt in their place.

[85] But as an olde booke sayth, who so wyll assaye,
Aboute the Cats necke to hang on a bell,
Had fyrst nede to cut the Cats clawes awaye,

[64] Thus hoysted high on Fortunes whyrling wheele, *F.*
[67] flie away: *C–G.*
[71] For Fortunes floode thus running with *C–G.*
[72] And I a Duke discended of great Kinges, *C–G.*
[73] officer of the *G.*
[74] with assuraunce in *F.* with desperaunce in *G.*
[76] high estate. *C–G.*
[84] to settle in *C–G.*
[86] on any bell, *C–G.*

Least yf the Cat be curst, or not tamed well,
She haply with her nayles may clawe him to the fell:
For doyng on the bell about the cats necke,   [90]
By beyng to busy I caught a sore checke.

Reade well the sentence of the Rat of renoune,
Which Pierce the plowman discribes in his dreame,
And who so hath wyt the sense to expoune,
Shall fynde that to bridle the prince of a realme,   [95]
Is euen (as who sayeth) to striue with the streame:
Note this all subiectes, and construe it well,
And busy not your braine about the cats bell.

But in that ye be Lyeges learne to obaye,
Submytting your wylles to your princes lawes,   [100]
It fytteth not a subiecte to haue his owne waye,
Remember this bywurde of the Cats clawes:
For princes lyke Lyons haue long and large pawes
That reache at raundon, and whom they once twitch,
They clawe to the bone before the skyn itch.   [105]

But to my purpose, I beyng once bent,
Towardes the atchiuyng of my attemptate,
Fower bolde Barrons were of myne assent,
By oth and allyaunce fastly confederate:
Fyrst Henry of Derby, an Earle of estate,   [110]
Richarde of Arundell, and Thomas of Warwicke,
With Mowbray erle Marshall a man most warlicke.

[88]   curst, and not C–G.
[90]   So putting on C–G.
[91]   a cruell checke. C–G.
[98]   brains C–G.
[102]   this prouerbe C–G.
[112]   Mowbray the Marshall, C–G.

[115] At Ratcote brydge assembled our bande,
The Commons in clusters cam to vs that day,
To daunte Robert Vere, then Duke of Irelande,
By whom king Rycharde was ruled alway:
We put hym to flyght, and brake his array,
Then maulgree the kyng, his leaue or assent,
By Constables power we called a parlyament.

[120] Where not in roabes, but with bastardes bright,
We cam for to parle of the Publyke weale,
Confyrming our quarell, with maine and with might
With swurdes and no wurdes we tryed our appeale,
In stede of Reason declaryng our Zeale,
[125] And whom so we knewe with the kyng in good grace
Playnely we depriued him of power and of place.

Sum with shorte proces were banysht the lande,
Sum executed with capytall payne,
Wherof who so lyst, the whole to vnderstande,
[130] In the parlyament roll it appeareth playne,
And furder howe stoutly we dyd the king strayne,
The Rule of his realme wholy to resygne,
To the order of those, whom we dyd assygne.

But note the sequele of suche presumption,
[135] After we had these myracles wrought,
The king enflamed with indignacion,
That to suche bondage he should be brought,
Suppressyng the yre of his inwarde thought:
Studyed nought els but howe that he myght
[140] Be highly reuenged of his high dispight.

[126] We playnlye depriued, of *C–E.*
[135] Myracles thus wrought, *F.*
[137] By Subiectes thus in bondage to bee brought, *F.*
[140] of this high *C–G.*

Aggreued was also this latter offence,
with former matter his yre to renue:
For once at wyndsore I brought to his presence,
The Mayor of London with all his retinue,
To axe a reckening of the Realmes reuenue: [145]
And the soldiers of Brest were by me made bolde,
To clayme entertainment the towne being solde.

These griefes remembred, with all the remnaunt,
Of hate in his hert hourded a treasure,
Yet openly in shewe made he no semblaunt,   [150]
By wurde nor by deede to beare displeasure:
But loue dayes dissembled do neuer endure,
And who so trusteth a foe reconcylde,
Is for the most parte alwayes begilde.

For as fyer yll quencht will vp at a starte,   [155]
And sores not well salued do breake out of newe,
So hatred hydden in an yrefull harte,
Where it hath had long season to brewe,
Vpon euery occasion doth easely renewe:
Not fayling at last, yf it be not let,   [160]
To paye large vsury besides the due det.

Euin so it fared by this frendship fained,
Outwardly sounde, and inwardly rotten:

[142] former cause of rancour to *F.*
[145] aske accoumpt of *F.*
[146] Brest by me were made *C–G.*
[147] Their wages to claime when the town was solde. *C–G.* [*Read* To
       clayme their wages, *for* Their wages to claime *F.*]
[149] Hourded in his harte hate out of measure, *C–G.* [*Read* Fulfyld his
       hart with *for* Hourded in his harte *F.*]
[151] woord or by *C–G.*
[152] But Frendship fayned, in proofe is found vnsure. *F.*
[158] hath not had *F.*

[165] For whan the kinges fauour in semyng was gained,
All olde dyspleasures forgyuen and forgotten,
Euin than at a sodayne the shaft was shotten,
Whiche pearced my harte voyde of mistrust,
Alas that a prince should be so vniust.

[170] For lying at Plasshey my selfe to repose,
By reason of syckenes whiche helde me full sore:
The king espying me aparte from those,
with whom I confedered in bande before,
Thought it not meete, to tract the tyme more,
But glad to take me at suche auauntage,
[175] Came to salute me with friendly vysage.

Who hauyng a bande bounde to his bent,
By coulour of kyndenes to vyset his Eame,
Tooke tyme to accomplysh his cruell intent:
And in a small vessell downe by the streame,
[180] Conueyed me to Calays out of the realme,
where without proces or doome of my peres,
Not nature but murder abridged my yeres.

This acte was odious to God and to man,
Yet rygour to cloke in habyte of reason,
[185] By crafty compas deuise they can,
Articles nyne of ryght haynous treason:
But doome after death is sure out of season,
For who euer sawe so straunge a presydent,
As execucion doen before iudgement.

[170] With long sicknesse diseased very sore: *F.*
[172] I was confedered before, *F.*
[189] execution to goe before *F.*

Thus hate harboured in depth of mynde,   [190]
By sought occasyon burst out of newe,
And cruelty abused the lawe of kynde,
whan that the Nephewe the Vncle slewe,
Alas king Rycharde sore mayst thou rewe:
whiche by this facte preparedst the waye,   [195]
Of thy harde destynie to hasten the daye.

For blood axeth blood as guerdon dewe,
And vengeaunce for vengeaunce is iust rewarde,
O ryghteous God thy iudgementes are true,
For looke what measure we other awarde,   [200]
The same for vs agayne is preparde:
Take heed ye princes by examples past,
Blood wyll haue blood, eyther fyrst or last.

[195]   preparedst a playne waye, F.
[200]   measure to others we awarde, F.

WHan maister *Ferrers* had ended this fruytfull tragedye, be-   [Prose 3]
cause no man was readye with another, I, hauyng perused
the story whiche cam next, sayd: Because you shall not say
my maisters but that I wyll in sumwhat do my parte, I wyll vnder your
correction declare the tragedy of the Lord Mowbray, the chiefe wurker   [5]
of the Dukes destruction: who to admonysh all Counsaylers to beware
of flattering princes, or falsely enuying or accusyng theyr Peregalles,
may lament his vices in maner folowyng.

> [1] ended his fruitfull G.
> [2] with any other, C–EG. an other, hauing F.
> [4] wyll somewhat C–G.
> [5] of Thomas Mowbray, Duke of Northefolke, the C–G.
> [6] the Duke of Glocesters destruction: C–G.

Howe the Lorde Mowbray promoted by   [Tragedy 4]
Kyng Richarde the seconde, was by
hym banyshed the Realme,
and dyed miserably
in exyle.

THough sorowe and shame abash me to reherce
My lothsum lyfe and death of due deserued,
Yet that the paynes thereof may other perce,
To leaue the lyke, least they be lykely serued,
Ah Baldwin marke, I wil shew thee how I swarued: [5]
Dyssemblyng, Enuy, and Flattery, bane that be
Of all their hostes, haue shewed their power on me.

> [Title] second, to the state of a Duke, was C–G.
> Realme, thé yeare of Christe. 1398. and after died C–G. [*Read*
> *in the D–F.*]
> [4] be like wyse serued, C–G.
> [5] marke, and see how that I swerued: C–G.

I blame not Fortune though she dyd her parte,
And true it is she can doo lytell harme,
[10]   She gydeth goods, she hampreth not the harte,
A vertuous mynde is safe from euery charme:
Vyce, onely vyce, with her stoute strengthles arme,
Doth cause the harte to euyll to enclyne,
Whiche I alas, doo fynde to true by myne,

[15]   For where by byrth I came of noble kynde,
The Mowbrayes heyre, a famous house and olde,
Fortune I thanke her, was to me so kynde,
That of my prince I had what so I wolde:
Yet neyther of vs was muche to other holde,
[20]   For I through flattery abused his wanton youth,
And his fonde trust augmented my vntruth.

He made me fyrst the earle of Notyngham,
And Marshall of the realme, in whiche estate,
The Piers and people ioyntly to me came,
[25]   with sore complaynt against them that of late
Made offycers, had brought the king in hate
By makynge sale of Iustice, ryght and lawe,
And lyuyng nought, without all dreede or awe.

I gaue them ayde these euyls to redresse,
[30]   And went to London with an army strong,
And caused the king against his wyll oppresse
By cruell death, all suche as led hym wrong:
The lorde chiefe Iustice suffred these among,
So dyd the Stuarde of his housholde head,
[35]   The Chauncelour scapte, for he aforehande fled.

[11]   A minde well bent, *C–G.*
[13]   hart from good to yll encline, *C–G.*
[15]   noble race, *C–F.*
[17]   thanke, gaue me so good a grace, *C–G.*
[19]   Yet neyther was, to other greatly holde, *C–G.*
[23]   Marshall of England, *F.*

These wicked men thus from the king remoued,
who best vs pleased, succeded in theyr place:
For whiche both kyng and commons muche vs loued
But chiefely I with all stoode high in grace,
The kyng ensued my rede in euery case,   [40]
whence selfe loue bred: for glory maketh proude,
And pryde aye looketh alone to be allowde.

wherfore to thende I might alone enioye
The kinges good wyll I made his lust my lawe:
And where of late I laboured to destroye,   [45]
Suche flatryng folke as thereto stoode in awe,
Nowe learned I among the rest to clawe:
For pride is suche, yf it be kindely caught,
As stroyeth good, and styrreth vp every nought.

Pryde pricketh men to flatter for the pray,   [50]
To oppresse and pol for mayntenaunce of the same,
To malyce suche as matche vnethes it may:
And to be briefe, pride doth the harte enflame,
To fyer what myschief any fraude maye frame,
And euer at length the euyls by it wrought   [55]
Confounde the wurker, and bring him vnto nought.

Beholde in me due proofe of euerye parte:
For pryde fyrst forced me my prince to flatter
So muche, that what so euer pleased his harte,
Were it neuer so evyll, I thought a lawfull matter,   [60]
Whiche caused the lordes afresh against him clatter,
Because he had his holdes beyonde sea solde,
And seen his souldiers of theyr wages polde.

[44]   Kinges fauour, I F.
[50]   Pryde prouoketh to F.
[51]   To poll, and oppresse for F.
[58]   pryde prickt me first my F.
[62]   Because of Holdes beyond the sea that he solde, F.

[65]

Though all these yls were doen by my assent,
Yet suche was lucke, that eche man deemed no:
For see the duke of Glocester for me sent,
With other lordes, whose hartes did blede for wo,
To see the Realme so fast to ruyne go.
In faulte whereof, they sayde the two dukes wer,
The one of Yorke, the other of Lancaster.

[70]

On whose remove fro beyng aboute the king
We all agreed, and sware a solempne oth,
And whyle the rest prouyded for this thyng,
I flatter I, to win the prayse of troth,
Wretche that I was brake fayth and promise both:
For I bewrayed the king theyr whole intent,
For whiche vnwares they all were tane and shent.

[75]

Thus was the warder of the common weale,
The Duke of Glocester gyltles made awaye,
With other moo, more wretche I so to deale,
Who through vntruth their trust dyd yll betraye:
Yet by this means obteyned I my praye,
Of king and Dukes I founde for this suche fauour
As made me Duke of Norfolke, for my labour.

[80]

But see howe pride and envy ioyntly runne,
Because my prince dyd more than me, preferre
Syr Henry Bolenbroke, the eldest sunne
Of Iohn of Gaunte, the Duke of Lancaster,
Proude I that would alone be blasyng sterre,
Envyed this Earle, for nought saue that the shine,
Of his desertes dyd glyster more then mine:

[85]

[90]

[64]   by mine assent, C–G.
[71]   from place about F.
[73]   whilst C–G.
[74]   I flattrer I, B–G.
[76]   bewrayed to'th King G.
[90]   this Duke, C–G.

To the ende therfore his lyght should be the lesse,
I slyly sought all shyftes to put it out:
But as the peyze that would the palme tree presse,
Doth cause the bowes sprede larger rounde about,　　　[95]
So spyte and enuy causeth glory sprout.
And aye the more the top is ouertrode,
The deper doth the sounde roote sprede abrode.

For when this Henry Erle of Harforde sawe,
What spoyle the kyng made of the noble blood,　　　[100]
And that without all Iustice, cause, or lawe:
To suffer him so he thought not sure nor good.
Wherfore to me two faced in a hood,
As touching this, he fully brake his mynde,
As to his frende that should remedy fynde.　　　[105]

But I, although I knewe my prince dyd yll,
So that my heart abhorred sore the same,
Yet myschief so through malyce led my wyll,
To bring this Earle from honour vnto shame,
And towarde my selfe, my souerayne to enflame:　　　[110]
That I bewrayed his wurdes vnto the king,
Not as a rede, but as a most haynous thyng.

Thus where my duty bounde me to have tolde,
My prince his fault, and wylde him to refrayne,
Through flattery loe, I dyd his yll vpholde,　　　[115]
whiche turnde at length both hym and me to payne:
Wo, wo, to kynges whose counsaylours do fayne,
Wo, wo to realmes where suche are put in trust,
As leave the lawe, to serve the princes lust.

[93]　　put him out: G.
[99]　　Henry Duke of C–G.
[103]　　in hood, B. in one hoode, C–G.
[109]　　this Duke C–G.

[120] And wo to him that by his flatteryng rede,
Maynteyneth a prince in any kynde of vyce:
wo wurth hym eke for envy, pryde, or mede,
That mysreportes any honest enterpryse,
Because I beast in all these poyntes was nyce,
[125] The plages of all together on me lyght,
And due, for yll ylldoers doth acquite.

For when the Earle was charged with my playnt,
He flatte denyed that any parte was true,
And claymde by armes to aunswere his attaynt,
[130] And I by vse that warly feates well knewe,
To his desyre incontinently drewe:
wherwith the king dyd seme ryght well content,
As one that past not muche with whom it went.

At tyme and place apoynted we apearde,
[135] At all poyntes armde to proue our quarels iust,
And whan our frendes on eche parte had vs chearde,
And that the Haroldes bad vs do our lust,
with spere in rest we tooke a course to iust:
But ere our horses had run halfe theyr way,
[140] A shoute was made, the kyng dyd byd vs stay.

And for to avoyde the sheddyng of our bloode,
with shame and death, which one must nedes haue had
The king through counsaile of the lordes thought good
To banysh both, whiche iudgement strayt was rad:
[145] No maruayle than though both were wroth and sad,
But chiefely I that was exylde for aye,
My enmy straunged but for a ten yeares daye.

[121] Maynteyns C–G.
[127] the Duke C–G.
[130] warlyke G.
[138] in brest wee G.
[140] kyng commaunded stay. B–G.
[147] for ten yeares daye. F.

The date expirde, whan by this doulfull doome
I should departe to lyve in banysht bande,
On payne of death, to Englande not to coome,   [150]
I went my way: the kyng seasde in his hande,
My offyces, my honours, goods and lande,
To paye the due, as openly he tolde,
Of myghty summes, whiche I had from hym polde.

See Baldwin see, the salarye of synne,   [155]
Marke with what meede vile vyces are rewarded.
Through pryde and envy I lose both kyth and kynne,
And for my flattring playnte so well regarded,
Exyle and slaunder are iustly me awarded:
My wife and heyre lacke landes and lawful right   [160]
And me theyr lorde made dame Dianaes knyght.

If these mishaps at home be not inough,
Adioyne to them my sorowes in exyle:
I went to Almayne fyrst, a lande ryght rough,
In whiche I founde suche churlysh folke and vyle,   [165]
As made me loth my lyfe ech other whyle:
There loe, I learned what it is to be a gest
Abrode, and what to lyve at home in rest.

For they esteme no one man more than eche,
They vse as well the Lackey as the Lorde,   [170]
And lyke theyr maners churlysh is theyr speche,
Their lodging hard, their bourd to be abhord:
Their pleyted garmentes herewith well accorde,

[148]   this doubtfull dome, F.
[152]   Myn offices, C–G.
[156]   are regarded D–F.
[158]   well rewarded, D–F.
[159]   are iust to mee awarded: F.
[171]   churlish in theyr C–G.
[173]   garments therewith G.

[175]
All iagde and frounst, with diuers coloures dekt,
They swere, they curse, and drynke tyll they be flekt.

They hate all suche as these their maners hate,
Which reason would no wise man should allow:
With these I dwelt, lamenting mine estate
Till at the length they had got knowledge, how
[180]
I was exilde because I dyd auow
A false complaynt agaynst my trusty frende:
For which they named me traytour styl vnende,

That what for shame, and what for werynes
I stale fro thence, and went to Venise towne,
[185]
Where as I founde more ease and frendlynes,
But greater gryefe: for now the great renowne
Of Bolenbroke whom I would haue put downe
Was waxt so great in Britaine and in Fraunce,
That Venise through ech man did him auaunce.

[190]
Thus loe his glory grew through great despyte
And I therby increased in defame:
Thus enuy euer doth her host acquyte
Wyth trouble, anguysh, sorow, smart and shame,
But sets the vertues of her foe in flame:
[195]
To water lyke, whych maketh clere the stone,
And soyles it selfe by running thervpon.

[182]   styll vnhende, C–EG. Which made them thinke, mee worse then
        any feende. F.
[183]   and what for other griefe, F.
[184]   I parted thence, F.
[185]   more pleasure and reliefe, F.
[186]   Which was not longe: for F.
[190]   Loo! thus his Glory grewe great, by my dispite, F.
[192]   her most acquite C–EG. So enuy euer, her hatred doth acquite F.
[193]   and selfe Shame, F.
[194]   Whereby her Foes do shine in higher Fame: F.
[195–96] Lyke water waues, which clense the muddy stone,
        And soyles them selues by beatyng thervpon. B–G.

Or ere I had soiurned there a yere
Strange tidinges came he was to England goen,
Had tane the king, & that which touched him nere
Enprisoned him, with other of his foen,   [200]
And made hym yelde hym vp his crowne and throne:
When I these thinges for true by serche had tryed,
Griefe griped me so I pined away and dyed.

Note here the ende of pride, se Flateries fine,
Marke the reward of enuy and false complaint,   [205]
And warne all princes from them to declyne
Lest likely fault do find the like attaynt.
Let this my life be to them a restraynt,
By others harmes who lysteth take no hede
Shall by his owne learne other better rede.   [210]

[206]   all people from *B–G*.

[Prose 4] THis tragicall example was of all the cumpany well liked, how be it a doubte was founde therin, and that by meanes of the diuersity of the Chronicles: for where as maister Hall whom in this storye we chiefely folowed, maketh Mowbray accuser, and Boleyn-

[5] broke appellant, mayster Fabian reporteth the matter quite contrary, & that by the reporte of good authours, makyng Boleynbroke the accuser, and Mowbray the appellant. Which matter sith it is more harde to desise, than nedefull to our purpose, which minde onely to diswade from vices and exalte vertue, we referre to the determinacion of the Haroldes, or

[10] such as may cum by the recordes and registers of these doinges, contented in the mean while with the best allowed iudgement, and which maketh most for our forshewed purpose. This doubt thus let passe, I would (quoth one of the cumpany) gladly say sumwhat for king Richard. But his personage is so sore intangled as I thinke fewe benefices

[15] be at this day: for after his imprisonment, his brother and diuers other made a maske, minding by Henries destruction to haue restored him, which maskers matter so runneth in this, that I doubt which ought to go

[3-4] wher as Hall whose Chronicle in this worke, we chiefely C-G. [*Read* was *for* we *F.*]

[4-5] Mowbray appellant & Bolinbroke defendant, Fabian C-G.

[6-7] by record of the parliament rolle, wherin it is playne that Bolinbroke was appellant and Mowbrey defendant. Wherfore what so euer shalbe saide here in the person of Mowbray, (who being a most noble prince had to much wrong to be so causeles defamed after his death) imagin that same to be spoken against his accuser. Which C-G. [*In ll.* 2-3 *above omit* here *after* saide *D-F. In l.* 4 *read* the *for* that *F. Omit same G.*]

[5]

[7] to decide, *F.*

[9-12] refer to such as may com by the records of the acts of the parliamente, contented in the mean while with maister Halles iudgement, which maketh best for our forshewed purpose. This C-G. [*In l.* 1 *above omit* of the acts *F.*]

[13] woulde (sayde master *Ferrers*) saye C-G.

[14-15] Richard, after whose depriuing, his brother C-G. [*Read* Rich. the 2. *for* Richard *F.*]

[16] by king Henries C-G.

before. But seing no man is redy to say ought in their behalfe, I will
geue who so listeth leasure to thinke thervppon, and in the meane time
to further your enterprise, I will in the kinges behalfe recount such part [20]
of his story as I thinke most necessary. And therfore imagine *Baldwin*
that you see him al to be mangled, with blew woundes, lying pale and
wanne al naked vpon the cold stones in Paules church, the people
standing round about him, and making his mone in this sort.

[19] to looke therevpon, *G.* thereon, *F.*
[20] in king Rychards behalfe *C–G.*
[22] that you see the corps of thys Prince all to *C–G.*
[23] wanne, naked vpon a Beere in *F.*
[24] makynge his complainte in maner as foloweth. *C–G.*

Howe kyng Richarde the seconde was for his euyll gouernaunce deposed from his seat, and miserably murdred in prison.

[Tragedy 5]

Appy is the prince that hath in welth the grace
To folowe vertue, keping vices vnder,
But wo to him whose will hath wisedomes place:
For who so renteth ryght and law a sunder
On him at length loe, al the world shall wunder, [5]
Hygh byrth, choyse fortune, force, nor Princely mace

[Title] seate, in the yeare. 1399. and *C–G.* and murdered in *G.* prison the
        yere folowing. *C–G.*
[2] Vertue to folow and vyces to keepe vnder, *F.*
[5] length all the *C–G.*
[6] Boast of high byrth, sword, scepter, ne mace. *F.*

Can warrant King or Keysar fro the case,
Shame sueth sinne, as rayne drops do the thunder.
Let Princes therfore vertuous life embrace
[10]   That wilfull pleasures cause them not to blunder.

Beholde my hap, see how the sely route
Do gase vpon me, and eche to other saye:
Se where he lieth for whome none late might route,
Loe howe the power, the pride, and riche aray
[15]   Of myghty rulers lightly fade away.
The Kyng whych erst kept all the realme in doute,
The veryest rascall now dare checke and lowte:
What moulde be Kynges made of, but carayn clay?
Beholde his woundes, howe blew they be about,
[20]   Whych whyle he lived, thought neuer to decay.

Me thinke I heare the people thus deuise:
And therfore Baldwin sith thou wilt declare
How princes fell, to make the liuing wise,
My vicious story in no poynt see thou spare,
[25]   But paynt it out, that rulers may beware
Good counsayle, lawe, or vertue to despyse.

[8]   rayne do drops of thunder, *F.*
[9]   Let kinges therfore the Lawes of God embrace, *F.*
[10]   That vayne delightes cause *F.*
[12]   On me do gase, and *C–G.*
[13]   lyeth, but late that was so stout, *C–G.*
[14]   and cyche araye *B.*
[15]   mighty Princes lightly *F.*
[17]   and floute: *G.* Dead and least dread, to graue is caryed out, *F.*
[18]   of but earth and clay: *F.*
[19]   Behold the woundes his body all about, *F.*
[20]   Who liuing here, thought *F.*
[22]   Wherfore Baldwin, *C–G.* wilt nowe declare *C–F.*
[24]   My lawlesse life, in *C–G.*

For realmes haue rules, and rulers haue a syse,
Which if they kepe not, doubtles say I dare
That eythers gryefes the other shall agrise
Till the one be lost, the other brought to care.   [30]
    I am a Kyng that ruled all by lust,
That forced not of vertue, ryght, or lawe,
But alway put false Flatterers most in trust,
Ensuing such as could my vices clawe:
By faythful counsayle passing not a strawe.   [35]
What pleasure pryckt, that thought I to be iust.
I set my minde, to feede, to spoyle, to iust,
Three meales a day could skarce content my mawe,
And all to augment my lecherous minde that must
To Venus pleasures alway be in awe.   [40]
    For mayntenaunce wherof, my realme I polde
Through Subsidies, sore fines, loanes, many a prest,

[27]   haue rulers, and *F.*
[28]   they breake, thus much to say I dare. *C–G.*
[30]   Tyll one be *C–G.*
[31]   I was a King, who ruled *C–G.*
[32]   Forcyng but light, of Iustice, right, or Lawe, *C–G.* [*Read* Without
          respect of *for* Forcyng but light, of *F.*]
[33]   Putting always flatterers false in trust, *C–EG.*
          In false Flatterers reposinge all my trust, *F.*
[34]   Embracinge sutch *F.*
[35]   passing not an hawe, *C–EG.* Fro counsell sage I did alwayes
          withdrawe, *F.*
[36–37]   As pleasure pricte, so needes obay I must:
          Hauing delite to fede and serue the gust, *C–G.*
[38]   Of God or man I stoode no wise in awe, *F.*
[39]   And to augment *B.* [*Corrected in* Be *to the original reading.*]
[39–40]   Me liked least to Torney or to Iust.
          To Venus sporte my fansy did me drawe. *C–G.*
          [*In l.* 40 *read* games *for* sporte *and* more *for* me *F.*]
[41–42]   Which to maintaine, my people were sore polde
          With Fines, Fiftenes, and loanes by way of prest, *C–G.*
          [*In l.* 41 *read* I gathered heapes of golde *for* my people were sore
          polde *F. In l.* 42 *read* By *for* With *F.*]

Blanke charters, othes, & shiftes not knowen of olde,
For whych my Subiectes did me sore detest.
[45] I also made away the towne of Brest,
My fault wherin because mine vncle tolde
(For Prynces vyces may not be controlde)
I found the meanes his bowels to vnbrest.
The Piers and Lordes that did his cause vphold,
[50] With death, exile, or greuous fines opprest.

Neyther lakt I ayde in any wicked dede,
For gaping Gulles whom I promoted had
Woulde furder all in hope of higher mede.
A king can neuer imagine ought so bad
[55] But most about him will perfourme it glad
For sickenes seldeme doth so swiftely brede
As vicious humors growe the griefe to feede.
Thus kinges estates of all be wurst bastad,
Abusde in welth, abandoned at nede,
[60] And nerest harme whan they be least adrad.

My life and death the truth of this can trye:
For while I fought in Ireland with my foes,

[44] which the commons, did C–EG. which the people, my doinges did detest. F.
[45] also sould the noble towne C–G.
[47] Princes actes, may no wise be C–G.
[48] His lyfe I tooke, vntried without Quest, F.
[49] The worthy Peeres, which his cause did vphold, C–EG.
And all sutch Lordes as did F.
[50] With long exile, or cruell death opprest. C–G.
[51] None ayde I lackt, in C–G.
[54] There can no King ymagin C–G.
[55] But shall fynde some that will C–EG. But shall fynde some, to do the same most glad: F.
[57] As humours yll, do growe C–G.
[58] estates, bee worst of all bestad, F.
[61] this hath tryde: C–G.

Mine vncle Edmunde whom I left to gide
My realme at home, right traytrously arose
To helpe the Percies plying my depose,   [65]
And cald fro Fraunce Erle Bolenbroke, whom I
Condemned ten yeres in exyle to lye:
Who cruelly did put to death all those
That in myne ayde durst looke but once awry,
Whose number was but slender I suppose.   [70]

For whan I was cum back this stur to stay,
The Erle of Worcester whom I trusted moste
(Whiles we in Wales at Flint our castell lay
Both to refresh and multiply mine oste)
Did in my hall in sight of least and moste   [75]
Bebreake his staffe, my housould office stay,
Bad eche man shifte, and rode him selfe away.
See princes, see the power wherof we boste,
Whome most we trust, at nede do vs betray,
Through whose false faith my land and life I lost.   [80]

[63]	vncle Edward *F.*
[64]	traytrously *is misprinted* trayteously *in the text.* home, rebelliously arose, *C–G.*
[65]	Percyes to helpe, which plied my depose: *C–G.* [*Read* Traytors *for* Percyes *F.*]
[67]	Exiled had for ten yeares there to lye: *C–G.*
[68]	Who tyrantlike did execute all those, *F.*
[70]	Of which sort soone after some their liues did lose. *F.*
[71]	For comming backe this soden stur *C–G.*
[72]	My Steward false to whom I trusted most: *F.*
[73]	(Whiles I in *C–G.* Flint my Castle *C–G.*
[75]	There in *C–G.* Hall, mindinge to fly the Coast, *F.*
[76]	His staffe did breake, which was my householde stay, *C–G.*
[77]	ech make shyfte, *B–G.*
[78]	the strength whereof *C–G.*
[80]	No better stay, then in a rotten Post. *F.*

For whan my trayterous Stuard thus was goen,
My seruauntes shranke away on euery side,
That caught I was, and caryed to my foen:
Who for theyr prince a prison dyd provide,
[85] And therin kept me, til duke Henryes pride
Dyd cause me yeld him vp my crowne and throne.
Whych shortly made my frendly foes to grone:
For Henry seing in me their falshode tryde
Abhorde them all, and would be rulde by none,
[90] For whych they sought to stoppe him strayt a tyde.

    The chiefe conspirde by death to drive him down,
For which exployte, a solemne othe they swore
To render me my libertie and crown,
Wherof them selues deprived me before.
[95] But salues helpe seeld an overlong suffred sore.
To stoppe the brech no boote to runne or rowne
When swelling fluds have overflowen the town:

[81–90]   My Stuard false, thus being fled and gone,
       My seruauntes slye shranke of on euery syde,
       Then caught I was, and led vnto my foen,
       Who for theyr Prince, no pallace did prouide,
       But prison strong, where henry puft with pride,
       causd me resigne, my Kingly state and throne,
       And so forsaken and left as post alone,
       These holowe frendes, by Henry soone espyed,
       Became suspect and fayth was geuen to none,
       Which caused them from faith agayne to slyde. *C–G.*
       [*In l.* 86 *read* abandoning my *for* my Kingly state and *F.*]
[91]   And strayt conspierd, theyr newe King to put downe, *C–G.* [*Read*
       Conspiring streight *for* And strayt conspierd, *Read* Prince *for*
       King *F.*]
[92]   And to that end a *C–EG.* Which to performe a *F.*
[93]   my royall seate and *C–EG.* my scepter and my crowne, *F.*
[95–97]   But late medcynes can helpe no sothbynde sore:
       When swelling floodes hath ouer flowen the towne
       To late it is, to saue them that shall drowne, *C–G.*
       [*In l.* 95 *read* festred *for* sothbynde *F.*]

Til sailes be spred the ship may kepe the shore.
The Ankers wayed, though al the frayte do frowne,
With streame and steere perforce it shalbe bore. [100]

For though the piers set Henry in his state,
Yet could they not displace him thence agayne:
And where they easily put me downe of late,
They could restore me by no maner payne:
Thinges hardly mende, but may be mard amayne. [105]
And whan a man is falne in froward fate
Still mischeves light one in anothers pate:
And wel meant meanes his mishaps to restraine
Waxe wretched mones, wherby his ioyes abate.
Due proofe wherof in me appereth playne. [110]

For whan king Henry knew that for my cause
His lordes in maske would kil him if they might,
To dash all dowtes, he tooke no farther pause
But sent sir Pierce of Exton a traytrous knight
To Pomfret Castell, with other armed light, [115]

[98] spred, a shyp *C–G.*
[99] No ankerholde can kepe the vessell downe, *C–G.*
[100] it will be bore. *C–EG.* When winde and streame hath set the seas in rore. *F.*
[101] in such state, *F.*
[103] easely, depriued me of *C–EG.* where with ease my pride they did abate. *F.*
[106] fallen by *F.*
[107] one on anothers *B–G.*
[108] And meanes well ment all mishaps *C–G.*
[110] in this appeared playne. *C–G.*
[111] whan the King did knowe that *C–G.*
[112] him on a night, *C–EG.* would murder him by night, *F.*
[114] But Pierce of Exton a cruell murdering knight, *C–G.* [*Read* cuttthroate *for* murdering *F.*]
[115] Castell, sent hym armed bright, *C–EG.* Castel sent with great dispite, *F.*

Who causeles kild me there agaynst all lawes.
Thus lawles life, to lawles deth ey drawes.
Wherfore byd Kynges be rulde and rule by right,
Who wurketh his wil, & shunneth wisedomes sawes
[120]   In flateries clawes, & shames foule pawes shal light.

[116]   Who reft my life by force against *F.*
[119–20] And so I end concluding with this clause:
           That God though late, at last wil surely smyte. *F.*
[120]   In snares of woo, ere he beware shall lyght. *C–EG.*

TO THE READER

Han he had ended this so wofull a tragedy, and to all [Prose 5]
Princes a ryght wurthy instruction, we paused: hauing
passed through a miserable time full of piteous tragedyes.
And seing the reyne of Henry the fourth ensued, a man more ware &
prosperous in hys doynges although not vntroubled with warres both of [5]
outforth and inward enemies, we began to serch what Piers were fallen
therin, wherof the number was not small: and yet because their examples were not much to be noted for our purpose, we passed ouer all
the Maskers (of whom King Richardes brother was chiefe) which were
all slayne and put to death for theyr trayterous attempt. And finding [10]
Owen Glendour next, one of fortunes owne whelpes, and the Percyes
his confederates, I thought them vnmete to be over passed, and therfore
sayde thus to the silent cumpany: what my maysters is euery man at
once in a browne study, hath no man affeccion to any of these storyes?
you minde so much sum other belyke, that these do not move you: [15]
And to say the troth there is no speciall cause why they should. Howbeit
Owen Glendour because he was one of fortunes darlinges, rather than

[1]   WHan master Chaloner had X. WHen Maister Ferrers had F. so eloquent a X.
[2]   right notable and wurthy X. instruction: hauing F.
[3]   Tragedies, we paused awhile. F.
[4]   a Prince more F. more wary and G.
[4-5]   a man more prosperous although X.
[6]   what Princes X.
[11]   Glendour, a great Prince in Wales, next in succession of ill Fortune with the
        stout Percies F.
[12]   thought it not meete to ouerpasse, so great persons with silence, and. F.
[16]   to say troth X.
[17]   he is a man of that countrey whence (as the welchmen beare me in hand) my
        Petigre is discended, althoughe he be but a slender prince, yet rather X.
        Fortunes owne darlinges, and affected to be Prince of wales, althoughe to
        his own mischiefe and destruction, rather C–G. [Read Monark for Prince F.]

he should be forgotten, I wil tel his tale for him vnder the priuilege of
Martine Hundred: whych Owen cumming out of the wilde mount-
[20] aynes like the Image of death in all poyntes (his dart onely excepted) so
sore hath famine and hunger consumed hym, may lament his folly after
thys maner.

[18–19] I will take vpon me by your fauour to say somwhat in his person: which
C–EG. I wil pray Maister Phaer who of late hath placed hymselfe in that
country, & haply hath met with his ghost in the forest of Kylgarran that
he wil say somwhat in his person: which F.

[19]   comming naked out X.

[19–20] mountaynes of Wales C–G.

[20]   his hart C²–G.

[20–22] excepted) as a ghost forpined with extreme famine, colde, & hunger, may
lament his great misfortune after this manner. C–G. [*Read* in sutch maner
as you maister Phaer are able most aptly to vtter and set forth. *for* after this
manner. F.]

[21]   him, lamenteth his infortune after X.

[Tragedy 6]

Howe Owen Glendour seduced by false prophesies tooke vpon him to be prince of Wales, and was by Henry then prince therof, chased to the mountaynes, where he miserably dyed for lacke of foode.

I Pray the Baldwin sith thou doest entend
To shewe the fall of such as clymbe to hye,
Remember me, whose miserable ende
May teache a man his vicious life to flye:

[Title] by Henrye Prince of England chased C–G. foode. Anno. 1401.
C–EG. miserably starued for hunger. Anno. 1401. F.

[2]   the falles of X.

[4]   teach all men Ambition to F.

Oh Fortune, Fortune, out on her I crye,　　　　　　　　[5]
My body and fame she hath made leane and slender
For I poore wretch am sterued Owen Glendour.

　A Welshman borne, and of a gentle blud,
But ill brought vp, wherby full wel I find,
That neither birth nor linage make vs good　　　　　　[10]
Though it be true that Cat wil after kinde:
Fleshe gendreth fleshe, so doeth not soule or minde,
They gender not, but fowly do degender,
When men to vice from vertue them do surrender.

　Ech thing by nature tendeth to the same　　　　　　[15]
Wherof it came, and is disposed like:
Downe sinkes the mold, vp mountes the fiery flame,
With horne the hart, with hoofe the horse doth strike:
The Wulfe doth spoyle, the suttle Fox doth pyke,
And generally no fish, flesh, fowle, or plant　　　　[20]
Doth any property that their dame had, want.

　But as for men, sith seuerally they haue
A mind whose maners are by learning made,
Good bringing vp alonly doth them save
In vertuous dedes, which with their parentes fade.　　[25]

[5]　on thee I *C–EG*. Oh false Fortune, Fortune vengeaunce on thee I *F*.
[6]　My liuely corps thou hast made *C–EG*.
[6–7]　Which offeringe a Sop of sweete receyt,
　　Haste made me byte the Hooke in steede of Bayt. *F*.
[7]　sterued *is printed* steruen *but is corrected in Ae. B prints* sterued *but
　　Be corrects to* starued. For lacke of foode, whose name was Owen
　　C–EG.
[8]　A Brytton borne, *F*. of the Troyan blood, *C–G*.
[10]　make men good *X*.
[12]　but not the soule *C–G*.
[14]　doo render. *X*. them surrender. *B–EG*. they surrender. *F*.
[20]　And to conclude, no *C–G*.
[21]　Of theyr true dame, the property doth want. *C–G*.
[25]　In honest acts, which *C–G*.

So that true gentry standeth in the trade
Of vertuous life, not in the fleshly line:
For blud is Brute, but Gentry is diuine.

[30]

Experience doth cause me thus to say,
And that the rather for my countreymen,
Which vaunt and boast their selues aboue the day
If they may strayne their stocke for wurthy men:
Which let be true, are they the better than?
Nay farre the wurse if so they be not good,

[35]

For why they steyne the bewty of theyr blood.

How would we mocke the burden bearing mule
If he would brag he wer an horses sunne,
To presse his pride (might nothing els him rule,)
His boast to proue, no more but byd him runne:

[40]

The horse for swiftenes hath his glory wunne,
To which the mule could neuer the more aspier
Though he should prove that Pegas was his sier.

Ech man may crake of that which is his own,
Our parentes vertues theirs are and not oures:

[45]

Who therfore wil of noble kind be knowen
Ought shine in vertue like his auncestors,

[27]   Of vertues life, F.
[31]   boast them selfes XB–G.
[32]   stocke fro worthy B–G.
[38]   presse the pryde B.
[39]   His boastes to C–G.
[41]   The mule could neuer the more aspyer, C–G.
[42]   Pegas wer his X. Pegas is hys B.
[43]   Ech man crake F. which was his C–G.
[44]   vertues, are theyrs and no whit oures: C–G.
[45]   Noble byrth be C–G.

Gentry consisteth not in landes and towers:
He is a Churle though all the world be his,
He Arthurs heyre if that he liue amys.

For vertuous lyfe doth make a gentleman [50]
Of her possessour, all be he poore as Iob,
Yea though no name of elders shewe he can:
For proofe take Merlyn fathered by an Hob.
But who so settes his mind to spoyle and rob,
Although he cum by due discent fro Brute, [55]
He is a Chorle, vngentle, vile, and brute.

Well thus dyd I for want of better wyt,
Because my parentes noughtly brought me vp:
For gentle men (they sayd) was nought so fyt
As to attaste by bolde attemptes the cup [60]
Of conquestes wyne, wherof I thought to sup:
And therfore bent my selfe to rob and ryue,
And whome I could of landes and goodes depryue.

For Henry the fourth did then vsurpe the crowne,
Despoyled the kyng, with Mortimer the heyre: [65]
For whych his subiectes sought to put him downe.
And I, whyle Fortune offred me so fayre,
Dyd what I myght his honour to appeyre:
And toke on me to be the prynce of Wales,
Entiste therto by many of Merlines tales. [70]

[48]   world were his, *C–G*.
[49]   Yea Arthurs *B–G*.
[50]   life a Gentleman doth make *C–G*.
[52]   elders he can take: *C–G*.
[53]   Merlin whose father was an hob. *X*.
[58]   naughtely *C–G*.
[70]   by prophecies and tales. *C–G*.

For whych, such Idle as wayte vpon the spoyle,
From euery parte of Wales vnto me drew:
For loytring youth vntaught in any toyle
Are redy aye all mischiefe to ensue.
[75] Through help of these so great my glory grew,
That I defyed my Kyng through lofty hart,
And made sharp warre on all that tooke his part.

See lucke, I tooke lord Reynolde Grey of Rythen,
And him enforst my doughter to espouse,
[80] And so vnraunsomed held him still: and sithen
In Wygmore land through battayle rygorous
I caught the ryght heyre of the crowned house
The Erle of March syr Edmund Mortymer,
And in a dungeon kept hym prysoner,

[85] Then al the marches longyng vnto Wales
By Syverne west I did inuade and burne:
Destroyed the townes in mountaynes and in vales,
And riche in spoyles did homward safe retourne:
Was none so bold durst once agaynst me spurne.
[90] Thus prosperously doth Fortune forward call
Those whom she mindes to geue the sorest fall.

Whan fame had brought these tidinges to the king
(Although the Skots than vexed him ryght sore)
A myghty army agaynst me he dyd bryng:
[95] Wherof the French Kyng beyng warned afore,
Who mortall hate agaynst kyng Henry bore,
To greve our foe he quyckely to me sent
Twelve thousand Frenchmen armed to war, & bent.

[80]   vnraunsomed I held C–G.
[88]   And with rich X. spoyles had homward B–G.

124

A part of them led by the Erle of Marche
Lord Iames of Burbon, a valiaunt tryed knyght　　　　[100]
Withheld by winds to Wales ward forth to marche,
Tooke lande at Plymmouth pryuily on a nyght:
And when he had done al he durst or myght,
After that a mayny of his men were slayne
He stole to shyp, and sayled home agayne.　　　　　　[105]

Twelve thousand moe in Mylford dyd aryue,
And came to me, then lying at Denbygh
With armed Welshmen thousandes double fiue:
With whom we went to wurcester well nigh,
And there encampte vs on a mount on high,　　　　　[110]
To abide the kyng, who shortly after came
And pitched his feild, on a Hyll hard by the same.

Ther eyght dayes long, our hostes lay face to face,
And neyther durst the others power assayle:
But they so stopt the passages the space　　　　　　　[115]
That vitayles coulde not cum to our auayle,
Wherthrough constrayned our hartes began to fayle
So that the Frenchmen shrancke away by night,
And I with mine to the mountaynes toke our flight:

The king pursued vs, greatly to his cost,　　　　　　　[120]
From Hyls to wuds, fro wuds to valeyes playne:
And by the way his men and stuf he lost.
And whan he see he gayned nought saue payne,
He blewe retreat, and got him home agayne:
Then with my power I boldly came abrode　　　　　　[125]
Taken in my cuntrey for a very God.

[103]　all that he C–G.
[106]　thousand other in X.
[114]　durst others power C–G.
[120]　pursued greatly C–G.
[123]　he saw he C–G. nought but paine, C–G.
[124]　and gat hym B–G.

Immediatly after fell a Ioly Iarre
Betwene the king, and Percies worthy bluds,
Which grew at last vnto a deadly warre:

[130] For like as drops engendre mighty fluds,
And litle seedes sprut furth great leaues and buds,
Euen so small strifes, if they be suffred run
Brede wrath and war, and death or they be don.

The kyng would haue the raunsum of such Scots
[135] As these the Percyes had tane in the feeld:
But see how strongly Luker knits her knottes,
The king will haue, the Percies wil not yeeld,
Desire of goodes soone craues, but graunteth seeld:
Oh cursed goodes desire of you hath wrought
[140] All wyckednes, that hath or can be thought.

The Percies deemed it meter for the king
To haue redeemed theyr cosin Mortymer,
Who in his quarel all his power did bryng
To fight with me, that tooke him prisoner
[145] Than of their pray to rob his Souldier:
And therfore willed him see sum mean wer found,
To quit furth him whom I kept vily bound.

Because the king misliked their request,
They came them selues and did accord with me,
[150] Complayning how the kyngdome was opprest,
By Henries rule, wherfore we dyd agre
To put him downe, and part the realme in three:
The North part theirs, Wales wholy to be mine
The rest to rest to therle of Marches line.

[131]   sprout G.
[135]   Percyes tane had in B–G.
[138]   goods some craues, C–G.
[152]   To plucke him G.

And for to set vs hereon more agog [155]
A prophet came (a vengeaunce take them all)
Affirming Henry to be Gogmagog
Whom Merlyn doth a Mouldwarp euer call,
Accurst of god, that must be brought in thrall
By a wulf, a Dragon, and a Lyon strong, [160]
Which should deuide his kingdome them among.

This crafty dreamer made vs thre such beastes
To thinke we were these foresayd beastes in deede:
And for that cause our badges and our creastes
We searched out, whych scarcely wel agreed: [165]
Howbeit the Haroldes redy at such a neede,
Drew downe such issues from olde auncestours,
As proued these ensignes to be surely oures.

Ye crafty Welshemen, wherfore do you mocke
The noble men thus with your fayned rymes? [170]
Ye noble men why flye you not the flocke
Of such as haue seduced so many times?
False Prophesies are plages for divers crymes
Whych god doth let the divilish sorte devise
To trouble such as are not godly wyse. [175]

And that appered by vs thre beastes in dede,
Through false perswasion highly borne in hand
That in our feat we could not chuse but spede
To kyll the kyng, and to enioye his land:
For which exployt we bound our selues in band [180]
To stand contented ech man with his part,
So fully folly assured our folysh hart.

[169] do ye mocke, C–G.
[171] fly ye not C–G.

But such they say as fysh before the net
Shal seldome surfyt of the pray they take,
[185] Of thinges to cum the haps be so vnset
That none but fooles may warrant of them make:
The full assured, succes doth oft forsake.
For Fortune findeth none so fyt to flout,
As suresby sots whych cast no kinde of doute.

[190] How sayest thou Henry Hotspur, do I lye?
For thou right manly gauest the king a feeld,
And there was slayn because thou wouldest not fly:
Sir Thomas Percie thine vncle (forst to yeeld)
Did cast his head (a wunder seen but seeld)
[195] From Shrewsbury town to the top of London bridge.
Lo thus fond hope did theyr both liues abridge.

Whan Henry king this victory had wunne,
Destroyed the Percies, put their power to flyght,
He did appoynt prince Henry his eldest sunne
[200] With all his power to meete me if he might:
But I discumfit through my partners fight
Had not the hart to mete him face to face,
But fled away, and he pursued the chase.

Now Baldwin marke, for I cald prince of Wales,
[205] And made beleve I should be he in dede,
Was made to flye among the hilles and dales,
Where al my men forsooke me at my nede.
Who trusteth loyterers seeld hath lucky spede:
And whan the captaynes corage doth him fayle
[210] His souldiers hartes a litle thing may quayle.

[189] As surebe sots G.
[196] did both theyr lyues C–G.
[197] Whan King Henry this C–G.

And so Prince Henry chased me, that loe
I found no place wherin I might abide:
For as the dogges pursue the selly doe,
The brach behind the houndes on euery side,
So traste they me among the mountaynes wide: [215]
Wherby I found I was the hartles hare
And not the beast Colprophete did declare.

And at the last: like as the litle roche,
Must eyther be eat, or leape vpon the shore
Whan as the hungry pickrel doth approch,   [220]
And there find death which it eskapte before:
So double death assaulted me so sore
That eyther I must vnto my enmy yeeld,
Or starue for hunger in the barayne feeld.

Here shame and payne a whyle were at a strife,   [225]
Payne prayed me yeeld, shame bad me rather fast:
The one bad spare, the other spend my life,
But shame (shame haue it) ouercam at last.
Than hunger gnew, that doth the stone wall brast
And made me eat both gravell, durt and mud,   [230]
And last of all, my dung, my fleshe, and blud.

This was mine ende to horrible to heare,
Yet good ynough for a life that was so yll.

[220] pickerell G.
[226] Payn bad me C–G.
[227] other bad spend C–G.
[229] hunger stronge, that F.
[230] Forst mee to feede on Barke of trees, and Wood, F.
[231] all, to gnaw my flesh and bloud. F.
[233] that did so F.

[235]

Wherby (O Baldwin) warne all men to beare
Theyr youth such loue, to bring them vp in skill
Byd Princes flye Colprophetes lying byll:
And not presume to clime aboue their states,
For they be faultes that foyle men, not their fates

[234]   warne men to forbeare, *F.*
[235]   The vayne desires, when wit doth yeld to will: *F.*
[236]   lyinge skill, *F.*

WHan starued Owen had ended his hungry exhortacion, it [Prose 6]
was well inough liked. Howbeit one found a dout wurth
the mouing, & that concerning this title, erle of March:
for as it appereth, there were .iii. men of .iii. diuers nacions together in
one time entitled by that honour: Fyrst sir Edmund Mortimer, whom [5]
Owen kept in prison, an Englishman: the second the lord George of
Dunbar a valiante Scot. banished out of his countrey, & well estemed of
Henry the fowerth: the third lord Iames of Burbon a frenchman, sent by
the french king to helpe Owen Glendour. These thre men had this title
all at once, which caused him to aske how it was true that euery one of [10]
these could be Earle of Marche? Wherto was aunswered, that euery
countrey hath Marches belonging vnto them, and those so large, that
they were Earledomes, & the lordes therof intituled therby, so that Lord
Edmund Mortimer was Earle of Marche in Englande, lord Iames of
Burbon of the marches of Fraunce, and Lord George of Dunbar erle of [15]
the marches in Scotland. For otherwise nether could haue interest in
others title. Thys doubt thus dissolued mayster Ferrers sayde: If no man
haue affeccion to the Percies, let vs pas the times both of Henry the
fowerth & the fifte, and cum to Henrye the syxte: in whose time fortune
(as she doth in the minoritie of princes) bare a great stroke among the [20]
nobles. And yet in Henry the fourths time are examples which I would
wish *Baldwin* that you should not forget, as the conspiracie made by the
bishop of Yorke, and the lorde Mowbray, sonne of him whom you late
treated of: prycked forward by the earle of Northumberland, father to
sir Henry Hotspur, who fled him selfe, but his partners were appre- [25]
hended and put to death, with Baynton and Blinkinsops, which could

[1-2]   WHan mayster Phaer had ended the Tragedy of thys hunger staruen Prynce
        of Wales, it was well liked of all the company that a Saxon would speake
        so mutch for a Brytton, then sodenly one found *F*.
[3]   title, Thearle of *F*.
[13]   so the lord *C–G*.
[19]   the fyfth, *B*.

not see theyr duty to theyr King, but tooke part with Percy that banished Rebell. As he was proceding, he was desired to stay by one whych had pondered the story of the Percies, who briefly sayd. To thende *Baldwin*
[30] that you may know what to say of the Percyes, whose story is not all out of my memory, (and it is a notable story) I wyll take vpon me the person of lord Henry earle of Northumberland, father of Henrye Hotspur, in whose behalfe thys may be sayd.

[31]   of memorye C–G. (and is G. an notable C–F.
[32]   of the Lorde Henry Percy Erle C–G. of syr Henry C–G.
[33]   saide as followeth C–G.

[Tragedy 7]

How Henry Percy Earle of Northhumberland, was for his couetous and trayterous attempt put to death at Yorke.

Morall Senec true find I thy saying,
That neyther kinsfolke, ryches, strength, or fauour
Are free from Fortune, but are ay decaying:
No worldly welth is ought save doubtful labour,
[5]   Mans life in earth is like vnto a tabour:
Which now to mirth doth mildly men provoke
And strayt to war, with a more sturdy stroke.

All this full true I Percy find by proofe,
Which whilom was erle of Northumberland:
[10]   And therfore Baldwin for my Piers behoof
To note mens falles sith thou hast tane in hand,

[Title] Yorke. Anno. 1407. C–G.
[2]   neyther kin, riches, C–G.

132

.I would thou shouldest my state well vnderstand:
For fewe kinges were more then I redouted,
Through double Fortune lyfted vp and louted.

As for my kinne their noblenes is knowen,   [15]
My valiauntise were folly for to prayse,
Wherthrough the Scottes so oft were ouerthrowen
That who but I was doubted in my dayes:
And that kyng Rychard found at all assayes,
For neuer Scottes rebelled in his rayne   [20]
But through my force were eyther caught or slayne.

A brother I had was Erle of Worcester
Alwayes in fauour and office with the king,
And by my wife Dame Elinor Mortimer,
I had a son which so the Scottes did sting,   [25]
That being yong, and but a very spring
Syr Henry Hotspur they gaue him to name,
And though I say it, he did deserue the same.

We thre tryumphed in king Richards time,
Til Fortune ought both him and vs a spite: [30]
But chiefly me, whom clere from any crime,
My king did banish from his favour quite,
And openly proclaymed trayterous knight:
Wherethrough false slaunder forced me to be
That which before I did most deadly flee.   [35]

[12]   thou should my C–G.
[14]   Whome double C–G.
[16]   My valiaunt acts were C–G.
[23]   Alwayes in office and fauour with C–G.
[25]   A sonne I had C–G.
[27]   Henry Hotspur they C–G. him vnto C–EG.
[31]   whom clearly from D–G.
[33]   Proclayming me a trayterous C–G.

Let men beware how they true folke defame,
Or threaten on them the blame of vices nought,
For infamy bredeth wrath, wreke foloweth shame:
Eke open slaunder, oftentimes hath brought
[40] That to effect, that erst was neuer thought:
To be misdemed men suffer in a sort,
But none can beare the griefe of misreport.

Because my king did shame me wrongfully,
I hated him, and in dede became his foe:
[45] And while he did at war in Ireland lye,
I did conspire to turne his weale to woe:
And through the duke of Yorke and other moe,
All royall power from him we quickely tooke
And gaue the same to Henry Boleynbroke.

[50] Neyther dyd we this alonely for this cause,
But to say truth, force draue vs to the same:
For he dispising god and all good lawes
Slew whom he would, made sinne a very game.
And seing neither age nor counsayle could him tame,
[55] We thought it wel done for the kingdomes sake,
To leaue his rule that did al rule forsake.

But whan sir Henry had attaynde his place,
He strayt becam in all poyntes wurse than he:
Destroyed the piers, & slewe kyng Rychards grace,
[60] Agaynst his othe made to the lordes and me:
And seking quarelles how to disagre,
He shamelesly required me and my sonne
To yeld him Scottes which we in field had wun.

[44]   and so became *F.*
[50]   this onely for *C–G.*
[52]   all his lawes, *C–G.*

My Nephew also Edmund Mortymer
The very heyre apparaunt to the Crowne,　　　　　　[65]
Whom Owen Glendour held as prisoner,
Vilely bound, in dungeon depe cast downe,
He would not raunsum: but did felly frowne
Agaynst my brother and me that for him spake,
And him proclaymed traytour for our sake.　　　　　　[70]

　This fowle despite did cause vs to conspire
To put him downe as we did Richard erst,
And that we might this matter set on fyre
From Owens iayle, our cosin we remerst,
And vnto Glendour all our griefes reherst,　　　　　　[75]
Who made a bonde with Mortymer and me.
To pryue the king, and part the realme in thre.

　But whan king Henry heard of this devise
Toward Owen Glendour he sped him very quyck
Mynding by force to stop our enterprise:　　　　　　[80]
And as the deuell would, then fell I sick,
Howbeit my brother, & sonne, more politike
Than prosperous, with an oast fro Scotland brought,
Encountred him at Shrewsbury, wher they fought.

　The one was tane and kild, the other slayne,　　　　[85]
And shortly after was Owen put to flight:
By meanes wherof I forced was to fayne,
That I knew nothing of the former fight.
Fraude oft avayles more than doth sturdy might:
For by my fayning I brought him in belief　　　　　　[90]
I knew not that wherin my part was chief.

[69]　　me which for C–G.
[80]　　stop hur enterprise: C–G.

135

And while the king thus tooke me for his frend
I sought all meanes my former wrong to wreake,
Which that I might bring to the sooner ende
[95]   To the bishop of Yorke I did the matter breake,
And to Therle Marshall likewise did I speake,
Whose father was through Henries cause exyled
The bishops brother with trayterous death defiled.

These strayt assented to do what they could,
[100] So did lorde Hastinges and lord Fauconbridge:
Which altogether promised they would
Set all their power the kinges dayes to abridge.
Be se the spite, before the byrdes wer flidge
The king had woord, and seysoned on the nest
[105] Wherby alas my frendes wer al opprest.

The bluddy tyrant brought them all to ende
Excepted me, which into Scotland skapte
To George of Dunbar therle of March, my frend,
Who in my cause al that he could ey skrapte:
[110] And when I had for greater succour gapte
Both at the Frenchman and the Flemminges hand,
And could get none, I toke such as I fand.

And with the helpe of George my very frend,
I did invade Northumberlande ful bold,
[115] Whereas the folke drew to me stil vnend,
Bent to the death my party to vphold:
Through helpe of these ful many a fort and hold.
The which the king right manfully had mand,
I easely wunne, and seysed in my hand

[93]   all meane my G.
[100]   dyd the lorde Hastinges B–F. [*Corrected in Be to the original reading.*]
[115]   styll on end, C–G.
[116]   Bent to death C–G.

Not so content (for vengeaunce drave me on)   [120]
I entred Yorkeshire there to waste and spoyle,
But ere I had far in the countrey gon
The shirif therof, Rafe Rekesby did assoyle
My troubled hoost of much part of our toyle,
For he assauting freshly, tooke through power   [125]
Me and lord Bardolph both at Bramham more.

And thence conueyed vs to the towne of Yorke
Vntil he knew, what was the kinges entent:
There loe Lord Bardolf kinder than the Storke,
Did lose his head, which was to London sent,   [130]
With whom for frendshippe mine in like case went.
This was my hap, my fortune, or my fawte,
This life I led, and thus I came to naught.

Wherfore good Baldwin wil the pyers take hede
Of slaunder, malyce, and conspiracy,   [135]
Of couetise, whence al the rest procede:
For couetise ioynt with contumacy,
Doth cause all mischief in mens hartes to brede.
Ad therfore this to *Esperance*, my wurd.
Who causeth bludshed shall not skape the swurd.   [140]

[139]   And therefore B–G. [*Corrected in Be to the original reading.*]
[140]   not escape the C–G.

[Prose 7] BY that this was ended, I had found out the storie of Richard earle of Cambridge: and because it conteyned matter in it, though not very notable, yet for the better vnderstanding of the rest, I thought it mete to touche it, and therfore sayd as foloweth, You haue
[5] sayd wel of the Percies and favourably. For in dede as it should appere, the chyefe cause of theyr conspiracie agaynst kyng Henry, was for Edmund Mortimer theyr cosins sake, whom the king very maliciously proclaymed to haue yelded hym selfe to Owen colourably, whan as in deede he was taken forcibly against his wil, & very cruelly ordered in
[10] prison. And seing we are in hand with Mortimers matter, I wyll take vppon me the person of Richard Plantagenet Earle of Cambridge, who for his sake likewise died. And therfore I let passe Edmund Holland erle of Kent, whom Henry the fowerth made Admirall to skoure the Seas, because the Brittons were abrode: whiche Earle (as many thynges
[15] happen in warre) was slayne with an arrowe at the assaulte of Briake: shortly after whose death thys king dyed, and his sonne Henry, the fyft of that name, succeded in his place. In the beginning of this Henry the fyfts rayne, dyed this Rychard, and with him Henry the lord Scrope & others, in whose behalfe this may be sayd.

[19] other in *B–G*.

How Richard erle of Cambridge en-
tending the kinges destruction
was put to death at
Southhampton.

HAst maketh wast, hath commonly ben sayd,
And secrete mischiefe seeld hath lucky spede:
A murdering mind with proper peyze is wayd,
Al this is true, I find it in my Crede.
And therfore Baldwin warne all states take hede,   [5]
How they conspire any other to betrappe,
Least mischiefe meant light in the miners lappe.

    For I lord Richard, heyre Plantagenet
Was Erle of Cambridge, and right fortunate,
If I had had the grace my wit to set   [10]
To have content me with mine owne estate:
But o false honours, breders of debate,
The loue of you our lewde hartes doth allure
To lese our selues by seking you vnsure.

    Because my brother Edmund Mortimer,   [15]
Whose eldest sister was my wedded wife,
I meane that Edmund that was prisoner
In Wales so long, through Owens busy strife,

[Title] Richard Plantagenet Earle *C–G*. Southampton. Anno. Dom. 1415.
     C–G.
[3]   poyze *C–G*.
[4]   this most true *F*. it, as my *F*.
[7]   the meaners lappe. *D–F*.
[13]   do allure, *F*.

[20]
Because I say, that after Edmundes life,
His rightes and titles must by law be mine,
(For he ne had, nor could encrease his line)

Because the right of realme & crowne was ours,
I serched means to helpe him thervnto.
And where the Henries held it by their powers
[25]
I sought a shift their tenures to vndo,
Which being force, sith force or sleyt must do,
I voyde of might, because their power was strong
Set privy sleyte agaynst theyr open wrong.

But sith the deathes of most part of my kinne
[30]
Did dash my hope, throughout the fathers dayes
I let it slip, and thought it best beginne
Whan as the sonne shuld dred lest such assayes:
For force through spede, sleyght spedeth through delayes
And seeld doth treason time so fitly find
[35]
As whan al dangers most be out of minde.

Wherfore while Henry of that name the fifte,
Prepared his army to go conquer Fraunce,
Lord Skrope and I thought to attempt a drifte
To put him downe my brother to avaunce:
[40]
But were it gods wil, my luck, or his good chaunce,
The king wist wholy wherabout we went,
The night before the king to shipward bent.

Then were we strayt as traytours apprehended,
Our purpose spied, the cause therof was hid,
[45]
And therfore loe a false cause we pretended
Wherthrough my brother was fro daunger ryd:

[29] the death of C–G.
[42] before to shypward he hym bent. B–G.

140

We sayd for hier of the French kinges coyne, we did
Behight to kil the king: and thus with shame
We stayned our selves, to save our frend fro blame.

Whan we had thus confest so foule a treason, [50]
That we deserved, we suffred by the lawe.
Se Baldwin see, and note (as it is reason)
How wicked dedes to wofull endes do drawe,
All force doth fayle, no crafte is wurth a straw,
To attayne thinges lost, and therfore let them go, [55]
For might ruleth right, and wil though God say no.

[47]   of French *C–G*.
[56]   though truth say *C–G*.

[Prose 8] WHan stout Richarde had stoutly sayd his mind, belike quoth one, this Rychard was but a litle man, or els litle fauoured of wryters, for our Cronicles speake very litle of him. But seyng we be cum now to king Henries viage into Fraunce, we [5] can not lack valyant men to speake of: for among so many as were led and sent by the Kyng out of thys realme thyther, it can not be chosen but sum, and that a great summe, were slayne among theym: wherfore to speake of them all, I thynke not nedefull. And therfore to let passe Edwarde Duke of Yorke, and the Earle of Suffolke slayne both at the [10] battayle of Aginecourte, as were also many other, Let vs ende the time of Henry the fyfth, and cum to hys sunne Henry the syxt: whose nonage brought Fraunce and Normandy out of bondage, and was cause that fewe of our noble men died aged. Of whom to let passe the numbre, I wyll take vppon me the person of Thomas Mountague earle [15] of Salysburye, whose name was not so good at home (and yet he was called the good erle) as it was dreadful abrode: who exclaming vpon the mutability of fortune, iustly may say thus.

[2] saide one, C–G.
[3] of the writers, G.
[7] s in slayne *is not printed in the HN copy of the text.*
[13] that so fewe C–G.
[17] Fortune may iustly saye in manner as followeth. C–G.

How Thomas Montague the earle of Salysbury in the middes of his glory, was chaunceably slayne with a piece of ordinaunce.

WHat fooles be we to trust vnto our strength,
Our wit, our courage, or our noble fame,
Which time it selfe must nedes deuour at length
Though froward Fortune could not foyle the same.
But seing this Goddes gideth al the game,   [5]
Which still to chaunge doth set her onely lust,
Why toyle we so for thinges so hard to trust.

A goodly thing is surely good reporte,
Which noble hartes, do seke by course of kinde,
But seen the date so doubtful and so short,   [10]
The wayes so rough wherby we do it find:
I can not chuse but prayse the princely minde
That preaseth for it, though we find opprest
By foule defame those that deserve it best.

Concerning-whom marke Baldwin what I say,   [15]
I meane the vertuous hindred of their brute,
Among which number reken wel I may
My valiaunt father Iohn lord Montacute,

[Title] Montague Earle *C–G.* slaine at Orleaunce with *C–G.* Ordinaunce
    the .3. of Nouember. Anno. 1428. *C–G. The text misprints a comma
    for a period after* ordinaunce.
[8]   thyng it is *B–G.* [*Corrected in Be to the original reading.*]
[10]   But seeing the *G.*
[11]   The way so *C–G.*

143

Who lost his life (I iudge) in iust pursute:
[20] I say the cause and not the casual spede,
Is to be wayed in euery kinde of dede.

This rule obserued, how many shall we find
For vertues sake with infamy opprest?
How many agayn through helpe of fortune blind,
[25] For yll attemptes atchiued, with honour blest?
Succes is wurst ofttimes whan cause is best,
Therfore say I: god send them sory happes,
That iudge the causes by their after clappes.

The ende in dede, is iudge of euery thing,
[30] Which is the cause, or latter poynt of time:
The first true verdyct at the first may bryng,
The last is slow, or slipper as the slime,
Oft chaunging names of innocence and crime.
Duke Thomas death was Iustice two yeres long,
[35] And euer sence sore tiranny and wrong.

Wherfore I pray the Baldwin waye the cause,
And prayse my father as he doth deserue:
Because erle Henry, king agaynst all lawes,
Endeuoured king Richard for to starve
[40] In iayle, wherby the regal crowne might swarve
Out of the line to which it than was due,
(Wherby God knowes what euil might ensue)

My lord Iohn Holland duke of Excester,
Which was dere cosin to this wretched king,
[45] Did mooue my father, and the erle of Glocester,
With other lordes to ponder well the thyng:
Who seing the mischiefe that began to spring,
Did all consent, this Henry to depose,
And to restore kyng Richard to the rose.

[19]   iudge through iust C–G.

And while they did deuise a prety trayne [50]
Wherby to bring their purpose bettre about,
Which was in maske, this Henry to haue slayne:
The duke of Awmerle blew their counsayle out,
Yet was their purpose good there is no doubt.
What cause can be more wurthy for a knight, [55]
Than save his king, and helpe true heires to right?

For this with them my father was destroyed,
And buryed in the dounghil of defame.
Thus evil chaunce theyr glory did auoyde,
Wheras their cause doth clayme eternal fame. [60]
Whan dedes therfore vnluckely do frame,
Men ought not iudge the authours to be naught,
For right through might is often overraught.

And God doth suffer that it should be so,
But why, my wit is feble to decise, [65]
Except it be to heape vp wrath and wo
Vpon their heades that iniuries devise.
The cause why mischiefes many times arise,
And light on them that wold mens wronges redresse,
Is for the rancour that they beare, I gesse. [70]

God hateth rigour though it furder right,
For sinne is sinne, how euer it be vsed:
And therfore suffereth shame and death to light,
To punish vice, though it be wel abused.
Who furdereth right is not therby excused, [75]
If through the same he do sum other wrong:
To every vice due guerdon doth belong.

[66]   heape of wrath *F.*
[67]   On wicked heades *C–G.*
[71]   God hath *B.* [*Corrected in Be to the original reading.*] God hates *C–G.*

What preach I now, I am a man of warre,
And that my body (I dare say) doth professe,
[80]   Of cured woundes beset with many a skarre,
My broken Iaw vnheald can say no lesse.
O Fortune, Fortune, cause of all distresse
My father had great cause thy fraude to cursse.
But much more I, abused ten times wursse.

[85]   Thou neuer flatteredst him in all his life,
But me thou dandledst like thy darling deare:
Thy giftes I found in every corner rife,
Where ever I went, I met thy smyling cheare:
Which was not for a day, or for a yeare,
[90]   But through the rayne of thre right worthy kynges,
I found the forward in al kind of thinges.

The while king Henry conquered in Fraunce
I sued the warres, and still found victory.
In all assaultes so happy was my chaunce,
[95]   Holdes yelde or wunne did make my enmies sory:
Dame Prudence eke augmented so my glory,
That in all treaties ever I was one
Whan weyghty matters were agreed vpon.

But whan this king this mighty conquerour,
[100]   Through death vnripe, was both his realmes bereft,
His sely infant did receyue his power,
Pore litle babe ful yong in cradell left,
Where crowne and Scepter hurt him with the heft:
Whose wurthy vncles had the governaunce,
[105]   The one at home, the other abrode in Fraunce.

[85]   flattredst *C–G.* all thy life, *C–G.*
[86]   lyke the darlyng *B.*

146

And I which was in peace and war wel skilled,
With both these rulers greatly was estemed:
Bare rule at home as often as they willed,
And fought in Fraunce whan thei it nedeful demed.
And every where so good my seruice semed,   [110]
That Englishmen to me great loue did beare,
Our foes the French, my force fulfilled with feare.

I always thought it fitly for a prince,
And such as haue the regiment of realmes,
His subiectes hartes with mildnes to convince,   [115]
Wyth iustice myxt, auoyding all extremes.
For like as Phebus with his chearfull beames,
Doth freshly force the fragrant floures to florish,
So rulers mildnes subiectes loue doth norish.

This found I true: for through my mild behauour   [120]
Their hartes I had with me to liue and dye:
And in their speache for to declare their fauour,
They called me styll good earle of Salisbury,
The lordes confest the commons did not lye.
For vertuous life, fre hart, and lowly mind,   [125]
With high and low shal always fauour find.

Which vertues chief becum a man of war,
Wherof in Fraunce I founde experyence,
For in assaultes due mildnes passeth farre
Al rigour, force, and sturdy violence: [130]
For men wil stoutly sticke to their defence
When cruel captaynes covet them to spoyle,
And so enforst, oft geue their foes the foyle.

[119] loue do norish. *F.*
[122] speche bewrayer of their *C–G.*
[132] couet after spoile, *C–G.*

But when they know they shall be frendly vsed,
[135] They hazard not their heades, but rather yelde,
For this, my offers neuer were refused
Of any towne, or surely very seelde:
But force and furies fyt be for the feelde.
And there in dede I vsed so the same,
[140] My foes would flye if they had heard my name.

For whan lord Steward and erle Vantadore,
Had cruelly besieged Crauant towne,
Which we had wunne, and kept long time before,
Which lieth in Awxer on the riuer Youne,
[145] To rayse the siege the Regent sent me downe:
Where as I vsed all rigour that I might,
I killed all, that were not saued by flight.

When the erle of Bedford then in Fraunce lord regent,
Knew in what sort I had remoued the syege,
[150] In Brye and Champayne he made me vice gerent,
And Lieutenaunt for him and for my Lyege:
Which caused me go to Bry, and ther besyege
Mountaguillon, with twenty wekes assaut,
Which at the last was yelded me for naught.

[155] And for the duke of Britayns brother, Arthur,
Both erle of Richmonde and of Yvery,
Against his othe from vs had made departure,
To Charles the Dolphin, our chief enemy,
I with the regent went to Normandy,
[160] To take his towne of Yvery, which of spight
Did to vs dayly al the harme they might.

[140] they but heard C–G.
[143] Which he had C–G.

They at the first compounded by a day
To yeeld, if rescues did not cum before.
And whiles in hope to fight, we at it lay,
The Dolphin gathered men two thousand skore,   [165]
With erles, lordes, and captaynes ioly store:
Of which the duke of Alanson was gide,
And sent them downe to see if we would bide.

But they left vs and downe to Vernoile went,
And made their vaunt they had our army slayne,   [170]
And through that lye, that towne from vs they hent,
Which shortly after turned to their payne:
For there both armies met vpon the plaine,
And we .viii. M. whom they flew, not slewe before,
Did kil of them, ten thousand men and more.   [175]

When we had taken Vernoile thus againe,
To driue the Dolphin vtterly out of Fraunce,
The Regent sent me to Aniowe and to Mayne,
Wher I besieged the warlik towne of Mawns:
Ther lord of Toysers Baldwins valiaunce   [180]
Did well appere, which wold not yeeld the towne,
Till all the towres & walles wer battred downe.

But here now Baldwin take it in good part,
Though that I brought this Baldwin ther to yeeld:
The Lion fearce for all his noble hart,   [185]
Being overmatched, is forst to flye the feeld.
If Mars him selfe had there ben with his sheeld,
And in my stormes had stoutly me withstoode,
He should haue yeeld, or els haue shed my bloode.

[186] to flée B.
[187] him selfe there had ben C–G.

[190]   This wurthy knight both hardy, stout, and wise,
Wrought well his feate: as time and place require,
Whan fortune fayles, it is the best advice
To strike the sayle, least al lie in the mire.
This have I sayd to thend thou take no yre,
[195]   For though no cause be found, so nature frames,
Men haue a zeale to such as beare their names.

But to returne, in Mayne wan I at length,
Such towns & fortes as might either helpe or hurt,
I manned Mayon & Suzans townes of strength,
[200]   Fort Barnarde, Thanceaux, & S. Cales the curt,
With Lile sues Bolton, standing in the durt:
Eke Gwerland, Susze, Loupeland and Mountsure,
With Malicorne, these wan I and kept full sure.

Besides al this, I tooke nere forty holdes,
[205]   But those I razed even with the grounde.
And for these dedes, as sely shepe in foldes
Do shrinke for feare at every litle sound,
So fled my foes before my face ful round:
Was none so hardy durst abide the fight,
[210]   So Mars and Fortune furdered me their knight.

I tel no lye, so gastful grewe my name,
That it alone discomfited an host:
The Scots and Frenchmen wil confesse the same,
Els wil the towne which they like cowardes lost.
[215]   For whan they sieged Bewron with great bost,
Being fourty .M. Britayns, French, and Scottes,
Fiue hundred men did vanquish them like sottes.

[199] Suzans town of *C–G.*
[209] hardy that durst *C–G.* abyde my fight, *F.*
[213] frenchmen well confesse *C–G.*

For while the Frenchmen did assault them stil,
Our Englishmen came boldly furth at night,
Criyng sainct George, Salisbury, kil, kil, kil,   [220]
And offred freshly with their foes to fight,
And they as frenchly tooke them selves to flight,
Supposing surely that I had ben there.
Se how my name did put them all in feare.

Thus was the Dolphins power discomfited,   [225]
Fower .M. slayne, their campe tane as it stoode,
Wherby our towne and souldiers profited,
For there were vitayles plentifull and good:
This while was I in England by the rood
To appeace a strife that was right foule befall,   [230]
Betwene Duke Humfrey and the Cardinall.

The Duke of Exceter shortly after died,
Which of the king at home had gouernaunce,
Whose roume the earle of Warwike then supplied,
And I tooke his, and sped me into Fraunce.   [235]
And hauing a zeale to conquer Orlyaunce,
With much ado I gat the regentes ayde,
And marched thither and siege about it layde.

But in the way I tooke the towne of Yayn,
Wher murdred wer for stoutnes many a man: [240]
But Baugency I tooke with litle payne,
For which to shew them fauour I began:
This caused the townes of Mewne and Iargeman,
That stoode on Loyer, to profer me the keyes,
Ere I came nere them, welny by two dayes.   [245]

[218]   Frenchmen freshly assaulted still, C–G.
[236]   hauing zeale to F.

See here how Fortune forward can allure,
What baytes she layeth to bring men to their endes.
Who having hap like this, but would hope sure
To bring to bale what euer he entendes?
[250] But soone is sowre the sweete that Fortune sendes:
Whan hope and hap, whan helth and welth is hyest,
Than wo and wracke, desease, and nede be nyest.

For while I, suing this so good successe,
Layd siege to Orlyaunce on the river syde,
[255] The Bastard (Cuckold Cawnyes sonne I gesse,
Tho thought the dukes) who had the towne in gide,
Came fearcely forth, when he his time espide,
To raise the siege, but was beat backe agayne,
And hard pursued both to his losse and payne.

[260] For there we wan the bulwarke on the bridge
With a mighty tower standing fast therby.
Ah cursed tower that didst my dayes abridge,
Would god thou hadst bene furder, eyther I.
For in this tower a chamber standes on hie,
[265] From which a man may view through al the towne
By certayne windowes yron grated downe.

Where on a day (now Baldwin note mine ende)
I stoode in vewing where the towne was weake,
And as I busily talked with my frend,
[270] Shot fro the towne, which al the grate did breake,
A pellet came, and drove a mighty fleake,
Agaynst my face, and tare away my cheeke,
For payne wherof I dyed within a weeke.

[246] Fortune froward G.
[248] but hopeth sure, C–G.

152

See Baldwin see the vncertaynty of glory,
How sodayne mischief dasheth all to dust.   [275]
And warne all princes by my broken story,
The happiest Fortune chiefly to mistrust.
Was neuer man that alway had his lust.
Than such be fooles, in fancy more then mad,
Which hope to haue that neuer any had.   [280]

[274]   the vncertayne of glory, C–E. the vncertayne glorye, FG.
[279]   Then sure be G.

[Prose 9] THis straunge aduenture of the good erle drave vs al into a
dumpne, inwardly lamenting his wofull destynye, out of which
we wer awaked, after this sort.

To what ende (quoth one) muse we so much on this matter. This
[5] Earle is neyther the first nor the last whom Fortune hath foundered in
the heyth of their prosperitye. For all through the raine of this vnfortunate king Henry, we shall find many whych haue bene likewise serued,
whose chaunces sith they be marcial, and therfore honorable, may the
better be omitted: And therfore we wil let go the lordes Morlines and
[10] Poyninges, slayne both at the siege of Orleans shortly after the death of
this earle. Also the valiaunt earle of Arundle destroyed with a bowlet
at the assault of Gerbory, whose storyes neuertheles are wurth the
hearyng. And to quicken vp your spirites, I wil take vpon me a tragicall
person in deede, I meane kyng Iamy slayne by his seruauntes in his pryvy
[15] chamber, who although he be a Skot, yet seing he was brought vp in
Englande where he learned the language, hys example also so notable,
it were not meete he shoulde be forgotten.

And therfore marke Baldwin what I thinke he may say.

[2]   dumpe B–G.
[4]   (saide one) C–G. on the matter. B–G.
[5]   neither the fyrste nor laste F. neyther first nor last G.
[9]   Molynes C–G.
[17] mete it should B–G.

How king Iames the first for breaking
his othes and bondes, was by gods
suffrauns miserably murdred
of his owne subiectes.

IF for examples sake thou write thy booke,
I charge the Baldwin thou forget me not:
Whom Fortune alwayes frowardly forsooke,
Such was my lucke, my merite, or my lot.
I am that Iames king Roberts sonne the Skot,   [5]
That was in England prisoner all his youth,
Through mine vncle Walters trayterous vntruth.

For whan my father through disease and age,
Vnwieldy was to gouerne well his land,
Because his brother Walter semed sage,   [10]
He put the rule therof into his hand.
Than had my father you shall vnderstand
Of lawfull barnes, me, and one only other,
Nempt Dauy Rothsay, who was mine elder brother

This Dauy was prince of Scotland, and so take,   [15]
Till his aduoutry caused men complayne:
Which that he might by monyshment forsake,
My father prayed mine vncle take the payne
To threaten him, his vices to refrayne.
But he false traytour, butcherly murdring wretch,   [20]
To get the crowne, began to fetch a fetch.

[Title] subiectes. An: 1437. *C–G.*
[1]   thou wrote thy *FG.*

And finding now a proffer to his pray,
Deuised meanes my brother to deuower,
And for that cause convayed him day by day,
[25] From place to place, from castell vnto tower,
To Faulkland fort, where like a tormentour
He starued him, and put to death a wife
Whom through a reede he sukt to saue his life.

O wretched death, fye cruel tiranny,
[30] A prince in prison lost for fault of foode?
Was neuer enmy wrought such villany.
A trusted brother stroye his brothers blood
Wo wurth foe frendly, fye on double hood.
Ah wretched father, see thy sonne is lost,
[35] Sterved by thy brother, whom thou trustedst most.

Of whom whan sum began to find the fraud,
And yet the traytor made him selfe so clere,
That he should seeme to haue deserued laud,
So wofull did he for his death appeare,
[40] My doubtful father louing me ful deere
To auoyde all daunger that might after chaunce,
Sent me away, but nine yeres olde, to Fraunce.

But windes and wether wer so contrary,
That we wer driuen to the English coast,
[45] Which realme with Skotland at that time did vary
So that they tooke me prisoner, not as oste:
For which my father fearing I wer lost,

[30]   for want of foode! G.
[32]   A trusty brother D–G. brother distroy his C–G.
[33]   wurth so fryndly, B–G.
[39]   his prince appere, C–G.
[46]   me as prisoner D–G. not an hoast: G.
[47]   I was lost, FG.

Conceiued shortly such an inward thought
As to the graue immediatly him brought.

   Than had mine vncle all the regiment   [50]
At home, and I in England prisoner lay,
For to him selfe he thought it detryment,
For my releace any raunsum for to pay,
For (as he thought) he had possest his pray:
And therfore wisht I might in durauns dure   [55]
Till I had dyed, so should his rayne be sure.

   But good king Henry seing I was a child,
And heyre by ryght vnto a realme and crowne,
Dyd bring me vp, not lyke my brother, wylde
But vertuously in feates of high renowne: [60]
In liberall artes in instrumentall sowne:
By meane wherof whan I was after king,
I did my realme to ciuil order bring.

   For ere I had been prisoner eyghtene yere,
In which short space two noble princes dyed,   [65]
Wherof the first in prudence had no peere
The other in warre most valyant throwly tryed,
Whose rowme his sonne babe Henry eke supplyed
The pyers of England which did gouerne all,
Did of their goodnes helpe me out of thrall.   [70]

   They maried me to a cosin of their king
The Duke of Somersets daughter rich & fayre.
Releast my raunsome saue a trifling thing:
And after I had done homage to the hayer,
And sworne my frendship neuer should appayre,   [75]
They brought me kingly furnisht to my lande,
Which I receyued at mine vncles hand.

[80]

Wherof my lordes and commons wer ful glad,
So was mine vncle chiefly (as he sayed)
Who in his mouth no other matter had,
Saue punish such as had my brother trayed.
The faut wherof epparantly he layed,
To good duke Murdo, his elder brothers sonne,
Whose father dyed long ere this dede was doen.

[85]

My cursed vncle slyer than the snake
Which would by craft vnto the crowne aspier,
Because he sawe this Murdo was a stake
That stayed vp the stop of his desier,
(For his elder brother was Duke Murdoes sier)

[90]

He thought it best to haue him made away,
So was he suer (I goen) to haue his pray.

And by his craftes the traytour brought to passe
That I destroyed Duke Murdo, and his kin
Poore innocentes, my louing frendes, alas.

[95]

O kinges and Princes what plight stand we in,
A trusted traytour shal you quickely winne
To put to death your kin and frendes most iust:
Take hede therfore, take hede whose rede ye trust.

And at the last to bring me hole in hate

[100]

With god and man, at home and eke abrode,
He counsayled me for surance of my state:
To helpe the Frenchmen, then nye overtrode
By Englishmen, and more to lay on lode,
With power and force al England to invade,

[105]

Against the othe and homage that I made.

[84]   ere this was don. *C–G.*
[88]   the top of *C–G.*

And though at first my conscience did grudge
To breake the bondes of frendship knit by oth,
Yet after profe (see mischiefe) I did iudge
It madnes for a king to kepe his troth.
And semblably with all the world it goth.   [110]
Sinnes ofte assayed are thought to be no sinne,
So sinne doth soyle, the soule it sinketh in.

But as diseases common cause of death,
Bring daunger most, whan least they pricke & smart
Which is a signe they haue expulst the breth   [115]
Of liuely heat which doth defende the hart:
Euen so such sinnes as felt are on no part
Haue conquered grace, and by their wicked vre,
So kild the soule that it can haue no cure.

And grace agate, vice stil succedeth vice,   [120]
And all to haste the vengeaunce for the furst.
I arede therfore all people to be wise,
And stoppe the bracke whan it begins to burst.
Attaste no poyson (vice is venim wurst,
It mates the mind) beware eke of to much,   [125]
All kil through muchnes, sum with only touche.

Whan I had learned to set my othe at nought,
And through much vse the sence of sinne exyled,
Agaynst king Henry, what I could I wrought,
My fayth, my othe, vniustly foule defiled.   [130]
And while sly Fortune at my doinges smiled,
The wrath of God which I had wel deserued,
Fell on my necke, for thus loe was I serued.

[107]   the boundes of C–G.
[112]   So soyleth synne, the B–G.
[123]   brake G.

[135]

Ere I had raygned fully fiftene yere,
While time I laye at Pertho at my place,
With the Quene my wife & children me to chere,
My murdring vncle with the double face,
That longed for my kingdome and my mace,
To slay me there suborned Robert Gram,
With whom his nephew Robert Stuart cam.

[140]

And whan they time fit for their purpose found,
Into my priuy chaumber they astart,
Where with their sweardes they gave me many a wound,
And slue al such as stucke vnto my parte:
There loe my wife dyd shewe her louing harte,
Who to defende me, felled one or twayne,
And was sore wounded ere I coulde be slayne.

[145]

See Baldwin Baldwin, the vnhappy endes,
Of suche as passe not for theyr lawfull oth:
Of those that causeles leaue theyr fayth or frendes,
And murdre kynsfolke through their foes vntroth,
Warne, warne all princes, all lyke sinnes to loth,
And chiefely suche as in my Realme be borne,
For God hates hyghly suche as are forsworne.

[150]

[141]   whan their time C–G. [F prints the   F² their]   for the
          purpose B.
[150]   fayth and frendes, G.
[154]   highly all that are C–G.

TO THE READER

WHan this was sayd, let King Iamy go quoth mayster [Prose 10]
Ferrers, & returne we to our owne story, & se what
broyls were among the nobility in the kinges minority.
How the cardinal Bewford maligneth the estate of good duke Humfrey
the kinges vncle & protector of the realme, & by what driftes he first [5]
banisheth his wife from him. And lastly howe the good duke is
murderously made away through conspiracy of Quene Margaret and
other: both whose tragedies I entend at leasure to declare, for they be
notable. Do so I pray you (quoth another) But take hede ye demurre
not vpon them. And I to be occupied the meane time, will shewe what [10]
I haue noted in the duke of Suffolkes doinges, one of the chiefest of duke
Humfreyes destroyers, who by the prouidens of God, came shortly
after in such hatred of the people, that the King him selfe could not saue
hym from a straunge and notable death, which he may lament after this
maner. [15]

[1]   go sayd mayster *C–F.*
[4]   the state of Duke *F.*
[6]   the sayd Duke *F.*
[8]   tragedies I haue here ioyned together, for *F.*
[9]   notable. That wil do very wel (*F.* (said an other) *CF.* (sayth another) *D–E.*
[9–16] ye stay not to long vppon them, I warrante you (quoth I) and therfore I would
        that first of al ye geeue eare, what the Duke himselfe doth say, as foloweth. *F.*
[10]   occupied in the *C–E.*
[11]   the chiefe of *C–E.*
[14]   death, for being banisht the realme for the terme of fyue yeares, to appease the
        contynuall rumors and inwarde grudges that not onely the Commons but
        most parte of the nobility of England bare towardes him for the death of the
        Duke of Glocester and sayling towardes Fraunce, was met with a ship of
        Deuonshyre, and beheaded forthwith the fyrste day of may Anno. 1450,
        and the dead corps thrown vp at Douer vpon the sandes, whiche may lament
        hys deathe after *C–E.*
        [*The cancel found in F² (see below, pp. 429–45) substituted another prose
        link to introduce Tragedy 28; added Prose 28 to introduce Tragedy 29; and for
        ll. 10–15 above substituted Prose 29. The cancel was incorporated in the 1587
        edition, and the original prose link discarded.*]

[Tragedy 11]

How Lorde William Delapole Duke of Suffolke was worthily punyshed for abusing his Kyng and causing the destruction of good Duke Humfrey.

𝕳Eauy is the hap wherto all men be bound,
I meane the death, which no estate may flye:
But to be banisht, headed so, and drownd,
In sinke of shame from top of honors hye,
[5] Was never man so served I thinke but I:
And therfore Baldwin fro thy grave of griefe
Reiect me not, of wretched princes chiefe.

My only life in all poyntes may suffise
To shewe howe base all baytes of Fortune be,
[10] Which thaw like yse, through heate of enuies eyes:
Or vicious dedes which much possessed me.
Good hap with vices can not long agree,
Which bring best fortunes to the basest fall,
And happiest hap to enuy to be thrall.

[Title] Howe William Delapoole *F.* worthely banished for *B–G.* of the
 good Duke Humfrey. An. 1450. *C–EG.* and procuringe the
 death of Duke Humfrey of Glocester, protector of England.
 Anno. 1450. *F.*
[3] banisht, beheded, and than drownd, *C–G.*
[6–7] Wherfore Baldwyn amongest the rest by ryght,
 I clayme of the my wofull case to wryte. *C–G.*
 [*In l. 6 read* good Baldwin *for* Baldwin *F.*]
[11] Of vicious *G.*
[12] with vice, long tyme cannot agree, *C–G.*

162

I am the prince duke William De la Poole [15]
That was so famous in Quene Margets dayes.
That found the meane Duke Humfreyes blud to coole
whose vertuous paynes deserve eternal prayse
Wherby I note that Fortune can not raise,
Any one aloft without sum others wracke: [20]
Fluds drowne no fieldes before they find a bracke.

But as the waters which do breake their walles
Do loose the course they had within the shore,
And dayly rotting stinke within their stalles
For fault of moouing which they found before: [25]
Euen so the state that over high is bore
Doth loose the lyfe of peoples love it had,
And rots it selfe vntil it fall to bad.

For while I was but Erle, eche man was glad
To say and do the best by me they might: [30]
And Fortune ever since I was a lad
Did smile vpon me with a chereful sight,
For whan my Kyng had doubed me a Knight
And sent me furth to serve at warre in Fraunce,
My lucky spede mine honor dyd enhaunce. [35]

Where to omit the many feites I wrought
Vnder others gyde, I do remember one
Which with my souldyers valiantly was fought
None other captayne save my selfe alone,
I meane not now the apprinze of Pucel Ione [40]
In which attempte my travayle was not smal,
Though the Duke of Burgoyn had the prayse of al.

[15]   Called I was Wyllyam C–G.
[16]   Of Suffolke Duke in C–G. Margarets C–G.
[18]   Whose worthy actes deserue C–G.
[22]   breake the walles C–G.
[23]   lose theyr course B–G.
[33]   douted DE.

But the siege of Awmarle is the feate I prayse
A strong built towne, with castes, walles, & vaultes,
[45]   With men and weapon armed at al assayes:
To which I gave nie five times five assaultes,
Tyl at the last they yelded it for naughtes.
Yet Lord Rambures like a valiaunt Knight
Defended it as long as euer he might.

[50]   But what prevayled it these townes to winne
Which shortly after must be lost againe,
Wherby I see there is more glory in
The keping thinges than is in their attayne:
To get and kepe not is but losse of payne.
[55]   Therfore ought men prouide to saue their winnings
In al attemptes, els lose they their beginninges.

Because we could not kepe the townes we wunne
(For they were more than we might easely wyelde)
One yere vndyd what we in ten had doen:
[60]   For envy at home, and treason abrode, dyd yelde
Kyng Charles his Realme of Fraunce, made barain fielde,
For bluddy warres had wasted al encreace,
Which causde the Pope helpe pouerty sue for peace,

So that in Tourayne at the towne of Toures
[65]   Duke Charles and other for their Prince appered,
So dyd Lord Rosse, and I than Erle, for oures:
And when we shewed wherein eche other dered,
We sought out meanes all quarels to haue clered,
Wherein the Lordes of Germany, of Spayne,
[70]   Of Hungary and Denmarke, tooke exceding paine.

[44]   with castles, *C–G.*
[49]   as ere he *F.*
[54]   losse and payne. *G.*
[59]   had don: *C–G.*
[64]   in *is misprinted* it *in the text.*

But sith we could no final peace induce,
For neither would the others couenants heare,
For eightene monthes we dyd conclude a truce:
And while as frendes we lay together there
Because my warrant dyd me therein beare,   [75]
To make a perfite peace, and through accorde,
I sought a mariage for my soueraine Lorde.

And for the French kinges doughters wer to small
I fancied most dame Margarete his niece,
A lovely lady, beautifull and tall,   [80]
Fayre spoken, pleasaunt, a very princely piece,
In wit and learning matcheles hence to Grece,
Duke Rayners daughter of Aniow, king by stile,
Of Naples, Ierusalem, and of Scicil yle.

But ere I could the graunt of her attayne,   [85]
All that our king had of her fathers landes,
As Mauntes the citee, the county whole of Mayne,
And most of Aniow duchy in our handes,
I did release him by assured bandes.
And as for dowry with·her none I sought,   [90]
I thought no peace could be to derely bought.

But whan this mariage throwly was agreed
Although my king were glad of such a make,
His vncle Humfrey abhorred it in deed,
Because therby his precontract he brake,   [95]
Made with the heire of the erle of Arminake,
A̕ noble maide with store of goodes endowed,
Which more than this with losse, the duke allowed.

[84]   and *Scicil* G.
[92]   And whan G.

[100]

But love and beauty in the king so wrought
That neither profite or promise he regarded,
But set his vncles counsayle still at nought:
And for my paynes I highly was rewarded.
Thus vertue starves, but lustfoode must be larded.
For I made Marquise went to Fraunce againe,

[105]

And brought this Bride vnto my soverayne.

At whom because Duke Humfrey aye repined,
Calling their mariage aduowtry (as it was)
The Quene did move me, erst therto enclined,
To helpe to bring him to his Requiem masse.

[110]

Which sith it could for no crime cum to passe
His life and doinges were so right and clere,
Through privy murder we brought him to his beere

Thus righteousnes brought Humfrey to rebuke
Because he would no wickednes allowe,

[115]

But for my doinges I was made a duke
So Fortune can both bend and smothe her browe
On whom she list, not passing why nor howe.
O lord how high, how soone she did me raise,
How fast she filde me both with prayes and prayse.

[120]

The Lordes and Commons both of like assent,
Besought my soverayne, kneling on their knees,
To recorde my doinges in the parliament,
As dedes deseruing everlasting fees.
In which attempt they did no labour leese,

[102]   was awarded. *C–G.*
[106]   At home because *G.*
[114]   he should no *C–F.*
[117]   why or how. *C–G.*

For they set not my prayse so fast in flame,   [125]
As he was ready to reward the same.

But note the ende, my dedes so wurthy demed
Of Kinge, of Lordes, and Commons altogether,
Wer shortly after treasons false estemed,
And al men curst Quene Margets cumming hither,   [130]
For Charles the french king, in his feates not lither
Whan he had rendred Rayner Mauntes & Mayne,
Found meane to winne all Normandy agayne.

This made the people curse the mariage
Esteming it the cause of every losse: [135]
Wherfore at me with open mouth they rage,
Affirming me to have brought the realme to mosse:
Whan king & Quene sawe thinges thus go a crosse,
To quiet all a parliament they called,
And caused me in prison to be thralled,   [140]

And shortly after brought me furth abrode.
Which made the Commons more than double wood:
And sum with weapons would have layed on lode,
If their graund captaine Blewberd, in his moode,
Had not in time with wisedome bene withstoode.   [145]
But though that he and mo wer executed
The people still their wurst against me bruted.

And so applyed the Parliament with billes,
Of haynous wronges, and open traytrous crimes,
That king & queene were forst against their willes   [150]
Fro place to place to adiourne it divers times,
For princes power is like the sandy slymes,
Which must perforce geve place vnto the wave,
Or sue the windy sourges whan they rave.

167

[155] Their life was not more dere to them than I,
Which made them search all shiftes to save me still.
But aye my foes such faultes did on me trye
That to preserve me from a wurser yll,
The king was fayne, ful sore agaynst his will,
[160] For five yeres space to send me in exile,
In hope to have restored me in a while.

But marke howe vengeaunce wayteth vpon vice.
As I was sayling toward the coast of Fraunce,
The Earle of Deuonshires barke, of litle price,
[165] Encountred me vpon the seas by chaunce,
Whose captaine tooke me by his valiaunce,
Let passe my shippes, with all the frayt and loade,
But led me with him into Dover roade.

Where whan he had recounted me my faultes,
[170] As murdring of Duke Humfrey in his bed,
And howe I had brought all the realme to naughtes
In causing the King vnlawfully to wed,
There was no grace, but I must loose my head.
Wherfore he made me shrive me in his boate,
[175] On the edge wherof my necke in two he smoat.

[163-4] To shun this storme, in sayling towardes Fraunce,
          A Pyrates Barke, that was of litle price, C–G.
[166]   captain there, tooke me ʼas in a traunce, C–G.
[167]   all their frayt C–G.
[168]   And led me backe agayne to Douer C–G.
[169]   Where vnto me recounting all my C–G.
[172]   Causing the C–G.
[174]   me to shryue C–G.
[175]   And on the brinke my C–G.

A piteous ende, and therfore Baldwin warne,
All pyers and princes to abhorre vntroth,
For vicious grayne must cum to fowl endes barne:
Who brueth breach of lawful bond or oth,
God wil ere long, cause all the world to loth.   [180]
Was never prince that other did oppresse
Unrighteously, but died in distresse.

[176–82]   This was myne end: which was by reason due
       To me, and such as others deaths procure.
       Therfore be bould to write, for it is true,
       That who so doth such practise put in vre,
       Of due reward at last shalbe most sure,
       For God is iust, whose stroke delayed long,
       Doth light at last with payn more sharpe and strong. C–G.

[Prose 11] WHan this was sayd: Every man reioyced to heare of a
wicked man so maruaylously well punished: For though
Fortune in many poyntes be iniurius to Princes, yet in this
and such lyke she is moost righteous: And only deserveth the name of a
[5] Goddes, whan she prouideth meanes to punish & distroye Tyrantes. And
whan we had a whyle considered the driftes of the Kyng and Quene to
haue saued this Duke, and yet they could not: It is wurth the labour
(sayd one) to way the workes and iudgementes of God: which seyng
they are knowen most euidently by comparyng contraryes, I wyll
[10] touche the story of Iacke Kade in order next folowynge. Whome
Kynge Henrye with all his puissauns was no more able for a while to
destroy (yet was he his rebellious enemie) than he was to preserve the
Duke of Suffolke his derest frend: by whiche two examples doeth
appere howe notably God dysposeth all thinges, and that no force
[15] stretcheth farther, than it pleaseth him to suffer. For this Cade beinge
but base borne, of no abilitye, and lesse power, accompanied with a few
naked Kentyshmen, caused the Kynge with hys armye at all poyntes
appoynted, to leaue the fyelde, and to suffer hym to doe what so euer he
lusted: In whose behalfe, seynge he is one of Fortunes whelpes, I wyll
[20] trouble you a while to heare the proces of his enterprise, Which he maye
declare in maner folowyng.

[2]   wicked person so righteously punished: C–G.
[15–16] being an Irisheman but of meane parentage, of C–G.
[18]   and suffer C–G.
[19]   lusted for a tyme, but in the ende hee was slaine at Hothfielde in Sussex, and
         caried thence to London in a cart, and there quartered. In C–G.

How Iacke Cade traiterously rebelling agaynst his Kyng, was for his treasons and cruell doinges wurthely punyshed.

[Tragedy 12]

SHal I cal it Fortune or my froward folly
That lifted me, and layed me downe below?
Or was it courage that me made so Ioly,
Which of the starres and bodyes grement grow?
What euer it were this one poynt sure I know,　　　[5]
Which shal be mete for euery man to marke:
Our lust and wils our evils chefely warke.

It may be wel that planetes doe enclyne,
And our complexions move our myndes to yll,
But such is Reason, that they brynge to fine　　　[10]
No worke, vnayded of our lust and wyl:
For heauen and earth are subiect both to skyl.
The skyl of God ruleth al, it is so strong,
Man may by skyl gyde thinges that to him long.

Though lust be sturdy and wyl inclined to nought,　　　[15]
This forst by mixture, that by heavens course,
Yet through the skyl God hath in Reason wrought
And geuen man, no lust nor wyl so course
But may be stayed or swaged of the sourse,
So that it shall in nothing force the mynde　　　[20]
To worke our wo, or leaue the proper kynde.

[Title] Cade naming hymselfe Mortimer, traterously rebelling agaynst his
　　　King in Iune. Anno. 1450. was C–G.
[2]　　me vp and C–G. That lifte mee vp, and F.
[4]　　Or strength of stars, whiche make men high to growe? F.
[18]　　wil to course, C–G.

171

But though this skil be geven every man
To rule the wyl, and kepe the minde aloft,
For lacke of grace ful fewe vse it can,

[25] These worldly pleasures tickle vs so oft:
Skyl is not weake, but wyl strong, flesh is soft
And yeldes it selfe to pleasure that it loueth,
And hales the mynde to that it most reproueth.

Now if this happe wherby we yelde our mynde

[30] To lust and wyll, be fortune, as we name her,
Than is she iustly called false and blynde,
And no reproche can be to much to blame her:
Yet is the shame our owne when so we shame her,
For sure this hap if it be rightly knowen,

[35] Cummeth of our selues, and so the blame our owne.

For who so lyveth in the skole of skyll
And medleth not with any worldes affaires,
Forsaketh pompes and honors that do spyl
The myndes recourse to Graces quiet stayers,

[40] His state no Fortune by no meane appayers:
For Fortune is the folly and plage of those
Which to the worlde their wretched willes dispose.

Among which Fooles (Marke Baldwyn) I am one
That would not stay my selfe in mine estate.

[45] I thought to rule, but to obey to none,
And therfore fel I with my Kyng at bate.
And to the ende I might him better mate,

[22]   geuen to euery C–G.
[45]   but would obay F.
[46–49] Wherefore I thought to be my Princes mate,
        And by some meane his power to abate,
        And for that ende, Mortimer would be nam'de,
        Heyre apparant, of England once proclaym'de. F.

172

Iohn Mortimer I caused my selfe be called,
Whose Kingly blood the Henries nye had thralled.

 This shift I vsed the people to perswade   [50]
To leave their Prince, on my side more to sticke,
Wheras in deede my fathers name was Kade
Whose noble stocke was never wurth a sticke.
But touching wit I was both rype and quicke,
Had strength of lims, large stature, cumly face, [55]
Which made men wene my lynage were not base.

 And seing stoutnes stucke by men in Kent
Whose Valiaunt hartes refuse none enterprise,
With false perswasions straite to them I went,
And sayd they suffred to great iniuryes: [60]
By meane wherof I caused them to rise,
And battayle wyse to cum to blacke heth playne
And thence their grefes vnto the Kyng complayne.

 Who being deafe (as men say) on that eare,
For we desired releace of subsidies,   [65]
Refused roughly our requestes to heare
And came against vs as his enemies.
But we to trap hym, sought out subtiltyes,
Remoued our campe, and backe to Senocke went,
After whom the Staffordes with their power wer sent. [70]

[51] Prince, and on my syde to *F.*
[60] And saye they *F.*
[67] as our enemies: *F.*
[68] To tray hym *B.* to tary him *C–E.* to tary sought *F.*
[70] power was sent. *C–EG.* [*In both HN copies of the* 1578 *text* wa *is
  followed by an indecipherable blur.* F² *has been emended in ink to read*
  "waer bent:".]

Se here how Fortune setting vs a flote
Brought to our nettes a porcion of our pray.
For why the Staffordes with their army hote
Assayled vs at Senocke, where we laye:

[75] From whence alive they parted not away,
Whiche whan the Kynges retinew vnderstode
They all affirmed my quarel to be good

Which caused the king, and quene whom al did hate,
To raise their campe, and sodaynly depart:

[80] And that they might the peoples grudge abate,
To imprison sum ful sore against their hart.
Lord Sayes was one, whom I made after smart.
For after the Staffordes & their oast was slaine,
To Blackheath fyelde I marched backe againe.

[85] And where the king would nothing heare before,
Nowe was he glad to send to know my minde:
And I therby enflamed much the more,
Refused his grauntes, so folly made me blind.
For this he flewe and left lord Skales behind,

[90] Mo helpe the towne, and strengthen London tower,
Towardes which I marched forward with my power.

And found there all thinges after my desier,
I entred London, did there what I list,
The Treasurer, lord Sayes, I did conspier

[95] To have condemned: wherof whan I mist,
(For he by lawe my malice did resist)
By force I tooke him in Guyld hall fro the heape,
And headed him before the crosse in cheape.

[82]   Lorde Saye C–G.
[83]   after Staffordes F. hoast C–G.
[92]   thinges at myne owne desire   C–G.
[94]   Lord Saye, C–G.

His sonne in law, Iames Cromer shrive of Kent,
I caught at Myle ende, where as than he laye: [100]
Beheaded him, and on a poale I sent
His head to London, where his fathers laye.
With these two heades I made a prety play,
For pight on poales I bare them through the strete,
And for my sport made ech kisse other swete. [105]

Than brake I prisons, let furth whom I woulde,
And vsed the citie as it had be mine:
Tooke fram the marchanntes, money, ware, & golde:
From sum by force, from other sum by fine.
This at the length did cause them to repine, [110]
So that lord Skales consenting with the mayre,
Forbad vs to their citie to repayre.

For al this while mine hoast in Southwarke lay,
Who whan they knewe our passage was denyed,
Came boldly to the bridge and made a fraye, [115]
For in we would, the townes men vs defied:
But whan with strokes we had the matter tryed,
We wan the bridge and set much part on fire,
This doen, to Southwarke backe we did retier.

The morowe after came the Chauncellour [120]
With generall pardon for my men halfe gone,
Which heard and read, the rest within an houre
Shranke all awaye, eche man to shift for one.
And whan I sawe they left me post alone,
I did disguise me like a knight of the post, [125]
And into Sussex roade away in poste.

[107]   had ben myne: *B–G.*

And there I lurked, till that cursed coyne
That restles begle sought and found me out.
For strayt the king by promise did enioyne
[130]   A thousand marke, to whosoever mought
Apprend my corse: which made men seke about.
Among the which one Alexander Iden,
Found out the hole wherin the fox was hidden.

But ere he tooke me, I put him to his trumpes,
[135]   For yeeld I would not while my handes would holde
But hope of money made him stur his stumpes,
And to assault me valiauntly and bolde.
Two howres and more our cumbate was not colde,
Til at the last he lent me such a stroke,
[140]   That downe I fell, and never after spoke.

Than was my carkas caried like a hog,
To Southwarke borow where it lay a night,
The next day drawen to Newgate like a dog,
All men reioycing at the rufull sight:
[145]   Than were on poales my parboylde quarters pight,
And set aloft for vermine to deuower,
Meete graue for rebels that resist the power.

Full litell knowe we wretches what we do.
Whan we presume our princes to resist.
[150]   We war with God, against his glory to,
That placeth in his office whom he list,
Therfore was never traytour yet but mist
The marke he shot, and came to shamefull ende
Nor never shall til God be forst to bend.

[131]   Apprehend *F.*
[138]   For two longe Howres, our *F.*

God hath ordayned the power, all princes be   [155]
His Lieutenauntes, or debities in realmes,
Against their foes still therfore fighteth he,
And as his enmies drives them to extremes,
Their wise deuises prove but doltish dreames.
No subiect ought for any kind of cause,   [160]
To force the lord, but yeeld him to the lawes.

And therefore Baldwin warne men folow reason
Subdue theyr wylles, and be not Fortunes slaues,
A troublous ende doth ever folowe treason,
There is no trust in rebelles, raskall knaues,   [165]
In Fortune lesse, whiche wurketh as the waves:
From whose assautes who lyst to stande at large,
Must folowe skyll, and flye all worldly charge.

[156]   deputies D–G.
[157]   foes therfore fighteth C–G.
[158]   And his F.
[161]   force the Prince, C–G.
[162]   Wherfore Baldwin C–G. men to folow F.
[164]   A shamefull ende C–G.
[167]   who listeth to stand fre, C–G.
[168]   Must know his state, F. and so contented be. C–G.

[Prose 12] **B**Y saint mary (quoth one) yf Iacke wer as well learned, as you
haue made his oracion, What so ever he was by byrth, I warraunt
hym a gentylman by his learnyng. Howe notably and Philosopher like hath he discrybed Fortune and the causes of worldly cum-
[5] braunce? howe vpryghtly also and howe lyke a deuine hath he determined the states both of officers and Rebelles. For in dede officers be
gods deputies, and it is gods office which they beare, and it is he whiche
ordeyneth thereto suche as himselfe lysteth, good whan he fauoreth the
people, and evyll whan he wyll punysh theim. And therefore whoso-
[10] ever rebelleth agaynst any ruler either good or bad, rebelleth against
GOD, and shalbe sure of a wretched ende: For God can not but main-
tein his deputie. Yet this I note by the waye concernyng rebelles and
rebellions. Although the deuyll rayse theim, yet God alwayes vseth
them to his glory, as a parte of his Iustice. For whan Kynges and chiefe
[15] rulers, suffer theyr vnder officers to mysuse theyr subiectes, and wil not
heare nor remedye theyr peoples wronges whan they complayne, than
suffreth GOD the Rebell to rage, and to execute that parte of his
Iustice, whiche the parcyall prince woulde not. For the Lord Saies a
very corrupt officer, & one whom notwithstanding the king alwaies
[20] mainteined, was destroyed by this Iacke, as was also the byshop of
Salysbury (a proude and coueitous prelate) by other of the rebelles. And
therefore what soever prince desyreth to lyue quyetlye without rebellion, must do his subiectes right in all thinges, and punyshe suche
officers as greue or oppresse theim, thus shall they be sure from all re-
[25] bellion. And for the clerer opening herof, it wer well doen to set forth
this Lord Sayes Tragedie. What neede that (quoth another) seyng the

[1]   (said one) C–G.
[4–5] cumbraunce? howe lyke C–G.
[6]   the office both of Magistrates and subiects F. in deede Magistrates be F.
[11] a shamefull ende: C–EG. God, and shal neuer see good end of hys attempt:
      for F.
[18] Lorde Saye C–G.
[24] Officers as oppresse his People: thus F.
[26] (sayd another) C–G.

lyke example is seen in the duke of Suffolke, whose doinges are declared
sufficiently alredy. Nay rather let vs go forward, for we haue a great
mayny behynde that maye not be omytted, and the tyme as you see,
passeth away. As for this Lorde Sayes whom Cade so cruelly kylled [30]
and spytefully vsed after his death (I dare say) shalbe knowen thereby
what he was to all that reade or heare this storie. For God would never
have suffred him to haue been so vsed, except he had fyrst deserved it.
Therefore let hym go, and with hym the Bushop, and all other slaine in
that rebellion: which was raysed as it may be thought, through sum [35]
dryft of the duke of Yorke, who shortly after began to endeuoure all
meanes to attayne the Crowne, and therefore gathered an armye in
Wales, and marched towarde London: but the kyng with his power
taried and met him at S. Albones. Where whyle the king & he wer about
a treatye, therle of Warwyke set vpon the kings army, and slewe the [40]

[28]   Nay let *C–G*.
[30]   Lorde Saye *C–G*.
[35–36] raysed by some sly drift *F*.
[36]   endeuour him selfe by all *C–EG*.
[36–37] Yorke, who shortly after by open War, manifested his title to the crowne, *F*.
[38]   towards *C–G*.
[38–41] London: And preuentinge the kinge, goinge northward to prepare an army,
          in the waye at Sayncte Albanes: Who for want of a sufficient power to take
          the field, was forced with sutch smal power as he had about him, to defend
          the Lanes, & backsydes of the towne, and to send out the Duke of Bucking-
          ham for a treaty, which the Duke of Yorke beinge head of the contrary
          faction, woulde not allow without fyrst hauinge the Duke of Somerset and
          other at his will, duringe which treaty Richard Neuill Earle of Warwike,
          the stout maintayner of yorckes title entred the Towne by force, fought a
          Battayle in the high streat, where of the Kinges part were slayne the sayd
          Duke of Somerset called Edmond Beauford, Henry Percy the second of
          that surname, Earle of Northumberlande, *F*.
[40–41] treaty, Richarde Neuile Earle of Warwicke, cheefe of the faction of the house
          of Yorke, set vpon the kinges army, gate the victorye and slue Eadmund
          Beauford Duke of Somerset. Where also the same day were slaine in the
          quarrell of king Henry the syxt, Henry Percy the seconde of that surname,
          Earle of Northumberland, *C–EG*.

duke of Somerset, the Erle of Northumberlande, the Lorde Clyfforde, and other, and in conclusion got the victorie, and the duke was made Lord Protector. Whiche so greved the Queene and her accomplices, that pryvy grutches and open dissemblyng never ceassed tyl the duke

[45] and his allies were glad to flye the field and Realme, he into Irelande, they to Calayes, whence they came agayne, with an army, wherof the Erle of Salisburye was leader, and marched toward Coventry where the king than was, and had gathered an armye to subdue them, and encountred them at Northhampton, and fought and lost the fyelde and

[50] was taken hym selfe, the duke of Buckingham, the erle of Shrewesbury,

[41-42] Northumberland, Humfrey Earle of Stafford son and heyre to Humfrey Stafford Duke of Buckingham, Iohn Lord Clifford, Babthorp the kinges Attorney and his son and heyre, besydes many mo of the nobility. But because the Duke of Somerset was the chiefe of that parte, passing ouer the

[5] rest, let vs onely heare hym speake for all. C–G. [*In l. 2 above omit* Stafford *In l. 3 read* a great number of Knightes, Esquiers, Gentlemen, & yeomen of the kinges houshold & of other Lordes seruauntes, on whom al the slaughter, and bochery fell, beinge all for the more part vnarmed. *for many mo of the nobility. In l. 4 read* the Kinges *for that F.*]

[*In the* 1571 *and all subsequent editions the Duke of Somerset's tragedy was inserted after that of Jack Cade, where it evidently was to have been placed originally (see Introduction, p. 11). This prose link, therefore, was broken at l. 42. The second part was treated as a new prose link and was placed after the Duke of Somerset's tragedy and before that of the Duke of York. The rest of the collation of texts C–G is given from this new-formed prose link.*]

[42-43] After this tragedye ended, one saide seinge this Duke hath so vehementlye exclamed agaynste the Duke of Yorkes practises, it were well done to heare what hee can saye for hym selfe. For after the fyrst battell at S. Albanes hee was made protectoure, whiche so muche greeued Quene Margaret & her

[5] complices, C–G. [*In l. 3 above insert* when he toke K. Henry prisoner, *after* S. Albanes *F.*]

[45]   were fayn to fly both field C–G.

[45-46] Ireland & they C–G.

[46-47] whereof Richard Neuil earle C–G.

[48]   kinge was, C–G.

[49]   Northhampton on the 10 day of Iuly in the yeare of grace 1460. fought with them, lost C–G.

[50-60] himselfe, & many of his frendes slayne, as Humfrey Stafford Duke of Bucking-

the vicounte Beaumount, the Lord Egermount, and many other of his retinue slayne. Yf no man haue any minde to any of these noble personages because they were honourably slaine in battayle, let sum man els take the Booke, for I mynde to say sumwhat of this duke of Somerset.

☞ Whyle he was deuisyng thereon, and every man seking farder notes, [55] I looked on the Cronicles, and fynding styl fyelde vpon fyelde, & manye noble men slayne, I purposed to haue ouerpassed all, for I was so wearye that I waxed drowsye, and began in dede to slumber: but my imaginacion styll prosecutyng this tragicall matter, brought me suche a fantasy. me thought there stode before vs, a tall mans body full of fresshe [60] woundes, but lackyng a head, holdyng by the hande a goodlye childe, whose brest was so wounded that his hearte myght be seen, his louely face and eyes disfigured with dropping teares, his heare through horrour standyng vpryght, his mercy cravyng handes all to bemangled, & all his body embrued with his own bloud. And whan through the gastfulnes [65] of this pyteous spectacle, I waxed afeard, and turned awaye my face, me thought there came a shrekyng voyce out of the weasande pipe of the headles bodye, saying as foloweth.

ham, Iohn Talbot the second of that name earle of Shrewesbury, Iohn Vicount Beaumont, Thomas Lorde Egremont, Syr William Lucy and dyuers other, But ouerpassing all these & many mo because they were
[5] honourably slain in the field, let vs come to hym who was the chief cause therof, that is to saye, Richarde Plantagenet Duke of Yorke slayn in the battell at Wakefield on Christmas euen, and Eadmund earle of Rutland his yong son, who was there murdered by the Lord Clifforde as he would haue fled into the towne to haue saued himselfe.
[10]   Therfore imagine that you se a tall C–G.
[59]   tragicall is misprinted ragicall in the text.
[65–68] bloud. Out of the wesand pipe of whiche headles bodye came a shrekinge voice sayinge as followeth. C–G.

[Tragedy 13]

How Richard Plantagenet duke of York was slayne through his over rash boldnes, and his sonne the earle of Rutland for his lack of valiauns.

TRust Fortune (quoth he) in whom was neuer trust,
O folly of men that haue no better grace,
All rest, renowne, and dedes lie in the dust
Of al the sort that sue her slipper trace.

[5]   What meanest thou Baldwin for to hide thy face?
Thou nedest not feare although I misse my head:
Nor yet to mourne, for this my sonne is dead.

The cause why thus I lead him in my hand,
His skin with blud and teares so sore bestaynd.

[10]   Is that thou mayst the better vnderstand
How hardly Fortune hath for vs ordaynde:
In whom her love and hate be hole contaynde.
For I am Richard prince Plantagenet,
The duke of Yorke in royall rase beget.

[Title]   valyaunce. Anno. Do. 1460. *CG.* valiaunce Anno. 1460. *DE.*
       Sonne Earle of Rutland an Infant cruelly murdered Anno. 1460.
       F.
[2]   O Beastes most brute, that *F.*
[5]   How now? Why dost thou Baldwin hide *F.*
[7]   See this poore Boy, whom by the hand I lead. *F.*
[9]   With bloud, and teares halinge his body staynd, *F.*
[13–14] Rychard I am Plantagenet by name,
       Whilom of Yorke the Duke of worthy fame. *F.*

For Richarde erle of Cambridge, eldest sonne　　　　[15]
Of Edmund Langley, third sonne of king Edward,
Engendred me of Anne, whose course did runne
Of Mortimers to be the issue garde:
For when her brother Edmund died a warde,
She was sole hayer by due discent of line,　　　　　[20]
Wherby her rightes and titles al wer mine,

But marke me now I pray thee Baldwin marke,
And see how force oft overbeareth right:
Waye how vsurpers tyrannously warke,
To kepe by murder that they get by might,　　　　[25]
And note what troublous daungers do alight
On such as seke to reposses their owne,
And how through rigour right is overthrowen.

The earle of Herford, Henry Bolenbrooke,
Of whom duke Mowbray tolde thee now of late,　　[30]
Whan voyde of cause he had King Richard tooke:
He murdred him, vsurped his estate,
Without all right or title, sauing hate
Of others rule, or love to rule alone:
These two excepted, title had he none.　　　　　[35]

The realme and crowne was Edmund Mortimers
Whose father Roger, was king Richardes hayre,

[16]　　Of Duke Edmond, thirde *F.*
[17]　　me whereof the course *C–G.*
[19]　　when Edmond her brother dyed Warde, *F.*
[26]　　what troubles daungers *C–E.* what troubles and daungers *F.*
[28]　　how by might, oft right *F.*
[29]　　Duke of Hereford, *C–EG.* Duke Henry of Hereforde called
　　　　Bolenbrooke, *F.*
[31]　　Whan traytourlike he *F.*
[32]　　Kild him in prison, vsurped *F.*
[36]　　The Crowne by right came to Edmond Mortimer *F.*

Which caused Henry and the Lancasters
To seeke all shiftes, our housholdes to appayre,
[40]   For sure he was to sit beside the chayre
Wer we of power to clayme our lawfull right,
Wherfore to stroye vs he did all he might.

His cursed sunne ensued his cruel path.
And kept my giltles cosin strayt in duraunce:
[45]   For whom my father hard intreated hath.
But liuing hopeles of his liues assuraunce
He thought it best by politik procuraunce,
To prive the king, and so restore his frend:
Which brought him selfe to an infamous ende.

[50]   For whan king Henry of that name the fift,
Had tane my father in this conspiracy,
He from Sir Edmund all the blame to shift,
Was fayne to say the French king, his ally,
Had hyred him this trayterous act to trye,
[55]   For which condemned, shortly he was slayne.
In helping right this was my fathers gayne.

[38]	and them of Lancaster, *F.*	
[39]	our houses to *F.*	
[42]	And therfore thought good, to extirpe vs quight. *F.*	
[43]	ensued the fathers trade, *F.*	
[44]	cosin guiltlesse in sure hold, *F.*	
[45]	father ful often did perswade, *F.*	
[46–49]	With his allies and cousins that they would.	
	Their Kinsmans right mainteyn and vphold,	
	And to depose by pollicy or power,	
	The heyre of him that was an vsurper. *F.*	
[50]	Whereof when Henry *F.*	
[51]	Had heard, and knew of this *F.*	
[53]	Sayd that my Father was the *F.* French Kings ally, *C-G.*	
[54–56]	And hyred by him to worke this trecherye,	
	For which at Hampton as it came to passe,	
	His lyfe he lost, and there beheaded was. *F.*	

184

Thus whan the linage of the Mortimers
Were made away by this vsurping line,
Sum hanged, sum slayne, sum pined prisoners:
Because the crowne by right of law was mine,　　　　[60]
They gan as fast agaynst me to repine:
In feare alwayes least I should sturre them strife.
For gilty hartes have never quiet life.

　　Yet at the last in Henryes dayes the sixt,
I was restored to my fathers landes,　　　　[65]
Made duke of Yorke, wherthrough my minde I fixt,
To get the crowne and kingdome in my handes.
For ayde wherin I knit assured bandes
With Nevels stocke, whose doughter was my make
Who for no wo would ever me forsake.　　　　[70]

　　O lord what happe had I through mariage,
Fower goodly boyes in youth my wife she boore.
Right valiaunt men, and prudent for their age.
Such bretherne she had and nephewes stil in store,
As none had erst, nor any shal haue more:　　　　[75]

[57–62]　　Thus was the name of Mortimer extinct,
　　　　Whose right and title descended vnto me,
　　　　Being forst to lyue, within a precinct
　　　　For feare I would to other countries flee
　　　　And so beeing at myne owne libertee,
　　　　Might haplye moue sedicion or strife, *F.*
[58]　　by hys vsurpyng *B–EG.* [*Corrected in* Be *to the original reading.*]
[62]　　them to stryfe, *C–EG.*
[63]　　hartes, can leade no quiet *F.*
[70]　　Whereby great frendes I had my part to take. *F.*
[71]　　I by mariage, *F.*
[72]　　Fowre fayre Sonnes my yong wife to me bore, *F.*
[73]　　Valiaunt men *F.*
[74]　　Such brothers she *F.*
[75]　　As none of the kin had any time before: *F.*

The erle of Salisbury, and his sonne of Warwike,
Wer matchles men from Barbary to Barwike.

Through helpe of whom and Fortunes lovely looke
I vndertooke to clayme my lawful right,

[80] And to abash such as agaynst me tooke,
I raysed power at all poyntes prest to fight:
Of whom the chiefe that chiefly bare me spite,
Was Somerset the Duke, whom to annoy
I alway fought, through spite, spite to distroy.

[85] And maugre him, so choyse loe was my chaunce,
Yea though the quene that all rulde tooke his part,
I twise bare stroke in Normandy and Fraunce,
And last liuetenant in Ireland, where my hart
Found remedy for euery kind of smart.

[90] For through the love my doinges there did brede,
I had their helpe at all times in my nede.

This spiteful duke, his silly king and quene,
With armed hostes I thrise met in the field,
The first vnfought through treaty made betwene,

[95] The second ioynde, wherin the king did yeeld,
The duke was slayne, the quene enforst to shylde

[77]   Were knights peerelesse, from *F.*
[78]   Fortunes liuely loke *DE.* Fortunes frendly grace, *F.*
[79]   I first began to *F.*
[80]   And my chiefe foes with stoutnesse to deface. *F.*
[84]   Al my hole force, I dayly did employ. *F.*
[86]   Queene was wholy on hys syde, *F.*
[87]   bare rule in *C–G.*
[88]   Ireland I did byde, *F.*
[89]   Ful often driuen of force my head to hyde, *F.*
[90]   Yet through *F.*
[92]   This doutye Duke most deare to King and Queene, *F.*
[93]   hoaste *F.*
[96]   Queene her partie helde *F.*

Her selfe by flight. The third the quene did fight,
Where I was slaine being overmacht by might.

Before this last were other battayles three,
The first the erle of Salisbury led alone,　　　　　　　　　　　[100]
And fought on Bloreheth, and got the victory:
In the next was I and my kinsfolke euerychone.
But seing our souldiers stale vnto our foen,
We warely brake our cumpany on a night,
Dissolved our hoaste, and tooke our selues to flight.　　　　　[105]

This boye and I in Ireland did vs save,
Mine eldest sonne with Warwicke and his father,
To Caleys got, whence by the reade I gave
They came againe to London, and did gather
An other hoast, wherof I spake not rather:　　　　　　　　[110]
And met our foes, slew many a lord and knight,
And tooke the King, and drave the Queene to flight.

This done came I to England all in haste.
To make my claime vnto the realme and crowne:
And in the house while parliament did last,　　　　　　　　[115]
I in the kinges seat boldly sat me downe,

[97–98]　Farre in the North, where ouermatcht with power
　　　　　My life I lost, in an vnlucky howre. *F.*
[100]　　Salisburie alone, *F.*
[101]　　Fought on *F.* got vyctory: *B–E.*
[102]　　euery one, *C–EG.*
[102–5]　I at the next was present in persone
　　　　　With my chiefe kin, whereas by one and one,
　　　　　Our souldiers false, withdrew away by night,
　　　　　Vnto our foes and wee put all to flight. *F.*
[110]　　spake no rather: *C–G.*
[113]　　done I came to *C–G.*
[114]　　To make clayme *C–E.* To make a claime *G.* New claime to make
　　　　　vnto *F.*
[116]　　In the Kinges seate, I boldly *F.*

And claymed it: wherat the lordes did frowne,
But what for that, I did so wel procede,
That al at last confest it mine in dede.

[120] But sith the king had rayned now so long,
They would he should continue til he died,
And to the ende that than none did me wrong,
Protectour and heire apparant they me cryed:
But sith the Quene and others this denied,
[125] I sped me toward the North, where than she lay,
In minde by force to cause her to obey.

Wherof she warnde prepared a mighty power,
And ere that mine were altogether ready,
Came bold to Boswurth, and besieged my bower,
[130] Where like a beast I was so rashe and heady,
That out I would, there could be no remedy,
With skant fiue thousand souldiers, to assayle
Fower times so many, encampt to most avayle.

And so was slayne at first: and while my childe
[135] Skarce twelve yere olde, sought secretly to part,

[117]	Clayming the place, whereat F.
[119]	last to my demaund agreed. F.
[120]	sith Henry had raigned than so F.
[122]	to thend to make my title strong, F.
[123]	Apparant heire of England they F. they my cryed. C.
[125]	sped me straight Northward whereas she F. towardes G.
[126]	Meaning by F.
[127]	She thereof warned, F.
[128]	ere my men were F.
[129]	Came swyft to Sandale and B–EG. To Sandale came, where in a dismal houre F.
[130–33]	I like a Beast, so rash was, and so heddy To trie Fortune, which alwaies is vnsteddy With thousands fiue, of souldiers to assayle The double number, in campe to their auayle. F.
[134]	my pore infant F.
[135]	sought way himselfe to saue, F.

That cruell Clifford, lord, nay Lorell wilde,
While the infant wept, and praied him rue his smart
Knowing what he was, with his dagger clave his hart:
This doen he came to the campe where I lay dead,
Dispoylde my corps, and cut away my head.   [140]

    And whan he had put a paper crowne theron,
As a gawring stocke he sent it to the Queen,
And she for spite, commaunded it anon
To be had to Yorke: where that it might be seen,
They placed it where other traytours been.   [145]
This mischiefe Fortune did me after death,
Such was my life, and such my losse of breath.

    Wherfore see Baldwin that thou set it furth
To the ende the fraude of Fortune may be knowen,
That eke all princes well may way the wurth: [150]
Of thinges, for which the sedes of warre be sowen:
No state so sure but soone is overthrowen.
No worldly good can counterpeyze the prise,
Of halfe the paynes that may therof arise.

[136]   Clifford that fel bloudy tyrant, *F.*
[137–38] While the pore chyld with tears did mercy craue,
          With dagger sharp his hart a sunder claue. *F.*
[138]   cloue *C–EG.*
[141–42] And set a crowne of paper theruppon
          Which for a sport he sent vnto the Quene *F.*
[142]   gawzing *DE.*
[144]   Yorke and set vp to be sene. *F.*
[145–47] In some such place as theuis & Traitors bene,
          This mocke I had of fortune for rewarde,
          After long hope that she wold me regard *F.*
[148]   Baldwin see that *F.* set her forth *F.*
[149]   With her slipper pranks so as they may *F.*
[150]   And warne all *F.* wel to way *F.*
[151]   sede *F.*
[152]   The gaine no surer but as of dice throwen *F.*

[155]   Farre better it wer to loose a piece of right,
Than limmes and life in sousing for the same.
It is not force of frendship nor of might,
But god that causeth thinges to fro or frame.
Not wit, but lucke, doth wield the winners game.
[160]   Wherfore if we our follies would refrayne,
Time would redres all wronges, we voyd of payne.

    Wherfore warne princes not to wade in warre,
For any cause, except the realmes defence:
Their troublous titles are vnwurthy farre,
[165]   The blud, the life, the spoyle of innocence.
Of frendes and foes behold my foule expence.
And never the nere: best therfore tary time,
So right shall raigne, and quiet calme ech crime.

[155]	Better it *F.*
[156]	in wrestling for *F.*
[158]	god aboue that kingdomes set in frame *F.*
[159]	but chance doth *F.*
[162]	warne Lordes no wise to *F.*
[163]	cause, saue their countries defence, *F.*
[166]	frendes of foes *C–G.* my long expence, *F.*
[167]	best than to tary *F.*
[168]	Low by the ground, than ouer high to clyme. *F.*

With this, mayster *Ferrers* shooke me by the sleve, saying: [Prose 13]
why how now man, do you forget your selfe? belike you
mind our matters very much: So I do in dede (quoth I)
For I dreame of them. And whan I had rehearced my dreame, we had
long talke concerning the natures of dreames, which to stint and to bring [5]
vs to our matter againe, thus sayde one of them: I am glad it was your
chaunce to dreame of Duke Richard, for it had bene pity to have over-
passed him. And as concerning this lord Clyfford whych so cruelly
killed his sonne, I purpose to geve you notes: who (as he wel deserved)
came shortly after to a sodayne death, & yet to good for so cruell a [10]
tiraunt. Wherfore as you thought you sawe and heard the headles duke
speake thorow his necke, so suppose you see this lord Clifford all armed
save his head, with his brest plate all gore bloud running from his
throte, wherin an hedles arrow sticketh, thrugh which wound he sayeth
thus: [15]

[1]   WIth that *C–G.*
[3]   (said I) *C–G.*
[5]   nature *B–G.*
[10]   for a cruell *F.*
[11]   tyrant. For on Palmesonday nexte followinge, being the Nine and twenty
        daye of Marche, in the yeare of Christ a thousand four hundreth threscore
        & one, thys Lord Clyfford wyth Henry Percy, the 3. Earle of Northumber-
        land, the Erle of Westmerland, the Lorde Dacres, the Lorde Welles & other
        were slaine at Towton in Yorkeshyre. Wherfore *C–G.*
[12]   so now suppose *C–G.*
[14–15] he ratleth out this Rhime. *F.*

[Tragedy 14]

How the lord Clyfford for his straunge and abhominable cruelty, came to as straunge and sodayne a death.

OPen confession axeth open penaunce,
And wisedome would a man his shame to hide:
Yet sith forgeuenes cummeth through repentaunce
I thinke it best that men their crimes ascried,

[5]
For nought so secrete but at length is spied:
For couer fire, and it wil neuer linne
Til it breake furth, in like case shame and sinne.

As for my selfe my faultes be out so playne
And published so brode in every place,

[10]
That though I would I can not hide a grayne.
All care is bootles in a cureles case,
To learne by others griefe sum haue the grace,
And therfore Baldwin write my wretched fall,
The brief wherof I briefly vtter shall.

[Title] death. Anno. 1461. *C-EG.* his extreame crueltie, came to a cruel, straunge, & sodaine death. Anno. 1461. *F.*
[2] Yet wisdome *F.* his fault should hide: *F.*
[3-5] But sith pardon commeth by repentaunce,
Playnesse is best when truth is plainly tryde,
Open or hid, al faultes at length be spyed. *F.*
[6] fyer neuer so close within, *F.*
[7] Yet out it will. and so will secret synne. *F.*
[9] so abroade in *C-EG.* Bruted and knowne abroade in *F.*
[10] cannot them reteyne, *F.*
[12] others some have had the *F.*
[13] Wherfore Baldwin, write thou my *F.*

LORD CLIFFORD

I am the same that slue duke Richardes childe [15]
The louely babe that begged life with teares.
Wherby my honour fowly I defilde.
Poore selly lambes the Lyon neuer teares:
The feble mouse may lye among the beares:
But wrath of man his rancour to requite, [20]
Forgets all reason, ruth, & vertue quite.

I mean by rancour the parentall wreke
Surnamde a vertue (as the vicious say)
But litle know the wicked what they speake,
In boldning vs our enmyes kin to slay, [25]
To punish sinne, is good, it is no nay.
They wreke not sinne, but merit wreke for sinne,
That wreke the fathers faultes vpon his kyn.

Because my father lord John Clifford died
Slayne at S. Albons, in his princes ayde, [30]
Agaynst the duke my hart for malyce fryed,
So that I could from wreke no way be stayed.
But to avenge my fathers death, assayde
All meanes I might the duke of Yorke to annoy.
And all his kin and frendes to kill and stroy. [35]

[15]   Clifford I am that F.
[16]   that craued lyfe F.
[17]   mine honour G. my fame, most fouly F.
[19]   among great beares F.
[21]   ruth and mercy quyte. F.
[22]   meane such wrath as works parental F.
[23]   (as these reuengers say) F.
[24]   know those people what F.
[25]   Which kyndle vs, our F. boldenyng B–EG.
[28]   fault G. The fathers faultes that wreake vpon the kinne. F.
[32]   way by stayed. C–E.

This made me with my bluddy daggar wound.
His giltles sunne that never agaynst me sturde:
His fathers body lying dead on ground,
To pearce with speare, eke with my cruell swurd
[40] To part his necke, and with his head to bourd,
Envested with a paper royal crowne,
From place to place to beare it vp and downe.

But cruelty can never skape the skourge
Of shame, of horror, and of sodayne death.
[45] Repentaunce selfe that other sinnes may pourge,
Doth flye from this, so sore the soule it slayeth,
Dispayre dissolves the tirauntes bitter breath:
For sodayne vengeaunce sodaynly alightes
On cruell heades, to quite thier cruel spightes.

[50] This find I true, for as I lay in stale
To fight agaynst duke Richardes eldest sonne,
I was destroyed not far from Dintingdale:
For as I would my gorget haue vndoen
To event the heat that had me nye vndoen,

[36]   This caused me with bloudy *F.*
[38–42] The fathers corps dead lying on the ground,
        The necke I cut asunder with my sword
        The bleding head I pight by way of borde,
        Vpon a speare, with a white paper crowne
        And in great scorne I sent it to Yorke towne. *F.*
[41]   a royall paper crowne, *G.*
[43]   But cruel deedes can *F.*
[44]   horror, or of *C–EG.* Of open shame, or of some bloudy death, *F.*
[47]   tyrants blustring breath: *F.*
[48–49] For vengeance due doth sodaynly alight,
        On cruel deedes the mischiefe to requite, *F.*
[49]   cruell deedes, to *C–EG.*
[51]   Agaynst Edward Duke *F.*
[52]   My death I caught not *F.*
[54]   To vent out heate traueiling in the sonne *F.*

An headles arrow strake me through the throte   [55]
Wherthrough my soule forsooke his filthy coate.

Was this a chaunce? no suer, gods iust award,
Wherin due iustice playnly doth appere:
An headles arrowe payed me my reward,
For heading Richard lying on the bere.   [60]
And as I would his child in no wise heare,
So sodayn death bereft my tounge the power,
To aske for pardon at my dying hower.

Wherfore good Baldwin warne the bluddy sort,
To leave their wrath, their rigour to refrayne: [65]
Tell cruel iudges, horror is the port
To which they sayle through shame, & sodayn payne:
Hel haleth tirauntes downe to death amayne.
Was never yet nor shalbe cruell deede,
Left vnrewarded with as cruel meede.   [70]

[55]   arrowe percyd my throte boule *F.*
[56]   Which parted straight my body from the soule. *F.*
[58]   Wherin his iustice *F.*
[60]   on his bere, *C–G.*
[63]   aske mercy at my last dying *F.*
[64]   Wherfore Baldwin perswade the *F.*
[65]   wrath, and rigour *F.*
[67]   Through which they sayle to shame *G.* sayle to suffer endles payne *F.*
[68]   halleth *G.*
[70]   Vnquyted left but had as *F.*

[Prose 14] WHan this tragedy was ended, O Lord quoth an other, how horrible a thing is division in a realme, to howe many myschiefes is it the mother, what vyce is not therby kindled, what vertue left vnquenched? For what was the cause of the
[5] Duke of Yorks death, and of the cruelty of thys Clyfford, save [the] vary-aunce betwene king Henry and the house of Yorke: whych at length besides millions of the commons, brought to destruction all the nobility. For Edward the dukes eldest sonne immediatly after his father was slayne, through helpe of the Nevels, gave the King a battayle, wherat,
[10] besides this Clifford and .xxxvi. thousand other souldiers wer slayne their captaynes, the earles of Northumberland & Westmerland, with the lordes Dacres and Welles: the winning of which fielde brought Edward to the crowne, and the losse drave King Henry and his wyfe into Skotland. But as few raines begin without blud, so kyng Edward
[15] to kepe order, caused the Erles of Devonshire and Oxford with diuers other his enemies, to be attaynted and put to death. And shortly after he did execution vppon the Duke of Somerset, and the lordes Hunger-ford & Rosse, whom he tooke prisoners at Exham field. For thither

[1]   Lord said an other, *C–G.*
[5]   the *is printed as the catchword on the page but is omitted in the text. It is incorporated in the text of later editions.*
[5]   cruelty shewed to his young sonne by this mercilesse man, saue *F.*
[7]   destruction most part of the *F.*
[8]   after Richarde his *F.*
[9]   battaile at Towton in Yorkshire, whereat *F.*
[10–11] Clifford, were slayne the Earles of *F.*
[12] Welles, besydes mo then 3000. men, the winning *F.*
[14] without *is divided at the end of a line in the text, and the hyphen after* with *misprinted as a comma.*
[15] keepe the common course, *F.* caused Thomas Courtney erle of Deuonshyre, and Iohn Veer Earle of Oxeforde, and Aubrey Veer eldest son to the said earle, wyth *C–G.* [*Read* Oxenford *for* Oxeforde *F.*]
[16] other of King Henries parte, to bee *F.*
[16–17] after did *F.*
[18–19] thyther came those Lordes with *F.*

they came with king Henry out of Skotland, with an army of Skottes, & fought a battaile, which was lost, & most part of the army slayne. [20] And because these are all noble men, I will leave them to Baldwins discretion. But seing the earle of Wurcester was the chiefe instrument, whom king Edward vsed as well in these mens matters, as in like bluddy affayres, because he should not be forgotten, ye shal heare what I have noted concerning his tragedy. [25]

[20]   of them slayne. *B–EG.* lost, wherein most part of theym were slaine. *F.*
[24–25] what may bee noted by his ende. *F.*

The infamous ende of Lord Iohn Tip- [Tragedy 15]
toft Earle of Wurcester, for cru-
elly executing his princes
butcherly commaun-
dementes.

𝕿He glorious man is not so loth to lurke,
As the infamous glad to lye vnknowen:
Which maketh me Baldwin disalow thy wurke,
Where princes faultes so openly be blowen.
I speake not this alonely for mine owne [5]
Which wer my princes (if that they wer any)
But for my Pyers, in numbre very many.

[Title] Lord Tiptoft *B.* of the Lorde Tiptoft *C–G.* commaundementes. Anno. 1470. *C–EG.* for executing his princes crueltie. Anno. 1470. *F.*

Or might report vprightly vse her tong,
It would lesse greue vs to augment thy matter.
[10] But suer I am thou shalt be forst among,
To frayne the truth, the liuing for to flatter:
And otherwhiles in poyntes vnknowen to smatter.
For time neuer was, nor euer I thinke shall be,
That truth vnshent should speake in all thinges fre.

[15] This doeth appere (I dare say) by my story,
Which diuers writers diuersly declare,
But story writers ought for neyther glory,
Feare, nor fauour, truth of thinges to spare.
But still it fares as alway it did fare,
[20] Affection, feare, or doubtes that dayly brue,
Do cause that stories neuer can be true.

Vnfruytfull Fabyan folowed the face
Of time and dedes, but let the causes slip:
Whych Hall hath added, but with double grace,
[25] For feare I thinke least trouble might him trip:
For this or that (sayeth he) he felt the whip.
Thus story writers leaue the causes out,
Or so rehears them, as they wer in dout.

But seing causes are the chiefest thinges
[30] That should be noted of the story wryters,
That men may learne what endes al causes bringes
They be vnwurthy the name of Croniclers,
That leaue them cleane out of their registers.
Or doubtfully report them: for the fruite
[35] Of reading stories, standeth in the suite.

[9] augment the matter. *C–G.*
[13] nor neuer I *C–G.*
[21] stories alwayes be not true. *F.*
[24] added some with better grace, *F.*
[27] This story *F.*
[28] Or shew them so as they were in some dout. *F.*

And therfore Baldwin eyther speake vpright
Of our affayres, or touche them not at all:
As for my selfe I waye al thinges so light,
That nought I passe how men report my fall.
The truth wherof yet playnly shew I shall,   [40]
That thou mayst write, and other therby rede,
What thinges I did, wherof they should take hede.

Thou hast heard of Tiptoftes erles of Wurcester
I am that Iohn that lived in Edwardes dayes
The fourth, and was his frend and counsayler,   [45]
And Butcher to, as common rumor sayes.
But peoples voyce is neyther shame nor prayse:
For whom they would alive devour to day,
To morow dead, they wil wurship what they may.

But though the peoples verdit go by chaunce,   [50]
Yet was there cause to cal me as they did.
For I enforst by meane of gouernaunce,
Did execute what euer my king did byd.
From blame herein my selfe I can not ryd,
But fye vpon the wretched state, that must   [55]
Defame it selfe, to serue the princes lust.

The chiefest crime wherwith men do me charge,
Is death of the Earle of Desmundes noble sonnes.
Of which the kinges charge doth me clere discharge,
By strayt commaundement and Iniunctions: [60]
Theffect wherof so rigorously runnes,
That eyther I must procure to se them dead,
Or for contempt as a traytour lose my head.

[36]   Wherfore Baldwin *F.* speake thou vpryght *F.*
[44]   that Lorde that *B–G.*
[51]   *Be corrects to read* Yet had they cause.

199

[65]

What would mine enemies do in such a case,
Obey the king, or proper death procure?
They may wel say their fancy for a face,
But life is swete, and love hard to recure.
They would haue doen as I did I am sure:
For seldome wil a welthy man at ease

[70]

For others cause his prince in ought displease.

How much lesse I, which was lieutenant than
In the Irishe yle, preferred by the king:
But who for love or dread of any man,
Consentes to accomplish any wicked thing,

[75]

Although chiefe fault therof from other spring,
Shall not eskape Gods vengeaunce for his dede,
Who skuseth none that dare do yl for drede.

This in my king and me may wel appere,
Which for our faultes did not eskape the scourge:

[80]

For whan we thought our states most sure and clere
The wind of Warwick blew vp such a sourge
As from the realme and crowne the king did pourge,
And me both from mine office, frendes, and wife,
From good report, from honest death, and life.

[85]

For Therle of Warwick through a cancard grudge,
Which to king Edward causeles he did beare,
Out of his realme by force did make him trudge,
And set king Henry agayne vpon his chaire.
And then all such as Edwardes louers were

[90]

As traytours tane, were greuously opprest,
But chiefly I, because I loved him best.

[80]   our state most *B–G.*
[82]   did vrge, *F.*
[83]   me also from *F.*
[85]   The Earle of Warwicke, through mallice and grudge, *F.*

And for my goodes and livinges wer not small,
The gapers for them bare the world in hand
For ten yeres space, that I was cause of all
The executions done within the land.   [95]
For thys did such as did not vnderstand
My enmies drift, thinke all reportes wer true:
And so to hate me wurse than any Iewe.

For seeldome shall a ruler lose his life,
Before false rumours openly be spred: [100]
Wherby this proverbe is as true as rife,
That rulers rumours hunt about a head.
Frowne Fortune once all good report is fled:
For present shew doth make the mayny blind,
And such as see, dare not disclose their mind.   [105]

Through this was I king Edwardes butcher named,
And bare the shame of all his cruell dedes:
I cleare me not, I wurthely was blamed,
Though force was such I must obey him nedes.
With hyest rulers seldome wel it spedes,   [110]
For they be ever nearest to the nip,
And fault who shall, for all fele they the whip.

For whan I was by parliament attaynted,
King Edwardes evilles all wer counted mine.
No truth avaylde, so lyes wer faste and paynted,   [115]
Which made the people at my life repine,
Crying: Crucifige, kill that butchers line:
That whan I should have gone to Blockam feast,
I could not passe so sore they on me preast.

[92]   And sith my F.
[93]   Some greedy gulles did beare F.
[95]   Murder, and mischiefe, done F.
[97]   Myne enmies C–G.
[98]   so did hate G.

[120]   And had not bene the officers so strong
           I thinke they would have eaten me aliue,
           Howbeit hardly haled from the throng,
           I was in the Fleete fast shrowded by the shrive.
           Thus one dayes life their malice did me give:
[125]   Which whan they knew, for spite the next day after,
           They kept them calme, so suffred I the slaughter.

           Now tel me Baldwin, what fault doest thou find,
           In me, that iustly should such death deserve?
           None sure, except desire of honour blind,
[130]   Which made me seke in offices to serve.
           What minde so good, that honors make not swerve?
           So mayst thou see, it only was my state
           That caused my death, and brought me so in hate.

           Warne therfore all men, wisely to beware,
[135]   What offices they enterprise to beare:
           The hyest alway most maligned are,
           Of peoples grudge, and princes hate in feare.
           For princes faultes his faultors all men teare.
           Which to auoyde, let none such office take,
[140]   Save he that can for right his prince forsake.

[121] haue swalowed me *F*.
[127] fault thou doest fynd *B*. [*Corrected in Be to the original reading.*]

TO THE READER

THis Earles tragedy was not so soone finished, but one of the [Prose 15] cumpany had prouided for an other, of a notable person, lord Tiptoftes chiefe enemy: concerning whom he sayd: Lord god, what trust is there in worldly chaunces? what stay in any prosperity? for see, the Earle of Warwicke which caused the earle of Wurcester to be [5] apprehended, attaynted, and put to death, triumphing with his olde imprisoned, and newe vnprisoned prince king Henry, was byandby after (and his brother with him) slayne at Barnet field by kyng Edward, whom he had before time damaged divers wayes. As first by his frendes at Banbury field, where to revenge the death of his Cosin Harry [10] Nevel, Sir Iohn Conyers and Iohn Clappam his seruauntes slewe five thousand Welshemen, and beheaded theyr captaynes, the earle of Penbroke, and syr Rychard Harbert his brother after they wer yelded prisoners: of whom syr Rychard Harbert was the tallest gentleman both of his person and handes that ever I reade or heard of. At which time [15] also, Robyn of Ridsdale, a rebell of the earle of Warwyks raysing, tooke the earle Rivers king Edwardes wifes father, and his sonne Iohn, at his manour of Grafton, and caryed them to Northhampton, & there without cause or proces beheaded them. Whych spites to requite, king Edward caused the lord Stafford of Southwike one of Warwikes [20] chyefe frendes to be taken at Brent march, and headed at Bridgewater. This caused the Earle shortly after to raise his power, to encounter the king which came agaynst him with an army beside Warwike, at Woulney wher he wan the field, tooke the king prisoner, and kept him a while at Yorkeshire in Middleham castel: whence (as sum say) he [25] released him agayne, but other thinke he corrupted his kepers, and so escaped. Then through the lordes the matter was taken vp betwene them, & they brought to talk together: but because they could not

[1]   THis Typtoftes Tragedye *F.*
[10] cosin Henry *C–G.*
[16] of *Kidsdale, G.*
[25] while in Yorkshire *C–G.*

203

agree, the earle raysed a new army, wherof he made captayne the lord
[30] Welles sonne. which broyle kinge Edward minding to appeace by
pollicy, fowly distayned his honor committing periury. For he sent for
the lord Welles & his brother sir Thomas Dimocke, vnder safeconduyte
promising them vpon his fayth to kepe them harmles: But after, because
the Lord Welles sonne would not dissolve his army, beheded them both,
[35] and went with his power downe into Lincolnshire, & there fought with
sir Robert Welles, & slewe ten thousand of his souldiers (yet ran they
away so fast, that the casting of of their clothes for the more spede,
caused it to be called loosecoate fyeld) & tooke sir Robert & other, and
put them to deth in the same place. This misfortune forced the earle of
[40] Warwike to saile into Fraunce wher he was wel entertained of the king
awhile, and at last with such poore helpe as he procured ther of duke
Rayner & other he came into England againe, & increased such a power
in Kyng Henries name, that as the lord Tiptoft, sayd in his tragedy, king
Edwarde vnable to abide him, was faine to flye over the washes in
[45] Lincolnshire to get a ship to saile out of his kingdome to his brother in
lawe the duke of Burgoyne: So was king Henry restored again to the
kingdome. Al these despites & troubles the Earle wrought agaynst king
Edward, but Henry was so infortunate that ere halfe a yeare was
expyred, king Edwarde came backe agayne, and imprisoned him, and
[50] gave the erle a fielde, wherein he slew both him and his brother. I have
recounted thus much before hande for the better opening of the story,
which if it should have bene spoken in his tragedy, would rather have
made a volume than a Pamphlete. For I entende onelye to say in the
tragedy, what I have noted in the Earle of Warwycks person wyshing
[55] that these other noble men, whom I have by the waye touched, should
not be forgotten.

[29] earle arraysed B–G.
[35] power into C–G.
[37] that casting of their C–G.
[38] Losecoate C–G.
[40] was entertained C–G.
[46] to his G.

And therfore imagine that you see this Earle lying with his brother
in Paules church in his coat armure, with such a face & countenaunce as
he beareth in portrayture ouer the dore in Poules, at the going downe
to Iesus Chappell fro the south ende of the quier stayres, and saying [60]
as foloweth.

[60] from C–G.

How sir Richard Nevell Earle of War- [Tragedy 16]
wike, and his brother Iohn Lord Mar-
quise Mountacute through their to-
much boldnes wer slayne
at Barnet field.

ᴁMong the heauy heape of happy knyghtes,
Whom Fortune stalde vpon her stailesse stage,
Oft hoyst on hye, oft pight in wretched plightes,
Behold me Baldwin, a per se of my age,
Lord Richard Nevell, Earle by mariage [5]
Of Warwike duchy, of Sarum by discent,
Which erst my father through his mariage hent.

Wouldest thou beholde false Fortune in her kind
Note well my life so shalt thou see her naked:
Ful fayre before, but toto foule behind, [10]
Most drowsy still whan most she semes awaked:

[Title] at Barnet. the 14. of Aprill. Anno. 1471. C–G.
[2]   stailesse *is printed* stayles *but is corrected in* Ae.
[7]   through thys maryage B.
[9]   my selfe so C–G.
[10]   to to C–E. too too FG.

My fame and shame her shift full oft hath shaked,
By enterchaunge, alowe and vp alofte,
The Luysard like that chaungeth hewe ful oft.

[15]   For while the Duke of Yorke in life remayned
Mine vncle deare, I was his happy hand:
In all attemptes my purpose I attayned,
Though King and Quene & most Lordes of the land
With all their power did often me withstand,
[20]   For god gaue Fortune, and my good behaviour,
Did from their prince steale me the peoples fauour,

So that through me in feldes right manly fought,
By force mine vncle tooke king Harry twise:
And for my cosin Edward so I wrought,
[25]   When both our syers were slayne through rashe aduice:
That he atchieved his fathers enterprise:
For into Scotland King and Quene we chased,
By meane wherof the kingdome he embraced.

Which after he had enioyde in quiet peace,
[30]   (For shortly after was king Henry take,
And put in prison) his power to encreace,
I went to Fraunce, and matched him with a make,
The French kinges doughter, whom he did forsake:
For while with payne I brought his sute to passe,
[35]   He to a widowe rashly wedded was.

This made the French king shrewdly to suspecte,
That all my treaties had but yll pretence,

[23]   Kyng Henry C–G.
[24]   As for C–G. Edward I so wrought, C–G.
[32]   and match hym C–G.
[33]   whom I dyd B. [*Corrected in Be to the original reading.*]
[34]   brought this sute C–G.
[36]   to mystrust, B–G.

206

And whan I sawe my king so bent to lust,
That with his fayth he past not to dispence,
Which is a princes honors chiefe defence, [40]
I could not rest til I had found a meane.
To mende his misse, or els to marre him cleane.

Wherfore I allyed me with his brother George,
Encensing him his brother to maligne
Through many a tale I did agaynst him forge: [45]
So that through power we did from Calays bring
And found at home, we frayed so the king,
That he to go to Freseland ward amayne,
Wherby king Henry had the crowne agayne.

Then put we the earle of Wurcester to death [50]
King Edwardes frend, a man to fowle defamed:
And in the while came Edward into breath,
For with the duke of Burgoyne so he framed.
That with the power that he to him had named,
Vnlooked for he came to England strayt, [55]
And got to Yorke, and tooke the towne by sleyte.

And after through the sufferans of my brother,
Which like a beast occasion fowly lost,
He came to London safe with many other,
And tooke the towne to good king Harries cost, [60]
Which was through him from post to piller tost,
Til therle of Oxeford, I, and other more,
Assembled power his fredome to restore.

[43] I me allyed with C–G.
[46] power that we from C–G.
[48] That he did fly to C–G.
[51] lo towle B. [Corrected in Be to the original reading.] lo foule C–G.
[60] kyng Henryes cost: B–G.
[61] Who was C–G.

Wherof king Edward warned came with spede,
And camped with his oste at Barnet towne,
Where we right fierce encountred him in dede
On Easter day, right early on the downe,
There many a man was slayne and striken downe
On eyther side, and neyther part did gayne
[70] Til I and my brother both at length were slayne.

For we to harten our overmatched men,
Forsooke our stedes, and in the thickest throng,
Ran preacing furth on foote, and fought so then,
That down we drave them wer they never so strong.
[75] But ere this lucke had lasted very long:
With numbre and force we wer so fowlye cloyed.
And rescue fayled, that quite we wer destroyed.

Now tell me Baldwin hast thou heard or read,
Of any man that did as I have done?
[80] That in his time so many armies led,
And victory at every vyage wunne?
Hast thou ever heard of subiect vnder sonne,
That plaaste and baaste his soveraynes so oft,
By enterchaunge, now low, and than aloft?

[85] Perchaunce thou thinkest my doinges were not such
As I and other do affirme they were.
And in thy minde I see thou musest much
What meanes I vsed, that should me so prefer:
Wherin because I wil thou shalt not erre,
[90] The truth of all I wil at large recite,
The short is this: I was no hippocrite.

[65]   oast in Barnet *B–G.*
[70]   Till that I *C–G.* both were *C–G.*
[71]   to hart our *C–G.*
[83]   souerayne *F.*

I never did nor sayd, save what I mente,
The common weale was still my chiefest care,
To priuate gayne or glory I was not bent,
I never passed vpon delicious fare.   [95]
Of nedeful foode my bourde was never bare.
No creditour did curs me day by day.
I vsed playnnes, ever pitch and pay.

    I heard olde soldiers, and poore wurkemen whine
Because their dutyes wer not duly payd.   [100]
Agayne I sawe howe people did repine,
At those through whom their paimentes wer delayd:
And proofe did oft assure (as scripture sayd)
That god doth wreke the wretched peoples griefes,
I sawe the polles cut of fro polling theves.   [105]

    This made me alway iustly for to deale.
Which whan the people playnly vnderstoode,
Bycause they sawe me mind the common weale
They still endeuoured how to do me good,
Ready to spend their substaunce, life, and blud,   [110]
In any cause wherto I did them move
For suer they wer it was for their behove.

    And so it was. For whan the realme decayde,
By such as good king Henry sore abused,
To mende the state I gave his enmies ayde: [115]
But whan king Edward sinful prankes stil vsed,
And would not mend, I likewise him refused:
And holpe vp Henry the better of the twayne,
And in his quarel (iust I thinke) was slayne.

[94]   pryuate payne B. [*Corrected in Be to the original reading.*] glory was
       I neuer bent, C–G.
[99]   heard pore souldiers C–G.
[100]   not truely payde. C–G.
[102]   theyr payment was G.
[118]   holp Henry, G. Henry, better C–G.

[120]   And therfore Baldwin teach by proofe of me,
That such as covet peoples love to get,
Must see their wurkes and wurdes in all agree:
Live liberally, and kepe them out of det,
On common weale let al their care be set,
[125]   For vpright dealing, dets payd, poore sustayned,
Is meane wherby all hartes are throwly gayned.

[124]   common welth G.
[126]   *The text misprints a comma for a period after* gayned.

TO THE READER

AS soone as the Erle had ended his admonicion, sure (quoth one) [Prose 16]
I thinke the Erle of Warwike although he wer a glorious man,
hath sayd no more of him selfe than what is true. For if he had
not had notable good vertues, or vertuous qualities, and vsed lawdable
meanes in his trade of lyfe, the people woulde never have loved him as [5]
they did: But god be with him, and send his soule rest, for sure his
bodye never had any. And although he dyed, yet ciuil warres ceased
not. For immediatlye after his death, came Quene Margarete with a
power out of Fraunce, bringing with her her yong sonne prince Edwarde,
and with such frendes as she found here, gave king Edward a battel at [10]
Tewxbury, where both she & her sonne wer taken prisoners, with
Edmund duke of Somerset her chiefe captayne: whose sonne lord Iohn,
and the earle of Deuonshire, were slayne in the fight, and the duke him
selfe with divers other immediatlye beheaded: whose infortunes are
wurthy to be remembred, chiefely Prince Edwardes, whom the king [15]
for speaking truth, cruelly stroke with his gauntlet, and his bretherne
tirannously murdered. But seinge the time so farre spente, I will passe
them over, and with them Fawconbridge that ioly rover, beheaded at
Southhampton: whose commocion made in Kent, was cause of sely
Henries destruccion. And seing king Henrye him selfe was cause of the [20]
destruccion of many noble princes, being of all other most vnfortunate
him selfe, I will declare what I have noted in his vnlucky lyfe: who
wounded in prison with a dagger, maye lament his wretchednes in
maner folowing.

[1]   ended this admonicion, *B–G.* (said one) *C–G.*
[13]   slaine in fight, *C–G.*
[16–17] brethren cruelly murdered, *C–F.*
[21]   infortunate *G.*
[24]   folowing *is misprinted* falowing *in the text.*

[Tragedy 17]

How king Henry the syxt a vertuous prince, was after many other mi- series cruelly murdered in the Tower of London.

JF ever woful wight had cause to rue his state,
Or by his rufull plight to move men moane his fate,
My piteous playnt may preace my mishaps to rehearce,
wherof the least most lightly heard, the hardest hart may pearce

[5]   What hart so hard can heare, of innocens opprest
By fraude in worldly goodes, but melteth in the brest
Whan giltles men be spoylde, imprisoned for theyr owne,
who wayleth not their wretched case to whom the cause is
    knowen

   The Lyon licketh the sores of selly wounded shepe,
[10] The dead mans corse may cause the Crocodile to wepe,
The waves that waste the rockes, refresh the rotten redes,
Such ruth the wracke of innocens in cruel creature bredes.

   What hart is than so hard, but wyl for pitye blede,
To heare so cruell lucke so cleare a life succede?
[15] To see a silly soule with woe and sorowe souste,
A king deprived, in prison pente, to death with daggars doust.

[Title] London the 22. of May. Anno. 1471. *C–G.*
[3]   mishap *C–G.*
[4]   lightly hard, *F.*
[8]   the case is *C–G.*
[9]   licks *C–G.*
[10]   Corse cause *F.*
[12]   creatures *C–G.*
[15]   sounst, *G.*
[16]   dounst. *G.*

Woulde god the day of birth had brought me to my beere,
Than had I never felt the chaunge of Fortunes cheere.
Would god the grave had gript me in her gredy woumbe,
Whan crowne in cradle made me king, with oyle of holy
    thoumbe. [20]

Would god the rufull toumbe had bene my royall trone,
So should no kingly charge have made me make my mone:
O that my soule had flowen to heaven with the ioy,
When one sort cryed: God save the king, another, *Vive le roy.*

So had I not been washt in waves of worldly woe, [25]
My mynde to quyet bent, had not bene tossed so:
My frendes had bene alyve, my subiectes vnopprest:
But death or cruell destiny, denyed me this rest.

Alas what should we count the cause of wretches cares,
The starres do styrre them vp, Astronomy declares: [30]
Or humours sayth the leache, the double true divines,
To the will of god, or yll of man, the doubtfull cause assignes.

Such doltish heades as dreame that all thinges drive by haps,
Count lack of former care for cause of afterclaps.
Attributing to man a power fro God bereft, [35]
Abusing vs, and robbing him, through their most wicked theft.

But god doth gide the world, and every hap by skyll.
Our wit and willing power are paysed by his will:
What wyt most wisely wardes, and wil most deadly vrkes,
Though al our power would presse it downe, doth dash our
    warest wurkes. [40]

[27]   subiects not opprest: *C–G.*
[31]   Our humours *B–G.*
[32]   th'will *C–G.*
[35]   Attributing *is printed* Astributing *but is corrected in Ae.*

Than destiny, our sinne, Gods wil, or els his wreake,
Do wurke our wretched woes, for humours be to weake:
Except we take them so, as they prouoke to sinne,
For through our lust by humours fed, al vicious dedes beginne

[45]   So sinne and they be one, both wurking like effect,
And cause the wrath of God to wreake the soule infect.
Thus wrath and wreake divine, mans sinnes and humours yll,
Concur in one, though in a sort, ech doth a course fulfill.

If likewise such as say the welken fortune warkes,
[50] Take Fortune for our fate, and sterres therof the markes,
Then destiny with fate, and Gods wil al be one:
But if they meane it otherwise, skath causers skyes be none.

Thus of our heavy happes, chiefe causes be but twayne,
Wheron the rest depende, and vnderput remayne.
[55] The chiefe the wil diuine, called destiny and fate,
The other sinne, through humours holpe, which god doth highly
hate,

The first appoynteth payne for good mens exercise,
The second doth deserve due punishment for vice:
This witnesseth the wrath, and that the love of God,
[60] The good for love, the bad for sinne, God beateth with his rod.

Although my sundry sinnes do place me with the wurst,
My happes yet cause me hope to be among the furst:
The eye that searcheth all, and seeth every thought.
Doth know how sore I hated sinne, and after vertue sought.

[65]   The solace of the soule my chiefest pleasure was,
Of worldly pompe, of fame, or game, I did not pas:

[42]   wretched *is misprinted* wrethed *in the text.*
[64]   Is iudge how C–G.
[65]   of my soule C–G.
[66]   worldly *is misprinted* wordly *in the text.*

My kingdomes nor my crowne I prised not a crum:
In heaven wer my rytches heapt, to which I sought to cum.

Yet wer my sorowes such as never man had like,
So divers stormes at once, so often did me strike: [70]
But why, God knowes, not I, except it wer for this
To shew by patarne of a prince, how britle honour is.

Our kingdomes are but cares, our state deuoyde of stay,
Our riches redy snares, to hasten our decay:
Our pleasures priuy prickes our vices to prouoke,   [75]
Our pompe a pumpe, our fame a flame, our power a smouldring
    smoke.

I speake not but by proofe, and that may many rue.
My life doth crie it out, my death doth trye it true:
Wherof I will in briefe, rehearce my heavy hap,
That Baldwin in his woful warpe, my wretchednes may wrap. [80]

In Windsore borne I was: and bare my fathers name,
Who wanne by war all Fraunce to his eternall fame:
And left to me the crowne, to be receyued in peace,
Through mariage made with Charles his haire, vpon his lifes
    decease.

Which shortly did ensue, yet died my father furst,   [85]
And both their realmes were mine, ere I a yere were nurst:
Which as they fell to soone, so faded they as fast,
For Charles and Edward got them both, or fortye yeres were
    past.

This Charles was eldest sonne of Charles my father in law,
To whom as heire of Fraunce, the Frenchmen did them draw. [90]
But Edward was the heire of Richard duke of Yorke.
The hayer of Roger Mortimer, slayne by the kerne of Korke.

[79]   rehearce the heauye B–G.
[86]   both the realmes C–G.

Before I came to age Charles had recovered Fraunce,
And kilde my men of warre, so lucky was his chaunce:
[95] And through a mad contract I made with Rayners daughter,
I gave and lost all Normandy, the cause of many a slaughter.

First of mine vncle Humfrey, abhorring sore this acte,
Because I therby brake a better precontracte:
Than of the flattring duke that first the mariage made,
[100] The iust rewarde of such as dare their princes yll perswade.

And I poore sely wretche abode the brunt of all:
My mariage lust so swete was mixt with bitter gall.
My wife was wise and good had she bene rightly sought,
But our vnlawful getting it, may make a good thing nought.

[105] Wherfore warne men beware how they iust promise breake
Least proofe of paynful plagues do cause them waile the wreke:
Aduise wel ere they graunt, but what they graunt, perfourme.
For god wil plage all doublenes, although we feele no wourme

I falsly borne in hand beleued I did wel,
[110] But al thinges be not true that learned men do tell:
My cleargy sayd a prince was to no promis bounde,
Whose wordes to be no gospel tho, I to my griefe haue found.

For after mariage ioynde Quene Margarete and me,
For one mishap afore, I dayly met with three:
[115] Of Normandy and Fraunce Charles got away my crowne,
The Duke of Yorke & other sought at home to put me downe.

Bellona rang the bell at home and all abrode,
With whose mishaps amayne fel Fortune did me lode:
In Fraunce I lost my fortes, at home the foughten fielde,
My kindred slaine, my frendes opprest, my selfe enforste to
[120]   yelde

[95]   Raynerds C–G.

Duke Richard tooke me twise, and forst me to resigne,
My crowne, and titles, due vnto my fathers ligne:
And kept me as a warde, did all thinges as him list,
Til time my wife through bluddy sword had tane me from his
    fyst.

But though she slew the duke, my sorowes did not slake,   [125]
But like to hiders head, stil more and more awake:
For Edward through the ayde of Warwick and his brother,
From one field drave me to the Skots, and toke me in another.

Then went my frendes to wracke, for Edward ware the crowne
Fro which for nine yeres space his prison held me downe: [130]
Yet thence through Warwikes wurke I was againe releast,
And Edward driven fro the realme, to seke his frendes by East.

But what prevayleth payn, or prouidens of man
To helpe him to good hap, whom destiny doth ban?
Who moyleth to remove the rocke out of the mud,   [135]
Shall myer him selfe, & hardly skape the swelling of the flud.

This al my frendes have found and I have felt it so.
Ordayned to be the touche of wretchednes and woe,
For ere I had a yeare possest my seat agayne,
I lost both it and liberty, my helpers all were slayne.   [140]

For Edward first by stelth, and sith by gadered strength,
Arrived and got to Yorke and London at the length:
Tooke me and tyed me vp, yet Warwike was so stout,
He came with power to Barnet fyelde, in hope to helpe me out.

[124] Till that my C–G.
[125] though we slew C–G.
[126] to *Hydraes* head G.
[130] Fro *is misprinted* For *in the text and in B–G.* [*Corrected in Ae and Be.*]

[145]   And there alas was slayne, with many a wurthy knight.
O Lord that ever such luck should hap in helping right:
Last came my wife and sonne, that long lay in exyle,
Defyed the King, and fought a fyelde, I may bewaile the while.

For there mine only sonne, not thirtene yere of age,
[150] Was tane and murdered strayte, by Edward in his rage:
And shortly I my selfe to stynt al furder strife
Stabbed with his brothers bluddy blade in prison lost my life.

Loe here the heauy happes which happened me by heape,
See here the pleasaunt fruytes that many princes reape,
[155] The payneful plagues of those that breake their lawful bandes,
Their mede which may & wil not save their frendes fro bluddy
      handes.

God graunt my woful haps to greuous to rehearce,
May teache all states to know how depely daungers pearce:
How frayle al honours are, how brittle worldly blisse,
[160] That warned through my fearful fate, they feare to do amys.

[149]   yeares G.
[160]   do misse. C.

TO THE READER

This tragedy ended, an other said: eyther you or king Henry are [Prose 17] a good philosopher, so narowly to argue the causes of misfortunes: but ther is nothing to experience, which taught, or might teach the king this lesson. but to procede in our matter, I finde mencion here shortly after the death of this king, of a duke of Excester [5] found dead in the sea betwene Dover and Calays, but what he was, or by what adventure he died, master Fabian hath not shewed, and master Hall hath overskipped him: so that excepte we bee frendlier vnto him, he is like to be double drowned, both in the sea, and in the gulfe of forgetfulnes. About this matter was much talke, but because one tooke [10] vppon him to seeke out that story, that charge was committed to him. And to be occupied the meane while, I found the storye of one drowned likewise, and that so notably, though priuily, that al the world knew of it: wherfore I sayd: because night approcheth, and that we wil lose no time, ye shall heare what I have noted concerning the duke of Clarens, [15] king Edwardes brother, who altobewashed in wine, may bewayle his infortune after this maner.

[9] in sea, *C–G*.
[12] ocupied in the *C–G*. I haue found *C–G*.
[13] notable, *F*.

[Tragedy 18]

How George Plantagenet third sonne of the Duke of Yorke, was by his bro- ther King Edward wrongfully imprisoned, and by his bro- ther Richard misera- bly murdered.

THe foule is fowle men say, that files the nest.
which maketh me loath to speak now, might I chuse,
But seing time vnburdened hath her brest,
And fame blowen vp the blast of all abuse,

[5] My silence rather might my life accuse
Than shroud our shame, though fayne I would it so:
For truth wil out, though all the world say no.

And therfore Baldwin hartely I the beseche.
To pause awhile vpon my heauy playnt,

[10] And though vnneth I vtter spedy spech,
No fault of wit, or folly maketh me faynt:
No heady drinkes have geven my tounge attaynte
Through quaffing craft, yet wine my wits confound
Not which I dranke of, but wherin I dround.

[Title] murdered. The 11. of Ianuary. Anno. 1478. *C–G.* [*Read* 1448 *for*
         1478. *D–F.*]
[2]   makes *C–G.*
[7]   out, although the world *C–G.*
[8]   Wherefore Baldwin with tearis I *F.*
[10]   And vnneth though I *C–EG.*
[11]   wit nor folly makes *C–G.*
[14]   Not of which I dranke, but *C–EG.* Not which I drancke, but
         wherein I was dround. *F.*

What prince I am although I nede not shewe. [15]
Because my wine bewrayes me by the smell,
For never was creature sowst in Bacchus dewe
To death but I, through Fortunes rigour fel:
Yet that thou mayst my story better tell,
I will declare as briefly as I may, [20]
My welth, my woe, and causers of decay.

The famous house sournamed Plantagenet,
Wherat dame Fortune frowardly did frowne,
While Bolenbroke vniustly sought to set
His lord king Richard quite beside the crowne, [25]
Though many a day it wanted due renowne,
God so preserved by prouidens and grace,
That lawful heires did never faile the race.

For Lionell king Edwardes elder childe,
Both vncle and haire to Richard yssulesse, [30]
Begot a doughter Philip, whom vnfilde
The earle of March espousde, and god did blesse
With fruyte assinde the kingdome to possesse:
I mean sir Roger Mortimer, whose hayer
The earle of Cambridge maried Anne the fayer. [35]

This earle of Cambridge Richard clept by name,
Was sonne to Edmund Langley duke of Yorke:
Which Edmund was fift brother to the same
Duke Lyonel, that al this line doth korke:
Of which two houses ioyned in a forke, [40]
My father Richard prince Plantagenet
True duke of Yorke, was lawful heire beget.

[17]   neuer creature was soust C–G.
[24]   While *is misprinted* White *in the text.*
[27]   so preferred B–G. [*Corrected in* Be *to the original reading.*]
[29]   Edwardes eldest child, B–EG. Edwards second child, *F.*
[30]   Both eame and C–G.
[31]   whom vndefylde C–G.

Who tooke to wife as you shal vnderstand
A mayden of a noble house and olde,
[45] Raulfe Nevels daughter Earle of Westmerland:
Whose sonne Earle Richard was a baron bolde,
And had the right of Salysbury in holde,
Through mariage made with good Earle Thomas hayer,
Whose earned prayses never shal appaire.

[50] The duke my father had by this his wife,
Fower sonnes, of whom the eldest Edward hight,
The second Iohn, who lost in youth his life,
At wakefield slayne by Clifford cruell knight.
I George am third of Clarence duke by right.
[55] The fowerth borne to the mischiefe of vs all,
Was duke of Glocester, whom men Richard call.

Whan as our syer in sute of right was slayne,
(Whose life and death him selfe declared earst,)
My brother Edward plyed his cause amayne,
[60] And got the crowne, as Warwick hath rehearst:
The pride wherof so depe his stomacke pearst,
That he forgot his frendes, dispisde his kin,
Of oth or office passing not a pinne.

Which made the earle of Warwike to maligne.
[65] My brothers state, and to attempt a waye,

[43]   as ye shall B–G.
[52]   second Eadmund who in youth did lose his C–G.
[56]   men did Richard C–G.
[59]   Edward, the Quarell styrd agayne, F.
[60]   And wan the F.
[62–63] That litle passinge on them that brought him in,
        Forgat his frendes, and set at naught his kin. F.
[65]   His dealinge ingrate, and F.

To bring from prison Henry selly king,
To helpe him to the kingdome if he may.
And knowing me to be the chiefest staye,
My brother had, he did me vndermine
To cause me to his treasons to encline. [70]

   Wherto I was prepared long before,
My brother had bene to me so vnkinde:
For sure no cankar fretteth fleshe so sore,
As vnkinde dealing doth a louing minde.
Loves strongest bandes vnkindnes doth vnbinde, [75]
It moveth love to malice, zele to hate,
Chiefe frendes to foes, and bretherne to debate.

   And though the Earle of Warwike subtile syer,
Perceyved I bare a grudge agaynst my brother,
Yet towarde his feat to set me more on fire, [80]
He kindeled vp one firebrand with another:
For knowing fansie was the forcing rother,
Which stiereth youth to any kinde of strife,
He offered me his daughter to my wife.

   Wherthrough and with his crafty filed tounge, [85]
He stale my hart, that erst vnstedy was:
For I was witles, wanton, fonde, and younge,
Whole bent to pleasure, brittle as the glas:
I can not lye, *In vino veritas.*
I did esteme the beawty of my bryde, [90]
Above my selfe and all the world beside.

[66]   From prison to enlarge Henry the sely Kinge, *F.*
[67]   Him to restore to Kingdome *F.*
[70]   To his ill practise the sooner to *F.*
[72]   Because the king to me was so *F.*
[73]   No canker sure, soft flesh doth fret so *F.*
[81]   vp *is misprinted* vy *in the text.*

These fond affeccions ioynt with lacke of skyll,
(Which trap the hart, and blinde the iyes of youth,
And pricke the minde to practise any yll)
[95] So tickled me, that voyd of kindly truth:
(Which where it wantes, all wickednes ensueth)
I stinted not to persecute my brother,
Till time he left his kingdome to an other.

Thus karnall love did quench the loue of kind,
[100] Til lust were lost through fansy fully fed.
But whan at length I came vnto my minde,
I sawe how lewdly lightnes had me led,
To seeke with payne the peril of my hed:
For had king Henry once bene setled sure,
[105] I was assured my dayes could not endure.

And therfore though I bound my selfe by othe
To helpe king Henry al that ever I might,
Yet at the treaty of my bretherne both,
Which reason graunted to require but right,
[110] I left his part, wherby he perisht quite:
And reconsilde me to my bretherne twayne,
And so came Edward to the crowne againe.

This made my father in lawe to fret and fume,
To stampe and stare, and call me false forsworne,
And at the length with all his power, presume
[115] To helpe king Henry vtterly forlorne.
Our frendly profers stil he tooke in skorne,
Refused peace, and came to Barnet field,
And there was kilde, bicause he would not yeeld:

[94]   prickt C–G.
[96]   (Which if it wante all wretchednes B–G.
[106]   with oth C–G.

His brother also there with him was slayne,   [120]
Wherby decayed the kayes of chiualrie.
For never lived the matches of them twaine,
In manhode, power, and marciall pollicy,
In vertuous thewes, and frendly constancy,
That would to god, if it had bene his wil   [125]
They might have turnde to vs, and liued stil.

But what shal be, shal be: there is no choyse,
Thinges nedes must drive as destiny decreeth:
For which we ought in all our haps reioyce,
Because the eye eterne all thing forseeth,   [130]
Which to no yll at any time agreeth,
For yls to yll to vs, be good to it,
So farre his skilles excede our reach of wit.

The wounded man which must abide the smart,
Of stitching vp, or searing of his sore,   [135]
As thing to bad, reproves the Surgeons art,
Which notwithstanding doth his helth restore.
The childe likewise to science plied sore,
Countes knowledge yll, his teacher to be wood,
Yet Surgery and sciences be good.   [140]

But as the pacientes griefe and Scholers payne,
Cause them deme bad such thinges as sure be best,
So want of wisedome causeth vs complayne
Of every hap, wherby we seme opprest:
The poore do pine for pelfe, the rich for rest,   [145]
And whan as losse or sicknes vs assayle:
We curse our fate, our Fortune we bewayle.

[129]   which ought C–F. For which ne ought B. [*Corrected in Be to the
        original reading.*]

Yet for our good, god wurketh every thing.
For through the death of those two noble peres
[150] My brother lived and raignde a quiet king,
Who had they lived perchaunce in course of yeares,
Would have delivered Henry from the breres,
Or holpe his sonne to enioye the careful crowne,
Wherby our lyne should have be quite put downe.

[155] A careful crowne it may be iustly named,
Not only for the cares therto annext,
To see the subiect wel and duly framed,
With which good care few kinges are greatly vext
But for the dread wherwith they are perplext,
[160] Of losing lordship, liberty, or life:
Which woful wrackes in kingdomes happen rife.

The which to shun while sum to sore have sought
They have not spared all persons to suspect:
And to destroy such as they gilty thought:
[165] Though no apparaunce proved them infect.
Take me for one of this wrong punisht sect,
Imprisoned first, accused without cause,
And doen to death, no proces had by lawes.

Wherin I note how vengeaunce doth acquite
[170] Like yll for yll how vices vertue quell:
For as my mariage love did me excite
Against the king my brother to rebell,
So love to have his children prosper well,
Prouoked him against both lawe and right,
[175] To murder me, his brother, and his knight.

[154]   haue ben quyte B–G.
[156]   Not for the cares which thereto bene annext, F.
[162]   That which C–E.

For by his quene two goodly sonnes he had.
Borne to be punisht for their parentes sinne:
Whose fortunes kalked made their father sad,
Such wofull haps were founde to be therin:
Which to auouch, writ in a rotten skinne   [180]
A prophecy was found, which sayd a G,
Of Edwardes children should destruccion be.

  Me to be G, because my name was George
My brother thought, and therfore did me hate.
But woe be to the wicked heades that forge   [185]
Such doubtful dreames to brede vnkinde debate:
For God, a gleve, a gibet, grate or gate,
A Grave, a Griffeth or a Gregory,
As well as George are written with a G.

  Such doubtfull riddles are no prophecies.   [190]
For prophecies, in writing though obscure,
Are playne in sence, the darke be very lyes:
What god forsheweth is euident and pure.
Truth is no Harold nor no Sophist sure:
She noteth not mens names, their shildes nor creastes,   [195]
Though she compare them vnto birdes and beastes.

  But whom she doth forshewe shal rule by force,
She termeth a Wulfe, a Dragon or a Beare:
A wilful Prince, a raynles ranging horse.
A bolde, a Lyon: a coward much in feare,   [200]
A hare or hart: a crafty, pricked eare:
A lecherous, a Bull, a Goote, a Foale:
An vnderminer, a Moldwarp, or a mole.

[176]   two pryncelyke sonnes *B–G*.
[178]   made the father *B–G*.
[185]   to that wicked *C–F*.
[197]   shal rayne by *B–G*.
[199]   raging horse *C–G*.
[200]   A Bore a Lyon: *D–F*.

By knowen beastes thus truth doth playne declare
[205] What men they be, of whom she speakes before.
And who so can mens properties compare
And marke what beast they do resemble more,
Shall soone discerne who is the griesly bore.
For God by beastes expresseth mens condicions,
[210] And not their badges, haroldes supersticions.

And learned Merline whom God gave the sprite,
To know, and vtter princes actes to cum,
Like to the Iewish prophetes, did recite
In shade of beastes, their doinges all and sum:
[215] Expressing playne by maners of the dum,
That kinges and lordes such properties should have
As had the beastes whose name he to them gave:

Which while the folish did not well consider,
And seing princes gave, for difference
[220] And knowledge of their issues myxt together,
All maner beastes, for badges of pretence,
They tooke those badges to expres the sence
Of Merlines minde, and those that gave the same,
To be the princes noted by their name.

[225] And hereof sprang the false namde prophecies,
That go by letters, siphers, armes, or signes:
Which all be foolish, false and crafty lies,
Deuised by gesse, or Guiles vntrue diuines:
For whan they sawe that many of many lines
[230] Gave armes alike, they wist not which was he,
Whom Merline meant the noted beast to be.

[211]   gaue *is misprinted* haue *in the text.* BC.
[217]   As have the B–G.

For all the broode of Warwickes geve the Bear,
The Buckinghames do likewise geve the swan:
But which Bear bearer shoulde the lyon teare
They wer as wise as Goose the fery man: [235]
Yet in their skil they ceased not to skan:
And to be demed of the people wise,
Set furth their gloses vpon prophecies.

And whom they doubted openly to name
They darkly termed, or by sum letter meant: [240]
For so they mought how ever the world did frame,
Preserve them selves from shame or being shent.
For howsoever contrary it went,
They might expound their meaning otherwise,
As haps in thinges should newly stil arise.   [245]

And thus there grew of a mistaken truth,
An arte so false, as made the true suspect:
Wherof hath cum much mischiefe, more the ruth,
That errours should our mindes so much infect.
True prophecies have fowly been reiect: [250]
The false which brede both murder, warre & strife,
Belyved to the losse of many a goodmans life.

And therfore Baldwin teach men to discerne,
Which prophecies be false and which be true:
And for a ground this lesson let them learne,   [255]
That all be false which are deuised newe:
The age of thinges is iudged by the hue.
All Riddels made by letters, names or armes,
Are yong and false, for wurse than witches charmes.

[232]   warwickes gaue the C–G.
[238]   gloses on prophecies. C–F.
[241]   they thought C–G.
[247]   And art D–F.
[250]   True prophets haue C–G.
[259]   false, far wurse B–G.

[260] I know thou musest at this lore of mine,
How I no student, should have learned it:
And doest impute it to the fume of wine
That styrs the tounge, and sharpeneth vp the wit,
But harke, a frende did teache me every whit.
[265] A man of mine, in al good knowledge rife,
For which he giltles, lost his learned life.

This man abode my servaunt many a day,
And stil in study set his hole delite:
Which taught me more than I could beare away
[270] Of every arte: and by his searching sight
Of thinges to cum he could forshew as right,
As I rehearce the pageantes that wer past:
Such perfectnes god gaue him at the last.

He knew my brother Richard was the Bore,
[275] Whose tuskes should teare my brothers boyes & me,
And gave me warning therof long before.
But wit nor warning can in no degree
Let thinges to hap, which are ordaynde to bee.
Witnes the paynted Lionesse, which slue
[280] A prince imprisoned, Lions to eschue.

He tolde me to, my youkefelow should dye,
(Wherin would God he had bene no diuine)
And after her death, I should woe earnestly
A spouse, wherat my brother should repine:
[285] And finde the meanes she should be none of mine.
For which such malice, should among vs rise,
As save my death no treaty should decise.

[271]   he would for shew B–G.
[281]   me eke, my B–G.
[284]   brother would repyne: B–G.
[285]   none myne. B.

And as he sayd, so all thinges came to passe:
For whan King Henry and his sonne wer slayne,
And every broyle so throughly quenched was,   [290]
That the King my brother quietly did rayne,
I, reconsiled to his love agayne,
In prosperous health did leade a quiet life,
For five yeares space with honors laden rife.

And to augment the fulnes of my blisse,   [295]
Two lovely children by my wife I had:
But froward hap, whose maner ever is,
In chiefest ioy to make the happy sad,
Bemixt my swete with bitternes to bad:
For while I swam in ioyes on every side,   [300]
My louing wife, my chiefest iewel died.

Whose lacke whan sole I had bewaylde a yeare,
The Duke of Burgoynes wife dame Margarete
My louing sister, willing me to cheare,
To mary againe did kindly me intreat: [305]
And wisht me matched with a mayden nete
A stepdaughter of hers, duke Charles, his hayer,
A noble damesell, yong, discrete and fayer.

To whose desyer, because I did encline,
The King my brother doubting my degree,   [310]
Through prophecies, against vs did repine:
And at no hande, would to our willes agree.
For which such rancor pearst both him and me
That face to face we fell to flat defiaunce,
But were appeased by frendes of our aliaunce.   [315]

[300]   I swim in F.
[302]   Whose *is printed* Who se *but is corrected in* Ae.
[307]   Duke Charls hayre, C–G.
[314]   fell at flat C–G.

Howbeit my mariage vtterly was dasht:
Wherein because my servaunt sayd his minde,
A meane was sought wherby he might be lasht.
And for they could no crime agaynst him finde,
[320] They forged a fault the peoples iyes to blinde,
And tolde he should by sorceries pretende,
To bring the King vnto a spedy ende.

Of all which poyntes he was as innocent,
As is the babe that lacketh kindely breth:
[325] And yet condemned by the Kinges assent,
Most cruelly put to a shamefull death.
This fierd my hart, as foulder doth the heath:
So that I could not but exclame and crye,
Against so great and open an iniury.

[330] For this I was commaunded to the tower,
The king my brother was so cruel harted:
And whan my brother Richard saw the hower
Was cum, for which his hart so sore had smarted,
He thought best take the time before it parted.
[335] For he endeuoured to attayne the crowne,
From which my life must nedes have held him downe.

For though the king within a while had died,
As nedes he must, he surfayted so oft,
I must have had his children in my gyde
[340] So Richard should beside the crowne have coft:
This made him plye the while the waxe was soft,
To find a meane to bring me to an ende,
For realme rape spareth neither kin nor frend.

[327] foulder *is printed* soulder *but is corrected in* Ae.
[329] open iniury, C–G.
[334] thought it best C–G. take time G.

And whan he sawe how reason can asswage
Through length of time, my brother Edwardes yre,   [345]
With forged tales he set him new in rage,
Til at the last they did my death conspire.
And though my truth sore troubled their desire,
For all the world did know mine innocence,
Yet they agreed to charge me with offence.   [350]

And covertly within the tower they called,
A quest to geve such verdite as they should:
Who what with fear, and what with fauour thralde,
Durst nought pronounce but as my brethern would
And though my false accusers never could   [355]
Prove ought they sayd, I giltles was condemned:
Such verdites passe where iustice is contemned.

This feat atchieved, yet could they not for shame
Cause me be kilde by any common way,
But like a wulfe the tirant Richard came,   [360]
(My brother, nay my butcher I may say)
Vnto the tower, when all men wer away,
Save such as wer provided for the feate:
Who in this wise did straungely me entreate.

His purpose was, with a prepared string   [365]
To strangle me. but I bestird me so,
That by no force they could me therto bring,
Which caused him that purpose to forgo.
Howbeit they bound me whether I would or no.
And in a butte of Malmesey standing by,   [370]
Newe Christned me, because I should not crie.

[358]   could the not B.
[359]   Bereue my lyfe by F.
[361]   nay Butcher I may rightly say) F.
[362]   Tower, commaundinge all away, F.
[369]   bound whether F.

Thus drounde I was, yet for no due desert,
Except the zeale of Iustice be a crime:
False prophecies bewitched king Edwardes hert.

[375] My brother Richard to the crowne wold clime.
Note these thre causes in thy ruful ryme:
And boldly say they did procure my fal,
And death, of deathes most straunge and hard of al.

And warne all princes prophecies to eschue

[380] That are to darke or doubtful to be knowen:
What God hath sayd, that can not but ensue,
Though all the world would have it overthrowen.
When men suppose by fetches of their owne
To flye theyr fate, they further on the same,

[385] Like quenching blastes, which oft reuiue the flame.

Will princes therfore not to thinke by murder
They may auoide what prophecies behight,
But by their meanes theyr mischiefes they may furder,
And cause gods vengeaunce heauier to alight:

[390] Wo wurth the wretch that strives with gods forsighte.
They are not wise, but wickedly do arre,
Which thinke yll dedes, due destinies may barre.

For if we thinke that prophecies be true,
We must beleve it can not but betide

[395] Which God in them forsheweth shall ensue:
For his decrees vnchaunged do abide.
Which to be true my bretherne both have tried.
Whose wicked warkes warne princes to detest,
That others harmes may kepe them better blest.

[374]   Edwardes harte. *B–G.*
[379]   warne Princes *F.*
[385]   Like Blasts of Winde, which *F.*

BY that this tragedy was ended, nyghte was so nere cum that we [Prose 18] could not conveniently tary together any longer: and therfore sayd mayster *Ferrers*: It is best my masters to staye here. For we be cum now to the ende of Edwarde the fowerth his raygne. For the last whom we finde vnfortunate therein, was this Duke of Clarens: In [5] whose behalfe I commende much that which hath be noted. Let vs therfore for this time leave with him. And this daye seuen nightes hence, if your busines will so suffer, let vs all mete here together agayne. And you shal se that in the mean season I will not only deuise vppon this my selfe, but cause divers other of my acquayntauns, which can do [10] very well, to helpe vs forwarde with the rest. To this every man gladly agreed, howbeit (quoth an other) seing we shall end at Edward the fowerthes ende, let him selfe make an ende of our daies labour with the same oracion which mayster Skelton made in his name, the tenour wherof so farre as I remember, is this. [15]

[4]   be now cum *B–F.* of Edward the fourths raigne. *C–G.*
[5]   the Duke *D–G.*
[7–8]   and some other day when your leasure will beste serue let vs mete here altogether agayne. *F.*
[10]   *The text mistakenly prints* but but.
[12]   (saide another) *C–G.*
[12–13] at Edwards the fourth end, *D–F.*
[14–15] name, the true copy wherof as hee wrote the same I haue here readye to be red *F.*
[15]   is as foloweth. *C–EG.*

[Tragedy 19]

How king Edward through his surfeting and vntemperate life, sodainly died in the mids of his prosperity.

*M*Iseremini *mei* ye that be my frendes,
This world hath formed me downe to fall:
How may I endure whan that every thing endes?
What creature is borne to be eternall,

[5] Now there is no more but pray for me all.
Thus say I Edward that late was your King,
And .xxiii. yeares ruled this imperiall:
Sum vnto pleasure and sum to no liking:
Mercy I aske of my misdoing,

[10] What auayleth it frendes to be my foe?
Sith I can not resist, nor amend your complayning,
Quia ecce nunc in pulvere dormio.

I slepe now in molde as it is naturall,
As earth vnto earth hath his reuerture:

[15] What ordeyned God to be terrestriall,
Without recourse to the earth by nature?
Who to live ever may him selfe assure?
What is it to trust on mutability?
Sith that in this world nothing may endure?

[20] For now am I gone that was late in prosperity.

[Title] Edwarde the fourth through *C–G.* prosperity. the nynth of Aprill.
Anno. 1483. *C–G.* [*Read* 1485 *for* 1483 *D–F.*]
[1]   *B mistakenly prints the initial* M *as* S.
[7]   And xxii. yeares *C–EG.* And yeres xxii. bare Scepter ryall, *F.*
[12] *Et ecce F.*
[15] God in the world vniuersall, *F.*
[18] trust to mutabylyty? *B–G.*

To presume therupon it is but a vanitye,
Not certayne, but as a chery fayre ful of wo.
Rayned not I of late in great prosperitye?
Et ecce nunc in pulvere dormio.

Where was in my life such an one as I,   [25]
While Lady Fortune with me had continuaunce?
Graunted not she me to have victory,
In England to rayne, and to contribute Fraunce?
She toke me by the hand and led me a daunce,
And with her sugred lyppes on me she smyled.   [30]
But what for her dissembled countenaunce,
I could not be ware tyl I was begiled.
Now from this worlde she hath me exiled,
Whan I was lothest hence for to goe,
And am in age as who saieth but a childe.   [35]
Et ecce nunc in pulvere dormio.

I had ynough I helde me not contente,
Without remembraunce that I should dye:
And moreover to encroch ready was I bent,
I knew not how long I should it occupy,   [40]
I made the tower strong I wist not why.
I knew not to whom I purchased Tattersall.
I amended Dover on the mountayne hye,
And London I prouoked to fortify the wall.

[21]   but vanity, *C–G.*
[23]   great felicity, *F.*
[25]   such a one *F.*
[26]   Fortune had with me continuaunce: *G.*
[31]   for dissembled *B–G.*
[35]   age who sayeth *B–G.* [*Corrected in Be to the original reading.*]
[43]   mended *B–G.*

[45] I made Notingham a place full royall.
Windsore, Eltam, and many other mo.
Yet at the last I went from them all,
Et ecce nunc in pulvere dormio.

Where is now my conquest and victory?
[50] Where is my ritches, and royall array?
Where be my coursers and my horses hye?
Where is my mirth, my solas, and playe?
As vanity to nought all is wyddred away:
O Lady Bes, long for me may you call,
[55] For I am departed vntill doomes day:
But love you that lord that is soveraine of all.
Where be my castels and buyldinges royall?
But Windsore alone now have I no moe.
And of Eton the prayers perpetuall,
[60] *Et ecce nunc in pulvere dormio.*

Why should a man be proude or presume hye?
Saynt Barnard therof nobly doth treat,
Saying a man is but a sacke of stercory,
And shall returne vnto wurmes meat:
[65] Why what became of Alexander the great?
Or els of strong Sampson, who can tell?
Wer not wurmes ordayned their flesh to freate?
And of Salomon that was of wit the well?
Absolon profered his heare for to sell,
[70] Yet for all his beauty, wurmes eat him also.
And I but late in honour did excell,
Et ecce nunc in pulvere dormio.

[52] solace and my play? *B–G.*
[53] nought els is *F.*
[64] into wormes *F.*
[69] *Absolon* preferred his *G.*
[70] for his *C–G.*
[71] honours *C–G.*

I have playd my pageaunt: now am I past,
Ye wote well all I was of no great elde.
This all thing concluded shall be at the last,   [75]
Whan death approcheth, than lost is the felde:
Than seing this world me no longer vphelde,
For nought would conserve me here in my place,
In manus tuas domine my spirite vp I yelde,
Humbly beseching the o God, of thy grace.   [80]
O you curteous commons your hartes enbrace,
Beningly now to pray for me also,
For right well you know your king I was.
Et ecce nunc in pulvere dormio.

[75]   Thus all *C–G.* thinges *F.*
[77]   lengar *B–E.*
[78]   in any place, *B.* in this place, *C–G.*
[80]   Humbly *is misprinted* Humby *in the text.*
[83]   well ye know *C–F.*

[Prose 19] WHan this was sayde, every man tooke his leave of other and departed: And I the better to acquyte my charge, recorded and noted all such matters as they had wylled me.

FINIS.

[1]   was red euery *F.* man for the time tooke *C–G.* [*Read* that *for* the *G.*]
[2–3] departed (for then it waxed darke) appointing a new day of meting *C–G.*
        [*B substitutes* Thus endeth the first parte *for* FINIS. *In editions C–G there is no break between the tragedies of edition A and those added in B, this prose link being combined with Preface 3. See also, therefore, the variants listed for Preface 3.*
[4]   *The text misprints a comma for a period after* FINIS.

TRAGEDIES ADDED IN THE EDITION OF 1563

¶ A MYRROVR FOR
Magiſtrates.

Wherein maye be ſeen by
example of other, with howe greuous plages vices are puniſhed: and
howe frayle and vnſtable worldly
proſperity is founde, even of
thoſe whom Fortune ſe-
meth moſt highly
to fauour.

Felix quem faciunt aliena pericula cautum.

Anno. 1 5 6 3.

¶ Imprinted at London in Fleteſtrete
nere to Saynct Dunſtans Churche
by Thomas Marſhe.

The seconde
PARTE OF THE
Mirrour for Magistrates.

Wylliam Baldwyn
to the Reader.

[Preface 3]

THe tyme beynge cum, whan (according to our former ap-
poyntment) we shuld meete together agayne to deuyse vpon
the tragicall affayres of our English Rulers, I with suche
storyes as I had procured & prepared, went to the place wherein we had
debated the former parte. There founde I the prynter and all the rest of [5]
our frendes and furderers assembled & tarying for vs, Save Maister
Ferrers, who shortly after according to hys promys came thyther.

Whan we had blamed hym for hys long tarying, he satisfyed vs fully
with this reasonable excuse. I haue been letted (quoth he) dyuers wayes,
but chyeflye in taryeng for suche tragedyes, as many of our frendes at [10]
myne instauns, vndertoke to discours, wherof I am sure you wyll be
right glad: For moe wits are better then one, & diuersity of deuice is
alway most plesante. And although I have presentlye brought but a
fewe, becaus no moe are redye, yet shall you be sure hereafter to have
all the rest, which notable men haue vndertaken: wherof sum are half [15]
doen, sum more, sum less, sum scarce begun, which maketh me thynke
that the dyuersytye of braynes in divisyng, is lyke the sundrynes of
beastes in engendryng: For sum wyttes are readye, & dispatch many
matters spedilye, lyke the Conye which lyttereth every moneth: sum

[*Preface* 3 *is continuous with Prose* 19 *in all editions after* B. *This collation should,
therefore, be read in connection with the collation of Prose* 19, *on p.* 240.]

[1–53] a new day of meting which being come, wee met all together againe. And
when wee had saluted one an other, then C–G.

[20] other are slowe lyke the Olyfaunt, skarce delyueryng any matter in .x. yeares. I dysprayse neyther of these byrthes, For both be naturall: But I commende most the meane, whiche is neyther to slowe nor to swyft, for that is Lion lyke, and therfore most noble. For the ryght poet doth neyther through haste bring furth swift feble Rabettes, neither doth he

[25] weary men in lookyng for hys strong ioyntles Olyphantes: But in reasonable tyme he bryngeth furth a perfect & liuely Lion, Not a Bear-whelp that must be longar in lyckyng than in breedynge. And yet I knowe manye that dooe hyghly lyke that lumpysh deliuery. But every man hath hys gyft, and the diversitie of our mindes maketh every thing

[30] to be liked. And therfore while the oliphantes are in bredyng (to whom I haue therfore geuen the latter storyes) I haue brought you such as are allready doen, to be publyshed in the mean season: wherin there nedeth no furder labour, but to place them in due order.

Loe you Baldwyne, here is of myne owne the duke of Somerset slain

[35] at .S. Albons with other which I promysed, whom I wysh you shoulde place last: there is also Shores wyfe, trimly handled by Master Church-yard, which I pray you place where you thynk most conuenient. here are other also of other mens, but they are rabettes, Do with them as you thynk best. I would tary with a good wyll & helpe you in the order,

[40] save that my busines is great & weighty, but I know you can do it wel inough, & therfore, tyl we meet agayne I wyll leaue you. Than de-liuered he the tragedyes vnto me, and departed.

Dyuers of the rest lykyng hys deuyse, vsed the lyke maner: For the prynter delyuered vnto me the lord Hastynges penned by maister

[45] Dolman, & kyng Rychard the third compiled by Frauncis Segars. Then sayd I: wel my masters sith you thinke yt good to charge me with the order, I am contented therwith: For as you haue doen, so have I lyke-wyse procured sum of my frendes to ayd vs in our labour. For master Sackvyle hath aptly ordered the duke of Buckkynghams oracion, and

[50] Master Cavyl the black smythes, and other. I pray you (quoth one of the cumpany) let vs heare them. Nay soft (quoth I) we wyl take the cronycles, & note theyr places, & as they cum, so wil we orderly reade

[45]   Frauncis *is misprinted* Fraũncis [Fraunncis] *in the text.*

244

them al. To thys they all agreed. Then one tooke the cronicle whom
therfore we made, & call the reder, & he began to rede the story of
prince Edward called the fift king of that name: & whan he came to the [55]
apprehending of the lord Riuers: stay ther I pray you (quoth I) For here
is hys complaynt: for the better vnderstanding wherof, you must
ymagin that he was accompanyed with the Lord Richard Graye, and
with Hault and, Clappam whose infortunes he bewayleth after this
manner.   [60]

[53–54] tooke the booke and began C–G.
[54–55] of king Edward the fift: (for there wee left) and when C–G.
[56]   (said I) C–G.
[58–59] Gray, Hawt & Clapeham, C–G.

How Sir Anthony Wudvile Lorde Rivers [Tragedy 20]
and Skales, Gouernour of prince Edward,
was with his Neuew Lord Richard Gray
and other causeles imprisoned, and
cruelly murdered.

𝕬S sylly suiters letted by delayes
To shew theyr prynce the meanyng of theyr mynde,
That long have bought theyr brokers yeas & nayes
And neuer the nyer: do dayly wayte to fynde
The prynces grace, from waighty affayres vntwind: [5]
Which tyme attayned, by attendyng all the yeare,
The weryed prince wyll than no suters heare:

[Title] murdered. Anno. 1483. C–G.
[2]   of the mynd F.

My case was such not many dayes agoe.
For after brute had blased all abrode
[10] That Baldwyn through the ayd of other moe,
Of fame or shame fallen prynces would vnloade
Out from our graues we got without abode,
And preaced forward with the rufull rout,
That sought to have theyr doynges bulted out.

[15] But whan I had long attended for my turne
To tell my tale as dyvers other dyd:
In hope I should no longar whyle soiourne
But from my suytes haue spedily been ryd,
Whan course and place both orderly had byd
[20] Me shew my mynde, and I prepared to saye,
The hearers paused, arose and went theyr way.

These doubtfull doynges draue me to my dumpes,
Vncertayne what should moeue them so to doe:
I feared least affeccions lothly lumpes
[25] Or inwarde grudge had dryven them therto,
Whose wycked stynges all storyes truth vndoe.
Oft causyng good to be reported yll,
Or dround in suddes of Lethes muddy swyll.

For hytherto slye wryters wyly wittes
[30] Which haue engrossed princes cheefe affayres,
Have been lyke horses snaffled with the byttes
Of fansye, feare, or doubtes full diepe dispayres,
Whose raynes enchayned to the chefest chayres,

[8]   My cause *D–F*.
[10] That one Baldwin by help of *F*.
[12] we stert without *F*.
[13] preaced forth among the *F*.
[15] long tended *C–G*.
[20] prepared *is misprinted* prpared *in the text*.
[25] had moued them *F*.

Have so ben strayned of those that bare the stroke
That truth was forst to chow or els to choke. [35]

   Thys caused such as lothed lowd to lye,
To passe with sylence sundry prynces lyues.
Lesse faut it is to leave, than leade awry:
And better dround, that ever bound in gyves.
For fatall fraude this world so fondly dryves, [40]
That whatsoeuer writers braines may brue
Be it neuer so false, at length is tane for true.

   What harme may hap by helpe of lying pennes
How wrytten lyes may lewdly be maynteyned.
The lothly rytes, the divilysh ydoll dennes [45]
With gyltles blud of vertuous men bestayned,
Is such a proofe as all good hartes haue playned.
The taly groundes of storyes throughly tryes,
The deth of martyrs vengeauns on it cryes.

   Far better therfore not to wryte at all [50]
Than stayne the truth for any maner cause,
For this they meane to let my story fall
(Thought I) and ear my tyme theyr volume clause.
But after I knew it only was a pause,
Made purposely, most for the readers ease, [55]
Assure thée Baldwyn, highly it dyd me please.

   For freshest wits, I know wyll sone be weary,
In redyng long what ever booke it be,
Except it be vayne matter, straunge or mery,
well saust with lyes, and glared all with glee, [60]
With which becaus no grave truth may agre,
The closest style for storyes is the metest,
In ruful moanes the shortest fourme is swetest.

[39]   dround, than euer *C–G*.
[53]   time my volume *C–G*.
[63]   rufull moads *F*. rufull meanes *G*.

[65]
And syth the playntes alredy by the pende,
Are briefe ynough, the number also small,
The tediousnes I thynk doeth none offend,
Save such as have no lust to learne at all,
Regarde none such: no matter what they brall.
Warne thou the wary, least they hap to stumble.
[70]
As for the carelesse, care not what they mumble.

My lyfe is such as (if thou note it wel)
May cause the witty wealthy to beware.
For theyr sakes therfore playnly will I tell,
How false and combrous worldly honors are,
[75]
How cankred foes, bryng careles folk to care.
How tyrantes suffered, and not queld in tyme
Do cut theyr throates that suffre them to clime.

Neyther wyll I hyde the chiefest poynt of all
Which wysest rulers least of all regarde,
[80]
That was and wyll be cause of many a fall.
This can not be to ernestly declarde
Becaus it is so seelde, and slackly heard.
The abuse and skornyng of gods ordynaunces,
Is chefest cause of care & wofull chaunces.

[85]
Gods holly orders hyghly are abused
When men do chaunge their endes for straunge respects:
They skorned are, whan they be cleane refused
For that they can not serve our fond affectes.
The one our shame, the other our synn detectes.
[90]
It is a shame for christians to abuse them,
But deadly synne for skorners to refuse them.

[72]   the wise, and welthy F.
[82]   stackly harde. G.

I meane not this all onlye of degrees
Ordeynde by God for peoples preseruacion,
But of hys law, good orders, and decrees,
Prouyded for his creatures conseruacion. [95]
And specially the state of procreacion
Wherin we here the number of them encreace
Which shall in heauen enioye eternall peace.

The only ende why god ordayned thys,
Was for the encreasyng of that blessed number [100]
For whome he hath prepared eternall blysse.
They that refuse it for the care or cumbre
Beyng apt therto, are in a synful slumber:
No fonde respect, no vayne devised vowes
Can quit or bar what God in charge allowes. [105]

It is not good for man to lyve alone
Sayd God: and therfore made he hym a make:
Sole lyfe sayd Chryste is graunted few or none,
All seedsheders are bound lyke wyues to take:
Yet not for lust, for landes, or ryches sake, [110]
But to beget and foster so theyr frute
That heauen and earth be stored with the suite.

But as thys state is damnably refused
Of many apt and able thervnto,
So is it lykewyse wyckedly abused [115]
Of all that vse it as they should not doe:
Wherin are gyltye all the gredy: who
For gayne, for frendshyp, landes or honors wed,
And these pollute the vndefyled bed.

[95] Prouyded for his *is printed* Prouyded his *but is corrected in Be.* Prouided
    his *C–F.*
[96] specially *is misprinted* specalliy *in the text.*
[109] All seedsheders *is printed* Allseed sheders *but is corrected in Be.* like wife
    to *F.*
[113] damnable *F.*

[120] And therfor god through iustice can not ceas
To plage these faultes with sundry sortes of whips:
As disagrement, healthes or wealthes decreas,
Or lothyng sore the neuer lyked lyppes.
Disdayne also with rygor sumtyme nips
[125] Presumyng mates, vnequally that matche:
Sum bytter leauen soures the musty batche.

We worldly folke account hym very wyse
That hath the wyt moste wealthily to wed.
By all meanes therfor alwayes we devyse
[130] To see our issue ryche in spousals sped.
We buy and sell rych orphans: babes skant bred
Must mary ere they know what maryage meanes,
Boyes mary old trots, old fooles wed yong queanes.

We call thys weddyng, which in any wyse
[135] Can be no maryage, but pollucion playne.
A new found trade of humane marchandyse,
The devyls net, a fylthy fleshly gayne:
Of kynde and nature an vnnaturall stayne,
A fowle abuse of gods most holy order,
[140] And yet allowed almost in every border.

Would god I were the last that shall haue cause
Agaynst thys crepyng cancar to complayne,
That men would so regarde theyr makers lawes,
That all would leaue the lewdnes of theyr brayne,
[145] That holly orders, holly myght remayne.
That our respectes in weddyng should not choke
The ende and frute of gods most holy yoke.

The sage kyng Solon after that he sawe,
What myschiefes folow missought maryages,
[150] To bar all baytes, establyshed thys lawe.
No frende nor father shall gyue herytages,

Coyne, catall, stuffe, or other caryages
With any mayd for dowry or weddyng sale,
By any meane, on payne of bannyng bale.

Had thys good law in England bene in force   [155]
My father had not so cruelly been slayne.
My brother had not causeles lost hys corps.
Our maryage had not bred vs such disdayne,
My selfe had lackt great part of grevous payne,
We wedded wyves for dignitie and landes,   [160]
And left our lyves in envyes bluddy handes.

My father hyght Syr Richard Wudvyle: he
Espoused the duches of Bedford, and by her
Had issue males my brother Iohn, and me
Called Anthony. Kyng Edward dyd preferre   [165]
Vs far aboue the state wherein we were.
For he espoused our syster Elizabeth,
Whom Syr Iohn Gray made wedow by his deth.

How glad wer we, thinke you of this alyaunce?
So nerely coupled with so noble a kyng.   [170]
Who durst with any of vs be at defyauns
Thus made of myght the myghtyest to wryng?
But fye, what cares do hyghest honours bryng,
What carelessenes our selves or frendes to know,
What spyte and envye both of high and lowe.   [175]

Becaus the kyng had made our sister Queene
It was his honor to prefer her kyn.
And syth the readyest way, as wysest ween,
Was first by weddyng welthy heyres to wyn,
It pleased the prynce by lyke meane to begyn.   [180]

[161]   in enmies bloudy *F.*
[171]   vs bene at *F.*
[180]   prince in like *F.*

To me he gaue the rych lord Skales hys heir,
A vertuous mayd, in myne eye very fayre.

He ioyned to my brother Iohn, the olde
Duches of Norfolke, notable of fame.
[185] My nephue Thomas (who had in hys holde
The honor and rightes of Marquis Dorcets name)
Espoused Cicilie a ryght wealthy Dame,
Lorde Bonuyles heyr: by whom he was possest
In al the rites wherthrough that house was blest.

[190] The honors that my father attaynde were dyuers
Fyrst Chamberlayn, than Constable he was.
I do omyt the gainfullest, Erle Ryvers.
Thus glystred we in glory clere as glas.
Such myracles can prynces bryng to passe
[195] Among theyr lieges whom they mynde to heave
To honors false, who all theyr gestes deceyve.

Honors are lyke that cruel kyng of Thrace,
With newcum gestes that fed his hungry horses.
Or lyke the tyrant Busiris: whose grace
[200] Offered hys gods all straungers strangled corses.
To forreyners so hard false honors force is
That all her bourders straungers eyther geastes
She spoyles to feede her gods & gredy beastes.

Her Gods be those whome God by law or lot,
[205] Or kynde by byrthe, doth place in highest rowmes.
Her beastes be such as gredilye haue got
Office or charge to gyde the sely growmes.
These officers in lawe or charge are browmes,

[182] in my minde G.
[186] right C–G.
[193] wee to glory G.
[202] her bourdens, F.

That swepe away the sweet from symple wretches,
And spoyle the enryched by their crafty fetches. [210]

   These plucke downe those whom princes set aloft,
By wrestyng lawes, and false conspyracyes:
Yea kynges them selues by these are spoyled oft.
Whan wylfull prynces carelesly despyse
To hear the oppressed peoples heavy cryes, [215]
Nor wyll correct theyr pollyng theues, than God
Doeth make those Reues the retchles princes rod.

   The seconde Richard is a proofe of thys
Whom crafty Lawyers by theyr lawes deposed.
An other paterne good kyng Henry is [220]
Whose ryght by them hath dyversly been glosed,
Good whyle he grew, bad whan he was vnrosed.
And as they foaded these and dyuers other
With lyke deceyt they vsed the kyng my brother.

   Whyle he prevayled they said he owed the crown, [225]
All Lawes and ryghtes agreed with the same:
But whan by dryftes he seemed to be downe,
All lawes and ryght extremely dyd him blame
Nought saue vsurpyng traytor was hys name.
So constantly the Iudges construe lawes, [230]
That all agree styll with the stronger cause.

   These as I sayd, and other lyke in charge
Are honors horses whom she feedes with gestes.
For all whome princes frankly do enlarge
With dignities, these bark at in theyr brestes: [235]
Theyr spite, theyr myght, their falshod neuer rests
Tyll they devour them: sparyng neyther blud,
Ne Lym nor Lyfe, and all to get theyr good.

[221]   them haue diuersly F.
[223]   they foadred these C–G. [F reads the for they]
[238]   lim ne life, C–G.

[240]
The Earle of Warwyck was a praunsyng courser
That hauty hart of hys could beare no mate:
Our welth through him waxt many a time the wurser
So cancardlye he had our kyn in hate.
He troubled oft the kynges vnstedy state
And that becaus he would not be hys warde
[245]
To wed and wurke, as he shuld lyst awarde.

He spyted vs becaus we were preferred
By maryage to dignytyes so great,
But craftely hys malyce he deferred
Tyll trayterously he found meanes to entreate
[250]
Our brother of Clarens to assyst hys feat:
whome whan he had by maryage to hym bound
Than wrought he strayght our linage to confound.

Through slaunderous brutes he brued many a broil
Through out the realme agaynst the king my brother:
[255]
And raised traiterous rebels thirstyng spoyle
To murder men: of whome among all other
One Robin of Riddesdal many a soul did smother:
His raskall rabble at my father wroth
Took syer and sonne, & quicke beheaded bothe.

[260]
Thys haynous act although the king detested,
Yet was he fayne to pardone: for the rowte
Of Rebels all the realme so sore infested,
That every way assayled, he stoode in doubte:
And though he were of courage high & stoute,
[265]
Yet he assayed by fayre meanes to asswage
His enemyes yre, reveled by rebels rage.

[257]   Robin of Kiddesdale G.
[265]   meane D–F.
[266]   ire, reueild by C–F.

But Warwick was not pacyfyed thus,
Hys constant rancor causeles was extreme.
No meane coulde serve the quarell to discus,
Tyl he had driuen the king out of the realme.   [270]
Neither would he then be waked from his dream.
For whan my brother was cum and placed again,
He stynted not tyll he was stoutly slayne.

Than grew the kyng and realme to quyet rest,
Our stocke and frendes styll flying higher an higher: [275]
The Quene with chyldren frutefully was blest:
I gouerned them, It was the kynges desyer.
This set theyr vncles furyously on fyer,
That we the quenes blud wer assygned to governe
The prynce, not they, the kynges own blud & bretherne. [280]

This caused the duke of Clarens so to chafe
That with the kyng he braynles fell at bate:
The counsayle warely for to kepe hym safe
From raysyng tumultes as he dyd of late,
Imprysoned hym: where through his brothers hate   [285]
He was condempned, and murdered in such sort
As he hym selfe hath truly made report.

Was none abhorred these mischiefes more than I,
Yet coulde I not be therwith discontented,
Consyderyng that hys rancour touched me nye.   [290]
Els would my conscience neuer have consented
To wyshe hym harme, could he have been contented.
But feare of hurt, for safegard of our state
Doth cause more myschiefe than desert or hate.

[269] serue my quarel F.
[271] be awaked from F.
[275] higher and higher: C-G.

[295] Such is the state that many wyshe to beare,
That eyther we must with others blud be stained,
Or leade our lyves contynually in feare.
You mountyng myndes beholde here what is gayned
By combrous honor, paynfully attayned:
[300] A damned soule for murdryng them that hate you,
Or doubtfull lyfe, in daunger lest they mate you.

The cause (I think) why sum of hygh degree
Do deadly hate all sekers to assend,
Is this: The cloyne contented can not be
[305] With any state, tyll tyme he apprehend
The highest top: for therto clymers tende.
Which seeldome is attaynde without the wrack
Of those betwene, that stay and bear hym back.

To save theim selues they therfore are compeld
[310] To hate such clymers, and with wit and power
To compas meanes wherthrough they may be queld,
Ear they ascend theyr honors to devour.
This caused the duke of Clarence frown & lowre
At me and other whom the kyng promoted
[315] To dignities: wherin he madly doted.

For seing we wer his dere alyed frendes,
Our furderauns should rather have made him glad
Than enmye like to wyshe our wofull endes.
We were the nerest kynsfolk that he had.
[320] We ioyed with him, his sorowe made vs sad:
But he estemed so much hys paynted sheath
That he disdayned the love of all beneath.

[320] with him, his sorowe *is printed* withim, hish sorow *but is corrected in Be.*

But see how sharpely god revengeth synne:
As he malygned me and many other
Hys faythfull frendes, and kyndest of hys kyn,   [325]
So Rychard duke of Glocester, hys naturall brother,
Malygned hym: and beastly dyd hym smother.
A divelysh deede, a moste vnkyndly part,
Yet iuste revenge for his vnnaturall hart.

Although this brother queller, Tyraunt fell   [330]
Envyed our state as much and more than he:
Yet dyd hys clokyng flattery so excell
To all our frendesward, chiefly vnto me,
That he appeared our trusty stay to be:
For outwardly he wrought our state to furder,   [335]
Where inwardly he mynded nought save murder.

Thus in aperaunce who but I was blest?
The chiefest honors heaped on my head:
Beloved of all, enioying quyet rest.
The forward prynce by me alone was led,   [340]
A noble ympe, to all good vertues bread:
The Kyng my lyege without my counsayl knowen
Agreed nought: though wysest were his owne.

But quyet blisse in no state lasteth long
Assayled styll by mischefe many wayes: [345]
Whose spoylyng battry glowyng hote and stronge,
No flowyng wealth, no force nor wysdome stayes
Her smoakles poulder beaten souldyers slayes.
By open force foule mischief oft preuayles,
By secrete sleyght, she seeld her purpose fayles.   [350]

[326] his very brother, C–G.

The kyng was bent to much to folysh pleasure,
In banketyng he had to great delyght:
Thys made hym grow in grossnes out of measure,
Which, as it kyndleth carnall appetyte,
[355] So quencheth it the lyvelynes of spryte.
Wherof ensue such sycknes and diseases
As none can cure save death that all displeases.

Through this fault furdered by hys brothers fraude
(Now god forgeve me yf I iudge amys)
[360] Or through that beast hys rybald or hys baude
That larded styll those sinfull lustes of hys,
He sodaynly forsoke all worldly blysse.
That loathed leach, that never wellcum death,
Through spasmous humours stopped vp his breth.

[365] That tyme lay I at Ludloe wales hys border.
For with the prince the kyng had sent me thyther
To stay the robberyes, spoyle, and fowle disorder,
Of dyvers outlawes gathered there together:
Whose bandyng tended no man wyst well whyther.
[370] Whan these by wysdome safely wer suppressed,
Came wofull newes, our soveraygne was deceassed.

The gryefe wherof, whan reason had asswaged,
Becaus the prynce remayned in my guyde,
For hys defende great store of men I waged,
[375] Doubtyng the stormes which at such tymes betyde.
But whyle I there thus warely dyd provyde,
Commaundement came to send them home agayne
And bryng the kyng thence with his householde trayne.

[352] had so great D–G.
[355] of the sprite. CG. of the spirite. D–F.
[372] reason was asswaged, D–F.
[374] his defence D–G.
[375] tyme C–G.

This charge sent from the counsayle and the Queene
Though much agaynst my mynde I beast obeyed: [380]
The devyll hym selfe wrought all the dryft I weene,
Becaus he would have innocentes betrayed:
For ere the kyng wer halfe hys way convayed,
A sorte of traytors falsely hym betrapt
I caught afore, and close in pryson clapt. [385]

The duke of Glocestre that incarned devyll
Confedered with the Duke of Buckyngham,
With eke Lorde Hastynges, hasty both to evyll
To meete the kyng in mournyng habyt came,
(A cruell woulfe though clothed lyke a Lambe) [390]
And at Northhampton, where as than I bayted
They tooke their inne, as they on me had wayted.

The kyng that nyght at Stonystratford lay,
A towne to small to harbar all his trayne:
This was the cause why he was goen awaye [395]
While I with other dyd behynde remayne.
But wyll you see how falsely fyendes can fayne?
Not Synon sly, whose fraude best fame rebukes,
Was halfe so suttle as these double dukes.

Fyrst to myne Inne, cummeth in my brother false [400]
Embraceth me: wel met good brother Skales,
And wepes withall: the other me enhalse
With welcum coosyn, now welcum out of Wales
O happy day, for now all stormy gales
Of stryfe and rancor vtterly are swaged, [405]
And we your owne to Lyve or dye vnwaged.

[386]   that incarnate deuill C–G.
[397]   falsely fyendes *is printed* falsly frendes *but is corrected in* Be. falsely
        frends C–G.
[406]   we your owne *is printed* we our owne *but is corrected in* Be. we our
        own C–G.

Thys profered seruice, saust with salutacions
Immoderate, might cause me to suspect:
For commonly in all dissimulacions
[410] The exces of glaveryng doth the guyle detect.
Reason refuseth falshode to dyrect:
The wyll therfore for feare of being spyed
Excedeth mean, becaus it wanteth gyde.

This is the cause why such as fayne to weepe
[415] Do houle outryght, or waylyng cry ah,
Tearyng them selves, & straynyng syghes moste depe.
Why such dissemblers as would seme to laugh
Breth not Tihhy, but braye out, hah hah hah.
Why beggers faynyng bravery are the proudest
[420] Why cowardes braggyng boldnes, wrangle loudest.

For commonly all that do counterfayte
In any thyng, excede the naturall mean,
And that for feare of faylyng in theyr feat.
But these conspyrers couched all so cleane,
[425] Through close demeanour, that theyr wyles dyd wean
My hart from doubtes, so many a fals device
They forged fresh, to hyde theyr enterprise.

They supped with me, propoundyng frendly talke
Of our affayres, styll gevyng me the prayse.
[430] And ever among the cups to mewarde walke:
I drynk to you good Cuz ech traytor sayes:
Our banquet doen whan they should go theyr wayes
They tooke theyr leave, oft wyshyng me good nyght
As hartily as any creature myght.

[415] cry ah, ah, G.
[427] They *is misprinted* The *in the text and in* C.

A noble hart they say is Lyon lyke,   [435]
It can not couche, dissemble, crouch nor fayne.
Howe villaynous wer these, and how vnlyke?
Of noble stocke the moste ignoble stayne.
Theyr wulvysh hartes, theyr traytrous foxly brayne
Eyther prooue them base, of raskall race engendred   [440]
Or from hault lynage bastardlyke degendred.

Such pollyng heades as prayse for prudent pollicie
False practises, I wysh wer pact on poales.
I meane the bastard law broode, which can mollyfie
All kynd of causes in theyr crafty nolles.   [445]
These vndermyne all vertue, blynde as molles,
They bolster wrong, they rack and strayne the ryght
And prayse for law both malyce fraude, and myght.

These quenche the wurthy flames of noble kynde,
Provokyng best borne to the basest vyces,   [450]
Through craftes they make the bouldest courage blinde,
Dislyking hyghly valeaunt enterpryses:
And praysyng vyly villanous devices.
These make the boare a Hog, the Bul an oxe.
The Swan a Goose, the Lyon a Wulfe or foxe.   [455]

The Lawyer Catesby and hys crafty feeres
A rowte that never did good in any realme,
Are they that had transformed these noble peeres:
They turned theyr blud to melancholick fleume.
Theyr courage hault to cowardyse extreame.   [460]
Theyr force and manhode into fraude and malyce,
Theyr wit to wyles: stout Hector in to Parys.

[439]   *The text prints two commas after* hartes
[440]   Or proue G.
[457]   that nere did G.

These glaverers goen, my selfe to rest I layd,
And doubtyng nothyng, soundly fel a slepe:
[465] But sodaynlye my seruantes sore afrayed
Awaked me: and drawyng sighes full deepe,
Alas (quoth one) my Lord we are betrayed.
How so (quoth I) the dukes are goen theyr wayes
They have barred the gates, and borne away the keyes.

[470] Whyle he thus spake, there came into my mynde
This fearefull dreame, whereout I waked was:
I saw a ryver stopt with stormes of wynde
Wherethrough a Swan, a Bull and Bore dyd passe.
Fraunchyng the fysh and frye, with teeth of brasse,
[475] The ryver dryed vp save a lytell streame
Which at the last dyd water all the realme.

My thought thys streame dyd drown the cruell bore
In lytle space, it grew so depe and brode:
But he had kylled the bull and swan before.
[480] Besydes all this I saw an ougly tode
Crall toward me, on which me thought I trode:
But what became of her, or what of me
My sodayne wakyng would not let me see.

These dremes consydered with this sodayne newes
[485] So dyvers from theyr doynges over nyght,
Dyd cause me not a lyttle for to muse,
I blest me, and ryse in all the hast I myght.
By this, Aurora spred abrode the lyght
Which fro the endes of Phebus beames she tooke
[490] Who than the bulles chiefe gallery forsooke.

[469] Th'haue G.
[476] the reame. G.
[477] Me thought C–G.

When I had opened the wyndow to looke out
There myght I see the streetes eche where beset,
My inne on ech syde compassed about
With armed watchmen, all escapes to let
Thus had these Neroes caught me in theyr net.   [495]
But to what ende, I could not throwly gesse,
Such was my playnnes, such theyr doublenes.

My conscince was so clere I could not doubt
Theyr deadly dryft, which lesse apparaunt lay
Becaus they caused theyr men returne the rout   [500]
That yode toward Stonystratford: as they say
Becaus the dukes wyll fyrst be there to day:
For this (thought I) they hynder me in least,
For gyltles myndes do easely deme the best.

By thys the Dukes were cum into myne inne   [505]
For they were lodged in an other by.
I gote me to them, thinkyng it a synne
Within my chamber cowardly to lye.
And meryly I asked my brother why
He vsed me so? he sterne in evyll sadnes   [510]
Cryed out: I arrest the traytor for thy badnes.

How so (quoth I) whence ryseth your suspicion?
Thou art a traytor (quoth he) I thee arrest.
Arrest (quoth I) why where is your commission?
He drew hys weapon, so dyd all the rest   [515]
Crying: yeld the traytor. I so sore distrest
Made no resystaunce: but was sent to ward
None save theyr seruauntes assygned to my gard.

[493] Inne one each G.
[501] That rode toward G.
[509] And merely C–F.

263

[520] Thys doen they sped them to the kyng in poste,
And after theyr humble reuerence to hym doen,
They trayterously began to rule the roste
They pycked a quarell to my systers sonne
Lord Richard Gray: The king would not be wonne
To agree to them, yet they agaynst all reason,
[525] Arrested hym. (they sayd) for haynous treason.

Syr Thomas Vaughan and Syr Richard Hault
To wurthy knyghtes were lykewyse apprehended,
These all were gylty in one kynde of fault,
They would not lyke the practyse then pretended:
[530] And seyng the kyng was herewith sore offended,
Back to Northhampton they brought him agayne
And thence discharged most part of his trayne.

There loe duke Richard made hym selfe protector
Of kyng and realme by open proclamation,
[535] Though neyther kyng nor Queene were his elector
Thus he presumed by lawles vsurpacion.
But wyll you see his depe dissimulacion?
He sent me a dyshe of deyntyes from his bourd
That day, and with it, this fals frendly wourd.

[540] Commende me to hym: All thynges shalbe well,
I am hys frende, byd hym be of good chere:
These newes I prayed the messanger go tell
My Nephue Richard, whome I loued full deare.
But what he ment by well, now shal you heare:
[545] He thought it well to have vs quickly murdered
Which not long after thorowly he furdered.

[519] sped him to CG.

For strayt from thence we closely wer convayed
For iayle to iayle Northward we wyst not whither:
Where after we had a while in sunder straied,
At last we met at Pomfret all together.   [550]
Syr Richard Ratclyf had vs welcum thither,
Who openly, all law and ryght contempned
Beheaded vs, before we were condempned.

My Cosyn Richard could not be content
To leave his lyfe, becaus he wyst not why,   [555]
Good gentle man that never harme had meant,
Therfore he asked wherfore he shuld dye:
The priest his gostly father dyd replye
With wepyng eyes: I know one wofull cause.
The realme hath neyther ryghteous lordes nor lawes. [560]

Syr Thomas Vaughan chafyng cryed styl:
This tyraunt Glocester is the graceles G
That will his brothers chyldren beastlye kyll.
And least the people through his talke might see
The mischiefes toward, and therto not agree   [565]
Our tormentour that false periured knyght
Bad stop our mouthes, with wurdes of high despyte.

Thus dyed we gyltles, proces heard we none,
No cause alleged, no Iudge, nor yet accuser,
No quest empaneld passed vs vppon.   [570]
That murderer Ratclyf, lawe and ryghtes refuser,
Dyd all to flatter Richard his abuser.
Vnhappy both that ever they were borne,
Through gyltles blud that have theyr soules forlorne.

[549]   Where, after a while wee had in sunder stayed, G.

[575]   In parte I graunt I well deserved thys,
Becaus I caused not spedy execution
Be doen on Richard for that murder of hys,
when fyrst he wrought kyng Henryes close confusion.
Nor for his brothers hatefull persecution.
[580]   These cruell murders paynfull death deserved
Which had he suffred, many had ben preserued.

Warne therfore all that charge or offyce beare
To se all murderers spedely executed:
And spare them not for favoure or for fear:
[585]   By gyltles blud the earth remaynes polluted.
For lack of Iustice kyngdomes are transmuted.
They that save murderers from deserved payne,
Shall through those murderers miserably be slayn.

[579]   Not for C–G.

TO THE READER

WHan I had read this, they liked it very wel. One wished [Prose 20] that the cumbat which he had with the bastard of Burgoine, and the honor which he wan bothe with speare and axe, shuld not be forgotten. An other moued a question about a great matter, and that is the varyaunce of the cronycles about the lord [5] Thomas Graye Marquis Dorcet: whome Fabian every where calleth the Queenes brother. Syr Thomas More and Hall call hym the Queenes sonne. Fabian sayeth he was governour of the prince, and had the conveyaunce of him from Ludlo towardes London. The other (whom we folowe) saye he was than at London with the queen prouydyng for [10] the kynges coronacion, and toke sanctuarye with her as soone as he heard of the apprehending of his vncle. This disagreynge of wryters is a great hinderaunce of the truthe, & no small cumbrauns to such as be diligent readers, besides the harme that may happen in succession of herytages. It were therfore a wurthye and a good dede for the nobilytie, [15] to cause al the recordes to be sought, & a true and perfecte cronicle therout to be wrytten. vnto which we refer the decydyng of this, & of all other lyke controversies, gevyng this to vnderstand in the mean tyme, That no man shall thinke his title eyther better or wurse by any thing that is wrytten in any part of thys treatyse. For the onlye thynge [20] which is purposed herin, is by example of others miseries, to diswade all men from all sinnes and vices. If by the way we touche any thing concernyng titles, we folow therin Halles cronicle. And where we seme to swarve from hys reasons and causes of dyuers doynges, there we gather vpon coniecture such thinges as seeme most probable, or at the least [25] most convenient for the furderaunce of our purpose.

Whan the reader would haue proceded in the cronicle which strayght entreateth of the vilannous destruction of the lord Hastynges, I wylled hym to surceas, becaus I had there his tragedye very learnedly penned. For the better vnderstandyng whereof, you must ymagyne that you [30] see hym newly crept out of his graue, and speakyng to me as followeth.

[2] he fought with C–G.
[8] son as he was in very dede. Fabian C–G.
[30] better *is misprinted* bettr *in the text.*

267

[Tragedy 21]

Howe the Lord Hastynges was betrayed by trustyng to much to his evyl counsayler Catesby, and vilanously murdered in the tower of London by Richarde Duke of Glocestre.

Hastynges I am, whose hastned death whoe knewe,
My lyfe with prayse, my death with plaint pursue.
With others, fearyng least my headlesse name
Be wrongd, by partiall bruite of flatteryng fame:

[5] Cleaving my tombe the waye my fame forewent,
Though bared of loanes which body & Fortune lent
Erst my proud vaunt: present present to thee
My honoure, fall, and forced destenye.

Ne feare to stayn thy credyt by my tale.

[10] In *Laethes* floud, long since, in Stigian vale
Selfe love I dreynt. what tyme hath fyned for true,
And ceasseth not, (though stale) styll to renewe:
Recount I wyl. wherof be this the proofe.
That blase I wyll my prayse, and my reproofe.

[15] We naked ghostes are but the verye man.
Ne of our selves more than we ought we skanne.

[Title] Glocester. the 13. of Iune. Anno. 1483. *C–G.*
[1–2]   I am that Hastings whose to hastye death,
         They blame that know wherefore I lost my breath. *D–F.*
[5–8]   Hearing O Baldwin that thou meanst to penne,
         The liues and falls of English noble men.
         My selfe here present do present to thee
         My life, my fall, and forced destenye. *D–F.*
[6]   of loyns which *C.*
[11]   I drownd. *D–F.*
[13]   whereof take this for proofe. *D–F.*

But doubte distracteth me, yf I should consent
To yeelde myne honourd name a martyrd Saynt.
Yf Martirdome rest in the mysers lyfe
Through tormentes wrongly reft by fatall knyfe: [20]
Howe fortunes Nurslyng I, and dearest babe,
Ought therto stoope, none maye me well perswade.
For howe maye myser martyrdome betyde,
To whome in Cradell Fortune was affyed?

Sée howe this grossest aier infecteth me since,   [25]
Forgot have I, of foyaltye to my prynce.
My happye meede is, Martir to be named?
And what the heavens embrace, the world aye blamed:
For, mens vniustyce wreaked but Gods iust Ire,
And by wrong end, turned wreake to Iustice hyre.   [30]
O Iudgmentes iust, by vniustice iustice dealt,
Whoe dowteth, of me may learne, the truth who felt.

So therfore, as my fall may many staye:
Aswell the prynce, from violent headlong swaie,
Of noble peeres, from honours throne to dust,   [35]
As nobles lesse in tyckle state to trust:
Shonning those synnes, that shake the golden leaves
Perforce from boughes, eare Nature bare the greaves:
So, what my lyfe professed, my death heare teacheth.
And, as with word so with example preacheth.   [40]

The hyllye heauens, and valey Earthe belowe,
Yet ryng hys Fame, whose dedes so great dyd grow.

[17–40]   *Omitted D–F.*
[20]   wrongly left by *G.*
[26]   of loyalty to *CG.*
[32]   Who douts of *CG.*
[36]   tyckle *is printed* title *but is corrected in* Be. title *C.* titles *G.*
[41]   The heauens hye, and earthly vale belowe, *D–F.*

Edward the fourth ye know vnnamed I meane.
Whose noble nature so to me dyd leane,
[45] That I hys staffe was, I his only ioye,
And even what Pandare was to hym of Troy.
Which moved hym fyrst, to create me chamberlayne.
To serve hys sweetes, to my most sower payne.

Wherein, to iustly praysed for secretnesse
[50] (For now my guylt with shrykyng I confesse)
To hym to true, to vntrue to the Queene,
Suche hate I wanne, as lasted longe betweene
Oure familyes. Shores wyfe was my nyce cheate.
The wholye whore, and eke the wyly peate.
[55] I fedd his lust with lovely peces so,
That Gods sharpe wrath I purchased, my iust woe.

See here of Nobles newe the dyverse source.
Some vertue rayseth, some clyme by sluttyshe sortes.
The fyrst, though onely of them selves begonne,
[60] Yet circlewyse into them selues doe ronne.
With in theyr Fame theyr force vnyted so,
Both endelesse is, and stronger gaynst theyr foe.
For, when endeth hit that neuer hath begonne?
Or by what force, maye circled knot be vndone?

[65] Thother, as by wycked meanes they grewe,
And raygned by flattery or violence: so sone rue.
First tomblyng stepp from honoures old, is vyce.
Which once discended, some lynger, none aryse

[44]   to me so CG.
[54]   holy hore, C–G.
[61]   Within themselues their D–F.
[64]   Or how may that that hath no end, be vndone? D–F.
[68]   once stept downe, D–F. once discend, CG.

To former type. but they catch vertues spraye,
Which mounteth them that clyme by lawfull waye. [70]
Beware to ryse by serving princely lust.
Surely to stand, one meane is rysyng iust.

Which learne by me. whome let it helpe to excuse,
That ruthfull nowe my selfe I do accuse.
And that my prynce I ever pleased with suche, [75]
As harmed none, and hym contented much.
In vyce, som favoure, or lesse hate let wynne,
That I ne wryed to worser end my sinne.
But vsed my favoure to the safetye of such,
As furye of Later warre to lyue dyd grutche. [80]

For as on durt (though durty) shyneth the sonne:
So, even amyds my vyce, my vertue shoane.
My selfe I spared with any his cheate to stayne,
For love and reverence so I could refrayne.
Gisippus wyfe erst Tytus would desyre [85]
With frendshyps breach. I quenchd that brutyshe fyre.
Manly hit is, to loth the fawnyng lust.
Small vaunt to flye, what of constraynt thou must.

These therfore rased, yf thou myne offyce skanne,
Loe none I hurt but furdered every manne. [90]
My chamber England was, my staffe the law:
Wherby sauns rygoure, all I held in awe.
So lovyng to all, so beloued of all,
As, (what ensued vppon my bloudy fall
Though I ne felt) yet surely this I thynke. [95]
Full many a tricklyng teare theyr mouthes did drynke.

[70]   Which rayseth them D–F.
[84]   loue or D–F.
[87]   the pleasing lust. D–F.
[88]   flye, that of D–F.
[89]   These faults except, if so my life thou skan, D–F.

Disdayne not prynces easye accesse, meeke cheare.
We knowe, then Angells statelyer port ye beare
Of God hym selfe: to massye a charge for sprytes.
[100] But then, my lordes, consyder, he delyghts
To vayle his grace to vs poore earthely wants,
To symplest shrubbes, and to the dunghyll plantes.
Expresse hym then, in myght and mercyes meane.
So shall ye wynne, as now ye welld, the realme.

[105] But all to long I feare I do delaye
The many meanes, wherby I dyd bewraye
My zelous wyll, to earne my prynces grace.
Least thou differ, to thynke me kynde percace
As nought may last, so Fortunes weathery cheare
[110] With powtyng lookes gan lower on my Syre,
And on her wheele, advaunsd hye in hys roome
The Warwick Earle, mase of Chrystendoome.

Besydes the temptyng prowesse of the foe,
His traytor brother dyd my prynce forgoe.
[115] The cause was lyked, I was hys lynked alye.
Yet, nor the cause, nor brothers trecherye,
Nor enmyes force, ne band of myngled bloude:
Made Hastynges beare hys prynce other mynd then good.
But tane and scaped from Warwicks gripyng pawes,
[120] With me he fled through fortunes frowardst flawes.

To London come, at large we might have seemed,
Had not we then the realme a pryson deemd.
Ech bush a barre, eche spray a banner splayed,
Eche house a fort our passage to haue stayed.

[104] ye rule the *D–F.*
[109] Fortunes chaunging cheare *D–F.*
[114] My Princes brother did him then forgo. *D–F.*
[117] force, nor bande *D–F.*
[120] frowards *G.*

To Linne we leape, where whyle we awayt the tyde,   [125]
My secrete fryndes in secrete I supplyed,
In mouth to mayntayne Henry syxt theyr kynge,
By deede to devoyre Edward to bryng in.

  The restles tyde, to bare the empty baye,
With waltryng waves roames wamblyng forth. Away   [130]
The mery maryner hayles. The braggyng boye,
To masts hye top vp hyes. In signe of ioye
The wauering flagge is vaunsd. The suttle Seas
Theyr swellyng ceasse: to calmest even peace
Sinkth down theyr pride. with dronkennes gainst al care [135]
The Seamen armed, awayte theyr noble fare.

  On Bord we come. The massye Anchors weyed,
One Englyshe shippe, two Hulkes of Holland, ayde
In suche a pynche. So small tho was the trayne,
Such his constraynt. that nowe, that one with payne   [140]
Commaund he myght, whoe erst mought many moe:
Then brought the ghastlye Greekes to Tenedo.
So nought is ours that we by happe maye lose,
What nearest seems, is farthest of in woes.

  As banished wightes, such ioyes we mought have made. [145]
Easd of aye thretnyng death, that late we dradde.
But once our countreyes syght (not care) exempt,
No harboure shewyng, that mought our feare relent,
No covert cave, No shrubbe to shroud our lyves,
No hollow wodde, no flyght, that oft depryves   [150]
The myghty hys pray, no Sanctuary left
For exyled prynce, that shroudes eche slave from theft:

[125]   wee wayte G.
[131]   mariner sayles. G.
[133]   The surging seas D–F.
[141]   who erst might CG. who late might D–F.
[142]   Then ghastly Greekes erst brought to D–F.

In pryson pent, whose woddye walles to passe
Of no lesse peryll than the dying was:
[155] With the Oceane moated, battered with the waves,
(As chaynd at Oares the wretched Galley slaves,
At mercy sit of Sea and enmyes shott,
And shonne with death what they with flyght may not)
But greenysh waves, and desert lowryng Skyes
[160] All comfort ells forclosed oure exyled eyes:

Loe loe from highest toppe, the Slavyshe boye
Sent vp with syght of land our hertes to ioye:
Descryes at hand whole fleet of easterlynges.
As then whote enmyes of the Britishe kynges.
[165] The mouse may somtyme help the Lyon in nede
The byttle bee once spylt the Aegles breed.
O prynces seke no foes. In your distresse,
The Earth, the seas, conspyre your heavinesse.

Oure foe descryed by flyght we shonne in hast,
[170] And lade with Canvase now the bendyng mast.
The shyppe was rackt to trye her saylyng then,
As Squirells clime the troupes of trusty men.
The stearesman sekes a redier course to ronne,
The souldyer stirres, the gonner hyes to gonne,
[175] The flemynges sweate, the englyshe shyp disdaynes
To wayte behynde to beare the flemynges traynes.

Forth flyeth the bark, as from the vyolent goonne
The pellet pearsth all stayes and stops eft soone.
And swift she swimmeth, as oft in sunny daye
[180] The dolphine fleetes in Seas in mery Maye.

[158] death that they *D–F*.
[159] and heauye lowring *D–F*.
[177] Forth flyes *G*.
[179] swimmeth *is printed* syngeth *but is corrected in Be*. singeth *CG*.
swyndgthe, *D–F*.

274

As we for lyves, so Theasterlynges for gayne,
Thwack on the sayles, and after make amayne.
Though laden they were, and of burthen great:
A Kyng to master yet, what swayne nold sweat?

So myde the vale, the greyhound seyng stert   [185]
His fearfull foe, pursueth. Before she flerteth.
And where she turnth, he turnth her there to beare.
The one pray prycketh, the other safetyes feare.
So were we chased, so fled we afore our foes.
Bett flyght then fyght, in so vneven close.   [190]
I end. Some think perhaps, to long he stayeth
In peryll present sheweng his fixed fayth.

This ventred I, this dread I dyd sustayne,
To trye my truth, my lyfe I dyd disdayne.
But, loe, lyke tryall agaynst his civile foe.   [195]
Faythes worst is tryall, which is reserued to woe.
I passe our scape, and sharpe retournyng home,
Where we were welcumd by our wonted fone.
To batayle mayne discendes the empyres ryght.
At Barnet ioyne the hostes in bloudy fyght.   [200]

There ioynd thre batayles ranged in such arraye,
As mought for terrour Alexander fray.
What should I staye to tell the long discourse?
Whoe wan the pallme? whoe bare away the worse?
Suffyseth to saye by my reserued band,   [205]
Oure enemyes fled, we had the vpper hand.
My Iron armye helld her steady place,
My prynce to shyeld, his feared foe to chace.

[183]   Though heauy they D–F.
[184]   swayne *is printed* Swyne *but is corrected in* Be. Swyne C–G.
[186]   The fearefull hare, D–F.
[189]   wee fore our G.
[195]   tryall gaynst G.

The lyke successe befell me in Tewkesbury field.

[210] My furyous force, there forsd perforce, to yelde
The traytour foe: and render to my kyng
Her onelye sonne, least he more bate myght bryng.
Thus hast thou a mirrour of a subiectes minde,
Suche as perhaps is rare agayne to fynd:

[215] The Carving cuts, that cleave the trusty steele,
My fayth, and due allegiaunce, could not fyle.

But out alas. what prayse maye I recount,
That is not spyced with spott, that doth surmount
My greatest vaunt? For bloudy warr to feete

[220] A Tyger was I, all for peace vnmeete.
A Souldyours handes must oft be dyed with goare,
Least starke with rest, they finewd wax, and hoare.
Peace could I wyn by warr, but peace not vse.
Fewe dayes enioy he, whoe warlyke peace doth choose.

[225] When Crofts a Knyght, presented Henryes heyre
To this our prynce, in furyous mood enquere
Of hym he gan, what folye or phrensye vayne,
With armes forsd hym to invade his realme?
Whome answeryng, that he claymd his fathers ryght:

[230] With Gauntlet smitt, commaunded from hys syght:
Clarence, Glocester, Dorcet, and I Hastyngs slewe.
The guylt whereof we shortly all dyd rue.

Clarence, as Cirus, drownd in bloudlyke wyne.
Dorcett I furthered to his spedy pyne.

[235] Of me, my selfe am speakyng presydent.
Nor easyer fate the brystled boare is lent.

[210]   there for so perforce, C.
[211]   My Princes foe: D–F.
[216]   feele. D–F.
[218]   not staind with D–F.
[219]   bloudy for Warre F.
[228]   With armyes G.

Oure bloudes have payd the vengeaunce of our guylt,
His fryed boanes, shall broyle for bloud he hath spilt.
O waltsome murther, that attaynteth our fame.
O horryble traytours wantyng worthy name.   [240]

Whoe more mischevouslye of all states deserve,
As better they, whoe fyrst dyd such preserve.
Yf those, for gyftes, we recken heavenly wyghtes,
These may we well deeme fends, and dampned sprytes.
And whyle on earth they walke, disguysed devyls,   [245]
Sworne foes of vertue, factours for all evylls.
Whose bloudye hands torment theyr goared hartes.
Through bloudsheds horrour, in soundest slepe he sterts.

O happy world were the Lyons men.
All Lyons should at least be spared then.   [250]
No suerty now, no lastyng league is bloude.
A meacock is, whoe dreadth to see blud shed.
Stale is the paterne, the fact must nedes be ryfe.
Whyle .ii. were armyes .ii., the issues of fyrst wyfe,
With armed Hert and hand, thone bloudy brother,   [255]
With cruell chase pursueth and murdreth thother.

Which whoe defyeth not? yet whoe ceasseth to sue?
The bloudy Caynes theyr bloudy Syre renew.
The horrour yet is lyke in common frayes.
For in eche murther, brother brother slayes.   [260]

[238]   he spilt. G.
[239]   attaynts G.
[241–42]   Who as mischieuously of all men deserue,
            As they merite well who do mens liues preserue. D–F.
[242]   who such did first preserue. CG.
[243]   those, therefore we D–F.
[252]   is he, who D–F.
[253]   Old is the practise of such bloudy strife, D–F.
[257]   who abhorreth not? D–F.

Traytours to nature, Countrey, kinne and kynde.
Whome no bande serveth in brothers zeale to bynd.
O symple age, when slaunder slaughter was.
The tonges small evyll, how doth this mischefe passe?

[265]   Hopest thou to cloake thy covert mischief wrought?
Thy conscience, Caytyf, shall proclayme thy thought.
A vysyon, Chaucer sheweth, discloasd thy cryme.
The Fox descrye the crowes and chatteryng Pyen.
And shall thy felow felons, not bewraye
[270]   The guiltlesse death, whome guilty hands doe slaye?
Vnpunished scaped for haynous cryme some one,
But vnadvenged, in mynde or bodye, none.

    Vengeaunce on mynd, the freatyng furyes take.
The synnefull coarse, lyke earthquake agewes shake.
[275]   Theyr frownyng lookes, their frounced mindes bewray.
In hast they runne, and mids theyr race they staye,
As gydded roe. Amyds theyr speache they whist,
At meate they muse. No where they may persyst
But some feare netleth them. Aye hang they so.
[280]   So never wanteth the wicked murtherer woe.

    An infant rent with lyons ramping pawes?
Whye slaunder I Lyons? They feare the sacred lawes
Of prynces bloud. Aye me, more brute than beast,
Wyth princes sydes, (Licaons pye) to feast?

[262]	no bond G. brothers loue to D–F.
[265]	cloake couert thy mischief CG.
[267]	difeldasd thy C. discloase thy G.
[273]	on my mynde, CG.
[274]	sinnefull corps, D–F.
[275]	their troubled minds D–F.
[280]	wants G.
[283]	Of royall bloud. D–F.
[284]	With enfants sides, D–F.

O Tyrant Tygres, O insatiable wolues,   [285]
O Englishe curtesye, monstrous mawes and gulfes.
My death shall forthwith preach my earned meede.
Yf fyrst to one lyke murther I procede.

Whyle Edward lyued, dissembled discord lurked:
In double hertes yet so his reuerence workd.   [290]
But when succedyng tender feble age,
Gave open gap to tyrants rushing rage:
I holpe the Boare, and Buck, to captyuate
Lord Rivers, Graye, Sir Thomas Vaughan and Hawte.
Yf land would hellp the Sea, well earnd that ground   [295]
Hit selfe, to be wyth Conqueryng waves surround.

Theyr spedy death by pryvy dome procured,
At Pomfret: tho my lyfe short whyle endured.
My selfe I slew, when them I damned to death.
At once my throate I ryved, and reft them breth.   [300]
For that selfe day, afore or neare the hower
That wythered Atropos nippd the spryngyng flower
With vyolent hand, of theyr foorth runnyng lyfe:
My head and body, in Tower twynd lyke knyfe.

[285]   insaciate D–F.
Insert between 286 *and* 287:
            Onely because our Prince displeasde we sawe
            With him, we slue him straight before all lawe.
                Before our Prince commaunded once his death,
            Our bloudy swords on him we did vnsheath.
            Preuenting law, and euen our Princes hest,
            Wee hid our weapons in the yonglings brest.
            Whom not desire of reigne did driue to field,
            But mothers pride, who longd the Realme to weld. D–F.
[287]   But straight my death shall shewe my worthy meede, D–F.
[288]   one another murther D–F.
[301]   day, before D–F.
[302]   nipt that springing CG.

[305] By this my paterne, all ye peeres beware.
Oft hangeth he hym selfe, whoe others weenth to snare,
Spare to be eche others butcher. Feare the kyte,
Whoe soareth aloft, whyle frogge and mouse do fyght
In civill Combatt, grapplyng voyd of feare
[310] Of foreyn foe. at once all both to beare.
Which playner by my pytied playnt to see,
A whyle anew your listnyng lend to me.

To true it is .ii. sondry assemblies kept,
At Crossbyes place, and Baynardes castell sett.
[315] The Dukes at Crossebyes, but at Baynards we.
The one to crown a kyng, the other to be.
Suspicious is secession of foule frends,
When eythers dryft to others myschefe tendes.
I feared the end. My Catesbyes beyng there
[320] Discharged all dowtes. Hym held I most entyre.

Whose great preferment by my meanes, I thought
Some spurre, to paye the thankfullnesse he ought.
The trust he ought me, made me trust him so:
That priuye he was bothe to my weale and woe.
[325] My harts one halfe, my chest of confydence,
My tresures trust, my ioye dwelt in his presence.
I loved hym Baldwyn, as the apple of myne eye.
I lothed my lyfe when Catesby would me dye.

Flye from thy chanell Thames, forsake thy streames,
[330] Leve the Adamant Iron, Phebus lay thy beames:
Ceasse heauenly Sphears at last your weary warke,
Betray your charge, returne to Chaos darke.

[318]   to thothers D–F.
[326]   Mine onely trust, D–F.
[330]   lay the beames: CG.

At least, some rutheles Tyger hange her whellpe,
My Catesby so with some excuse to hellp.
And me to comfort, that I aloane, ne seeme   [335]
Of all dame natures workes, left in extreme.

A Golden treasure is the tryed frend.
But whoe may gold from counterfaytes defend?
Trust not to sone, ne all to lyght mistrust.
With thone thy selfe, with thother thy frend thou hurtst. [340]
Whoe twyneth betwyxt, and steareth the golden meane,
Nor rashely loveth, nor mistrusteth in vayne.
For frendshyp poyson, for safetye mithridate
Hit is, thy frend to love as thou wouldest hate.

Of tyckle credyte ne had ben the mischiefe,   [345]
What needed Virbius miracle doubled lyfe?
Credulytye surnamed first the Aegean seas.
Mistrust, doth trayson in the trustyest rayse.
Suspicious Romulus, staynd his walls fyrst reard
With Brothers bloud, whome for lyght leape he feared.   [350]
So not in brotherhode ielousye may be borne,
The ialous cuckold weares the infamous horne.

A beast may preach by tryal, not foresyght.
Could I have shonnd this credyte, nere had lyght
The dreaded death, vpon my guylty head.   [355]
But fooles aye wont to learne by after reade.

[334]   Catesbies C.
[336]   workes least in C.
[339]   so soone, C. soone, nor yet to soone mistrust. D–F.
[343–44] In frendship soueraigne it is as mithridate
         Thy frend to loue as one whome thou mayst hate. D–F.
[354]   shond light credit, D–F.

Had Catesby kept vnstaynd, the truth he plyght,
Yet had ye enioyed me, and I yet the lyght.
All Derbyes doutes I cleared with his name.
[360] I knewe, no harme could happ vs, sauns hys blame.

But see the fruites of fickle lyght belief.
The Ambitious dukes corrupt the traytour theef,
To groape me, yf allured I would assent,
To bin a partner of theyr cursd entent.
[365] Wherto, when neyther force nor frendshyp vayld,
By tyraunt force theyr purpose they assailed.
And summond shortly a councell in the tower,
Of Iune the fyftenth, at apoynted hower.

Alas. are counsels wryed to catch the goode?
[370] Is no place now exempt from sheadyng bloud.
Sith counsells, that were carefull to preserve
The guyltlesse good, are meanes to make them starve.
What may not mischief of mad man abuse?
Religions cloake some one to vyce doth chuse,
[375] And maketh god protectour of his cryme.
O monstrous world, well ought we wyshe thy fine.

The fatall skyes, roll on the blackest daye,
When doubled bloudshed, my bloud must repay.
Others none forceth. To me, Syr Thomas Haward
[380] As spurre is buckled, to prouoke me forward.

[357]   kept vnstain, C.
[360]   hap me without his D–F.
[361]   of tickle light D–F.
[365]   Wherto, when as by no meanes frendship D–F.
[366]   force behold they me assailde. D–F.
[370]   No place is now exempt D–F.
[378]   must my bloud repay. G.

Darbie whoe feared the parted syttynges yore.
Whether, much more he knew by experyence hoare,
Or vnaffected, Clearer truth could see:
At midnight darke this message sendes to me.

Hastynges away. in slepe the Gods foreshew   [385]
By dreadfull dreame, fell fates vnto vs two.
Me thought a Boare with tuske so rased our throate,
That both our shoulders of the bloud dyd smoake.
Aryse to horse, strayght homewarde let vs hye.
And syth our foe we may not mate, o flye.   [390]
Of Chaunteclere you learne dreames sooth to know.
Thence wysemen conster, more then the Cock doth crow.

While thus he spake, I held within myne arme
Shores wyfe, the tender peece, to kepe me warme.
Fye on adultery, fye on lecherous lust.   [395]
Marke in me ye nobles all, Gods iudgmentes iust.
A Pandare, murtherer, and Adulterer thus,
Onely such death I dye, as I ne blushe.
Now, least my Dame mought feare appall my hart:
With eger moode vp in my bed I steart.   [400]

And, is thy Lord (quoth I) a sorcerer?
A wyse man now becumme? a dreame reader?
What though so Chaunteclere crowed? I reke it not.
On my part pledeth as well dame Partelott.
Uniudgd hangth yet the case betwixt them twaye,   [405]
Ne was his dreame Cause of hys hap I saye.

[381]   the party sittings *CG*.
[383]   Or better mynded, clearlyer truthe *D–F*.
[390]   we can not matche, *D–F*.
[399]   dame mought thinke appalld my *D–F*.
[403]   I reck it *D–F*.
[405]   Vniudge *F*.

Shall dremyng doutes from prynce my seruyce slacke?
Naye, then mought Hastynges lyfe and lyvyng lacke.

He parteth. I sleepe. my mynde surcharged with synne,
As Phebus beames by mysty clowde kept in,
Ne could missegeve, ne dreame of my mysse happe.
As block I tumbled to myne enemyes trappe.
Securitye causelesse through my carelesse frende,
Reft me foresyght of my approchyng end.
So Catesby clawed me, as when the Catt doth playe
Dalieng with mouse, whom straight he mindes to slaye.

The morow come, the latest lyght to me,
On Palfray mounted, to the Tower I hye.
Accompanyed with that Haward my mortall foe,
To slaughter led. thou God wouldest have yt so.
(O depe dissemblers, Honouryng with your cheare,
Whome in hydd hart ye trayterouslye teare.)
Never had realme so open signes of wrack.
As I had shewed me of my heavy happ.

The vysyon fyrst of Stanley, late descryed.
Then myrth so extreme, that neare for ioye I dyed.
Were hit, that Swannelyke I foresong my death,
Or merye mynde foresaw the loose of breath
That long it coueyted, from thys earthes annoye.
But even as syker as thende of woe is ioye,
And gloryous lyght to obscure night doth tend:
So extreame myrth in extreame moane doth ende.

[410]
[415]
[420]
[425]
[430]

[407]   my seruing slacke? D–G.
[413]   my fayned frende, D–F.
[416]   straight she myndes to CG. straight she meanes to D–F.
[420]   God didst suffer so. D–F.
[427]   foresong is printed forefong but is corrected in Be.

For whye, extreames are happs rackd out of course.
By vyolent myght far swinged forth perforce.
Which as thei are pearcingst while they violentst move,   [435]
For nearst they cleave to cause that doth them shove:
So soonest fall from that theyr hyghest extreame,
To thother contrary that doth want of meane.
So lawghed he erst, whoe lawghed out his breath.
So laughed I, whan I laughd my selfe to death.   [440]

   The pleasyngst meanes boade not the luckiest endes.
Not aye, found treasure to lyke plesure tendes.
Mirth meanes not myrth all tyme. thryse happy hyre
Of wyt, to shonne the excesse that all desyer.
But this I passe. I hye to other lyke.   [445]
My palfrey in the playnest paved streete,
Thryse bowed his boanes, thryse kneled on the flower,
Thryse shonnd (as Balams asse) the dreaded tower.

   What? shoulde I thynke he had sence of after happs?
As beastes forshew the drought or rayny drapps,   [450]
As humoures in them want or ells abound,
By influence from the heavens, or chaunge of grounde?
Or doe we enterprete by successe eche sygne?
And as we fansye of ech happ devyne?
And make that cause, that kynne is to theffect?   [455]
Not havyng ought of consequence respect?

   Bucephalus kneeling onely to his lorde,
Shewed onely, he was, monarche of the world.
Whye maye not then, the steede foreshew by fall,
What Casuall happ the sitter happen shall?   [460]
Darius horse by brayeng brought a realme.
And what letteth, why he ne is (as the Asse) Gods meane,
By speakyng sygne, to shew his hap to come,
Whoe is deaf hearer of his speakyng domme?

[436]   For that they are neare to cause *D–F*.

[465]   But forward yet. In tower streete I stayed.
Where (could I have seene) loe Haward al bewrayde.
For as I commond with a pryest I mett:
Away my lord quoth he. your tyme ne is yet
To take a pryest. Loe, Synon myght be seene,
[470]   Had Troyans eares, as they had hares foole eyen.
But, whome thou God allotted hast to dye
Some grace it is to dye with wympled eye.

       Ne was this all. For even at Towerwharfe,
Neare to those walles within whose syght I starfe,
[475]   Where erst, in sorowe sowst and depe distresse,
I emparted all my pynyng pensyfnesse
With Hastynges: (so my pursevaunt men call)
Even there, the same to meete hit did me fall.
Who gan to me most dolefully renewe,
[480]   The wofull conference had erst in that Lieu.

       Hastinges (quoth I) accordyng now they fare,
At Pomfret this daye dyeng, whoe caused that care.
My self have all the world now at my will,
With pleasures cloyed, engorged with the fyll.
[485]   God graunt it so quoth he whye doutest thou tho
Quoth I? and all in chafe, to hym gan shewe
In ample wyse, our drift with tedious tale.
And entred so the tower to my bale.

[468]   time is ne yet *FG.*
[470]   they haue hares foule eyen. *G.*
[470–71] Had not the Troyans hares foolishe forthright eyen,
         But since the time was come that I should dye, *D–F.*
[472]   it was to *D–F.*
[474]   within the which I *D–F.*
[481]   now thy fare, *CG.*
[483]   world now at my wyl, *is printed* worlde at my will, *but is corrected*
        in Be. world at my *C–G.*

What should we thinke of sygnes? They are but happs.
How maye they then, be sygnes of afterclaps?　　　　　[490]
Doth every Chaunce forshew or cause some other?
Or endyng at it selfe, extendth no furder?
As thoverflowyng floude some mount doth choake,
But to his ayde some other floud hit yoake:
So, yf with sygnes thy synnes once ioyne, beware.　　[495]
Els wherto chaunces tend, nere curyous care.

Had not my synne deserued my death as wreake,
What myght my myrth have hurt? or horses becke?
Or Hawardes bitter scoffe? or Hastinges talke?
What meane then foole Astrologers to calke,　　　　　[500]
That twyncklyng sterres flyng downe the fixed fate?
And all is guyded by the sterrye state?
Perdye, a certayne taxe assygnd they have
To shyne, and tymes divyde, not fate to grave.

But graunt they somwhat gyve: is at one instant　　　[505]
Of every babe the byrth in heauen so skannd,
That they that restlesse roll, and never staye,
Should in his lyfe beare yet so vyolent swaye:
That, not his actions onely next to byrth,
But even last fyne, and death be sweyed therwith?　　[510]
Howe may one mocion make so sundry effectes?
Or one impression tend to such respectes?

Some rule there is yet. Els, whye were differrd
Tyll nowe, these plages, so long ere now deserved?
Yf for they are tryfles, they ne seeme of care:　　　[515]
But toyes with god the statelyest scepters are.

[492]　　Or tending at *CG*.
[496]　　tend, doe neuer care. *D–F*.
[501–724] *Omitted CG.*
[503]　　certaine charge assignd *D–F.*
[505]　　geue it at *F.*
[510]　　But all his life, and *D–F.*

Yet in them to playne, doth appere foresett,
The certayne rule and fatall lymytes sett.
Yet thinke we not, this sure foresettyng fate.
[520] But Gods fast prouydence for eche pryncely state.

And hath he erst restraynd his provydence?
Or is he nygard of his free dispence?
Or is he vncertayne foresett dryfts to dryue?
That not Dame Chaunce but he all goods may gyve?
[525] A heathen god they hold, whoe fortune keepe,
To deal them happs, whyle god they ween a sleepe.
Mock godds they are, and many Gods induce,
Whoe fortune fayne to father theyr abuse.

Howe so it be, hit mought have warned me.
[530] But, what I could not, that in me see ye.
Whoe runne in race, the honour lyke to wynn,
Whose fayrest forme, nought maye deforme but synne.
Alas, when most I dyd defye all dread,
By syngle heare deaths sworde hong over my head.
[535] For herk the end and lysten now my fall.
This is the last, and this the fruit of all.

To Councell chamber come, awhyle we stayd
For hym, without whom nought was done or sayd.
At last he came, and curteously excused,
[540] For he so long our patience had abused.
And pleasantly began to paynt his cheare,
And sayd. My lord of Elye, would we had here
Some of the strawberyes, whereof you haue stoare.
The last delyghted me as nothyng more.

[540]   That he *D–F.*
[544]   me so as *D–F.*

Would, what so ye wyshe, I mought as well commaund, [545]
My lord (quoth he) as those. And out of hand.
His servant sendth to Elye place for them.
Out goeth from vs the restlesse devyll agayne.
Belyke (I thynk) scarce yet perswaded full,
To worke the mischiefe that thus maddeth his scull.   [550]
At last determynd, of his bloudy thought
And force ordaynd, to worke the wyle he sought:

Frownyng he enters, with so chaunged cheare,
As for myld May had chopped fowle Januere.
And lowryng on me with the goggle eye,   [555]
The whetted tuske, and furrowed forhead hye,
His Crooked shoulder bristellyke set vp,
With frothy Iawes, whose foame he chawed and suppd,
With angry lookes that flamed as the fyer:
Thus gan at last to grunt the grymest syre.   [560]

What earned they, whoe me, the kyngdomes staye,
Contryved have councell, trayterously to slaye?
Abashed all sate. I thought I mought be bolld,
For conscyence cleerenesse, and acquayntaunce olld.
Theyr hyre is playne quoth I. Be death the least,   [565]
To whoe so seekth your grace so to molest.
Withouten staye: the Queene, and the whore shores wyfe,
By witchcraft (quoth he) seeke to wast my lyfe.

Loe here the wythered and bewytched arme,
That thus is spent by those .ii. Sorceresse charme.   [570]
And bared his arme and shewed his swynyshe skynne.
Suche cloakes they vse, that seek to clowd theyr synne.

[545]   so you wyshe, D–F.
[550]   that did madde his D–F. [F mistakenly prints is for his]
[561]   What merite they, who D–F. [For who read whom F.]

But out alas, hit serueth not for the rayne.
To all the howse the coloure was to playne.

[575] Nature had gyven hym many a maymed marke,
And hit amonges, to note her monstrous warke.

My doubtfull hart distracted this replye.
For thone I cared not. Thother nyppd so nye
That whyst I could not. But forthwith brake forth.

[580] Yf so hit be, of death they are doutlesse worth.
Yf, traytour quod he? playest thou with yfs and ands?
Ile on thy body avowe it with these hands.
And therwithall he myghtely bounced the bord.
In rushd hys byll men. one hym selfe bestyrrd.

[585] Layeng at lord Stanley. whose braine he had suerly cleft
Had he not downe beneath the table crept.
But Elye, Yorke, and I, were taken strayght.
Imprysoned they: I should no longar wayt,
But charged was to shryue me, and shyft with hast.

[590] My lord must dyne, and now midday was past.
The boares first dyshe, not the boares head should be.
But Hastynges heade the boaryshe beast would see.

Whye staye I his dyner? vnto the chapell ioyneth
A greenish hyll, that body and sowle oft twyneth.

[595] There on a block my head was stryken of.
Iohn Baptists dishe, for Herode bloudy gnoffe.
Thus lyued I Baldwyn, thus dyed I, thus I fell:
This is the summe. which all at large to tell
Would volumes fyll. whence yet these lessons note

[600] Ye noble lords, to learne and kenne by roate.

By fylthy rysyng feare your names to stayne.
Yf not for vertues love, for dread of payne.

[596] As Baptists head, for *D–F.*

Whome so the myndes vnquyet state vpheaves,
Be hit for love or feare: when fancye reaves
Reason his ryght, by mockyng of the witt: [605]
Yf once the cause of this affection flytt,
Reason preuaylyng on the vnbrydled thought:
Downe tottreth whoe by fansy clombe aloft.

So hath the ryser fowle no staye of fall,
No not of those that raysd hym fyrst of all.   [610]
His surety standes, in maynteynyng the cawse
That heaved him first, which reft by reasons sawes,
Not onelye fallth he to hys former state,
But lyveth for ever in his prynces hate.
And marke my lordes, God for adultery sleaeth   [615]
Though ye it thynk to sweet a synne for death.

Serve truely your prynce and fear no rebells myght,
On princes halves the myghty god doth fyght.
O much more then forsweare a forein foe,
Whoe seeketh your realme and countrey to vndoe.   [620]
Murther detest, have hands vnstaynd with bloude.
Aye with your succour do protect the good.
Chace treason where trust should be. wed to your frend
Youre hart and power, to your lyves last end.

Flye tickle credyte, shonne alyke distrust.   [625]
To true hit is, and credyte it you must:
The Ialous nature wanteth no stormy stryfe,
The symple sowle aye leadeth a sower lyfe.

[605]   Reason hir right, *D–F.*
[608]   Down falth he who *D–F.* clymbe *F.*
[609]   staye from fall, *D–F.*
[617]   feare not rebels *F.*

[630] Beware of flaterers, frends in outward showe.
Best is of such to make thyne open foe.
What all men seek, that all men seek to fayne.
Some such to be, some such to seeme, them payne.

Marke gods iust iudgments, punishyng synne by synne.
And slyppery state wherin aloft we swymme.
[635] The prouerbe, all day vp yf we ne fall,
Agreeth well to vs hye heaued worldlynges all.
From dunghill couche vpsterte, in honours weed
We shyne: whyle fortune false, (whome none erst feed
To stand with staye and forswear ticklnesse:)
[640] Sowseth vs in myre of durtye brittlenesse.

And learne ye prynces by my wronged sprite,
Not to misseconster what is meant aryght.
The whinged wordes to oft preuent the wytt,
When sylence ceassth afore the lypps to sytt.
[645] Alas, what may the wordes yeeld worthy death?
The words worst is, the speakers stynkyng breath.
Words are but wynd. whye cost they then so muche?
The guylty kyck, when they to smartly touche.

Forth irreturnable flyeth the spoken word,
[650] Be hit in scoffe, in earest, or in bourd.
Without returne, and vnreceyued, hit hangs.
And at the takers mercy, or rygour, stands.
Which yf he sowerly wrest with wrathfull cheare,
The shyveryng word turns to the speakers feare.
[655] Yf frendly curtesye do the word resollve,
To the Speakers comfort sweetly hit dissolueth.

[630] make your open D–F.
[637] couche, vpsterte in B². From commen sort vpraisd, in D–F.
[655] word expounde, D–F.
[656] it doth redounde. D–F.

Even as the vapour which the fyer repells,
Turns not to earth, but in mydd aer dwells.
Where whyle it hangth, yf Boreas frosty flawes
With rygour rattle yt: not to rayne it thawes,　　　　[660]
But thonder, lyghtnynges, rattlyng hayle and snow
Sends downe to earth, whence first hit rose below.
But yf fayre phebus with his countenaunce sweete
Resolue it, downe the dewe, or Manna fleeteth.

The Manna dew, that in the easterne lands,　　　　[665]
Excellth the laboure of the bees small hands.
Els for her Memnon gray, Auroras teares,
On the earth hit stylleth, the partner of her feares.
Or sendeth sweete showers to gladd theyr mother earth,
Whence fyrst they tooke theyr fyrst inconstant byrth.　　[670]
To so great gryefes, ill taken wynd doth grow.
Of words well taken, such delyghtes do flowe.

This learned, thus be here at length an end.
What synce ensued, to the I wyll commend.
Now farewell Baldwyn, shyeld my torne name,　　　　[675]
From sclaunderous trompe of blastyng black defame.
But ere I part, hereof thou record beare.
I clayme no part of vertues reckned here.
My vyce my selfe, but god my vertues take.
So hence depart I, as I entred, naked.　　　　[680]

Thus ended Hastynges both his lyfe and tale,
Contaynyng all his blysse, and worldes bale.
Happye he lyved, to happye but for synne,
Happye he dyed whome ryght hys death dyd bryng.

[661]　　hayle or snow D–F.
[664]　　sleete. F.
[671]　　ill taken woordes do grow. D–F.
[682]　　his worldly blisse and bale. D–F.

[685]   Thus ever happy. For there rests no meane
Twyse blyssefull lyfes and balefull deathes extreame.
Yet feared not his foes to head his name.
And by these sclaunders to procure hys shame.

    In rousty armure as in extreame shyft,
[690]   They cladd them selues, to cloake theyr diuelysh dryft.
And forthwith for substancyall cytezyns sent,
·Declaryng to them, Hastynges forged entent
Was to haue slayne the duke: and to haue seysed
The kyngs yonge person, slayeng whom he had pleasd.
[695]   But god of Iustyce had withturnd that fate,
Which where hit ought, lyght on hys proper pate.

    Then fedd they fame by proclamation spredd,
Nought to forgett, that mought defame hym dead,
Which was so curyous, and so clerkly pennd,
[700]   So long with all: that when some dyd attend
Hys death so yonge: they saw, that longe afore
The Shroud was shaped, then babe to dye was boare.
So wonteth god to blynde the worldly wyse,
That not to see, that all the world espyes.

[705]   One hearyng hit, cryed out. A goodly cast,
And well contryved, fowle cast away for hast.
Wherto another gan in scoffe replye,
Fyrst pennd it was by enspyryng prophecye.
So can god reape vp secrete mischiefes wrought,
[710]   To the confusyon of the workers thought.

[685]   happy *is misprinted* happpy *in the text.* there is no *D–F.*
[686]   Twixt blissefull *D–F.* and mortall deathes *D–F.*
[687]   to staine his *D–F.*
[689]   extreame *is printed* exareame *but is corrected in Be.*
[697]   Then practised they by *D–F.*
[698]   mought *is printed* nought *but is corrected in Be.* nought *D–F.*
[701]   long before *D–F.*

My lords, the tubb, that drownd the Clarence duke,
Dround not his death, ne yet his deathes rebuke.

　Your polytyke secretes gard with trusty loyaltye
So shall they lurk in most assured secretye.
By Hastynges death, and after fame, ye learne,　　　　　[715]
The earth for murther cryeth out vengeaunce sterne.
Flye from his fautes, and spare his quyted fame.
The Eager houndes forbeare theyr slayne game.
Deade, deade. Avaunt Curres from the conquered chase.
Ill mought he lyue who loveth the deade to race.　　　　[720]

　Thus lyued this lord, thus dyed he, thus he slept.
Mids forward race when first to rest he stept,
Envyous death, that bounceth as well with mace
At Caysars courtes, as at the poorest gates:
When nature seemd to slow, by artes sloape meane,　　　[725]
Conueyghd him sooner to his liues extreame.
Happy, in preuenting woes that after happd,
In slomber swete his liuing lightes he lappd.

　Whose thus vntimely death, yf any grieve:
Knowe he, he lived to dye, and dyed to lyue.　　　　　[730]
Vntimely neuer comes the liues last mett.
In Cradle death may rightly clayme his dett.
Strayght after byrth due is the fatall beere.
By deathes permission the aged linger here.
Euen in thy Swathebands out commission goeth　　　　　[735]
To loose thy breath, that yet but yongly bloweth.

[712]　　*The text prints two commas after* death　death, nor *D–F.*
[714]　　secrecie. *D–F.*
[717]　　spare to hurte his fame. *D–F.*
[725]　　by this sloape *D–F.*
[729]　　Whose hasty death, if it doe any grieue: *D–F.*
[732]　　her debt. *G.*
[735]　　in the swathbands *C–G.*

Happy, thrise happy, who so loosth his breath,
As life he gayneth by his liuing death.
As Hastinges here. Whom time and truthe agree,

[740] To engrave by fame in strong eternitie.
Who spareth not spitting, if he spitte but bloud?
Yet this our lord, spared not for others good,
With one swete breath his present death to speake,
Agaynst the vsurpour Boare, that hellyshe freak.

[745] Worthy to liue, who liued not for him selfe
But prised his fame more then this worldly pelfe.
Whose name and line, if any yet preserue,
We wyshe they liue like honour to deserue.
Whether thou seke by Martial prowesse prayse,

[750] Or Pallas pollecie hygh thy name to rayse,
Or trustye seruice iust death to attayne:
Hastinges foreled. Trace here his bloudy trayne.

[738]   That life *D–F*. his godly death. *D–F*.
[741]   not speaking, with danger of his bloud? *D–F*.
[742–44] Yet loe this noble Lord did thinke it good
         To cleare the innocent not to spare to speake,
         Although his shoulders with his bloud should reake. *D–F*.
[745]   lyue, but lyu'd *G*.
[751]   seruice honour to *D–F*.
[752]   Tracke here *D–F*.

WHen I had read this, one sayd it was very darke, and hard [Prose 21] to be vnderstood: excepte it were diligently and very leasurely considered. I like it the better (quoth an other.) For that shal cause it to be the oftener reade, and the better remembred. Considering also that it is written for the learned (for such all Magistrates [5] are or should be) it can not be to hard, so long as it is sound and learnedly wrytten. Then sayd the reader: The next here whom I finde miserable are king Edwards two sonnes, cruelly murdered in the tower of London: Haue you theyr tragedy? No surely (quoth I) The Lord Vaulx vndertooke to penne it, but what he hath done therein I am not [10] certayne, & therfore I let it passe til I knowe farder. I haue here the duke of Buckingham, king Richardes chyefe instrument, wrytten by mayster Thomas Sackuille. Read it we pray you sayd they: with a good wyl (quoth I) but fyrst you shal heare his preface or Induction. Hath he made a preface (quoth one) what meaneth he thereby, seeing none [15] other hath vsed the like order? I wyl tell you the cause thereof (quoth I) which is thys: After that he vnderstoode that some of the counsayle would not suffer the booke to be printed in suche order as we had agreed and determined, he purposed with him selfe to haue gotten at my handes, al the tragedies that were before the duke of Buckinghams, [20] Which he would haue preserued in one volume. And from that time backeward euen to the time of William the conquerour, he determined to continue and perfect all the story him selfe, in such order as Lydgate (folowing Bocchas) had already vsed. And therfore to make a meete

[1–7]   saide the admonition giuen in the history was profitable for the auoyding of the vices conteyned in the sayde historie, and for the imitating of the vertues in the same mentioned and commended. Then *D–F*.
[3]   (saide an other.) *CG*.
[4]   bee oftner *G*.
[9]   (saide I) *C–G*.
[15]   (saide one) *C–G*.
[16–17] (said I) *C–G*.
[19]   purposed to *C–G*.

[25] induction into the matter, he deuised this poesye: which in my iudgement is so wel penned, that I woulde not haue any verse therof left out
of our volume. Nowe that you knowe the cause and meanyng of his
doing, you shal also heare what he hath done. His Induccion beginneth
thus.

The Induction.

THe wrathfull winter prochinge on a pace,
With blustring blastes had al ybared the treen,
And olde Saturnus with his frosty face
With chilling colde had pearst the tender green:
[5]   The mantels rent, wherein enwrapped been
The gladsom groves that nowe laye ouerthrowen,
The tapets torne, and euery blome downe blowen.

The soyle that earst so seemely was to seen
Was all despoyled of her beauties hewe:
[10] And soot freshe flowers (wherwith the sommers queen
Had clad the earth) now Boreas blastes downe blewe.
And small fowles flocking, in theyr song did rewe
The winters wrath, wherwith eche thing defaste
In woful wise bewayld the sommer past.

[15]   Hawthorne had lost his motley lyverye,
The naked twigges were shivering all for colde:
And dropping downe the teares abundantly,
Eche thing (me thought) with weping eye me tolde
The cruell season, bidding me withholde
[20] My selfe within, for I was gotten out
Into the fieldes where as I walkte about.

[Title] Mayster Sackuilles Induction. *B²*.
[7]   euery tree downe *B²–G*.
[12] fowles *is misprinted* sowles *in B but is corrected in B²; in both issues of B
the change is noted in Be.*
[21] fieldes *is printed* feldes *but is corrected in Be.*

When loe the night with mistie mantels spred
Gan darke the daye, and dim the azure skyes,
And Venus in her message Hermes sped
To bluddy Mars, to wyl him not to ryse,   [25]
While she her selfe approcht in speedy wise:
And Virgo hiding her disdaineful brest
With Thetis nowe had layd her downe to rest.

Whiles Scorpio dreading Sagittarius dart,
Whose bowe prest bent in sight, the string had slypt,   [30]
Downe slyd into the Ocean flud aparte,
The Beare that in the Iryshe seas had dipt
His griesly feete, with spede from thence he whypt:
For Thetis hasting from the Virgines bed,
Pursued the Bear, that ear she came was fled.   [35]

And Phaeton nowe neare reaching to his race
With glistering beames, gold streamynge where they bent,
Was prest to enter in his resting place.
Erythius that in the cart fyrste went
Had euen nowe attaynde his iourneyes stent.   [40]
And fast declining hid away his head,
while Titan couched him in his purple bed.

And pale Cinthea with her borowed light
Beginning to supply her brothers place,
was past the Noonesteede syxe degrees in sight   [45]
when sparklyng starres amyd the heauens face
with twinkling light shoen on the earth apace,
That whyle they brought about the nightes chare,
The darke had dimmed the daye ear I was ware.

[30]   in fight, C–G.
[45]   syxe *is misprinted* syre *in the text.*

[50] And sorowing I to see the sommer flowers,
The liuely greene, the lusty leas forlorne,
The sturdy trees so shattered with the showers,
The fieldes so fade that floorisht so beforne,
It taught me wel all earthly thinges be borne
[55] To dye the death, for nought long time may last.
The sommers beauty yeeldes to winters blast.

Then looking vpward to the heauens leames
with nightes starres thicke powdred euery where,
which erst so glistened with the golden streames
[60] That chearefull Phebus spred downe from his sphere,
Beholding darke oppressing day so neare:
The sodayne sight reduced to my minde,
The sundry chaunges that in earth we fynde.

That musing on this worldly wealth in thought,
[65] which comes and goes more faster than we see
The flyckering flame that with the fyer is wrought,
My busie minde presented vnto me
Such fall of pieres as in this realme had be:
That ofte I wisht some would their woes descryue.
[70] To warne the rest whom fortune left aliue.

And strayt forth stalking with redoubled pace
For that I sawe the night drewe on so fast,
In blacke all clad there fell before my face
A piteous wight, whom woe had al forwaste,
[75] Furth from her iyen the cristall teares outbrast,
And syghing sore her handes she wrong and folde,
Tare al her heare that ruth was to beholde.

[59]   glistred *F.*
[68]   in the realme *C–G.*
[75]   Forth on her eyes the *C–G.* teares foorth brast. *F.*

Her body small forwithered and forespent,
As is the stalke that sommers drought opprest,
Her wealked face with woful teares besprent,　　　　　　　　[80]
Her colour pale, and (as it seemd her best)
In woe and playnt reposed was her rest.
And as the stone that droppes of water weares,
So dented were her cheekes with fall of teares.

Her iyes swollen with flowing streames aflote,　　　　　　[85]
Wherewith her lookes throwen vp full piteouslye,
Her forceles handes together ofte she smote,
With dolefull shrikes, that eckoed in the skye:
Whose playnt such sighes dyd strayt accompany,
That in my doome was neuer man did see　　　　　　　　　[90]
A wight but halfe so woe begon as she.

I stoode agast beholding all her plight,
Tweene dread and dolour so distreynd in hart
That while my heares vpstarted with the sight,
The teares out streamde for sorowe of her smart:　　　　　[95]
But when I sawe no ende that could aparte
The deadly dewle, which she so sore dyd make,
With dolefull voice then thus to her I spake.

Vnwrap thy woes what euer wight thou be
And stint betime to spill thy selfe wyth playnt,　　　　　[100]
Tell what thou art, and whence, for well I see
Thou canst not dure wyth sorowe thus attaynt.
And with that worde of sorrowe all forfaynt
She looked vp, and prostrate as she laye
With piteous sound loe thus she gan to saye.　　　　　　[105]

[81]　　pale, (as it semed C–G.
[100]　stint in tyme C–G.

    Alas, I wretche whom thus thou seest distreyned
With wasting woes that neuer shall aslake,
Sorrowe I am, in endeles tormentes payned,
Among the furies in the infernall lake:
[110] Where Pluto god of Hel so griesly blacke
Doth holde his throne, and *Letheus* deadly taste
Doth rieue remembraunce of eche thyng forepast.

    Whence come I am, the drery destinie
And luckeles lot for to bemone of those,
[115] Whom Fortune in this maze of miserie
Of wretched chaunce most wofull myrrours chose
That when thou seest how lightly they did lose
Theyr pompe, theyr power, & that they thought most sure,
Thou mayest soone deeme no earthly ioye may dure.

[120]   Whose rufull voyce no sooner had out brayed
Those wofull wordes, wherewith she sorrowed so,
But out alas she shryght and never stayed,
Fell downe, and all to dasht her selfe for woe.
The colde pale dread my lyms gan overgo,
[125] And I so sorrowed at her sorowes eft,
That what with griefe and feare my wittes were reft.

    I strecht my selfe, and strayt my hart reuiues,
That dread and dolour erst did so appale,
Lyke him that with the feruent feuer stryves
[130] When sickenes seekes his castell health to skale:
With gathered spirites so forst I feare to auale.
And rearing her with anguishe all fordone,
My spirits returnd, and then I thus begonne.

[114]   bemoane al those *F.*
[117]   That thou *F.*

O Sorrowe, alas, sith Sorrowe is thy name,
And that to thee this drere doth well pertayne,   [135]
In vayne it were to seeke to ceas the same:
But as a man hym selfe with sorrowe slayne,
So I alas do comfort thee in payne,
That here in sorrowe art forsonke so depe
That at thy sight I can but sigh and wepe.   [140]

   I had no sooner spoken of a syke
But that the storme so rumbled in her brest,
As Eolus could neuer roare the like,
And showers downe rayned from her iyen so fast,
That all bedreynt the place, till at the last   [145]
Well eased they the dolour of her minde,
As rage of rayne doth swage the stormy wynde.

   For furth she paced in her fearfull tale:
Cum, cum, (quod she) and see what I shall shewe,
Cum heare the playning, and the bytter bale   [150]
Of worthy men, by Fortune ouerthrowe.
Cum thou and see them rewing al in rowe.
They were but shades that erst in minde thou rolde.
Cum, cum with me, thine iyes shall them beholde.

   What could these wordes but make me more agast? [155]
To heare her tell whereon I musde while eare?
So was I mazed therewyth, tyll at the last,
Musing vpon her wurdes, and what they were,
All sodaynly well lessoned was my feare:
For to my minde returned howe she telde   [160]
Both what she was, and where her wun she helde.

[141]   syke *is printed* stike *but is corrected in* Be. stike C–G.
[144]   eies C–G.
[151]   Fortunes G.

Whereby I knewe that she a Goddesse was,
And therewithall resorted to my minde
My thought, that late presented me the glas
[165] Of brittle state, of cares that here we finde,
Of thousand woes to silly men assynde:
And howe she nowe byd me come and beholde,
To see with iye that erst in thought I rolde.

Flat downe I fell, and with al reuerence
[170] Adored her, perceyuing nowe that she
A Goddesse sent by godly prouidence,
In earthly shape thus showed her selfe to me,
To wayle and rue this worldes vncertayntye:
And while I honourd thus her godheds might,
[175] With playning voyce these wurdes to me she shryght.

I shal the guyde first to the griesly lake,
And thence vnto the blisfull place of rest.
Where thou shalt see and heare the playnt they make,
That whilom here bare swinge among the best.
[180] This shalt thou see, but great is the vnrest
That thou must byde before thou canst attayne
Vnto the dreadfull place where these remayne.

And with these wurdes as I vpraysed stood,
And gan to folowe her that strayght furth paced,
[185] Eare I was ware, into a desert wood
We nowe were cum: where hand in hand imbraced,
She led the way, and through the thicke so traced,
As but I had bene guyded by her might,
It was no waye for any mortall wight.

[173] worlds certainty: *C–F*.

304

But loe, while thus amid the desert darke,   [190]
We passed on with steppes and pace vnmete:
A rumbling roar confusde with howle and barke
Of Dogs, shoke all the ground vnder our feete,
And stroke the din within our eares so deepe,
As halfe distraught vnto the ground I fell,   [195]
Besought retourne, and not to visite hell.

But she forthwith vplifting me apace
Remoued my dread, and with a stedfast minde
Bad me come on, for here was now the place,
The place where we our trauayle ende should finde.   [200]
Wherewith I arose, and to the place assynde
Astoynde I stalke, when strayt we approched nere
The dredfull place, that you wil dread to here.

An hydeous hole al vaste, withouten shape,
Of endles depth, orewhelmde with ragged stone,   [205]
Wyth ougly mouth, and grisly Iawes doth gape,
And to our sight confounds it selfe in one.
Here entred we, and yeding forth, anone
An horrible lothly lake we might discerne
As blacke as pitche, that cleped is Auerne.   [210]

A deadly gulfe where nought but rubbishe growes,
With fowle blacke swelth in thickned lumpes that lyes,
Which vp in the ayer such stinking vapors throwes
That ouer there, may flye no fowle but dyes,
Choakt with the pestilent sauours that aryse.   [215]
Hither we cum, whence forth we still dyd pace,
In dreadful feare amid the dreadfull place.

[200]   trauails G.
[201]   I rose, C–G.
[204]   And CG.

And first within the portche and iawes of Hell
Sate diepe Remorse of conscience, al besprent
[220] With teares: and to her selfe oft would she tell
Her wretchednes, and cursing neuer stent
To sob and sigh: but euer thus lament,
With thoughtful care, as she that all in vayne
Would weare and waste continually in payne.

[225] Her iyes vnstedfast rolling here and there,
Whurld on eche place, as place that vengeaunce brought,
So was her minde continually in feare,
Tossed and tormented with the tedious thought
Of those detested crymes which she had wrought:
[230] With dreadful cheare and lookes throwen to the skye,
Wyshyng for death, and yet she could not dye.

Next sawe we Dread al tremblyng how he shooke,
With foote vncertayne profered here and there:
Benumde of speache, and with a gastly looke
[235] Searcht euery place al pale and dead for feare,
His cap borne vp with staring of his heare,
Stoynde and amazde at his owne shade for dreed,
And fearing greater daungers than was nede.

And next within the entry of this lake
[240] Sate fell Reuenge gnashing her teeth for yre,
Deuising meanes howe she may vengeaunce take,
Neuer in rest tyll she haue her desire:
But frets within so farforth with the fyer
Of wreaking flames, that nowe determines she,
[245] To dye by death, or vengde by death to be.

[226] vengeaunce *is printed* vegeauns *but is corrected in Be.*
[228] with tedious *C–G.*

When fell Reuenge with bloudy foule pretence
Had showed her selfe as next in order set,
With trembling limmes we softly parted thence,
Tyll in our iyes another sight we met:
When fro my hart a sigh forthwith I fet   [250]
Rewing alas vpon the wofull plight
Of Miserie, that next appered in sight.

His face was leane, and sumdeale pyned away,
And eke his handes consumed to the bone,
But what his body was I can not say,   [255]
For on his carkas, rayment had he none
Saue cloutes & patches pieced one by one.
With staffe in hand, and skrip on shoulders cast,
His chiefe defence agaynst the winters blast.

His foode for most, was wylde fruytes of the tree,   [260]
Vnles sumtime sum crummes fell to his share:
Which in his wallet, long God wote kept he.
As on the which full dayntlye would he fare.
His drinke the running streame: his cup the bare
Of his palme closed, his bed the hard colde grounde.   [265]
To this poore life was Miserie ybound.

Whose wretched state when we had well behelde
With tender ruth on him and on his feres,
In thoughtful cares, furth then our pace we helde.
And by and by, an other shape apperes   [270]
Of Greedy care, stil brushing vp the breres,
His knuckles knobd, his fleshe deepe dented in,
With tawed handes, and hard ytanned skyn.

[258]   shoulder C–G.
[263]   would fare C–G.
[270]   other *is printed* ohter *but is corrected in* Be.

The morrowe graye no sooner hath begunne
[275] To spreade his light euen peping in our iyes,
When he is vp and to his worke yrunne,
But let the nightes blacke mistye mantels rise,
And with fowle darke neuer so much disguyse
The fayre bright day, yet ceasseth he no whyle,
[280] But hath his candels to prolong his toyle.

By him lay Heauy slepe the cosin of death
Flat on the ground, and stil as any stone,
A very corps, save yelding forth a breath.
Small kepe tooke he whom Fortune frowned on.
[285] Or whom she lifted vp into the trone
Of high renowne, but as a liuing death,
So dead alyve, of lyef he drewe the breath.

The bodyes rest, the quyete of the hart,
The travayles ease, the still nightes feer was he.
[290] And of our life in earth the better parte,
Reuer of sight, and yet in whom we see
Thinges oft that tide, and ofte that neuer bee.
Without respect esteming equally
Kyng Cresus pompe, and Irus pouertie.

[295] And next in order sad Olde age we found
His beard al hoare, his iyes hollow and blynde,
With drouping chere still poring on the ground,
As on the place where nature him assinde
To rest, when that the sisters had vntwynde
[300] His vitall threde, and ended with theyr knyfe
The fleting course of fast declining life.

[285] throne G.

There heard we him with broken and hollow playnt
Rewe with him selfe his ende approching fast,
And all for nought his wretched minde torment.
With swete remembraunce of his pleasures past,   [305]
And freshe delites of lusty youth forwaste.
Recounting which, how would he sob & shrike?
And to be yong againe of Ioue beseke.

But and the cruell fates so fixed be
That time forepast can not retourne agayne,   [310]
This one request of Ioue yet prayed he:
That in such withered plight, and wretched paine,
As elde (accompanied with his lothsom trayne.)
Had brought on him, all were it woe and griefe.
He myght a while yet linger forth his lief,   [315]

And not so soone descend into the pit:
Where death, when he the mortall corps hath slayne,
With retcheles hande in grave doth couer it,
Thereafter neuer to enioye agayne
The gladsome light, but in the ground ylayne,   [320]
In depth of darkenes waste and weare to nought,
As he had neuer into the world been brought.

But who had seene him sobbing, howe he stoode
Vnto him selfe and howe he would bemone
His youth forepast, as though it wrought hym good   [325]
To talke of youth, al wer his youth foregone,
He would haue mused, & meruayld muche whereon
This wretched age should life desyre so fayne,
And knowes ful wel life doth but length his payne.

[302]   broke and C–G.
[322]   nere into G.
[325]   as thought it D–F.

[330]   Crookebackt he was, toothshaken, and blere iyed,
Went on three feete, and sometime crept on fower,
With olde lame bones, that ratled by his syde,
His skalpe all pilde, & he with elde forlore:
His withered fist stil knocking at deathes dore,
[335] Fumbling and driueling as he drawes his breth,
For briefe the shape and messenger of death.

    And fast by him pale Maladie was plaste,
Sore sicke in bed, her colour al forgone,
Bereft of stomake, sauor, and of taste,
[340] Ne could she brooke no meat but brothes alone.
Her breath corrupt, her kepers euery one
Abhorring her, her sickenes past recure,
Detesting phisicke, and all phisickes cure.

    But oh the doleful sight that then we see,
[345] We turnde our looke and on the other side
A griesly shape of Famine mought we see,
With greedy lookes, and gaping mouth that cryed,
And roard for meat as she should there haue dyed,
Her body thin and bare as any bone,
[350] Wherto was left nought but the case alone.

    And that alas was knawen on euery where,
All full of holes, that I ne mought refrayne
From teares, to se how she her armes could teare
And with her teeth gnashe on the bones in vayne:
[355] When all for nought she fayne would so sustayne
Her starven corps, that rather seemde a shade,
Then any substaunce of a creature made.

    Great was her force whom stonewall could not stay,
Her tearyng nayles snatching at all she sawe:
[360] With gaping Iawes that by no meanes ymay

[360]   by ne meanes *C–F*.

310

Be satisfyed from hunger of her mawe,
But eates her selfe as she that hath no lawe:
Gnawyng alas her carkas all in vayne,
Where you may count eche sinow, bone, and vayne.

On her while we thus firmely fixt our iyes, [365]
That bled for ruth of such a drery sight,
Loe sodaynelye she shryght in so huge wyse,
As made hell gates to shyver with the myght.
Wherewith a darte we sawe howe it did lyght.
Ryght on her brest, and therewithal pale death [370]
Enthryllyng it to reve her of her breath.

And by and by a dum dead corps we sawe,
Heauy and colde, the shape of death aryght,
That dauntes all earthly creatures to his lawe:
Agaynst whose force in vayne it is to fyght [375]
Ne piers, ne princes, nor no mortall wyght,
No townes, ne realmes, cities, ne strongest tower,
But al perforce must yeeld vnto his power.

His Dart anon out of the corps he tooke,
And in his hand (a dreadfull sight to see) [380]
With great tryumphe eftsones the same he shooke,
That most of all my feares affrayed me:
His bodie dight with nought but bones perdye
The naked shape of man there sawe I playne,
All save the fleshe, the synowe, and the vayne. [385]

Lastly stoode Warre in glitteryng armes yclad.
With visage grym, sterne lookes, and blackely hewed
In his right hand a naked sworde he had,
That to the hiltes was al with blud embrewed:

[375] fyght: B^2.
[379] of his corps F.

311

[390] And in his left (that kinges and kingdomes rewed)
Famine and fyer he held, and therewythall
He razed townes, and threwe downe towers and all.

Cities he sakt, and realmes that whilom flowred,
In honor, glory, and rule above the best,
[395] He overwhelmde, and all theyr fame deuowred,
Consumed, destroyed, wasted, and neuer ceast,
Tyll he theyr wealth, theyr name, and all opprest.
His face forhewed with woundes, and by his side,
There hunge his targe with gashes depe and wyde.

[400] In mids of which, depaynted there we founde
Deadly debate, al ful of snaky heare,
That with a blouddy fillet was ybound,
Outbrething nought but discord euery where.
And round about were portrayd here and there
[405] The hugie hostes, Darius and his power,
His kynges, pryances, his pieres, and all his flower.

Whom great Macedo vanquisht there in sight,
With diepe slaughter, dispoylyng all his pryde,
Pearst through his realmes, and daunted all his might.
[410] Duke Hanniball beheld I there beside,
In Cannas field, victor howe he did ride,
And woful Romaynes that in vayne withstoode
And Consull Paulus covered all in blood.

Yet sawe I more the fight at Trasimene.
[415] And Trebey field, and eke when Hanniball
And worthy Scipio last in armes were seene
Before Carthago gate, to trye for all
The worldes empyre, to whom it should befal.

[390] King *C–G.*
[415] Trebey field *is printed* Trebery fyeld *but is corrected in Be.* Treberie fyeld, *C–G.*

There sawe I Pompeye, and Cesar clad in armes,
Theyr hostes alyed and al theyr civil harmes.   [420]

   With conquerours hands forbathde in their owne blood,
And Cesar weping ouer Pompeyes head.
Yet sawe I Scilla and Marius where they stoode,
Theyr great crueltie, and the diepe bludshed
Of frendes: Cyrus I sawe and his host dead,   [425]
And howe the Queene with great despyte hath flonge
His head in bloud of them she overcome.

   Xerxes the Percian kyng yet sawe I there
With his huge host that dranke the riuers drye,
Dismounted hilles, and made the vales vprere,   [430]
His hoste and all yet sawe I slayne perdye.
Thebes I sawe all razde howe it dyd lye
In heapes of stones, and Tyrus put to spoyle,
With walles and towers flat euened with the soyle.

   But Troy alas (me thought) aboue them all,   [435]
It made myne iyes in very teares consume:
When I beheld the wofull werd befall,
That by the wrathfull wyl of Gods was come:
And Ioues vnmooved sentence and foredoome
On Priam kyng, and on his towne so bent.   [440]
I could not lyn, but I must there lament.

   And that the more sith destinie was so sterne
As force perforce, there might no force auayle,
But she must fall: and by her fall we learne,
That cities, towres, wealth, world, and al shall quayle.   [445]
No manhoode, might, nor nothing mought preuayle,
Al were there prest ful many a prynce and piere
And many a knight that solde his death full deere.

[438] God C–G.
[443] perforce *is misprinted* perfore *in the text.*

[450]   Not wurthy Hector wurthyest of them all,
Her hope, her ioye, his force is nowe for nought.
O Troy, Troy, there is no boote but bale,
The hugie horse within thy walles is brought:
Thy turrets fall, thy knightes that whilom fought
In armes amyd the fyeld, are slayne in bed,
[455]   Thy Gods defylde, and all thy honour dead.

   The flames vpspring, and cruelly they crepe
From wall to roofe, til all to cindres waste,
Some fyer the houses where the wretches slepe,
Sum rushe in here, sum run in there as fast.
[460]   In euery where or sworde or fyer they taste.
The walles are torne, the towers whurld to the ground,
There is no mischiefe but may there be found.

   Cassandra yet there sawe I howe they haled
From Pallas house, with spercled tresse vndone,
[465]   Her wristes fast bound, and with Greeks rout empaled:
And Priam eke in vayne howe he did runne
To armes, whom Pyrrhus with despite hath done
To cruel death, and bathed him in the bayne
Of his sonnes blud before the altare slayne.

[470]   But howe can I descryve the doleful sight,
That in the shylde so liuelike fayer did shyne?
Sith in this world I thinke was neuer wyght
Could haue set furth the halfe, not halfe so fyne.
I can no more but tell howe there is seene
[475]   Fayer Ilium fal in burning red gledes downe,
And from the soyle great Troy Neptunus towne.

[456]   flames vprising, C–G.
[471]   so liuely fayre C–G.

314

Herefrom when scarce I could mine iyes withdrawe
That fylde with teares as doeth the spryngyng well,
We passed on so far furth tyl we sawe
Rude Acheron, a lothsome lake to tell   [480]
That boyles and bubs vp swelth as blacke as hell.
Where grisly Charon at theyr fixed tide
Stil ferreies ghostes vnto the farder side,

   The aged God no sooner sorowe spyed,
But hasting strayt vnto the banke apace   [485]
With hollow call vnto the rout he cryed,
To swarve apart, and geue the Goddesse place.
Strayt it was done, when to the shoar we pace,
Where hand in hand as we then linked fast,
Within the boate we are together plaste.   [490]

   And furth we launch ful fraughted to the brinke,
Whan with the vnwonted weyght, the rustye keele
Began to cracke as if the same should sinke.
We hoyse vp mast and sayle, that in a whyle.
We set the shore, where scarcely we had while   [495]
For to arryve, but that we heard anone
A thre sound barke confounded al in one.

   We had not long furth past, but that we sawe,
Blacke Cerberus the hydeous hound of hell,
With bristles reard, and with a thre mouthed Iawe,   [500]
Foredinning the ayer with his horrible yel.
Out of the diepe darke cave where he did dwell,
The Goddesse strayt he knewe, and by and by
He peaste and couched, while that we passed by.

[477]   could my eyes C–F.
[504]   whils C–F.

[505] Thence cum we to the horrour and the hel,
The large great kyngdomes, and the dreadful raygne
Of Pluto in his trone where he dyd dwell,
The wyde waste places, and the hugye playne:
The waylinges, shrykes, and sundry sortes of payne,
[510] The syghes, the sobbes, the diepe and deadly groane,
Earth, ayer, and all resounding playnt and moane.

Here pewled the babes, and here the maydes vnwed
with folded handes theyr sory chaunce bewayled,
Here wept the gyltles slayne, and louers dead,
[515] That slewe them selues when nothyng els auayled;
A thousand sortes of sorrowes here that wayled
with sighes and teares, sobs, shrykes, and all yfere,
That (oh alas) it was a hel to heare.

we stayed vs strayt, and wyth a rufull feare,
[520] Beheld this heauy sight, while from mine eyes,
The vapored teares downstilled here and there,
And Sorowe eke in far more woful wyse.
Tooke on with playnt, vp heauing to the skyes
Her wretched handes, that with her crye the rout
[525] Gan all in heapes to swarme vs round about.

Loe here (quoth Sorowe) Prynces of renowne,
That whilom sat on top of Fortunes wheele
Nowe layed ful lowe, like wretches whurled downe,
Euen with one frowne, that stayed but with a smyle,
[530] And nowe behold the thing that thou erewhile,
Saw only in thought, and what thou now shalt heare
Recompt the same to Kesar, King, and Pier.

[507] throne G.
[512] pewed C–F.
[527] whilom late on F.

Then first came Henry duke of Buckingham,
His cloke of blacke al pilde and quite forworne,
Wringing his handes, and Fortune ofte doth blame,　　　[535]
Which of a duke hath made him nowe her skorne.
With gastly lookes as one in maner lorne,
Oft spred his armes, stretcht handes he ioynes as fast,
With ruful chere, and vapored eyes vpcast.

His cloke he rent, his manly breast he beat,　　　[540]
His heare al torne about the place it laye,
My hart so molte to see his griefe so great,
As felingly me thought it dropt awaye:
His iyes they whurled about withouten staye,
With stormy syghes the place dyd so complayne,　　　[545]
As if his hart at eche had burst in twayne.

Thryse he began to tell his doleful tale,
And thrise the sighes did swalowe vp his voyce,
At eche of which he shryked so wythal
As though the heauens rived with the noyse:　　　[550]
Tyll at the last recovering his voyce,
Supping the teares that all his brest beraynde
On cruel Fortune weping thus he playnde.

[Tragedy 22]

The complaynt of Henrye duke of Buckingham.

𝕎Ho trustes to much in honours highest trone
And warely watche not slye dame Fortunes snare:
Or who in courte will beare the swaye alone,
And wysely weygh not howe to wyeld the care,
[5]   Beholde he me, and by my death beware:
Whom flattering Fortune falsely so begilde
That loe she slewe, where earst ful smooth she smylde.

   And Sackeuylle sith in purpose nowe thou hast
The woful fal of prynces to discryve,
[10]   Whom Fortune both vplyft, and gayn downe cast,
To shewe thereby the vnsuerty in this life,
Marke wel my fal, which I shal shewe belive.
And paynt it furth that all estates may knowe:
Haue they the warning, and be mine the woe.

[15]   For noble bloud made me both prince and pier
Yea pierles too, had reason purchast place,
And God with giftes endowed me largely here.
But what auayles his giftes where fayles his grace?
My mothers syer sprong of a kyngely race
[20]   And calde was Edmund duke of Somerset,
Bereft of lyef ere tyme by nature set.

[1]   much to honours C–G.
[2]   snares: G.
[3]   the swinge alone, C–G.
[6]   so begilde *is printed* so egylde *but is corrected in Be.*
[10]   and eke downe C–G.
[12]   belive *is misprinted* beliive *in the text.*
[16]   had season purchast F.

Whose faythfull hart to Henry syxt so wrought
That never he hym in weale or woe forsooke,
Tyl lastly he at Tewxbury fyeld was cought
Where with an axe his violent death he toke: [25]
He never could kyng Edwardes party brooke,
Tyll by his death he vouchte that quarell good,
In which his syer and graundsyer spylt theyr bloud.

And such was erst my fathers cruell chaunce,
Of Stafford Earle by name that Humfrey hyght,   [30]
Who ever prest dyd Henries parte auaunce,
And neuer ceast tyl at Saynt Albones fight
He lost his lyfe as than did many a knyght:
where eke my graundsyer duke of Buckingham
was wounded sore, and hardly skapte vntane.   [35]

But what may boot to stay the sisters three?
When Atropos perforce wil cut the threde:
The doleful day was come when you might see
Northhampton fyeld with armed men orespred,
where fate would algates haue my graundsyer dead: [40]
So rushyng furth amyds the fyercest fight,
He lived & dyed there in his maysters ryght.

In place of whom, as it befel my lot,
Like on a stage, so stept I in strayt waye,
Enioying there but wofully god wot,   [45]
As he that had a slender part to playe:
To teache therby, in earth no state may stay,
But as our partes abridge or length our age
So passe we all while others fyll the stage.

For of my selfe the drery fate to playne,   [50]
I was sometime a prince withouten pier,
When Edward fift began his ruful raygne,
Ay me, then I began that hatefull yeare,

To cumpas that which I have bought so deare:
[55] I bare the swynge, I and that wretched wyght,
The duke of Glocester that Rychard hyght.

For when the fates had reft that royal prince
Edward the fowrth, chiefe myrrour of that name,
The duke and I fast ioyned ever since,
[60] In faythfull love, our secrete driftes to frame:
What he thought best, to me so seemde the same,
My selfe not bent so much for to aspyer,
As to fulfyl that greedy dukes desyre.

Whose restles minde sore thyrsting after rule,
[65] When that he sawe his nephewes both to ben
Through tender yeares as yet vnfyt to rule,
And rather ruled by theyr mothers kyn,
There sought he first his mischyefe to begyn,
To plucke from them theyr mothers frendes assynde,
[70] For wel he wist they would withstand his mynde.

To folowe which, he ran so headlong swyft,
With eygre thyrst of his desired draught,
To seeke theyr deathes that sought to dashe his dryft,
Of whom the chiefe the Queenes allyes he thought,
[75] That bent thereto wyth mountes of mischiefe fraught,
He knewe theyr lyues would be so sore his let,
That in theyr deathes his only helpe he set.

And I most cursed caytief that I was,
Seeing the state vnstedfast howe it stood,
[80] His chief complyce to bryng the same to passe,
Vnhappy wretche consented to theyr blood:
Ye Kinges and Piers that swim in worldly good,

[69]   mother *DE.*
[82]   Yea Kings *C–G.*

320

In seekyng blud the ende aduert you playne,
And see if bloud ey aske not blud agayne.

Consyder Cyrus in your cruell thought, [85]
A makeles prynce in ryches and in myght,
And weygh in minde the bloudy dedes he wrought,
In sheading which he set his whole delyght:
But see the guerdon lotted to this wyght,
He whose huge power no man might ouerthrowe, [90]
Tomyris Queen with great despite hath slowe.

His head dismembred from his mangled corps,
Her selfe she cast into a vessell fraught
With clottered bloud of them that felt her force.
And with these wordes a iust reward she taught: [95]
Drynke nowe thy fyll of thy desyred draught.
Loe marke the fine that did this prynce befall:
Marke not this one, but marke the ende of all.

Behold Cambises and his fatal daye,
Where Murders mischief myrrour like is left: [100]
While he his brother Mergus cast to slaye,
A dreadful thing, his wittes were him bereft.
A sword he caught wherewith he perced eft
His body gored, which he of liefe benooms: [105]
So iust is God in al his dreadfull doomes.

O bluddy Brutus rightly didst thou rew,
And thou Cassius iustly came thy fall,
That with the swurd wherewith thou Cesar slewe
Murdrest thy selfe, and reft thy life withall.
A myrrour let him be vnto you all [110]
That murderers be, of murder to your meede:
For murder crieth out vengeance on your seede.

[107]   thou O *Cassius*, G.
[112]   murder cryes out G.

Loe Bessus he that armde with murderers knyfe,
And traytrous hart agaynst his royall kyng,
[115] With bluddy handes bereft his maysters life,
Aduert the fine his fowle offence dyd bryng:
And lothing murder as most lothly thing
Beholde in him the iust deserued fall,
That euer hath, and shall betide them all.

[120] What booted him his false vsurped raygne?
Wherto by murder he did so ascende?
When like a wretche, led in an yron chayne
He was presented by his chiefest frende
Vnto the foes of him whom he had slayne:
[125] That euen they should venge so fowle a gylt,
That rather sought to haue his bloud yspylt.

Take hede ye princes and ye prelates all
Of this outrage, which though it slepe a while
And not disclosde, as it doth seeld befall,
[130] Yet God that suffreth silence to beguyle
Such gyltes, wherwith both earth and ayre ye file,
At last discryes them to your fowle deface,
You see the examples set before your face.

And deepely grave within your stony hartes,
[135] The drery dewle that myghty Macedo,
With teares vnfolded wrapt in deadly smartes,
When he the death of Clitus sorowed so,
whom erst he murdred wyth the deadly blowe
Raught in his rage vpon his frende so deare,
[140] For which behold loe how his panges appere.

[114] And traytours hart *C–F.*

The launced spear he writhes out of the wound,
From which the purple blud spins on his face:
His heynous gylt when he returned found,
He throwes him selfe vpon the corpes alas.
And in his armes howe ofte doth he imbrace   [145]
His murdred frende? and kyssyng him in vayne,
Furth flowe the fluds of salte repentant rayne.

His frendes amazde at such a murder doen,
In feareful flockes begyn to shrynke away.
And he thereat with heapes of griefe fordoen,   [150]
Hateth him selfe, wishing his latter daye.
Nowe he him selfe perceyued in like staye,
As is the wilde beast in the desert bred,
Both dreading others and him selfe adred.

He calles for Death, and loathing lenger lyfe,   [155]
Bent to his bane, refuseth kyndely foode:
And ploungde in depth of death and dolours stryfe,
Had quelde him selfe, had not his frendes wythstoode.
Loe he that thus had shed the gylteles blud,
Though he wer Kyng and Kesar over all   [160]
Yet chose he death to guerdon death withall.

This prynce whose pyer was never vnder sonne,
Whose glystening fame the earth did overglyde,
Whych with his power welnye the world had wonne,
His bluddy handes him selfe could not abyde,   [165]
But fully bent with famine to have dyed:
The wurthy prynce deemed in his regarde,
That death for death could be but iust rewarde.

[142] spins in his C–G.
[152] he likewise perceiued C–G.
[159] thus hath shed C–G.
[166] But folly bent G.

Yet we that were so drowned in the depth
[170] Of diepe desyre to drinke the gylteles blud,
Lyke to the wulfe, with greedy lookes that lepth
Into the snare, to feede on deadly foode,
So we delyghted in the state we stoode,
Blinded so farre in all our blynded trayne
[175] That blind we sawe not our destruction playne.

We spared none whose life could ought forlet
Our wycked purpose to his pas to cum.
Fower wurthy knyghtes we headed at Pomfret
Gylteles (God wote) withouten lawe or doome.
[180] My heart even bleedes to tell you al and some,
And howe Lord Hastinges when he feared least,
Dispiteously was murdred and opprest.

These rockes vpraught, that threatned most our wreck
We séemde to sayle much surer in the streame:
[185] And Fortune faryng as she were at becke
Layed in our lap the rule of all the realme.
The nephewes strayt deposde were by the Eame.
And we advaunst to that we bought full deare,
He crowned king, and I his chyefest Pyer.

[190] Thus hauing wonne our long desired pray,
To make him king that he might make me chiefe,
Downthrow we strayt his sellie nephewes twaye,
From princes pompe, to woful prisoners lyfe:
In hope that nowe stynt was all furder stryfe.
[195] Sith he was king, and I chiefe stroke did beare
Who ioyed but we, yet who more cause to feare?

The gylteles bloud which we vniustly shed,
The royall babes deuested from theyr trone,

[198]   Trons, F.

324

And we like traytours raygning in theyr sted,
These heauy burdens pressed vs vpon,　　　　　　　　[200]
Tormenting vs so by our selues alone,
Much like the felon that pursued by night,
Startes at eche bushe as his foe were in sight.

　　Nowe doubting state, nowe dreading losse of life,
In feare of wrecke at euery blast of wynde,　　　　　[205]
Now start in dreames through dread of murdrers knyfe,
As though euen then revengement were assynde.
With restles thought so is the guylty minde
Turmoyled, and never feeleth ease or stay,
But lives in feare of that which folowes aye.　　　　[210]

　　Well gave that iudge his doome vpon the death
Of Titus Clelius that in bed was slayne:
Whan every wight the cruell murder leyeth
To his two sonnes that in his chamber layen,
The Iudge, that by the proofe perceyueth playne,　　[215]
That they were found fast sleping in theyr bed,
Hath deemde them gylteles of this blud yshed.

　　He thought it could not be, that they which brake
The lawes of God and man in such outrage
Could so forthwith them selves to slepe betake:　　[220]
He rather thought the horror and the rage
Of such an haynous gylt, could never swage.
Nor never suffer them to slepe or rest,
Or dreadles breath one breth out of theyr brest.

[200]　burdens passed vs C–G.
[205]　wracke C–G.
[212]　*Titus Glelius* F.
[215]　That Iudge, C–F.

[225] So gnawes the griefe of conscyence evermore
And in the hart it is so diepe ygrave,
That they may neyther slepe nor rest therfore,
Ne thynke one thought but on the dread they have.
Styl to the death fortossed with the wave
[230] Of restles woe, in terror and dispeyre.
They lead a lyef continually in feare.

Like to the Dere that stryken with the dart,
Withdrawes him selfe into some secrete place,
And feeling green the wound about his hart,
[235] Startles with panges tyl he fall on the grasse,
And in great feare lyes gasping there a space,
Furth braying sighes as though eche pang had brought
The present death which he doeth dread so oft:

So we diepe wounded with the bluddy thought,
[240] And gnawing wurme that grieved our conscience so,
Never tooke ease, but as our hart furth brought
The strayned syghes in wytnes of our woe,
Such restles cares our fault did well beknowe:
Wherewith of our deserved fall the feares
[245] In every place rang death within our eares.

And as yll grayne is never well ykept,
So fared it by vs within a while:
That which so long wyth such vnrest we reapt,
In dread and daunger by all wyt and wyle,
[250] Loe sée the fine, when once it felt the whele
Of slipper Fortune, stay it mought no stowne,
The wheele whurles vp, but strayt it whurleth downe.

[226]   so deepely graue, *F.*
[235]   Startlesse *C–F.*
[241]   hart outbrought *C–G.*
[242]   The stayned sighes *C–G.*

For hauyng rule and riches in our hand,
Who durst gaynsay the thing that we averde?
Wyl was wysedome, our lust for lawe dyd stand,   [255]
In sorte so straunge, that who was not afeard
When he the sound but of kyng Rychard heard?
So hatefull waxt the hearyng of his name,
That you may deeme the residewe by the same.

But what auaylde the terror and the fear,   [260]
Wherewyth he kept his lieges vnder awe?
It rather wan him hatred every where,
And fayned faces forst by feare of lawe:
That but while Fortune doth with fauour blaw
Flatter through feare: for in theyr hart lurkes aye   [265]
A secrete hate that hopeth for a daye.

Recordeth Dionisius the kynge,
That with his rigor so his realme opprest,
As that he thought by cruell feare to bryng
His subiectes vnder, as him lyked best: [270]
But loe the dread wherewyth him selfe was strest,
And you shal see the fine of forced feare,
Most myrrour like in this proud prynce appeare.

All were his head with crowne of golde ysprad,
And in his hand the royall scepter set: [275]
And he with pryncely purple rychely clad,
Yet was his hart wyth wretched cares orefret:
And inwardly with deadly fear beset,
Of those whom he by rygour kept in awe,
And sore opprest with might of Tyrants lawe.   [280]

[259]   residue of the C–G.

327

Agaynst whose feare, no heapes of golde and glie,
Ne strength of garde, nor all his hyred power,
Ne prowde hyghe Towers that preaced to the skye,
His cruel hart of safetie could assure:
[285] But dreading them whom he should deeme most sure,
Hym selfe his beard wyth burning brand would cear,
Of death deservde so vexed him the feare.

This might suffise to represent the fine
Of Tyrantes force, theyr feares, and theyr vnrest,
[290] But heare this one, although my hart repyne
To let the sound once synke wythin my brest:
Of fell Phereus, that above the rest,
Such lothsum crueltee on his people wrought,
As (oh alas) I tremble wyth the thought.

[295] Sum he encased in the coates of Beares,
Among wylde beastes deuoured so to be:
And sum for praye vnto the hunters speares,
Lyke savage beastes withouten ruth to dye.
Sumtime to encrease his horrible crueltye,
[300] The quicke with face to face engraved hee,
Eche others death that eche mought living see.

Loe what more cruell horror mought be found,
To purchase feare, if feare could staye his raygne?
It booted not, It rather strake the wounde
[305] Of feare in him, to feare the lyke agayne.
And so he dyd full ofte and not in vayne:
As in his life his cares could wytnes well
But moste of all his wretched ende doth tell.

[282] No strength *C–G*.
[307] And in *C–F*.

His owne dere wyfe whom as his life he loved,
He durst not trust, nor proche vnto her bed,   [310]
But causing fyrst his slave with naked sworde
To go before, him selfe with tremblyng dread
Strayt foloweth fast, and whorling in his head
His rolling iyen, he searcheth here and there
The diepe daunger that he so sore did feare.   [315]

For not in vayne it ran styll in his brest,
Sum wretched hap should hale him to his ende.
And therfore alwaye by his pillowe prest
Had he a sworde, and with that sworde he wende,
In vayne (God wote) all peryls to defende: [320]
For loe his wife foreyrked of his raygne,
Sleping in bed this cruel wretche hath slayne.

What should I more nowe seeke to say in this?
Or one Iote farder linger furth my tale?
With cruel Nero, or with Phalaris,   [325]
Caligula, Domician, and all
The cruell route? or of theyr wretched fall?
I can no more, but in my name aduert
Al earthly powers beware of Tyrants hart.

And as our state endured but a throwe,   [330]
So best in vs the staye of such a state
May best appeare to hang on overthrowe,
And better teache Tyrantes deserved hate
Than any Tyrantes death tofore or late.
So cruell seemde this Rychard thyrd to me,   [335]
That loe my selfe now loathde his crueltee.

[314]   searched G.
[319]   Sword bee wende, F.
[321]   foreyrking G.

For when alas, I saw the Tyrant kyng
Content not only from his nephewes twayne
To ryve worldes blysse, but also al worldes beyng,
[340]   Saunce earthly gylt ycausing both be slayne,
My hart agryesd that such a wretche should raygne,
Whose bluddy brest so salvaged out of kynde,
That Phalaris had never so bluddy a minde.

Ne could I brooke him once wythin my brest,
[345]   But wyth the thought my teeth would gnashe wythal:
For though I earst wer his by sworne behest,
Yet when I sawe mischiefe on mischiefe fall,
So diepe in blud, to murder prynce and all,
Ay then thought I, alas, and wealaway,
[350]   And to my selfe thus mourning would I say.

If neyther love, kynred, ne knot of bloud,
His owne alegeaunce to his prynce of due,
Nor yet the state of trust wherein he stoode,
The worlds defame, nor nought could tourne him true
[355]   Those gylteles babes, could they not make him rue?
Nor could theyr youth, nor innocence withal
Move him from reuing them theyr lyfe and all?

Alas, it could not move him any iote,
Ne make him once to rue or wet his iye,
[360]   Sturde him no more than that that styrreth not:
But as the rocke or stone that wyl not plye,
So was his hart made hard to crueltye,
To murder them, alas I weepe in thought,
To thinke on that which this fel wretche hath wrought

[341]   hart agriefde that *D–F*.
[343]   had nere so *G*.
[349]   welaway, *G*.
[354]   could forme him *C–G*.
[362]   hard with crueltie, *C–G*.

That nowe when he had done the thing he sought, [365]
And as he would, complysht and cumpast all,
And sawe and knewe the treason he had wrought
To God and man, to slaye his prynce and all,
Then seemde he fyrst to doubte and dread vs all,
And me in chiefe, whoes death all meanes he myght, [370]
He sought to wurke by malice and by might.

Such heapes of harmes vpharbard in his brest
With enuyous hart my honour to deface,
As knowyng he that I whych woted best
His wretched dryftes, and all his cursed case, [375]
If ever sprang within me sparke of grace,
Must nedes abhorre him and his hatefull race:
Now more and more can cast me out of grace.

Which sodayne chaunge, when I by secrete chaunce
Had well perceyved by proofe of enuious frowne, [380]
And sawe the lot that did me to aduaunce
Hym to a kyng that sought to cast me downe,
To late it was to linger any stowne:
Syth present choyse lay cast before myne iye,
To wurke his death or I my selfe to dye. [385]

And as the knyght in fyeld among his foes,
Beset wyth swurdes, must slaye or there be slayne:
So I alas lapt in a thousand woes,
Beholding death on every syde so playne,
I rather chose by sum slye secrete trayne [390]
To wurke his death, and I to lyve thereby,
Than he to lyve, and I of force to dye.

[375]   his wretched case, C–G.

Which heauy choyse so hastened me to chose,
That I in parte agryeved at his disdayne,
[395] In part to wreke the dolefull death of those
Two tender babes, his sillye nephewes twayne,
By him alas commaunded to be slayne,
With paynted chere humbly before his face,
Strayght tooke my leave, & rode to Brecknocke place.

[400] And there as close and covert as I myght,
My purposed practise to his passe to bryng,
In secrete dryftes I lingred day and night:
All howe I might depose this cruell kyng,
That seemd to all so much desyerd a thyng,
[405] As therto trusting I emprysde the same:
But to much trusting brought me to my bane.

For while I nowe had Fortune at my becke
Mistrusting I no earthly thing at all,
Vnwares alas, least looking for a checke,
[410] She mated me in turning of a ball:
When least I fearde, then nerest was my fall,
And when whole hoastes wer prest to stroy my foen,
She chaunged her chere, and left me post alone.

I had vpraysde a mighty band of men,
[415] And marched furth in order of array,
Leadyng my power amyd the forest Dene,
Agaynst that Tyrant banner to displaye:
But loe my souldiers cowardly shranke away.
For such is Fortune when she lyst to frowne,
[420] Who seemes most sure, him soonest whurles she down

[393] With heauy C–F.
[404] much a desyerd thing, F.
[411] feard, the nearest D–F.
[417] Agaynst the tyrant C–G.

O let no prynce put trust in commontie,
Nor hope in fayth of gyddy peoples mynde,
But let all noble men take hede by me,
That by the proofe to well the payne do fynde:
Loe, where is truth or trust? or what could bynde   [425]
The vayne people, but they will swarve and swaye,
As chaunce bryngs chaunge, to dryve & draw that way?

Rome thou that once aduaunced vp so hye,
Thy staye, patron, and flower of excellence,
Hast nowe throwen him to depth of miserye,   [430]
Exiled him that was thy whole defence,
Ne comptest it not an horryble offence:
To reuen him of honour and of fame,
That wan it thée when thou hadst lost the same.

Beholde Camillus, he that erst reuyved   [435]
The state of Rome, that dyeng he dyd fynde,
Of his owne state is nowe alas depryved,
Banisht by them whom he dyd thus det bynde:
That cruell folke, vnthankeful and vnkynde,
Declared wel theyr false inconstancye,   [440]
And Fortune eke her mutabilitye.

And thou Scipio, a myrrour mayst thou be
To all Nobles, that they learne not to late,
Howe they once trust the vnstable commontye.
Thou that recuredst the torne dismembred state,   [445]
Euen when the conquerour was at the gate,
Art now exylde, as though thou not deserved
To rest in her, whom thou hadst so preserved.

[440]   vnconstancie, G.

[450]
Ingrateful Rome hast shewed thy crueltye,
On hym, by whom thou lyvest yet in fame,
But nor thy dede, nor his desert shall dye,
But his owne wurdes shal witnes aye the same:
For loe hys grave doth thee most iustly blame.
And with disdayne in Marble sayes to thée:

[455]
Vnkynde countrey my bones shalt thou not see.

What more vnwurthy than this his exyle?
More iust than this the wofull playnt he wrote?
Or who could shewe a playner proofe the while,
Of moste false fayth, than they that thus forgot

[460]
His great desertes? that so deserved not?
His cindres yet loe, doth he them denye,
That him denyed amongst them for to dye.

Milciades, O happy hadst thou be,
And well rewarded of thy countrey men,

[465]
If in the fyeld when thou hadst forst to flye
By thy prowes, thre hundred thousand men,
Content they had bene to exyle thée then:
And not to cast thée in depth of pryson so,
Laden wyth gyves to ende thy lyfe in woe.

[470]
Alas howe harde and steely hartes had they
That not contented there to have thée dye,
With fettred gyves in pryson where thou laye,
Increast so far in hatefull crueltye,
That buryall to thy corps, they eke denye:

[475]
Ne wyl they graunt the same tyll thy sonne have
Put on thy gyves to purchase thée a grave.

[459] they thus *C–F*.
[465] thou *is misprinted* thon *in the text*.
[468] thee in prison *DE.* thee into Prison *F*.

Loe Hanniball as long as fixed fate,
And bryttle Fortune had ordeyned so,
Who ever more aduaunst his countrey state
Then thou, that lyvedst for her and for no moe?   [480]
But when the stormy waves began to grow,
Without respect of thy desertes erwhile,
Art by thy countrey throwen into exyle.

Vnfrendly Fortune shal I thée nowe blame?
Or shal I fault the fates that so ordayne?   [485]
Or art thou Ioue the causer of the same?
Or crueltie her selfe doth she constrayne?
Or on whom els alas shal I complayne?
O trustles world I can accusen none,
But fyckle fayth of commontye alone.   [490]

The Polipus nor the Chameleon straunge,
That turne them selves to every hewe they sée
Are not so full of vayne and fickle chaunge
As is this false vnstedfast commontye.
Loe I alas with mine adversitie   [495]
Have tryed it true, for they are fled and gone
And of an oast there is not left me one.

That I alas in this calamitie
Alone was left, and to my selfe mought playne
This treason, and this wretched cowardye,   [500]
And eke with teares bewepen and complayne
My hateful hap, styll lookyng to be slayne.
Wandryng in woe, and to the gods on hye
Cleapyng for vengeaunce of this treacherye.

[483]   by they Countrey G.

[505]   And as the Turtle that hath lost her make,
Whom grypyng sorowe doth so sore attaynt,
With dolefull voyce and sound whych she doth make
Mourning her losse, fylles all the grove wyth playnt,
So I alas forsaken, and forfaynt,
[510]   With restles foote the wud rome vp and downe,
Which of my dole al shyvering doth resowne.

      And beyng thus alone, and all forsake,
Amyd the thycke, forwandred in despayer,
As one dismayed ne wyst what waye to take,
[515]   Vntyll at last gan to my mynde repayer,
A man of mine called Humfrey Banastair:
Wherewyth me feeling much recomforted,
In hope of succour to his house I fled.

      Who beyng one whom earst I had vpbrought
[520]   Euen from his youth, and loved and lyked best,
To gentrye state auauncing him from nought,
And had in secrete trust above the rest,
Of specyal trust nowe being thus dystrest
Full secreatly to him I me conueyed
[525]   Not doubting there but I should fynde some ayde.

      But out alas on cruell trecherye,
When that this caytief once an ynklyng hard,
Howe that kyng Rychard had proclaymde, that he
Which me descryed should have for his rewarde
[530]   A thousand poundes, and farther be prefarde,
His truthe so turnde to treason, all distaynde
That fayth quyte fled, and I by trust was traynde.

[505] her mate, *D–F.*
[507] sound that she *C–F.*

For by this wretche I beyng strayt betrayed,
To one Iohn Mitton, shiriffe of Shropshire then,
All sodaynely was taken, and conuayed   [535]
To Salisbury, wyth rout of harnest men,
Vnto kyng Rychard there encamped then:
Fast by the citye with a myghtye hoste
Withouten doome where head and lyfe I lost.

And with these wordes, as if the axe even there   [540]
Dismembred had his head and corps aparte,
Dead fel he downe: and we in woful feare
Stoode mazed when he would to lyef revert:
But deadly griefes stil grewe about his hart,
That styll he laye, sumtyme reuived wyth payne,   [545]
And wyth a sygh becumming dead agayne.

Mydnyght was cum, and every vitall thyng
With swete sound slepe theyr weary lyms dyd rest,
The beastes were still, the lytle byrdes that syng,
Nowe sweetely slept besides theyr mothers brest: [550]
The olde and all were shrowded in theyr nest.
The waters calme, the cruel seas did ceas,
The wuds, the fyeldes, & all thinges held theyr peace.

The golden stars wer whyrlde amyd theyr race,
And on the earth did laugh wyth twinkling lyght,   [555]
When eche thing nestled in his restyng place,
Forgat dayes payne with pleasure of the nyght:
The Hare had not the greedy houndes in sight,
The fearfull Dear of death stoode not in doubt,
The Patrydge drept not of the Falcons foote.   [560]

[547]   come, when euery C–G.
[560]   Partridge C–G.

The ougly Beare nowe mynded not the stake,
Nor how the cruell mastyues do hym tear,
The stag laye still vnroused from the brake,
The fomy boar feard not the hunters spear.
[565] All thing was still in desert, bush and brear.
With quyet hart now from their trauailes rest,
Soundly they slept in midst of all their rest.

When Buckyngham amid his plaint opprest,
With surgyng sorowes and with pinching paynes
[570] In sort thus sowned, and with a sigh he ceast.
To tellen furth the treachery and the traynes,
Of Banastar, which him so sore distraynes.
That from a sigh he falles into a sounde,
And from a sounde lyeth ragyng on the ground

[575] So twiching wer the panges that he assayed,
And he so sore with rufull rage distraught.
To thinke vpon the wretch that hym betrayed,
Whom earst he made a Gentylman of naught.
That more and more agreued with this thought,
[580] He stormes out sighes, and with redoubled sore,
Stroke with the Furies, rageth more and more.

Who so hath seene the Bull chased with Dartes,
And with dyepe woundes forgald and gored so,
Tyl he oppressed with the deadlye smartes,
[585] Fall in a rage, and runne vpon his foe,
Let him I saye, beholde the ragyng woe
Of Buckyngham, that in these grypes of gryefe
Rageth gaynst him that hath betrayed his lyef.

[566] trauayles ceast, G.
[568] amid this plaint D–F.
[574] *The last letters in* ground *are blurred in the text.*
[576] ruthfull G.
[579] agreeued was his thought, F.

With blud red iyen he stareth here and there,
Frothing at mouth, with face as pale as cloute: [590]
When loe my lymmes were trembling all for feare,
And I amazde stoode styll in dread and doubt,
While I mought see him throwe his armes about:
And gaynst the ground him selfe plounge with such force
As if the lyfe forthwyth should leave the corps. [595]

With smoke of syghes sumtyme I myght beholde
The place al dymde, like to the mornyng myst:
And strayt agayne the teares how they downrolde
Alongst his cheekes, as if the ryuers hyst:
Whoes flowing streemes ne wer no sooner whist, [600]
But to the stars such dreadfull shoutes he sent,
As if the trone of mighty Ioue should rent,

And I the while with spirites wel nye bereft,
Beheld the plyght and panges that dyd him strayne.
And howe the blud his deadly colour left, [605]
And strayt returnde with flamyng red agayne:
When sodaynly amid his ragyng payne,
He gave a sygh, and with that sygh he sayed:
Oh Banastar, and strayt agayne he stayed.

Dead laye his corps as dead as any stone, [610]
Tyll swellyng syghes stormyng within his brest
Vpraysde his head, that downeward fell anone,
With lookes vpcast, and syghes that never ceast:
Furth streamde the teares recordes of his vnrest,
When he wyth shrykes thus groveling on the ground, [615]
Ybrayed these wordes with shryll and dolefull sound.

Heaven and earth, and ye eternal lampes
That in the heavens wrapt, wyl vs to rest,
Thou bryght Phebe, that clearest the nightes dampes
Witnes the playntes that in these panges opprest [620]

I woful wretche vnlade out of my brest.
And let me yeald my last wordes ere I part,
You, you, I call to record of my smart.

And thou Alecto feede me wyth thy foode
[625] Let fal thy serpentes from thy snaky heare,
For such relyefe wel sittes me in this moode,
To feede my playnt with horror and wyth feare,
While rage afreshe thy venomd worme arear.
And thou Sibilla when thou seest me faynte,
[630] Addres thy selfe the gyde of my complaynt.

And thou O Ioue, that with thy depe fordoome
Dost rule the earth, and raygne aboue the skyes,
That wrekest wronges, and geuest the dreadful doome
Agaynst the wretche that doth thy trone despyse,
[635] Receyue these wurdes, and wreake them in such wyse,
As heauen and earth may witnesse and beholde,
Thy heapes of wrath vpon this wretche vnfolde.

Thou Banaster, gaynst thée I clepe and call
Vnto the Gods, that they iust vengeaunce take
[640] On thée, thy bloud, thy stayned stocke and all;
O Ioue, to thée aboue the rest I make
My humble playnt, guyde me that what I speake,
May be thy wyll vpon thys wretche to fall,
On thée Banastar, wretche of wretches all.

[645] O would to God, that cruel dismal daye,
That gaue me light fyrst to behold thy face,
With fowle eclypse had reft my syght away:
The vnhappy hower, the tyme, and eke the place,

[631] with the deepe G.
[634] thy name despise, C–G.
[645] God the cruell C–G.
[648] eke the day: C–G.

The sunne and Moone, the sters, and all that was
In theyr aspectes helping in ought to thée, [650]
The earth, and ayer, and all accursed bee.

And thou caytief, that like a monstar swarved,
From kynde and kyndenes, hast thy mayster lorne,
Whom neyther truth, nor trust wherein thou served,
Ne his desertes, could move, nor thy fayth sworne, [655]
Howe shall I curse, but wyshe that thou vnborne
Had bene, or that the earth had rent in twaye,
And swallowed thee in cradle as thou laye.

To this did I even from thy tender youth
Witsafe to bryng thée vp? dyd I herefore [660]
Beleve the oath of thy vndoubted trouth?
Aduaunce thée vp, and trust thée evermore?
By trusting thée that I should dye therefore?
O wretche, and wurse than wretche, what shal I say?
But cleap and curse gaynst thee and thine for aye. [665]

Hated be thou, disdaynd of every wyght,
And poynted at where ever that thou goe,
A trayterous wretche, vnwurthy of the light,
Be thou estemed: and to encrease thy woe,
The sound be hatefull of thy name also: [670]
And in this sort with shame and sharpe reproche,
Leade thou thy life till greater grief approch.

Dole and despayer, let those be thy delight,
Wrapped in woes that can not be vnfolde,
To wayle the daye, and wepe the weary night, [675]
With rayny iyen and syghes can not be tolde,
And let no wyght thy woe seeke to withholde:
But coumpt thée wurthy (wretche) of sorrowes store,
That suffryng much, oughtest still to suffer more,

[660] Witsafe to bryng *is printed* Witsave to dryng *but is corrected in* Be.
Witsaue to C–G.

341

[680]   Deserve thou death, yea be thou demed to dye
A shamefull death, to ende thy shamefull lyfe:
A syght longed for, ioyful to euerye iye,
Whan thou shalt be arraygned as a thief,
Standing at bar, and pleadyng for thy lyef,
[685] With trembling toung in dread and dolors rage,
Lade with white lockes, and fowerskore yeres of age.

    Yet shall not death delyuer thee so soone
Out of thy woes, so happye shalt thou not bee:
But to the eternall Ioue this is my boone,
[690] That thou may liue thine eldest sonne to see
Reft of his wits, and in a fowle bores stye
To ende his dayes in rage and death distrest,
A wurthy tumbe where one of thyne should rest.

    And after this, yet pray I more, thou may
[695] Thy second sonne sée drowned in a dyke,
And in such sorte to close his latter daye,
As heard or seen earst hath not bene the lyke:
Ystrangled in a puddle not so deepe
As halfe a foote, that such hard losse of lyfe,
[700] So cruelly chaunst, may be thy greater gryefe.

    And not yet shall thy hugie sorrowes cease,
Ioue shal not so withholde his wrath fro thée,
But that thy plagues may more and more encreas,
Thou shalt still lyve, that thou thy selfe mayst sée

[688]   shalt not bee: G.
[690]   thou maist liue C–G.
[694]   Yet after C–G.
[698]   not halfe so C–G.
[700]   be the greater C–G.
[701]   thy huge sorowes C–G.
[704]   thy selfe shalt see F.

Thy deare doughter stroken with leprosye: [705]
That she that earst was all thy hole delyght,
Thou now mayst loath to haue her cum in sight.

And after that, let shame and sorrowes gryefe
Feede furth thy yeares continually in wo,
That thou mayest live in death, and dye in lyef,   [710]
And in this sorte forewayld and wearyed so,
At length thy ghost to parte thy body fro:
This pray I Ioue, and wyth this latter breath,
Vengeaunce I aske vpon my cruell death.

This sayd, he floung his retcheles armes abrode,   [715]
And groveling flat vpon the ground he lay,
Which with his teeth he al to gnasht and gnawed:
Depe groanes he fet, as he that would awaye.
But loe in vayne he dyd the death assay:
Although I thinke was never man that knewe,   [720]
Such deadly paynes where death dyd not ensewe.

So strove he thus a while as with the death,
Nowe pale as lead, and colde as any stone.
Nowe styl as calme, nowe storming forth a breath
Of smoaky syghes, as breath and al were gone: [725]
But every thing hath ende: so he anone
Came to him selfe, when wyth a sygh outbrayed,
With woful cheare these woful wurdes he sayd.

Ah where am I, what thing, or whence is this?
Who reft my wyts? or howe do I thus lye?   [730]
My lims do quake, my thought agasted is,
Why sygh I so? Or wherevnto do I
Thus grovle on the ground? and by and by
Vpraysde he stoode, and wyth a sygh hath stayed,
When to him selfe retourned, thus he sayed.   [735]

[733] graule on C–F.

Suffiseth nowe this playnt and this regrete,
Whereof my hart his bottome hath vnfraught:
And of my death let pieres and princes wete
The worldes vntrust, that they thereby be taught.
[740] And in her wealth, sith that such chaunge is wrought,
Hope not to much, but in the myds of all
Thinke on my death, and what may them befall.

So long as Fortune would permyt the same,
I lyved in rule and ryches wyth the best:
[745] And past my time in honour and in fame.
That of mishap no feare was in my brest:
But false Fortune whan I suspected least,
Dyd turne the wheele, and wyth a dolefull fall
Hath me bereft of honour life and all.

[750] Loe what auayles in ryches fluds that flowes?
Though she so smylde as all the world wer his?
Euen kinges and kesars byden Fortunes throwes,
And simple sorte must bear it as it is.
Take hede by me that blithd in balefull blisse:
[755] My rule, my riches, royall blud and all,
Whan Fortune frounde the feller made my fall.

For hard mishaps that happens vnto such,
Whoes wretched state earst neuer fell no chaunge,
Agryue them not in any part so much,
[760] As theyr distres to whome it is so straunge,
That all theyr lyues nay passed pleasures raunge:
Theyr sodayne wo that ay wield welth at will,
Algates their hartes more pearcingly must thril.

[747] Fortune whom I G.

344

For of my byrth, my blud was of the best,
Fyrst borne an Earle, than duke by due discent: [765]
To swinge the sway in court amonge the rest,
Dame Fortune me her rule most largely lent:
And kynd with corage so my corps had blent,
That loe on whom but me dyd she most smyle?
And whom but me lo, dyd she most begyle?   [770]

Now hast thou heard the whole of my vnhap,
My chaunce, my chaunge, the cause of all my care:
In wealth and wo, how Fortune dyd me wrap,
With world at will to win me to her snare.
Byd kynges, byd kesars, by all states beware,   [775]
And tell them this from me that tryed it true.
Who reckles rules, right soone may hap to rue.

[768] kynde courage *C–F.*
[771] my mishap *F.*
[775] Kesars, bid al *FG.*

[Prose 22] HOw like you this my maisters (quoth I?) very wel said one: The tragedy excelleth: the inuencion also of the induction, and the discriptions are notable. But where as he faineth to talke with the princes in hel, that I am sure will be mislyked, because it is [5] moste certayne, that some of their soules be in heauen. And although he herein do follow allowed Poetes, in theyr discription of Hel, yet it sauoreth so much of Purgatory, whiche the papistes haue digged thereout, that the ignorant maye therby be deceyued. Not a whit I warrant you (quoth I) For he meaneth not by his Hell the place eyther of [10] damned soules, or of such as lye for their fees, but rather the Graue, wherin the dead bodies of al sortes of people do rest till tyme of the resurrection. And in this sence is Hel taken often in the scriptures, & in the writynges of learned christians. And so (as he himselfe hath tolde me) he meaneth, and so would haue it taken. Tush (quoth an other) [15] what stande we here vpon? it is a Poesie and no diuinitye, and it is lawfull for poetes to fayne what they lyst, so it be appertinent to the matter: And therfore let it passe euen in such sort as you haue read it. With a good will (quoth I) But where as you say a poet may faine what he list: In deede my thynke it should bee so, and ought to be well taken of the [20] hearers: but it hath not at al times been so allowed. Ye saye troth quoth the reader: For here followeth in the story, that after the death of this duke, one called Collingborne was cruelly put to death for makyng of a ryme. I haue his Tragedie here (quoth I) For the better perceyuing whereof, you must ymagin that you se him a meruaylous wel fauoured [25] man, holdinge in his hand, his owne hart, newely ripped out of his brest, and smoaking forth the lively spirit: and with his other hand, beckening to and fro, as it were to warne vs to auoyde: and with his faynte tounge and voyce, sayeng as coragiously as he mav ,these wordes that folowe.

[9]   (saide I) C–EG. sayd one: F.
[13–14] Christians, & so wold F.
[19]   me thinke FG.
[23]   (said I) C–G.
[26]   his hand, C–G.

Howe Collingbourne was cruelly executed [Tragedy 23]
for making a foolishe rime.

BEware, take heede, take heede, beware, beware
You Poetes you, that purpose to rehearce
By any arte what Tyrantes doynges are,
Erinnis rage is growen so fell and fearce
That vicious actes may not be toucht in verse: [5]
The Muses freedoome, graunted them of elde,
Is barde, slye reasons treasons hye are held.

Be rough in ryme, and then they say you rayle,
Though Iuuenal so be, that makes no matter:
With Ieremye you shal be had to iayle, [10]
Or forst with Marciall, Ceasars faultes to flatter,
Clarkes must be taught to clawe and not to clatter:
Free Hellicon, & franke Pernassus hylles,
Are Helly hauntes, & ranke pernicious ylles.

Touche couertly in termes, and then you taunt, [15]
Though praysed Poetes, alway dyd the lyke,
Controll vs not, els traytour vyle auaunt,
What passe we what the learned do mislyke?
Our sinnes we see, wherin to swarme we seeke.
We passe not what the people saye or thynke. [20]
Theyr shyttle hate maketh none but cowardes shrinke.

We knowe say they the course of Fortunes wheele,
Howe constantly it whyrleth styll about,
Arrearing nowe, whyle elder headlong reele.
Howe al the riders alwaye hange in doubt. [25]

[6]   *Mules* G.
[9]   As *Iuuenal* was, but that *C–G.*
[21]   makes G.
[22]   knowe *is printed* vnowe *but is corrected in* Be.

But what for that? we count him but a lowte
That stickes to mount, and basely like a beast
Lyves temperately for feare of blockam feast.

[30] In deede we would of all be deemed gods
What ever we doe: and therfore partely hate
Rude preachers that dare threaten vs plages & rods,
And blase the blots whereby we stayne our state:
But nought we passe what any such do prate.
Of course and office they must say theyr pleasure,
[35] And we of course must heare and mend at leasure.

But when these pelting poetes in theyr rymes
Shall taunt, and iest, or paynt our wicked wurkes,
And cause the people knowe, and curse our crymes,
This ougly fault, no Tyrant lyves but vrkes.
[40] And therefore lothe we taunters worse than Turkes.
They minde thereby to make vs knowe our mis,
And so to amend, but they but doate in this.

We knowe our faultes as wel as any other,
We also doubt the daungers for them due:
[45] Yet styll we trust so ryght to guyde the rother,
That skape we shal the sourges that ensue.
We thinke we knowe moe shiftes than other knewe.
In vayne therfore for vs are counsayles wryt:
We knowe our faultes, and wil not mend a whit.

[37]   taunt, or ieast, C–G.
[40]   Wherfore we loth such C–G.
[41]   Whose meaning is to C–G.
[42]   to mend, C–G.
[44]   daungers from them G.
[45]   to rule the G.
[47]   more G.

These are the affections of the wycked sorte,   [50]
That preace for honours, welth, and pleasure vayne.
Ceas therfore Baldwyn, ceas I thée exhort,
Withdrawe thy pen, for nothing shalt thou gayne
Save hate, with losse of paper, ynke and payne.
Fewe hate theyr sinnes, all hate to heare them touched,   [55]
Howe covertly so ever they be couched.

Thy entent I knowe is godly, playne, and good,
To warne the wyse, to fraye the fond fro yll:
But wycked worldelinges are so wytles wood,
That to the wurst they all thinges construe styl.   [60]
Wyth rygour oft they recompence good wyll:
They racke the wurdes tyl tyme theyr synowes burst,
In doubtfull sences, strayning styll the wurst.

A paynefull proofe taught me the truth of this,
Through Tyrauntes rage, and Fortunes cruel tourne: [65]
They murdred me, for metryng thinges amys.
For wotst thou what? I am that Colingbourne
Whych rymed that whych made full many mourne:
The Cat, the Rat, and Lovel our Dog,
Do rule al England, vnder a Hog.   [70]

Whereof the meanyng was so playne and true,
That every foole perceyved it at furst:
Most liked it, for most that most thinges knewe,
In hugger mugger, muttred what they durst.

[50]   the feats of the vnhappy sort, C–G.
[55–56] Fewe hate their faults, all hate of them to heare.
        And fautiest, from fault would seme most cleare. C–G.
[57]   is honest, playne, C–G.
[63]   In dolefull sences G.
[68]   Which made the ryme, wherof I may well mourne. C–G. [For
        may well read wel may F.]
[72]   foole is misprinted fooole in the text.

[75]   The kyng him selfe of most was held accurst,
Both for his owne and for his faultours faultes,
Of whom were three, the naughtiest of all naughtes.

    The chyefe was Catisby whom I called a Cat,
A crafty lawyer catching all he could.
[80]   The second Ratclife, whom I named a Rat,
A cruel beast to gnawe on whom he should.
Lord Lovell barkt & byt whom Rychard would.
Whom therfore ryghtly I dyd terme our Dog,
Wherewyth to ryme I cleped the Kyng a Hog.

[85]   Tyll he vsurped the crowne, he gave the Bore,
In whych estate would God he had deceased,
Than had the realme not ruyned so sore.
His Nephewes raygne should not so soone have ceassd,
The noble blud had not bene so decreased.
[90]   His Rat, his Cat, and Bloudhound had not noyed
So many thousandes as they have destroyed.

    Theyr laweles dealynges al men dyd lament,
And so dyd I, and therfore made the rymes
To shewe my wyt, howe wel I could invent,
[95]   To warne withal the careles of theyr crymes,
I thought the freedome of the auncient tymes
Stoode styll in force. *Ridentem dicere verum
Quis vetat?* None, save clymers stil in *ferum*.

[75]	The tyrant prince, of C–G.
[76]	his counsails faults, C–G.
[77]	whom was three C–F.
[78]	Catesby was one whome C–G.
[83]	Whom I therfore did rightly terme C–G.
[84]	I calde C–G.
[85]	Tyll he the crowne had caught, he C–G.
[91]	Such liegemen true, as after they destroyed. C–G.
[92]	lawlesse acts, good subiects did C–G.
[98]	*vetat?* Nay nay, *Veritas est pessima rerum* C–G. [*Read* pessuma *for* pessima G.]

Belyke no Tyrantes were in Horace dayes,
And therefore Poetes freely blamed vyce.   [100]
Witnes theyr Satyr sharpe, and tragicke playes,
With chyefest Prynces chyefly had in pryce.
They name no man, they myxe theyr gall with spyce,
No more do I, I name no man outryght,
But ryddle wise, I meane them as I myght.   [105]

When bruyt had brought this to theyr gylty eares,
Who rudely named were noted in the ryme,
They all conspyred like most greedy Beares,
To charge me wyth most haynous traytrous cryme:
And damned me the gallow tree to clyme,   [110]
And strangled fyrst in quarters to be cut,
Whych should on hye over London gates be put.

This wicked iudgement vexed me so sore,
That I exclamed agaynst theyr tyranny:
Wherewyth encenst, to make my payne the more,   [115]
They practised a shamefull villanye:
They cut me downe alyve, and cruelly
Rypt vp my paunche and bulke to make me smart,
And lingred long eare they tooke out my hart.

Here Tyraunt Rychard played the eager Hog,   [120]
His grashyng tuskes my tender grystels shore:
His bloudhound Lovell playd the ravenyng Dog,
His wuluishe teeth, my gylteles carkas toar:

[101]   Satyrs C–G.
[103]   myxe *is misprinted* myre *in the text.* mixe C–G.
[107]   Whose right surnames were C–G.
[109]   me straight with this most greuous cryme: C–G.
[111]   And then strangled, in C–G.
[113]   This iudgement geuen so vehement and sore C–G. [*Read* so sore *F.*]
[114]   Made me exclame C–G.
[122]   the hungry Dog, G.

[125] His Rat, and Cat, did what they myght, and more,
Cat Catesby clawed my guts to make me smart,
The Rat Lord Ratclyve gnawed me to the hart.

If Iewes had kylde the iustest kyng alyve,
If Turkes had burnt vp churches, Gods, and all,
What greater payne could cruel hartes contryve,
[130] Than that I suffred, for this trespas smal?
I am not Prince nor Piere, but yet my fall
Is wurthy to be thought vpon for this,
To see how cankard Tyrantes malyce is.

To teach also all subiectes to take heade
[135] They meddle not with Magistrates affayres,
But praye to God to mende them if it nede:
To warne also all Poetes that be strayers,
To kepe them close in compas of their chayers,
And whan they touch thinges which they wish amended.
[140] To sause them so, that fewe nede be offended.

And so to myxe theyr sharpe rebukes with myrth,
That they maye pearce, not causyng any payne,
Saue such as followeth euery kyndly byrth,
Requyted strayte, with gladnes of the gayne.
[145] A poet must be plesaunt, not to playne,
No flatterer, no bolsterer of vyce,
But sound and swete, in all thinges ware and wyse.

The Greekes do paynt a Poetes office whole
In Pegasus, theyr fayned horse wyth wynges,

[126] Rat Ratcliffe C–G.
[131] I was no prince C–G.
[136] if they neede: F.
[139] touch, that they would wish C–G.
[146] Faults to controll, ne yet to flatter vice C–G.

Whom shaped so Medusaes blud did foale,   [150]
Who with his feete strake out the Muses sprynges
Fro flintie rockes to Hellicon that clynges.
And then flewe vp vnto the starrye skye,
And there abides among the heauens hye.

    For he that shal a perfect Poete be,   [155]
Must fyrst be bred out of Medusaes blud:
He must be chaste and vertuous as was she,
Who to her power the Ocean god wythstoode.
To thende also his doome be iust and good,
He must (as she had) have one onlye iye,   [160]
Regarde of truth, that nought maye leade awrye.

    In courage eke he must be like a horse,
He maye not feare to register the ryght.
And that no power or fansie do him force,
No byt nor reyne his tender Iawes may twight.   [165]
He must be armed wyth strength of wyt and spryght
To dashe the rockes, darke causes and obscure,
Tyll he attayne the sprynges of truth most pure.

    His hooves must also plyant be and strong,
To ryve the rockes of lust and errors blynde,   [170]
In brayneles heades, that alway wander wrong:
These must he bryse wyth reasons playne and kinde,
Tyll sprynges of grace do gushe out of the minde.
For tyl affections from the fond be dryven,
In vayne is truth tolde, or good counsayle geuen.   [175]

[153]   vp into C–G.
[154]   An there G. the gods on hye. C–G.
[160]   (as she) looke rightly with one eye C–G.
[161]   Truth to regarde and write nothing awrye. C–G.
[164]   What though some frowne, thereof he may not force, C–G.
[167]   To *is misprinted* Do *in the text.* To dash C–G.
[169]   hooues also must plyant C–G.

Like Pegasus a Poet must have wynges,
To flye to heaven, thereto to feede and rest:
He must have knoweledge of eternal thynges,
Almighty Ioue must harber in his brest.
[180] With worldly cares he may not be opprest,
The wynges of skyll and hope must heaue him hyer,
That al the ioyes which worldly wyts desyre.

He must be also nymble, free, and swyft
To trauayle farre to viewe the trades of men,
[185] Great knowledge oft is gotten by the shyft:
Thynges notable he must be quicke to pen,
Reprouyng vyces sharpely now and then.
He must be swyft when touched tyrants chafe,
To gallop thence to kepe his carkas safe.

[190] These propertyes yf I had well consydered,
Especially that whych I touched last,
With speedy flyght my feete should have delyvered
My feble body from the stormy blast:
They should have caught me, ere I had be cast.
[195] But trusting vaynely to the Tyrauntes grace,
I never shronke, nor chaunged porte or place.

I thought the Poetes auncient liberties
Had bene allowed plea at any barre.

[177] heauen or where him liketh best: C–G.
[181] of wit and skill must C–G.
[182] With greate delight to satisfye desyer. C–G.
[183] must also be lusty, fre, C–G.
[185] often D–F. this shift: G.
[186] Things that impart he C–G. [*For* impart *read* import G.]
[190] If I had well these quallities considered. C–G.
[193] from a most boistous blast, C–G. [*Read* boystrous FG.]
[194] bene F.
[195] But to much trust vnto C–F. [*For* trust vnto *read* trusting to G.]
[198] For pleas had bene allowed at the bar. C–G.

I had forgot howe newefound tyrannies
Wyth ryght and freedome were at open warre,   [200]
That lust was lawe, that myght dyd make and mar,
That with the lewde save this no order was,
Sic volo, sic iubeo, stet pro ratione voluntas.

   Where this is lawe, it booteth not to pleade,
No pryuilege or libertyes auayle.   [205]
But wyth the learnde whom lawe and wisedome lead
Although through rashenes Poetes hap to rayle,
A plea of dotage may all quarels quayle:
Their libertyes theyr wrytinges to expounde,
Doth quyt them clere from faultes by Momus founde.   [210]

   This auncient freedome ought not be debarred
From any wyght that speaketh ought, or wryteth.
The authours meanyng should of ryght be heard,
He knoweth best to what ende he endyteth:
Wordes sometyme beare more than the hart behiteth.   [215]
Admyt therefore the authours exposicion,
Yf playne, for truth: if forst, for his submission.

   Of slaunderers iust lawes requyre no more
Save to amend that seemed euel sayd:
Or to vnsaye the slaunders sayd afore,   [220]
And aske forgeuenes for the hasty brayd:

[200]   With truth and *C–G.*
[202]   That among tyrants this is and euer was *C–G.*
[204]   Where lust is *C–G.*
[205]   priuelege nor *C–G.*
[209]   Their olde license their *C–G.*
[211]   This fredome olde ought *C–G.*
[218]   In case of sclaunder the lawes *C–G.*
[219]   seemed not well sayde: *C–G.*

To Heretykes no greater payne is layed
Than to recant theyr errours or retract:
And wurse than these can be no wryters acte.

[225]   Yes (quoth the Cat) thy rayling wordes be treason
And treason is far worse than heresye.
Then must it folowe by this foolyshe reason,
That kynges be more than God in maiestie,
And soules be lesse than bodyes in degree.
[230] For Heretikes both soules and God offend,
Traytours but seeke to bryng mans lyfe to ende.

I speake not this to abase the haynous faulte
Of traytrous actes abhord of God and man,
But to make playne theyr iudgement to be naught
[235] That heresye for lesser sinne do ban,
I curse them both as deepe as any can,
And alway dyd: yet through my foolyshe ryme,
They arraynde & staynde me wyth that shameful crime.

I never meant the kyng or counsayle harme,
[240] Vnles to wyshe them safetye were offence.
Agaynst theyr power I neuer lyfted arme,
Neyther pen nor tounge for any yll pretence.
The ryme I made, though rude, was sound in sence,
For they therein whom I so fondly named,
[245] So ruled all that they were fowle defamed.

This was no treason but the very troth,
They ruled all, none could denye the same:
What was the cause then why they were so wroth?

[227]   this awkwarde reason, C–G.
[233]   abhorde by God C–G.
[238]   They stayned me with that most hatefull cryme. C–G.

What, is it treason in a riming frame
To clyp, to stretche, to adde, or chaunge a name?   [250]
And this reserved, there is no rime or reason,
That any craft can clowt to seeme a treason.

   For where I meant the kyng by name of Hog,
I only alluded to his badge the Boare:
To Lovels name I added more our Dog,   [255]
Because most Dogs have borne that name of yore.
These metafors I vse with other more,
As Cat, and Rat, the halfe names of the rest,
To hide the sence which they so wrongly wrest.

   I praye you nowe what treason fynde you here?   [260]
Enough: you rubbed the gylty on the gal,
Both sence and names do note them very nere.
I graunt that was the chiefe cause of my fall,
Yet can you finde therein no treason at all:
There is no worde agaynst the prynce or state,   [265]
Nor harme to them whom al the realme dyd hate.

   But sith the gylty alwayes are suspicious,
And dread the ruyne that must sewe by reason,
They can not chose but count theyr counsayle vicious
That note theyr faultes, and therfore cal it treason: [270]
All grace and goodnes with the lewde is geason.
This is the cause why they good thinges detest,
Whereas the good take yll thynges to the best.

[251]   ryme nor C–G.
[257]   vsde G.
[266]   No harme C–G.
[272]   things do wrest C–G.

And therfore Baldwyn boldly to the good
[275] Rebuke thou vice, so shalt thou purchase thankes
As for the bad thou shalt but move his mood,
Though plesantly thou touch his sinfull prankes:
Warne poetes therfore not to passe the bankes
Of Hellicon, but kepe them in the streames,
[280] So shall their freedome save them from extreames.

[275] Rebuke their falt, *C–G.*
[276] moue their moode, *C–G.*
[277] touch their naughty prankes: *C–G.*
[278] Poets all, no wyse to *C–G.*
[279] kepe within the bound: *C–G.*
[280] fredome vnto no harme redound. *C–G.* [*For* vnto *read* to *G.*]

GOds blessing on his heart that made thys (sayd one) specially [Prose 23]
for reuiuinge our auncient liberties. And I pray god it may
take suche place with the Magistrates, that they maye ratifie
our olde freedome, Amen (quoth another) For that shalbe a meane
bothe to staye and vpholde them selves from fallyng: and also to pre- [5]
serve many kinde, true, zealous, and well meaning mindes from
slaughter and infamie. If kyng Richard and his counsayloures had
allowed, or at the least but wynked at sum such wits, what greate com-
modities myght they have taken thereby. Fyrst, they should have
knowen what the people myslyked and grudged at, (which no one of [10]
theyr flatterers eyther would or durst have tolde them) & so mought
have found meane, eyther by amendment (whyche is best) or by some
other pollicie to have stayed the peoples grudge: the forerunner commonly of Rulers destructions. *Vox populi, vox dei*, in this case is not so
famous a proverbe as true: The experyence of all times doth approve it. [15]
They should also have bene warned of theyr owne sinnes, whyche call
continually for Gods vengeance, which never fayleth to fall on theyr
neckes sodaynely and horriblye, vnles it be stayed with harty repentaunce.

These weyghtye commodityes mought they have taken by Colling-
bornes vayne ryme. But as all thinges worke to the best in them [20]
that be good, so best thinges heape vp mischiefe in the wicked, and all
to hasten theyr vtter destruction. For after this poore wretches lamentable persecution, (the common reward of best endeuors) strayt folowed
the eternal destruction both of this Tyraunt, and of his tormentors.
Whiche I wyshe myght be so set furth, that they might be a warning for [25]
ever, to al in authoritye to beware howe they vsurpe or abuse theyr
offices. I haue here (quoth I) king Richards tragedie. Reade it we pray
you (quoth they). With a good wyll (quoth I) For the better vnderstanding whereof, imagine that you see him tormented with Dives in
the diepe pit of Hell, and thence howlinge this that foloweth. [30]

[4]   Amen saide another C–G.
[14]   destruction. G.
[15]   tymes do approue C–G.
[24]   the fatall destruction C–G.
[30]   this whiche followeth. C–G.

[Tragedy 24] How Richard Plantagenet duke of Glocester, murdered his brothers children vsurping the crowne, and
in the third yeare of his raygne was most worthely deprived of life and kingdome in Bosworth
playne by Henry Earle of Richemond
after called king Henry the .vii.

Hat hart so hard, but doth abhorre to heare
The ruful raygne of me the thyrd Rychard?
King vnkindely cald though I the crowne dyd weare,
Who entred by rigour, but ryght did not regard,
[5]   By tyranny proceding in kyllyng kyng Edward,
Fyft of that name, ryght heyre vnto the crowne,
With Rychard his brother, prynces of renowne.

    Of trust they were committed vnto my governaunce,
But trust turned to treason to truly it was tryed,
[10]   Both agaynst nature, duetye, and allegiaunce,
For through my procurement most shamefully they died
Desire of a kyngdome forgetteth all kynred,
As after by discourse it shalbe shewed here,
How cruelly these innocentes in pryson murdred were.

[15]   The Lordes and Commons all with one assent,
Protectour made me both of land and Kyng,
But I therewyth alas was not content:
For mindyng mischiefe I ment another thyng,
Which to confusion in short time dyd me bryng,
[20]   For I desyrous to rule and raygne alone,
Sought crowne and kingdome, yet title had I none.

[Title] the vii. the 22. of August. 1485. C–G.

To all Piers and princes a president I may be.
The like to beware howe they do enterpryse,
And learne theyr wretched falles by my fact to forsee,
Which ruful stand bewayling my chaunce before theyr eyes, [25]
As one cleane bereft of all felicities:
For ryght through might I cruelly defaced,
But might helped ryght, and me agayne dysplaced.

Alas that ever Prince should thus his honour stayne
With the bloud of Innocentes most shameful to be tolde [30]
For these two noble ympes I caused to be slayne,
Of yeares not ful rype as yet to rule and raygne.
For which I was abhorred both of yong and old,
But as the deede was odious in syght of god and man,
So shame and destruction in the ende I wan. [35]

Both God, nature, dutie, allegiaunce al forgott,
This vile and haynous acte vnnaturally I conspyred:
Which horrible deede done, alas, alas, god wot
Such terrors me tormented, and so my spyrytes fyred
As vnto such a murder and shameful deede requyred, [40]
Such broyle dayly felt I breeding in my brest,
Wherby more and more, increased myne vnrest.

My brothers children were right heyres vnto the crowne
Whom nature rather bound to defend than distroy,
But I not regarding theyr ryght nor my renowne [45]
My whole care and study to this ende did imploye,
The crowne to obtayne, and them both to put downe:
Wherein I God offended, prouoking iust his yre,
For this my attempt and most wicked desyre.

[37] vnnaturally conspyred: *C–G.*
[39] sprites *C–G.*
[43] the *is misprinted* rhe *in the text.* heires to the *D–F.*

[50]   To cruel cursed Cayn compare my carefull case,
Whych did vniustly slaye his brother iust Abel,
And did not I in rage make runne that rufull race
My brother duke of Clarens, whose death I shame to tell
For that so straunge it was, as it was horrible?
[55]   For sure he drenched was, and yet no water neare,
Which strange is to be tolde to al that shal it heare.

The But he was not whereat I dyd shoote,
But yet he stoode betwene the marke and me:
For had he lived, for me it was no boote
[60]   To tempt the thing that by no meanes could be,
For I thyrd was then of my brethren thrée:
But yet I thought the elder beyng gone,
Then nedes must I beare the stroke alone.

Desire to rule made me alas to rewe,
[65]   My fatal fall I could it not forsee,
Puft vp in pride, so hawtie then I grewe,
That none my peare I thought now could be,
Disdayning such as were of hygh degree:
Thus dayly rising and pulling other downe,
[70]   At last I shot howe to wyn the crowne.

And dayly deuising which was the best waye
And meane howe I myght my nephewes both deuoure
I secretely then sent wythout further delay
To Brackynbury then lieuetenaunt of the tower,
[75]   Requesting him by letters to helpe vnto his power,
For to accomplyshe this my desire and wyl,
And that he would secretely my brothers children kyll.

[50]   To cursed Cayn C–G.
[54]   that it was so straunge as G.
[60]   To attempt F.
[64]   Desyre of rule C–G.
[66]   to hawtye C–F.

He aunswered playnely with a flat naye,
Sayeng that to dye he would not doe that dede:
But finding then a proffer ready for my pray, [80]
Wel worth a frende (quoth I) yet in time of nede.
Iames Tyrryl hyte his name, whom wyth al speede,
I sent agayne to Brackynbury, as you heard before,
Commaunding him deliver the keyes of every dore.

The keyes he rendered, but partaker would not be [85]
Of that flagitious facte. O happy man I say,
And as you heard before, he rather chose to dye
Then on those silly lambes his violent handes to lay.
His conscience him prycked, his prynce to betray:
O constant minde, that wouldest not condyscend, [90]
Thee may I prayse, and my selfe discommend.

What though he refused, yet be sure you maye,
That other were as ready to take in hand the thyng,
Which watched and wayted as duely for theyr pray,
As ever dyd the Cat for the Mouse taking, [95]
And howe they might their purpose best to passe bryng:
Where Tyrryl he thought good to have no bloud shed,
Becast them to kyl by smothering in theyr bed.

The Wolves at hand were ready to devoure
The silly lambes in bed whereas they laye [100]
Abiding death and looking for the hower,
For well they wyst, they could not scape awaye.
Ah, woe is me, that did them thus betraye,
In assigning this vile dede to be done,
By Myles Forrest, and wycked Iohn Dyghton. [105]

[80]   proffer to my C–G.
[87]   As you haue heard C–G.
[88]   lay *is printed* lye *but is corrected in* Be.
[93]   hand that thing, C–G.

Who priuely into theyr chamber stale,
In secrete wyse somewhat before midnyght,
And gan the bed together tug and hale,
Bewrapping them alas in rufull plyght,
[110] Keping them downe, by force, by power, and might,
With haling, tugging, tormoyling, torne and tost,
Tyl they of force were forced yeeld the ghost.

Which when I heard, my hart I felt was eased
Of grudge, of gryefe, and inward deadly payne,
[115] But with this deede the Nobles were displeased,
And sayd: O God, shal such a Tyraunt raygne,
That hath so cruelly his brothers chyldren slayne?
Which brute once blowen in the peoples eares,
Theyr dolour was such, that they brast out in teares.

[120] But what thing may suffise vnto the bloudy man,
The more he bathes in bloud, the bloudier he is alway:
By proofe I do this speake, whych best declare it can,
Which only was the cause of this prynces decaye.
The wolfe was never greedier than I was of my pray,
[125] But who so vseth murder ful wel affirme I dare,
Wyth murder shal be quyt, ere he therof be ware.

And marke the sequell of this begonne mischiefe
Which shortly after was cause of my decaye,
For high and lowe conceyved such a gryefe
[130] And hate against me, whych sought day by daye,
All wayes and meanes that possible they may,
On me to be revenged for this sinne,
For cruell murdering vnnaturally my kyn.

[109] in wofull plight, *C–G.*
[111] turmoyling, turnde and *C–G.*
[114] griefe of inward *D–F.*
[120] the gredy man, *C–G.*
[133] cruelly *G.*

Not only kyn, but kyng the truth to saye
Whom vnkyndely of kyngdome I bereft,   [135]
His life also from him I raught away,
With his brothers, whych to my charge were left.
Of ambicion behold the worke and weft,
Prouoking me to do this haynous treason,
And murder them agaynst al right and reason.   [140]

After whose death thus wrought by violence,
The Lordes not liking this vnnaturall dede,
Began on me to have great diffidence,
Such brynnyng hate gan in their hartes to breede,
Which made me doubt, and sore my daunger drede: [145]
Which doubt and drede proved not in vayne,
By that ensewed alas vnto my payne.

For I supposing all thinges were as I wyshed,
When I had brought these silly babes to bane,
But yet in that my purpose farre I missed: [150]
For as the Moone doth chaunge after the wane,
So chaunged the hartes of such as I had tane
To be most true, to troubles dyd me turne,
Such rage and rancour in boyling brestes do burne.

And sodaynely a bruyte abrode was blowen,   [155]
That Buckingham the duke both sterne and stout,
In fyeld was ready, with divers to me knowen,
To gyve me battayle if I durst come out:
Which daunted me and put me in great doubt,
For that I had no armie then prepared,   [160]
But after that I litel for it cared.

[136]   lyfe from him I also raught C–G.
[137]   was left. C–F.
[154]   doth burne. G.

But yet remembryng, that oft a lytle sparke
Suffered doth growe vnto a great flame,
I thought it wysedome wisely for to warke,
[165] Mustered then men in every place I came.
And marching forward dayly wyth the same,
Directly towardes the towne of Salisbury,
Where I gat knowledge of the dukes army.

And as I passed over Salysbury downe,
[170] The rumour ran the duke was fled and gone,
His hoste dispersed besides Shrewisbury towne,
And he dismayd was left there post alone,
Bewayling his chaunce and makyng great mone:
Towardes whom I hasted with al expedicion,
[175] Making due serche and diligent inquisicion.

But at the first I could not of him heare,
For he was scaped by secrete bywayes,
Vnto the house of Humfrey Banystar,
Whom he had much preferred in his dayes,
[180] And was good lord to him in al assayes:
Which he ful euel requyted in the ende,
When he was driven to seeke a trustye frende.

For it so happened to his mishap, alas,
When I no knowledge of the Duke could heare
[185] A proclamacion by my commaundement was
Publyshed and cryed throughout euery shyre,
That who so could tel where the Duke were,
A thousand marke should have for his payne,
What thing so hard but money can obtayne?

[166] marched G.
[181] full ill requited G.

But were it for mony, mede, or drede,   [190]
That Banystar thus betrayed his ghest,
Divers have diversly deuined of this dede,
Some deeme the worst, and some iudge the best,
The doubt not dissolved nor playnely exprest,
But of the Dukes death he doubteles was cause,   [195]
Which dyed without iudgement or order of lawes.

Loe this noble Duke I brought thus vnto bane,
Whose doynges I doubted and had in great dred,
At Banysters house I made him to be tane,
And wythout iudgement be shortened by the head,   [200]
By the Shrive of Shropshire to Salisbury led.
In the market place vpon the scaffolde newe
Where all the beholders did much his death rewe.

And after this done I brake vp my hoste,
Greatly applauded with this happy happe,   [205]
And forthwyth I sent to every sea coste
To foresee al mischieues and stoppe every gappe,
Before they should chaunce and lyght in my lappe
Geving them in charge to have good regarde
The sea coast to kepe with good watche and warde.   [210]

Directing my letters vnto every shryve,
With strayt commaundement vnder our name,
To suffer no man in theyr partes to aryve
Nor to passe forth out of the same,
As they tendered our favour, and voyd would our blame,   [215]
Doyng therein their paine and industrye,
With diligent care and vigilant eye.

[204]   the hoaste, F.
[205]   this heauy hap, C–G.
[208]   chaunce or light C–G.

And thus setting thinges in order as you heare,
To prevent mischieves that myght then betyde,
[220] I thought my selfe sure, and out of all feare,
And for other thinges began to provyde:
To Notyngham castel strayt dyd I ride,
Where I was not very long space,
Straunge tydinges came whych dyd me sore amase.

[225] Reported it was, and that for certaynetye,
Therle of Rychemond landed was in Wales
At Mylford haven, wyth an huge armye,
Dismissing his navie which were many sayles:
Whych at the fyrst I thought fleing tales.
[230] But in the ende dyd otherwyse prove,
Which not a litle dyd me vexe and move.

Thus fawning Fortune began on me to frowne,
And cast on me her scorneful lowring looke:
Then gan I feare the fall of my renowne,
[235] My hart it faynted, my sinowes sore they shooke,
This heauy happe a scourge for sinne I tooke,
Yet dyd I not then vtterly despayre,
Hooping stormes past, the weather should be fayre.

And then with all speede possible I myght,
[240] I caused them muster through out every shyre,
Determining wyth the Earle spedely to fyght,
Before that his power much encreased were,
By such as to him great favour did beare:
Which were no smal number by true reporte made,
[245] Dayly repayring him for to ayde.

Directing my letters to divers noble men,
With earnest request theyr power to prepare,

[232] Fortune gan on C–G.

To Notyngham castel where as I laye then.
To ayde and assyst me in this weyghty affayre:
Where strayt to my presence did then repayre,   [250]
Iohn duke of Norfolke, his eldest sonne also,
With therle of Northhumberland and many other mo.

    And thus beyng furnysht with men and municion,
Forward we marched in order of battayle raye,
Makyng by scoutes every way inquisicion,   [255]
In what place the earle with his campe laye:
Towardes whom directly we tooke then our waye,
Evermore minding to seeke our most auayle,
In place convenient to gyve to him battayle.

    So long we laboured, at last our armies met   [260]
On Bosworth playne besydes Lecester towne,
Where sure I thought the garland for to get,
And purchase peace, or els to lose my crowne.
But fyckle Fortune alas on me dyd frowne,
For when I was encamped in the fyelde,   [265]
Where most I trusted I soonest was begyld.

    The brand of malyce thus kyndlyng in my brest
Of deadly hate which I to him dyd beare,
Prycked me forward, and bad me not desist,
But boldely fight, and take at all no feare,   [270]
To wynne the fyeld, and the earle to conquere:
Thus hopyng glory great to gayne and get,
My army then in order dyd I set.

    Betide me life or death I desperately ran,
And ioyned me in battayle wyth this Earle so stoute,   [275]
But Fortune so him fauoured that he the battayle wan
With force and great power I was beset about,
Which when I did behold, in myds of the whole rout

[273] Myne army C–G.
[278] in midst of G.

[280] With dent of sword I cast me on him to be revenged,
Where in the middest of them my wretched life I ended.

My body it was hurryed and tugged like a Dogge,
On horsebacke all naked and bare as I was borne.
My head, handes, & feete, downe hanging like a Hogge,
With dyrt and bloud besprent, my corps al to torne,
[285] Cursing the day that ever I was borne.
With greuous woundes bemangled most horrible to se
So sore they did abhorre this my vile crueltye.

Loe here you may beholde the due and iust rewarde
Of tiranny and treason which God doth most detest,
[290] For if vnto my duety I had taken regarde,
I myght haue lived stil in honour with the best,
And had I not attempt the thing that I ought lest.
But desire to rule alas dyd me so blinde,
Which caused me to do agaynst nature and kynde.

[295] Ah cursed caytive why did I clymbe so hye,
Which was the cause of this my baleful thrall.
For styll I thyrsted for the regal dignitie,
But hasty rising threatneth sodayne fall,
Content your selves with your estates all,
[300] And seeke not right by wrong to suppresse,
For God hath promist eche wrong to redresse.

See here the fine and fatall fall of me,
And guerdon due for this my wretched deede,
Whych to all prynces a myrrour nowe may be
[305] That shal this tragicall story after reede,
Wyshyng them all by me to take heede,
And suffer ryght to rule as it is reason,
For Time trieth out both truth and also treason.

[302] fine and fall D–F.

WHen I had read this, we had much talke about it. For it [Prose 24] was thought not vehement ynough for so violent a man as kyng Rychard had bene. The matter was wel ynough lyked of sum, but the meeter was mysliked almost of all. And when divers therefore would not allowe it, what (quoth one). You knowe [5] not wherevpon you sticke: elles you would not so much mislike this because of the vncertayne Meter. The cumlynes called by the Rhetoricians *decorum*, is specially to be observed in al thinges. Seyng than that kyng Rychard never kept measure in any of his doings, seing also he speaketh in Hel, whereas is no order: it were agaynst the *decorum* of his personage, [10] to vse eyther good Meter or order. And therfore, if his oracion were far wurse, in my opinion it were more fyt for him. Mars and the Muses did never agree. Neyther is it to be suffred that their milde sacred Arte shoulde seeme to proceede from so cruell and prophane a mouth as his: seynge they them selves do vtterly abhorre it. And although we read of [15] Nero, that he was excellent both in Musicke, and in versifieng, yet do not I remember that ever I saw any song or verse of his makyng: Minerua iustlye providing, that no monument should remayne of any such vniust vsurpacion. And therefore let thys passe euen as it is, which the wryter I know both could and would amend in many places, save for [20] kepyng the *decorum*, which he purposely hath observed herein.

In deede (quoth I) as you saye: It is not meete that so disorderly and vnnatural a man as kyng Rychard was, shuld observe any metrical order in his talke: which notwithstanding in many places of his oracion is very wel kept: It shall passe therefore even as it is, though to good for [25]

[*Folio 165, on the recto and verso of which is printed this prose link, is missing in the HN copy of F but is preserved in the copy of F².*]
[10]   against that *Decorum* G.
[15]   do abhorre it. *F.*

so yll a person. And to supplye that whych is lackinge in him, here I haue Shores wyfe, an eloquent wentch, whyche shall furnishe out both in meter and matter, that which could not comlily be sayd in his person. Marke I praye you what she sayeth, and tell me howe you like it.

[26]   so euell a C–G.
> *[Because of the rearrangement of the tragedies in later editions, the closing lines of the prose link are changed so that it may introduce the tragedy of the blacksmith. All editions after the first (B) substitute for the last two sentences the substance of Prose 26. See the collation of Prose 26. The passage after* person *in l. 26 is transferred in editions C–F to Prose 27 and is accordingly here collated with its variants found in Prose 27 when that link serves to introduce the tragedy of Jane Shore (C–F).]*

[26–27] But because these two persons last before rehersed were thoughte not onelye obscure in the matter but also crabbed in the meeter, (I haue here redy to supply that which lacked in them) Shores wyfe, *C–F. [Omit* the *before* matter *F.*]

[27]   fynish out *C–F.*
[28]   in their persons. *C–F.*

> *[In the edition of* 1587 *(G) a wholly new prose link serves to introduce Jane Shore, which link, on folio* 259, *follows directly the tragedy of Brampton, or Flodden Field (see Introduction, p.* 19*):*
>
> THe open bruite of Princes falles and such as bare sway in this Realme, made mee poore haplesse woman (though once in great place) presume to shew my selfe emong that infortunate flock. And making more haste then good speede, I appeared fyrst to one *Baldwine* a Minister and a Preacher:
>
> 5 whose function and calling disdaynes to looke so lowe, as to searche the secrets of wanton women, (though commonly a Preacher with sufferaunce may rebuke vice.) Wherefore I haue better bethought mee, and so doe sodaynly appeale and appeare to some martiall man, who hath more experience both in defending of womens honour, and knowes somwhat
>
> 10 more of theyr conditions and qualityes: and the rather, because my tragedy was in question among some that would not spare due commendation to the autor therof. I now appeare to him that fyrst set mee forth, a writer of good continuance, and one that dayly is exercised to set out both matter tragicall, and other prophane histories and verses, whose name is *Churchyard*:
>
> 15 hee shall not only haue the fame of his owne worke (which no man can deny) but shall likewise haue all the glory I can gieue him, if hee lend mee the hearing of my woefull tale, a matter scarce fit for womans shamefastnes to bewray. But since without blushing I haue so long beene a talkatiue wench, (whose words a world hath delighted in) I will now goe on boldly
>
> 20 with my audacious manner: and so step I on the stage in my shrowdeing sheete as I was buried.]

372

Howe Shores wife, Edwarde the fowerthes concubine, was by king Richarde despoyled of all her goodes, and forced to do open penance.

𝕬Mong the rest by Fortune overthrowen,
I am not least, that most may wayle her fate:
My fame and brute abrode the world is blowen,
Who can forget a thing thus done so late?
My great mischaunce, my fall, and heauye state,   [5]
Is such a marke whereat eche tounge doth shoote,
That my good name is pluckt vp by the roote.

This wandryng worlde bewitched me with wyles,
And wonne my wittes wyth wanton sugred ioyes,
In Fortunes frekes who trustes her when she smyles,   [10]
Shal fynde her false, and full of fyckle toyes,
Her tryumphes al but fyl our eares wyth noyse,
Her flatteryng gyftes are pleasures myxt wyth payne.
Yea al her wordes are thunders threatnyng rayne.

The fond desire that we in glory set,   [15]
Doth thirle our hartes to hope in slipper happe,
A blast of pompe is all the fruyt we get,
And vnder that lyes hidde a sodayne clappe:
In seeking rest vnwares we fall in trappe.
In groping flowers wyth Nettels stong we are,   [20]
In labouring long, we reape the crop of care.

[Title] wyfe, Kinge Edwarde C-G.

373

Oh darke deceyt with paynted face for showe,
Oh poysoned baite that makes vs egre styll,
Oh fayned frende deceyuing people so,
[25] Oh world of thée we can not speake to yll,
Yet fooles we are that bende so to thy skyll,
The plage and skourge that thousandes dayly feele,
Should warne the wise to shonne thy whyrling whele.

But who can stop the streame that runnes full swyft?
[30] Or quenche the fyer that crept is in the strawe?
The thirstye drinkes, there is no other shyft,
Perforce is such, that nede obeyes no lawe,
Thus bound we are in worldly yokes to drawe,
And can not staye, nor turne agayne in tyme,
[35] Nor learne of those that sought to hygh to clyme.

My selfe for proofe, loe here I nowe appeare,
In womans weede with wepyng watered eyes,
That bought her youth and her delyghtes ful deare.
Whose lowde reproche doth sound vnto the skyes
[40] And byds my corse out of the grave to ryse,
As one that may no longer hide her face,
But nedes must come and shewe her piteous case.

The shete of shame wherein I shrowded was
Did move me ofte to playne before this daye,
[45] And in mine eares dyd ryng the trumpe of brasse,
Which is defame that doth eche vice bewraye.
Yea though ful dead and lowe in earth I laye,
I heard the voyce of me what people sayd,
But then to speake alas I was affrayed.

[26] Yet fooles we *C.* that ben so *C–E.* are to bend *F.*
[30] that crept is in *is printed* that is crept is in *but is corrected in Be.* that is crept in *C–E.*
[39] vnto skies *DE.*
[46] each thing bewraye. *G.*

And nowe a time for me I see preparde, [50]
I heare the lives and falles of many wyghtes:
My tale therfore the better may be heard,
For at the torche the litle candle lightes.
Where Pageantes be, small thinges fil out the sightes.
Wherefore geve eare, good Baldwyn do thy best, [55]
My tragedy to place among the rest.

Because that truthe shal witnesse wel with thee,
I wil rehearse in order as it fell,
My life, my death, my dolefull destenie,
My wealth, my woe, my doing every deale, [60]
My bitter blisse, wherein I long dyd dwell:
A whole discourse of me Shores wife by name,
Now shalt thou heare as thou hadst sene the same.

Of noble bloud I can not boast my byrth,
For I was made out of the meanest molde, [65]
Myne heritage but seven foote of earth,
Fortune ne gave to me the gyftes of golde:
But I could bragge of nature if I would,
Who fyld my face with favour freshe and fayer,
Whose beautie shone like Phebus in the ayer [70]

My shape, some sayd, was seemely to eche sight,
My countenaunce did shewe a sober grace,
Myne eyes in lookes were never proved lyght,
My tongue in wordes were chaste in every case,
Myne eares were deafe, and would no lovers place, [75]
Save that (alas) a prynce dyd blot my browe,
Loe, there the strong did make the weake to bowe.

[55] good *Churcheyard* do G.
[57] Because the truth C–G.
[62] discourse by me C–G.
[66] of earth, *is printed* of the earth *but is corrected in Be.* of the earth, C–EG.
[74] wordes was chast FG.

The maiestie that kynges to people beare,
The stately porte, the awful chere they showe,
[80] Doth make the meane to shrynke and couche for feare,
Like as the hound, that doth his maister knowe:
What then, since I was made vnto the bowe:
There is no cloke, can serve to hyde my fault,
For I agreed the fort he should assaulte.

[85] The Egles force, subdues eche byrd that flyes,
What mettal may resist the flaming fyre?
Doth not the sonne, dasill the clearest eyes,
And melt the ise, and make the frost retire?
Who can withstand a puissaunt kynges desyre?
[90] The stiffest stones are perced through with tooles,
The wisest are with princes made but fooles.

Yf kynde had wrought my forme in common frames,
And set me forth in coloures black and browne,
Or beautie had bene parched in Phebus flames,
[95] Or shamefast waies had pluckt my fethers downe,
Then had I kept my name and good renowne:
For natures gyftes was cause of all my griefe.
A pleasaunt pray entiseth many a thiefe.

Thus woe to thee that wrought my peacocks pryde
[100] By clothing me with natures tapistrye,
Woe wurth the hewe wherein my face was dyed,
Whych made me thinke I pleased everye eye:
Like as the sterres make men beholde the skye,
So beauties showe doth make the wife ful fond.
[105] And bringes free hartes ful oft to endeles bond.

[94] percht G.
[96] my fame and C-G.
[97] gifts, were cause G.

But cleare from blame my frendes can not be found,
Before my time my youth they did abuse:
In maryage, a prentyse was I bound,
When that meere love I knewe not howe to vse.
But wealaway, that can not me excuse,   [110]
The harme is mine though they deuysed my care,
And I must smart and syt in slaundrous snare.

   Yet geve me leave to pleade my case at large,
Yf that the horse do runne beyond his race,
Or any thing that kepers have in charge   [115]
Do breake theyr course, where rulers may take place,
Or meat be set before the hungryes face,
Who is in fault? the offendour yea or no,
Or they that are the cause of all this wo?

   Note wel what stryfe this forced maryage makes,   [120]
What lothed lyves do come where love doth lacke,
What scratting bryers do growe vpon such brakes,
What common weales by it are brought to wracke,
What heavy loade is put on pacientes backe,
What straunge delyghtes this braunch of vice doth brede [125]
And marke what graine sprynges out of such a seede.

   Compel the hawke to syt that is vnmande,
Or make the hound vntaught to drawe the dere,
Or bryng the free agaynst his wil in band,
Or move the sad a pleasaunt tale to heare,   [130]
Your time is lost and you are never the nere:
So love ne learnes of force the knot to knyt,
She serves but those that feele sweete fancies fyt,

[109] Then that C–G.
[113] my cause C–G.
[122] What scratching breers C–G.
[131] you no whit the G.

The lesse defame redoundes to my disprayse,
I was entyste by traynes, and trapt by trust:
Though in my power remayned yeas or nayes,
Vnto my frendes yet nedes consent I must,
In every thing, yea lawfull or vniust:
They brake the boowes and shakte the trée by sleyght,
And bent the wand that might have growen ful streight

What helpe in this, the pale thus broken downe,
The Deere must nedes in daunger runne astraye:
At me therfore why should the world so frowne,
My weakenes made my youth a prynces praye.
Though wysedome should the course of nature stay,
Yet trye my case who lyst, and they shal prove,
The rypest wittes are soonest thralles to love.

What nede I more to cleare my selfe to much?
A kyng me wanne, and had me at his call:
His royall state, his pryncely grace was such,
The hope of will (that women seeke for all,)
The ease and wealth, the gyftes whych were not smal,
Besieged me so strongly rounde aboute,
My power was weake, I could not holde him out.

Duke haniball in all his conquest greate.
Or Ceaser yet, whose tryumphes did excede,
Of all their spoyles which made them toÿle and sweat,
Were not so glad to haue so ryche a meade.
As was this prince when I to hym agreed.
And yelded me a prisoner willynglye,
As one that knew no way awaye to flee.

[136] yeas and nayes, *C–G.*
[148] so much? *G.*
[152] ease, the wealth, *F.*
[161] to flye. *C–G.*

The Nightingale for all his mery voyce
Nor yet the Larke that stil delightes to syng,
Did never make the hearers so reioyce,
As I with wordes have made this worthy kyng: [165]
I never iard, in tune was every stryng,
I tempered so my tounge to please his eare,
That what I sayd was currant every where.

 I ioynde my talke, my gestures, and my grace
In wittie frames that long might last and stand,   [170]
So that I brought the kyng in such a case,
That to his death I was his chiefest hand.
I governed him that ruled all this land:
I bare the sword though he did weare the crowne,
I strake the stroke that threwe the mightye downe. [175]

 Yf iustice sayd that iudgement was but death,
With my sweete wordes I could the kyng perswade,
And make him pause and take therein a breath,
Tyl I wyth suyte the fawtors peace had made:
I knewe what waye to vse him in his trade,   [180]
I had the arte to make the Lyon meeke,
There was no poynt wherein I was to seeke.

 Yf I did frowne, who then did looke awrye?
Yf I dyd smyle, who would not laugh outryght?
Yf I but spake, who durst my wordes denye?   [185]
Yf I pursued, who would forsake the flyght?
I meane my power was knowen to every wyght.
On such a heyght good hap had buylt my bower,
As though my swete should never have turnd to sower.

[180] him is his C.
[189] nere haue G.

[190]   My husband then, as one that knewe his good,
        Refused to kepe a prynces concubine,
        Forseing the ende and mischiefe as it stoode,
        Agaynst the king did never much repyne,
        He sawe the grape whereof he dranke the wyne,
[195]   Though inward thought his hart did still torment,
        Yet outwardly he seemde he was content.

        To purchase prayse and winne the peoples zeale,
        Yea rather bent of kinde to do some good,
        I ever did vpholde the common weale,
[200]   I had delyght to save the gylteles bloud :
        Eche suters cause when that I vnderstoode,
        I did preferre as it had bene mine owne,
        And helpt them vp, that might have bene orethrowne.

        My power was prest to ryght the poore mans wrong,
[205]   My handes were free to geve where nede requyred,
        To watche for grace I never thought it long,
        To do men good I nede not be desyred.
        Nor yet with gyftes my hart was never hyred.
        But when the ball was at my foote to guyde,
[210]   I played to those that fortune did abide.

        My want was wealth, my woe was ease at wyll,
        My robes were ryche, and braver then the sonne :
        My Fortune then was farre above my skyll,
        My state was great, my glasse did ever runne,
[215]   My fatal threede so happely was spunne,
        That then I sat in earthly pleasures clad,
        And for the time a Goddesse place I had.

        [203]   helpe C–G.
        [212]   robes was rich D–F.

But I had not so sone this lyef possest,
But my good happe began to slyp asyde.
And fortune then dyd me so sore molest,   [220]
That vnto playntes was tourned all my pride.
It booted not to rowe agaynst the tyde:
Myne oares were weke my hart and strength did fayle,
the wynd was rough I durst not beare a sayle.

What steppes of stryef belonge to highe estate?   [225]
The clymynge vp is doubtfull to indure,
The seate it selfe doth purchase priuie hate,
And honours fame is fyckle and vnsure,
And all she brynges, is floures that be vnpure:
Which fall as fast as they do sprout and spring,   [230]
And cannot last they are so vayne a thyng.

We count no care to catche that we do wyshe,
But what we wynne is long to vs vnknowen,
Til present payne be served in our dyshe,
We skarce perceyve whereon our gryefe hath growen: [235]
What grayne proves wel that is so rashely sowen?
Yf that a meane dyd measure all our deedes,
In stead of corne we should not gather weedes.

The setled minde is free from Fortunes power,
They nede not feare who looke not vp aloft,   [240]
But they that clyme are carefull every hower,
For when they fall they light not very softe:
Examples hath the wysest warned ofte,
That where the trees the smallest braunches bere,
The stormes do blowe and have most rigor there.   [245]

Where is it strong but nere the ground and roote?
Where is it weake but on the hyghest sprayes?

Where may a man so surely set his foote,
But on those bowes that groweth lowe alwayes?
[250] The litle twigges are but vnstedfast stayes,
Yf they breake not, they bend wyth every blast,
Who trustes to them shal never stand full fast.

The wynde is great vpon the hyghest hilles,
The quiete life is in the dale belowe,
[255] Who treades on yse shal slide agaynst theyr wylles,
They want no care that curious artes would knowe,
Who lives at ease and can content him so,
Is perfect wise, and settes vs all to scoole,
Who hates this lore may wel be called a foole.

[260] What greater gryefe may come to any lyfe,
Than after sweete to taste the bitter sower?
Or after peace to fall at warre and stryfe,
Or after myrth to have a cause to lower?
Vnder such proppes false Fortune buyldes her bower,
[265] On sodayne chaunge her flitting frames be set,
Where is no way for to escape her net.

The hastye smart that Fortune sendes in spyte
Is hard to brooke where gladnes we imbrace,
She threatens not, but sodaynly doth smyte,
[270] Where ioye is moste there doth she sorowe place.
But sure I thinke, this is to strange a case,
For vs to feele such gryefe amyd our game,
And know not why vntil we taste the same.

[252] Who trustes *is printed* Whot rustes *but is corrected in* Be.
[256] want not cares C–G.
[265] her flitting frames *is noted, without change, in* Be. her flittring frames
C–G.
[266] escape the net. G.

As earst I sayd, my blisse was turnde to bale,
I had good cause to weepe and wring my handes,   [275]
And showe sad cheare with countenaunce full pale,
For I was brought in sorowes woful bandes:
A pyrrye came and set my shippe on sandes,
What should I hide, or colour care and noye?
Kyng Edward dyed in whom was all my ioye.   [280]

And when the earth receyved had his corse,
And that in tombe, this worthye prince was layd,
The world on me began to shewe his force,
Of troubles then my parte I long assayed:
For they, of whom I never was afrayed,   [285]
Vndyd me most, and wrought me such despyte,
That they bereft from me my pleasure quyte.

As long as life remaynd in Edwardes brest,
Who was but I? who had such frendes at call?
His body was no sooner put in chest,   [290]
But wel was him that could procure my fall:
His brother was mine enemy most of all
Protector then, whose vice did stil abound,
From yll to worse tyll death dyd him confound.

He falsely fayned, that I of counsayle was   [295]
To poyson him, which thing I never ment,
But he could set thereon a face of brasse,
To bring to passe his lewde and false entent,
To such mischiefe this Tyrantes heart was bent.
To God, ne man, he never stoode in awe,   [300]
For in his wrath he made his wyll a lawe.

[277]   in sorrow wofull C.
[286]   Vndyd me *is misprinted* Vndid wee *in* G.
[287]   bereft me from my C–G.
[288]   Edward D–F.
[291]   was he that C–G.

Lord Hastinges bloud for vengeauns on him cries,
And many moe, that were to long to name:
But most of all, and in most wofull wise
[305] I had good cause this wretched man to blame.
Before the world I suffred open shame,
Where people were as thicke as is the sand,
I penaunce tooke with taper in my hand.

Eche iye did stare, and looke me in the face,
[310] As I past by the rumours on me ranne,
But Patience then had lent me such a grace,
My quiete lookes were praised of every man:
The shamefast bloud brought me such colour than,
That thousandes sayd, which sawe my sobre chere,
[315] It is great ruth to see this woman here.

But what prevailde the peoples pitie there?
This raging wolfe would spare no gylteles bloud.
Oh wicked wombe that such yll fruite did beare,
Oh cursed earth that yeldeth forth such mud,
[320] The hell consume all thinges that dyd the good,
The heavens shut theyr gates against thy spryte,
The world tread downe thy glory vnder feete,

I aske of God a vengeance on thy bones,
Thy stinking corps corrupts the ayre I knowe:
[325] Thy shameful death no earthly wyght bemones,
For in thy lyfe thy workes were hated so,
That every man dyd wyshe thy overthrowe:
Wherefore I may, though percial nowe I am,
Curse every cause whereof thy body came.

[330] Woe wurth the man that fathered such a childe:
Woe worth the hower wherein thou wast begate,
Woe wurth the brestes that have the world begylde,
To norryshe thée that all the world dyd hate.
Woe wurth the Gods that gave thée such a fate,

To lyve so long, that death deserved so ofte.   [335]
Woe wurth the chaunce that set thee vp alofte.

    Ye Princes all, and Rulers everychone,
In punyshement beware of hatreds yre.
Before ye skourge, take hede, looke well thereon:
In wrathes yl wil yf malice kyndle fyre,   [340]
Your hartes wil bourne in such a hote desire,
That in those flames the smoake shal dym your sight,
Ye shal forget to ioyne your iustice ryght.

    You should not iudge til thinges be wel deserned,
Your charge is styll to mainteyne vpryght lawes,   [345]
In conscience rules ye should be throughly learned,
Where clemencie byds wrath and rashenes pawes,
And further sayeth, stryke not wythout a cause,
And when ye smite do it for Iustice sake,
Then in good part eche man your skourge wil take.   [350]

    Yf that such zeale had moved this Tyrantes minde,
To make my plague a warning for the rest,
I had small cause such fault in him to finde,
Such punishement is vsed for the best:
But by yll wil and power I was opprest.   [355]
He spoyled my goodes and left me bare and poore,
And caused me to begge from dore to dore,

    What fall was this, to come from Princes fare,
To watche for crummes among the blinde and lame?
When almes was delt I had a hungry share,   [360]
Bycause I knewe not howe to aske for shame,
Tyll force and nede had brought me in such frame,
That starve I must, or learne to beg an almes,
With booke in hand, and say S. Dauids psalmes.

[352]   warning *is printed* warrant *but is corrected in Be.* warrant *C–G.*
[360]   had *is misprinted* bad *in the text.* almes were delt I had an hungry *C–G.*
[364]   hand to say *C–G.*

[365] Where I was wont the golden chaynes to weare,
A payre of beades about my necke was wound,
A lynnen clothe was lapt about my heare,
A ragged gowne that trayled on the ground,
A dishe that clapt and gave a heavie sound,
[370] A stayeng staffe and wallet therewithal,
I bare about as witnesse of my fal.

I had no house wherein to hyde my head,
The open strete my lodging was perforce,
Ful ofte I went al hungry to my bed,
[375] My fleshe consumed, I looked like a corse,
Yet in that plyght who had on me remorse?
O God thou knowest my frendes forsooke me than,
Not one holpe me that suckered many a man.

They frownde on me that faund on me before,
[380] And fled from me that followed me ful fast,
They hated me, by whom I set much store,
They knewe ful wel my Fortune dyd not last,
In every place I was condemnd and cast:
To pleade my cause at barre it was no boote,
[385] For every man dyd tread me vnder foote.

Thus long I lyved all weary of my life,
Tyl death approcht and rid me from that woe:
Example take by me both maide and wyfe,
Beware, take heede, fall not to follie so,
[390] A myrrour make of my great overthrowe:
Defye this world, and all his wanton wayes,
Beware by me, that spent so yll her dayes.

[379] faund on me before, *is printed* fawnd on before *but is corrected in* Be.
[386] of my life, *is misprinted* of myfe, F.
[390] make by my C–G.
[391] Defye the world, G.

TO THE READER

THis was so well lyked, that all together exhorted me instantly, [Prose 25] to procure Maister Churchyarde to vndertake and to penne as manye moe of the remaynder as myght by any meanes be attaynted at his handes.

And when I had promysed I wold do my diligence therein, they [5] asked me if I had any mo tragedyes yet vnred, for the euenyng was nowe at hand and there were enow alredy red to make a handsum volume. In dede (quod I) I purpose here to ende the second parte of this volume, for here endeth the cruel reigne of kyng Rychard the thyrd: And in an other volume hereafter, to dyscourse the resydue from the [10] begynnyng of kyng Henry the seuenth to the ende of this king & Queenes raigne (if god so long will graunte vs lyfe) and I beseche you all that you wyll dylygently performe such storyes as you haue vndertaken, & procure your frendes such as be learned, to helpe vs with the rest: for ther is in this part mater enough to set al the poetes in England [15] in wurke, and I wold wishe that every fine apt wyt wold at the leest vndertake one. For so wold it be a notable volume. For my parte, I entende to be so impudente and importunate a suiter to so manye as I knewe or maye hereafter be acquaynted wyth, that no excuse shall serve to shake me of: and I desyre you all to be as earnest. And to occupye the [20] tyme whyle we be nowe together, I wyl reade vnto you Edmund the Duke of Somerset, which must be placed in the fyrst parte: and than the blacke Smyth, which must serve for [the] thyrde volume, to thende I maye knowe youre iudgement therein. Do so we pray you (quoth they).

[This prose link is omitted in all later editions, owing to the rearrangement of the tragedies. See Introduction, p. 15. See also pp. 180–81.]

[Tragedy 26]
The tragedie of Edmund duke of Somerset, slayne at the first battayle at Saynct Albanes, in the tyme of Henrye the sixte.

Some I suppose are borne vnfortunate,
Els good endeuours could not yll succede,
What shal I call it? yll Fortune or fate,
That some mens attemptes have never good speede,
[5]   Theyr trauayle thankeles, all bootles theyr hede:
Where other vnlyke in workyng or skyll,
Outwrestle the world, and wyeld it at wyll,

    Of the fyrst number I count my selfe one,
To all mishap I wene predestinate,
[10]   Beleve me Baldwyne there be fewe or none,
To whom Fortune was ever more ingrate.
Make thou therfore my lyfe a caveat,
That who so wyth force wil worke agaynst kynde,
Sayleth as who sayeth, agaynst the stream & wynde.

[15]   For I of Somerset which duke Edmund hight,
Extract by discent from Lancaster line,
Were it by folly or Fortunes fell despyte,
Or by yll aspecte of some crooked sygne,

[Title] slaine in the *C–G.* Albanes, the 23. day of May, in the 32. yeare of Henrye the sixte. Anno: 1454. *C–G.*
[2]   not so ill *F.*
[4]   some attempts *F.* neuer happy speede, *F.*
[5]   But trauayle *F.*
[6]   or in skill, *F.*
[7]   Wynne what they will, and wield the world at will. *F.*
[8]   first sorte, myselfe I count for one, *F.*
[17]   Fortunes despyte, *C–G.*

Of my workes never could see a good fine:
What so I began dyd seldome wel ende: [20]
God from such Fortune all good men defend.

Where I sought to save, most parte I dyd spyll,
For good hap with me was alway at warre.
The lynage of Yorke whom I bare so yll,
By my spite became bryght as the morning starre, [25]
Thus somewhiles men make when fayne they would marre.
The more ye lop trees, the greater they growe,
The more ye stop streames the hygher they flowe.

By malice of me his glory grewe the more,
And mine, as the moone in the wane, waxt lesse: [30]
For having the place which he had before,
Governour of Fraunce, nedes I must confesse,
That lost was Normandie wythout redresse,
Yet wrought I al wayes that wyt myght contryve,
But what doth it boote with the streame to stryve? [35]

Borne was I neyther to warre nor to peace
For Mars was maligne to all my whole trade:
My byrth I beleve was in Ioves decreas,
When Cancer in his course beyng retrograde,
Declyned from Sol to Saturnus shade, [40]

[19]   Of mine attempts could neuer se good fine: C–G.
[22]   I thought to C–EG.
[25]   bright, and shone like a Starre, F.
[29]   Maugre my spite, his C–G.
[33]   Normandy yet nethelesse, F.
[34]   Alwayes I wrought that wit might well contriue, F.
[35]   what bootes it, against the F.
[36]   war ne to C–G.
[37]   Mars was maligne, and enemy to my trade: F.
[39]   in course, F.
[40]   Swarued from Sol, vnto F.

Where aspectes were good, opposites did marre,
So grew myne vnhap both in peace and warre.

A straunge natiuitie in calculation,
As all my lyves course dyd after declare,
[45]　Whereof in a bryefe to make relacion,
That other by me may learne to beware,
Overlight credence was cause of my care.
And want of foresight in geuyng assent,
To condemne Humfrey the duke innocent,

[50]　　Humfrey I meane that was the protector,
Duke of Glocester of the royall bloud,
So long as he was Englandes dyrectour,
Kyng Henries tytle to the crowne was good.
This prynce as a pyller most stedfastly stood:
[55]　Or like to a proppe set vnder a vyne,
In state to vpholde al Lancasters line.

O hedeles trust, vnware of harme to cum,
O malice headlong swyft to serve fond wyll,
Did ever madnes man so much benomme
[60]　Of prudent forecast, reason wit, and skyll,
As me blinde Bayard consenting to spyll,
The bloud of my cosyn my refuge and staye,
To my destruction making open waye?

[44]　As my *F.* after well declare, *C–G.*
[45]　in briefe *FG.*
[49]　Humfrey that Duke *C–EG.* Humfrey to damme that Duke most
　　　innocent. *F.*
[50]　Humfrey meane I that *F.*
[54]　This worthy Prince, as a Piller longe stood: *F.*
[55]　like a *C–EG.* like a strong prop *F.*
[58–59] O mad malice where wit obeyeth will,
　　　Was there euer any, whom folly did so nome: *F.*
[60]　Of all forecast, right [*misprinted* rigth], reason, *F.*
[62]　My Coosyns bloud, my refuge, and my stay, *F.*

So long as the Duke bare the stroke and swaye,
So long no Rebelles quarelles durst begin,   [65]
But when that the post was once pulled awaye,
Which stoode to vpholde the king and his kyn,
Yorke and his banders proudly preased in.
To chalenge the crowne by title of ryght,
Beginning with lawe and ending with myght.   [70]

Abrode went bruites in countrey and in towne,
That Yorke of England was the heyre true,
And howe Henry vsurped had the crowne
Agaynst al right, which al the realme may rue:
The people then, embrasing titles newe,   [75]
Yrksome of present, and longing for a chaunge,
Assented soone bycause they love to raunge.

True is the text which we in scripture read,
Ve terrae illi cuius rex est puer.
Woe to the land whereof a chylde is head,   [80]
Whether chylde or childyshe the case is one sure,
Where kynges be yong we dayly see in vre,
The people awles wanting one to dread,
Lead theyr lives lawles by weakenes of the heade.

[64]   So long as he in England bare the sway, *F.*
[65]   long Rebelles no Quarelles *F.*
[66]   when the *C–G.* was pulled once away, *C–G.*
[68–69] The Duke of Yorke, than stoutly hee stept in,
        And chalenged the Crowne, by color of right, *F.*
[71]   countrey and towne, *C–EG.* And spred great brutes in England
          vp and downe, *F.*
[72]   That he of *F.*
[73]   Henry had vsurped the *C–G.*
[74]   realme myght rue: *C–EG.* right, by practise most vntrue: *F.*
[76]   for chaunge, *C–G.*
[80]   to that land *C–G.*
[83]   awlesse, by weakenes of their head, *C–G.*
[84]   lawlesse, hauing none to dread. *C–G.*

[85]   And no lesse true is this text agayne,
          Beata terra cuius rex est nobilis.
          Blest is the land where a stout kyng doth rayne,
          Where in good peace eche man possesseth his,
          Where ill men feare to fault or do amis,
[90]   Where the prynce prest hath alway sword in hand,
          At home and abrode his enemyes to wythstand.

          In case king Henry had bene such a one,
          Hardy and stoute as his fathers afore,
          Long mought he have sat in the royall throne,
[95]   Without any feare of common vprore.
          But dayly his weakenes shewed more and more,
          And that gave boldenes to the aduers bande,
          To spoyle him at last both of life and land.

          His humble hart was nothyng vnknowen,
[100]   To the gallantes of Yorke & theyr retinue,
          A ground lyeng lowe is soone overflowen,
          And shored houses can not long continue,
          Ioyntes can not knyt where as is no synowe,
          And so a prynce, not dred as well as loved
[105]   Is from his place, by practise soone removed.

[89]   For dread of whom, no man dare do amis, *F.*
[90]   Where a stout Prince is prest, with sword *C–EG.*
          Whose Prince is prest alwayes, and Sword *F.*
[91]   abroade, all enemies *F.*
[92]   In case the sonne had proued sutch *F.*
[94]   Sure had he sitten in *F.*
[95]   Dreadlesse, and carelesse of *F.*
[96]   But Henries weakenesse appeered more, and more, *F.*
[97]   Which boldnes gaue, to the aduersary band, *C–G.* [*Read* contrary
          for aduersary *F.*]
[100–101] To the gaye gallants, of Yorkes retinue,
          Any lowe ground, is highly ouerflowen, *F.*
[105]   By bold Traytours may bee soone remoued. *F.*

Well mought I see had I not wanted brayne,
The wurke begon to vndermine the state,
When the chiefe lynke was lewced fro the chayne,
And that men durst vpon bloud royal grate,
Howe tickle a holde had I of mine estate? [110]
When the head poste laye flat vpon the flore,
Mought not I thinke my staf next the dore?

So mought also dame Margarete the Queene,
By meane of whom this mischiefe fyrst began,
Dyd she trowe ye her selfe not overwéen [115]
Death to procure to such a noble man?
Whych she and hers afterward did ban,
On whom dyd hang as I before have sayd,
Her husbandes life, his honour and his ayde.

For whylest he lyved whych was our stable staye, [120]
Yorke and his ympes were kept as vnder yoke,
But when our poste removed was away,
Then burst out flame that late before was smoke,
The traytour covert then cast of his cloke,
And he that lay hyd came forth in open light, [125]
With titles blynde whych he set forth for ryght.

[109] that some durst *C–G.*
[110] How tickle hold I had of *F.*
[111] the chiefe post *C–G.*
[112] staffe then next *C–G.*
[113] mought I also *C–EG.*
[114] By whose malice this *F.*
[116] to that most worthy man? *C–G.*
[117] afterward mought well ban, *C–G.*
[122] when the piller remoued *C–G.*
[124] The close Traytoure, then *F.*
[125] And from his den came *C–G.* [*Read* the dark *for* his den *F.*]

Whych thyng to compasse him fyrst behooved,
The kyng and his kyn a sunder to set:
Who being perforce or practise remooved,

[130]   Then had they auoyded the pryncipall let,
Which kept the sought pray so long from the net:
The next poynt after, was them selves to place
In hyghest authoritie about his grace.

Therfore he wrought strayght me to displace,

[135]   No cause pretending but the common weale,
The crowne of England was the very case,
Why to the commons they burned so in zeale.
My faultes were cloakes theyr practise to conceale,
In counsayle hearing consider the entent,

[140]   For by pretence of truth treason ofte is ment,

So theyr pretence was only to remove
Counsayle corrupt from place about the kyng.
But O ye Prynces, you it doth behoove,
This case to construe as no fayned thyng,

[145]   That never traytour did subdue his kyng,
But for his plat ere he would furder wade,
Agaynst his frendes the quarel fyrst he made.

And if by hap he could so bryng about,
Them to subdue at his owne wyshe and wyll,

[127]   But this to bring about him *C–EG.* But this to achieue, first it
        him behoued, *F.*
[128]   asunder for to *C–F.*
[129]   Who once perforce, or practice ill remoued, *F.*
[133]   In rule aboue the rest, next vnto his *C–EG.* Next to the Prince,
        and other to abase. *F.*
[134]   I was the fyrst whome they put out of place, *C–G.* [*Read* Therefore
        was I first *for* I was the fyrst *G.*]
[140]   For in pretence *C–EG.*
[146]   he could furder *C–EG.*
[149]   subdue, and haue them at his will, *F.*

Then would he waxe so arrogant and stout,   [150]
That no reason his outrage myght fulfyll.
But to procede vpon his purpose styl
Tyll kyng and counsayle brought were in one case:
Loe to a rebell what it is to geve place.

   So for the fyshe casting forth his net,   [155]
The next poynt was in dryuing out his plat,
Common doltes to cause furiously to fret,
And to rebel, I can not tel for what,
Requyring redres of this and of that:
Who yf they speede, he standing at receyt,   [160]
Graspe would the pray that he long dyd awayte.

   Then by surmyse of sumthing pretended,
Such to displace as they may well suspect
Lyke to wythstand theyr practises entended,
And in theyr roomes theyr banders to elect,   [165]
The adverse party proudly to reiect.
And then wyth reportes the simple to abuse,
And when these helpes fayle, open force to vse.

   So this Dukes traynes were covert and not séene,
Which nought lesse meant, then he most pretended.   [170]
Lyke to a serpent covert vnder greene,
To the weale publycke séemed wholly bended:

[154] Such is their folly, to rebelles to geue place. *C–G*. [*Read* that geue
     for to geue *F*.]
[155] forth a net, *C–EG*. So for the fishe, when cast forth was the Net,
     F.
[156] out the plat, *C–G*.
[157] Commons to cause in rage to fume and fret, *C–G*.
[160] spede, the stander at *C–G*.
[161] Grasp wyll the pray for which he doth awayt. *C–G*.
[164] their mischief entended, *C–G*.
[170] Which ment no lesse, that he *C–EG*. Who little ment, that which
     hee *F*.
[171] Serpent lurkinge vnder *F*.

Zelous he was, and would have all thing mended,
But by that mendment nothyng els he ment,
[175] But to be kyng, to that marke was his bent.

For had he bene playne as he meant in dede,
Henry to depose from the royall place,
His haste had bene waste, and much worse his speede,
The kyng then standing in his peoples grace.
[180] This Duke therfore set forth a goodly face,
As one that meant no quarell for the crowne,
Such as bare rule he only would put downe.

But all for nought so long as I bare stroke,
Served these dryftes, and proved all vayne,
[185] Then dyd he attempt the people to provoke,
To make commocion and vprores amayne:
Which to appease, the kyng him selfe was fayne,
From Blackheath in Kent, to send me to the Tower.
Such was the force of rebels that hower.

[190] The tempest yet therewyth was not ceased,
For Yorke was bent his purpose to pursue,
Who seing howe soone I was released,
And yll successe of suffraunce to insue:
Then like a Iudas vnto his lord vntrue,
[195] Esteming time lost lenger to deferre,
By Warwykes ayde proclaymed open warre,

At S. Albanes towne both our hostes dyd mete,
Which to trye a fielde was no equal place,

[173]   thinges *FG*.
[184]   all but vayne, *C–G*.
[185]   The best helpe then, was people *C–G*.
[189]   rebels in that *C–G*.
[194]   lyke Iudas, *C–G*.
[195]   Thynkinge time *F*. lost any lenger *C–G*.
[197]   S. Albanes towne, where both *F*.
[198]   To trye a fielde was not an equall *F*.

EDMUND, DUKE OF SOMERSET

Forst we were to fyght in every lane and strete,
No feare of foes could make me shun the place: [200]
There I and Warwyke fronted face to face,
At an Inne dore, the Castel was the syne,
Where with a sword was cut my fatal line.

Oft was I warned to come in Castel none,
But thought no whit of any common sygne,   [205]
I dyd ymagine a Castel buylt wyth stone,
For of no Inne I could the same diuine:
In Prophetes skyl my wyt was never fine,
A Foole is he that such vayne dreames doth dread,
And more foole of both that wyl by them be led.   [210]

My life I lost in that vnlucky place,
With many Lordes that leaned to my parte:
The Erle Percy had there no better grace,
Clyfford for all his courage could not shun the darte,
Stafford although stout, free went not from this marte.   [215]
Babthorp the attorney for all his skyll in lawe,
In this poynt of pleading was found very rawe.

So thus this poore kyng disarmed of his bandes,
His frendes slayne wanting al assistence,

[199–200] For we were forst to fight within a streete,
　　　　　With fewe agaynst many, sutch was the case, *F*.
[205]　　Hauing no mistrust of *C–EG*. But little thought of *F*.
[208]　　wits was *DE*. wits were *F*.
[210]　　But more Foole hee, that *F*.
[213]　　had no *C–F*.
[214]　　Couragious Clifford could not eschewe the dart, *F*.
[215]　　Buckingham heyr was at this mortall marte, *C–G*. [*Read*
　　　　　Buckinghams *F*.]
[217]　　pleadyng apppered very *C–G*.
[218]　　So pore King Henry disarmed *C–EG*. So thus poore Prince dis-
　　　　　armed *F*.
[219]　　His frendes all slayne, wantinge good assistence, *F*.

[220] Was made a pray vnto his enemies handes,
Pryued of power, and pryncely reverence,
And as a pupyl voyd of all experience,
Innocent playne, and symply wytted
Was as a Lambe to the Wolfe committed.

[225] A Parlyament then was called wyth speede
A Parlyament, nay a playne conspiracye,
When all in poste it was by acte decreed,
That after the death of the syxt Henry,
Yorke should succede vnto the regally,
[230] And in his life the charge and protection,
Of kyng and realme at the dukes direction.

And thus was Yorke declared protectour,
Protector sayd I, nay proditor playne.
A ranke rebell the prynces director
[235] A liege to lead his lord and soveraygne,
What honest hart would not conceyve disdayne
To sée the foote appeare above the head,
A monster is in spyte of 'nature bred.

Some haply here wyl move a farder doubt,
[240] And for Yorkes parte allege an elder right,
O braynles heades that so run in and out.
Whan length of time a state hath firmely pyght:

[223] simple witted, *D–F*.
[224] Lambe vnto the *C–G*.
[227] When agaynst ryght it was decreede, *C–G*.
[229] The Duke of Yorke should haue the *F.* the eegally, *C–E.* the
regalty, *G*.
[235] A vassall to *C–G*.
[237] foote surmount aboue *C–G*.
[239] happyly *C–EG*.
[241] head, *F*.

And good accorde hath put all stryfe to flyght,
Were it not better such titles should slepe,
Than all a realme for theyr tryall to wepe?   [245]

    From the heyre female came Yorke and his lede,
And we of Lancaster from the heyre male,
Of whom thrée kinges in order dyd succede,
By iust discent: this is no fayned tale.
Who would have thought that any storme or gale   [250]
Our shyp could shake, having such anker hold?
None I thinke sure vnlesse God so would.

    After this hurle the kyng was fayne to flée,
Northward in poste for succour and relyefe.
O blessed God howe straunge it was to sée,   [255]
A ryghtfull prynce pursued as a thiefe:
To thée O England what can be more repryefe?
Then to pursue thy Prynce wyth armed hand,
What greater shame may be to any land?

    Traytours dyd triumphe, true men lay in the dust,   [260]
Reuing and robbing roysted every where,
Will stoode for skyll, and lawe obeyed lust,
Might trode downe right, of kyng there was no feare.
All thing was tried only by shield and speare.
Al which vnhappes that they were not foreséene,   [265]
I was in fault, or some about the Queene.

[244]   tytles still to slepe, *C–G.*
[245]   realme about the tryall wepe? *C–G.*
[246]   From the female, came Yorke and all his leede, *C–G.* [*Read* seede
      for leede G.]
[247]   wee Lancastrians, from *F.*
[252]   vnlesse that God *C–G.*
[253]   hurly *DE.*
[264]   The tytle was tryed *C–G.*
[266]   Suffolke was in fault who ruled King and Quene. *C–G.*

Thou lookest Baldwyn I should my selfe accuse,
Of some subtyle dryft or other lyke thyng,
Wherein I should my prynces eares abuse,

[270]   To the Dukes foes overmuch adhering,
Though some mens practise did me thereto bryng,
My fault only consisted in consent,
Forgeve it me, for sore I dyd repent:

Yf I at fyrst when brandes began to smoke,

[275]   The sparkes to quenche by any way had sought,
England had never felt this mortal stroke,
Which nowe to late lamenting helpeth nought.
Two poyntes of wyt to dearly have I bought,
The fyrst that better is timely to foresée,

[280]   Then after over late a counsaylour to be.

The second poynt, not easely to assent
To aduise geven agaynst thy faythful frende,
But of the speaker ponder the intent,
The meaning ful, the poynt, and final ende.

[285]   A saynt in showe, in proofe is found a fende,
The subtyle man the simple to abuse,
Much pleasaunt speache and eloquence doth vse.

And so was I abusde and other moe
By Suffolkes sleyghtes, who sought to please the quene,

[267–68]   Some here perhaps, do looke I should accuse
        My selfe of some sleight, or subtiltie vniust C–G.
        [In l. 268 omit some F.]
[270–71]   Agaynst the Duke, to bring him in mistrust
        Some parte whereof, though nedes confesse I must, C–G.
[273]   Leaning to my foes, whereof I do repent. C–EG. To my Foes
        driftes, which I could not preuent. F.
[276]   Neuer had England felt C–G.
[281]   The second is, not C–G.
[282]   To any aduice, agaynst F.
[288]   I, and other mo abused F.

Forecasting not the miserye and woe   [290]
Whych thereof came, and soone was after sene:
With glosing tonge he made vs fooles to weene,
That Humfrey dyd to Englandes crowne aspyre,
Which to prevent, his death they dyd conspyre.

What should I more of myne vnhaps declare,   [295]
Whereof my death at last hath made an ende?
Not I alone was cause of all this care,
Some besides me there were that did offend.
None I accuse, nor yet my selfe defend,
Faultes I know I had, as none lives wythout,   [300]
My chiefe fault was folly I put thée out of doubt.

Folly was the chiefe, the noughty time was next,
Which made my fortune subiect to the chiefe:
If England then wyth strife had not bene vext.
Glory might have growen where as ensewed gryefe   [305]
Yet one thing to me is comfort and relyefe,
Constant I was in my Prynces quarell,
To dye or lyve and spared for no parell.

What though Fortune enuious was my foe,
A noble hart ought not the sooner yelde,   [310]
Nor shrynke abacke for any weale or woe,
But for his Prynce lye bleeding in the feelde:
If priuie spyte at any time me helde,
The pryce is payed: and grevous is my guerdon,
As for the rest God I trust wyll pardon.   [315]

[290]   Forecast we lackt, which cannot be excused F.
[291]   Of thinges to come, as soone F.
[292]   Which glosinge F.
[297]   was voyde of C–EG.
[300]   I confesse, as no man liues F.
[301]   fault, was folly, out F.
[302]   was chiefe, F.
[306]   thing is, my comfort and C–G.

[Prose 26]   WHen they had sayde their myndes herein allowyng it very
                well, they willed me also to reade the blacke Smyth.
                Wyth a good wyll (quod I) but fyrst you must ymagine
that you see hym standynge on a ladder, ouershryned wyth the Tyborne,
[5] a meete trone for all suche rebelles and Trayters: and there corageouslye
sayenge as folowethe.

> [*In all later editions this prose link is substituted for the closing sentences of Prose 24.
> It should be regarded, therefore, as appended to Prose 24 at l. 26, after* person, *in
> editions C–G.*]
> [1–2] Then they wylled *C–F²G.*
> [5]   meete stage for *C–F²G.* there stoutlye *C–F²G.*
> [6]   *The text prints* say- *at the end of a line and* sayenge *at the beginning of the next line.*

[Tragedy 27]   The wilfull fall of Blacke Smyth,
                        and the foolishe ende of the
                              Lord Awdeley.

         WHo is more bolde then is the blynde Beard?
         Where is more craft than in the clowted shoen?
         Who catche more harme then such as nothing feard?
         Where is more guyle then where mistrust is none?
[5]   No playsters helpe before the gryefe be knowen.
         So semes by me who could no wysedome lere,
         Vntyll such time I bought my wyt to deare.

> [Title] of the blacke Smith, *G.* Awdeley in Iune anno. 1496. *C–G.*
> [4]   mistrust in none? *G.*

Who being boystous stout, and brayneles bolde,
Puft vp wyth pryde, with fyer and furies fret,
Incenst with tales so rude and playnely tolde,   [10]
Wherein deceyt wyth double knot was knyt,
I trapped was as sely fishe in net,
Who swift in swimming, not doubtful of disceyt,
Is caught in gyn wherein is layd no bayt.

Such force and vertue hath this doleful playnt,   [15]
Set forth wyth syghes and teares of Crocodyle,
Who seemes in sight as simple as a saynt,
Hath layd a bayte the wareles to begyle,
And as they weepe they worke disceyt the while,
Whose ruful cheare the rulers so relent,   [20]
To worke in hast that they at last repent.

Take hede therfore ye rulers of the land,
Be blynd in sight, and stop your other eare,
In sentence slowe tyl skyll the truthe hath skand,
In all your doomes both love and hate forbeare,   [25]
So shal your iudgement iust and ryght appeare:
It was a southfast sentence long agoe,
That hastye men shal never lacke much woe.

Is it not truth? Baldwyn what sayest thou?
Say on thy minde, I pray the muse no more,   [30]
Me thinke thou starest and lookest I wote not howe,
As though thou never sawest a man before:
By like thou musest why I teache this lore,
Els what I am that here so boldly dare,
Among the prease of princes to compare.   [35]

[8]   Boystrous, *FG*.
[9]   with fierce, and *F*.
[14]   whererein *F*.
[24]   truth haue scande, *D–F*.

Though I be bolde, I pray thée blame not me,
Lyke as men sowe, such corne nedes must they reape,
And nature hath so planted in eche degrée,
That Crabbes like Crabbes wil kindly cral and crepe:
[40] The sutell Foxe vnlike the silly shepe:
It is according to myne education,
Forward to prease in rout and congregacion.

Behold my cote burnt wyth the sparkes of fyer,
My lether apron fylde wyth horseshoe nayles,
[45] Behold my hammer and my pyncers here,
Behold my lookes a marke that seldome fayles:
My chekes declare I was not fed wyth quayles,
My face, my clothes, my tooles wyth al my fashion,
Declare full wel a prynce of rude creacion.

[50] A prynce I sayd, a prynce I say agayne,
Though not by byrth, by crafty vsurpacion,
Who doutes but some men pryncehoode do obtayne,
By open force and wrongful dominacion,
Yet whyle they rule are had in reputation:
[55] Even so by me, the whyle I wrought my feate,
I was a Prynce at least in my conceyte.

I dare the bolder take on me the name,
Because of him whom here I leade in hand,
Tychet Lord Audeley a lord of byrth and fame,
[60] Which with his strength and power servde in my band,
I was a Prynce whyle that I was so mande:
His Butterflye styll vnderneth my shielde,
Displayed was from Welles to Blackheath fyelde.

[40] sutell *is misprinted* sutlel *in the text.*
[44] with the horse shoe *CG.*
[60] hys power and strength serude *F.*

But nowe beholde he doth bewayle the same:
Thus after wittes theyr rashenes do deprave,   [65]
Beholde dismayd he dare not speake for shame,
He lookes like one that late came from the grave,
Or one that came forth of Trophonius cave,
For that in wyt he had so litle pyth,
As he a lord to serve a traytour smyth.   [70]

Such is the Corage of the noble hart,
Which doth despyse the vile and baser sorte,
He may not touch that savers of the Cart,
Him listeth not wyth eche Iacke lout to sporte,
He lets him passe for payring of his porte,   [75]
The iolly Egles catche not litle flees,
The courtly sylkes matche seeld with homly frees.

But surely Baldwyne if I were allowde
To saye the trouth, I could somewhat declare:
But Clarkes wyl say, this Smith doth waxe to proude,   [80]
Thus in preceptes of wysedome to compare,
But Smithes must speake that clarkes for feare ne dare.
It is a thyng that all men may lament,
When clarkes kepe close the truth least they be shent.

The Hostler, Barber, Myller, and the smyth,   [85]
Heare of the sawes of such as wysedome ken,
And learne some wyt although they want the pyth,
That Clarkes pretende: and yet both nowe and then,
The greatest Clarkes prove not the wisest men:
It is not right that men forbid should be,   [90]
To speake the truth all were he bond or free.

And for becavse I have vsed to fret and fome,
Not passing greatly whom I should displease,
I dare be bolde a while to play the mome,
Out of my sacke some others faultes to lease,   [95]

405

And let my owne behinde my backe to peyse.
For he that hath his owne before his iye,
Shal not so quicke anothers fault espye.

    I say was never no such woful case,
[100] As is when honour doth it selfe abuse:
The noble man that vertue doth imbrace,
Represseth pryde, and humblenes doth vse,
By wysedome workes, and rashenes doth refuse:
His wanton wyl and lust that brydel can,
[105] In dede is gentil both to God and man.

    But where the nobles want both wyt and grace,
Regard no rede, care not but for theyr lust,
Oppresse the poore, set wil in reasons place,
And in their wordes and doomes be found vniust,
[110] Wealth goeth to wracke tyl all lye in the dust:
There Fortune frownes, and spite beginth to growe,
Til high, and lowe, and al be overthrowe.

    Then syth that vertue hath so good rewarde,
And after vice so duely wayteth shame,
[115] Howe happth that Prynces have no more regarde,
Their tender youth wyth vertue to enflame?
For lacke whereof theyr wyt and wyl is lame,
Infecte with folly, prone to lust and pryde,
Not knowing howe them selfes or theyrs to guyde.

[120]   Whereby it hapneth to the wanton wyght,
As to a shyppe vpon the stormy seas,
Whych lacking sterne to guyde it selfe aryght,
From shore to shore the wynde and tide do téese,

[96]   let myne owne C–G.
[111]   begins G.
[123]   tyde to teese, G.

Finding no place to rest or take his ease,
Tyl at the last it synke vpon the sande: [125]
So fare they all that have not vertue cand.

   The Plowman fyrst his land doth dresse and torne,
And makes it apte or ere the seede be sowe,
Whereby he is full like to reape good corne,
Where otherwise no seede but wéede would growe: [130]
By whych ensample men may easely knowe,
When youth have welth before they can wel vse it,
It is no wonder though they do abuse it.

   Howe can he rule wel in a common welth,
Whych knoweth not him selfe in rule to frame? [135]
Howe should he rule him selfe in ghostly health,
Which never learnd one lesson for the same?
If such catche harme theyr parentes are to blame:
For nedes must they be blynde, and blyndly ledde,
Where no good lesson can be taught or red. [140]

   Some thinke theyr youth discrete and wysely taught,
That brag, and boste, and weare their fether brave,
Can royst, and rowt, both lowre, and looke alofte,
Can sweare and stare, and call their felowes knave,
Can pyll and poll, and catche before they crave, [145]
Can carde and dyse, both cogge and foyst at fare,
Play on vnthriftye, til theyr purse be bare.

   Some teache theyr youth to pype, to syng, and daunce,
To hauke, to hunt, to choose and kyl theyr game,
To wynde theyr horne, and with their horse to praunce, [150]
To play at Tenys, set the lute in frame,

[128]   seede hee sowe, G.
[149]   kill the game, F.

Runne at the ring and vse such other game:
Which fetes although they be not all vnfyt,
Yet can not they the marke of vertue hit.

[155]   For noble youth, there is no thyng so meete
As learning is, to knowe the good from yll:
To knowe the tounges, and perfectly endyte,
And of the lawes to have a perfect skyll,
Thinges to reforme as ryght and iustice will:
[160] For honour is ordeyned for no cause,
But to sée ryght maynteyned by the lawes,

It spytes my heart to heare when noble men
Can not disclose their secretes to theyr frende,
In savegarde sure wyth paper, ynke, and pen,
[165] But fyrst they must a secretary fynde,
To whom they shewe the bottome of theyr minde:
And be he false or true, a blabbe or close,
To him they must theyr counsayle nedes disclose.

And where they rule that have of lawe no skyll,
[170] There is no boote, they nedes must seke for ayde:
Then ruled are they, and rule as others wyll:
As he that on a stage his parte hath playd:
But he was taught nought hath he done or sayd.
Such youth therfore seeke scyence of the sage,
[175] As thynke to rule when that ye come to age.

Where youth is brought vp in feare and obedyence,
Kept from yll company, brydeld of theyr lust,
Do serve god duely and knowe theyr allegiaunce,
Learne godly wisedome which time nor age can rust:

[153] feates C–G.
[161] But see C–F.

Where Prince, people, & peares nedes prosper must: [180]
For happy are the people and blessed is that land,
Where truth and vertue have got the over hand.

I speake this Baldwyn of this ruful Lord,
Whom I perforce do here present to thée,
He fayntes so sore he may not speake a worde: [185]
I pleade his cause wythout rewarde or fée,
And am inforst to speake for him and me:
If in his youth he had bene wysely tought,
He should not nowe his wyt so deare have bought.

For what is he that hath but halfe a wyt, [190]
But may wel knowe that rebelles can not spede:
Marke wel my tale, and take good hede to it,
Recount it well and take it for good rede,
If it prove vntrue I wyl not trust my crede.
Was never rebell before the world, nor since, [195]
That could or shall preuayle agaynst his prynce,

For ere the subiect beginneth to rebell,
Within him selfe let hym consider well,
Foresée the daunger, and beat wel in his brayne,
Howe hard it is his purpose to obtayne, [200]
For if he once be entred to the breares,
He hath a raging Wolfe fast by the eares.

And when he is once entred to rule the beastly route
Although he would he can no way get out:
He may be sure none wyl to him resorte, [205]
But such as are the vile and rascall sorte:
All honest men, as well the most as lest,
To taste of Treason wyl vtterly detest.

Then let him way how long he can be sure,
[210] Where fayth nor frendshippe may no while endure:
He whom he trusteth moste, to gayne a grote
Wil fall him from and assay to cut his throte,
Among the knaves and slaves where vice is rooted,
There is no other frendshippe to be looked.

[215] With slashers, slaves, and snuffers so falshod is in price
That simple fayth is deadly sinne, & vertue counted vice.
And where the quarell is so vyle and bad,
What hope of ayde then is there to be had?
Thinkes he that men wyl runne at this or that,
[220] To do a thing they knowe not howe or what?

Nor yet what daunger may thereof betide,
Where wysedome would they should at home abyde,
Rather than seke and knowe not what to fynde.
Wise men wil first debate this in theyr minde:
[225] Ful sure they are yf that they go to wrecke,
Without all grace they lose both head and necke.

They lose theyr landes and goodes, theyr chyld & wyfe
With sorowe and shame shal lead a wofull life,
If he be slayne in fyeld he dyeth acurst,
[230] Which of all wreckes we should accompt the worst:
And he that dyeth defending his liege lord,
Is blyst and blyst agayne by Gods owne worde.

And where the souldiers wages is vnpayd,
There is the captayne slenderly obeyed,
[235] And where the souldyer is out of feare and drede,
He wil be lacke when that there is most nede,
And priuately he seekes his ease and leasure,
And wyl be ruled but at his wil and pleasure.

[216] The simple C–G.

And where some drawe forth, & other do drawe backe,
There in the ende must nedes be woe and wracke: [240]
To hope for aydes of lordes it is but vayne,
Whose foretaught wyt of treason knoweth the payne,
They knowe what power a prynce hath in his land,
And what it is with rebelles for to stand.

They knowe by treason honour is defaced,   [245]
Theyr ofspryng and theyr progeny disgraced,
They knowe to honour is not so worthy a thyng,
As to be true and faythfull to theyr kyng,
Above conysaunce or armes, or pedigrewe a farre,
An vnspotted cote is like a blasyng starre: [250]

Therfore the rebel is accurst and madde,
That hoopeth for that whych rebell never hadde:
Who trusting stil to tales doth hang in hope,
Tyll at the last he hang fast by the rope,
For though that tales be tolde that hope myght fede,   [255]
Such foolishe hope hath styll vnhappy spede.

It is a custome that never wyl be broken,
In broyles the bagge of lyes is ever open,
Such lyeng newes men dayly wyl invent,
As can the hearers fancie best content,   [260]
And as the newes do runne and never cease,
So more and more they dayly do increase.

And as they encrease they multiplye as fast,
That ten is ten hundred, ten thousand at the last.

[241]   ayde *C–G.*
[243]   his hand, *G.*
[249]   Aboue cognisaunce *C–G.* pedigrew far, *F.*
[255]   though such tales *F.*

[265] And though the rebell had ones got the fielde,
Thinkes he thereby to make his Prince to yelde?
A Princes power within his owne regyon,
Is not so soone brought vnto confusion.

For kinges by God are strong and stoutly harted,
[270] That they of subiectes wil not be subverted:
If kinges would yeeld, yet God would them restrayne,
Of whom the Prynce hath grace and power to raygne:
Who straytly chargeth vs above al thing,
That no man should resist agaynst his kyng.

[275] Who that resisteth his dread soveraygne lord,
Doth dampne his soule by Gods owne very worde.
A christen subiect should with honour due,
Obey his soveraygne though he were a Iue:
Whereby assured when subiectes do rebell,
[280] Gods wrath is kindled and threatneth fyer and hell.

It is soone knowen when Gods wrath is kyndled,
Howe they shall spéede with whom he is offended:
If God geve victorye to whom he liketh best,
Why looke they for it whom God doth most detest?
[285] For treason is hateful and abhord in Gods sight,
Example of Iudas that most wycked wyght:

Which is the chiefe cause no treason preuayles,
For yll must he spede whom Gods wrath assayles:
Let Traytors and Rebels looke to spede then,
[290] When Gods mighty power is subiect to men.
Much might be sayd that goeth more nere the pyth,
But this suffiseth for a rurall Smyth.

[277] Christian *D–G.*

THE BLACKSMITH

Baldwyn when thou hearest my reason in this case,
Belike thou thinkest I was not very wyse,
And that I was accurst, or els lacked grace, [295]
Which knowyng the ende of my fond enterpryse,
Would thus presume agaynst my prynce to ryse:
But as there is a cause that moveth every woe,
Somewhat there was wherof this sore did growe.

And to be playne and simple in this case, [300]
The cause why I such matter tooke in hand,
Was nothyng els but pryde and lacke of grace,
Vayne hope of helpe, and tales both false and fond:
By meane whereof my prynce I dyd wythstand,
Denyed the taxe assest by conuocacion [305]
To maynteyne warre agaynst the scottyshe nacion.

Whereat the Cornyshe men dyd much repyne,
For they of Golde and sylver were full bare,
And lyved hardly digging in the mine,
They sayd they had no money for to spare: [310]
Began fyrst to grudge and then to sweare and stare,
Forgot theyr due obeysaunce, and rashely fel to rauing,
And sayd they would not beare such pollinge & such shauing.

They fyrst accusde the kyng as author of theyr gryefe,
And then the byshop Moreton, and sir Reynold Bray, [315]
For they then were about the kyng most chiefe,
Because they thought the hole fault in them lay:
They did protest to ryd them out of the waye.
Such thanke have they that rule about a prynce,
They beare the blame of others mens offence. [320]

[295] else wanted grace, *G.*
[301] matter *is misprinted* mattter *in the text.*
[304] meanes *F.* wherof I did my prince withstand, *C–G.*
[306] the *Sottishe* nation. *G.*
[319] rule aboue a *G.*
[320] other *C–G.*

413

When I perceyved the commons in a roare,
Then I and Flamoke consulted both together,
To whom the people resorted more and more,
Lamenting and cryeng, helpe vs nowe or never,
[325] Breake this yoake of bondage then are we frée for ever:
Wherat we inflamed in hope to have a Fame,
To be theyr capitaynes toke on vs the name.

Then myght you heare the people make a shoute,
And crie, God save the Captens, & send vs al good spede
[330] Then he that faynted was counted but a lowt,
The ruffians ran abrode to sowe sedicious sede:
To call for company then there was no nede
For every man laboured an other to entyce,
To be partaker of his wicked vice.

[335] Then al such newes as made for our avayle,
Was brought to me, but such as sounded yll,
Was none so bolde to speake or yet bewayle:
Everich was so wedded vnto his wyll,
That forth they cryed wyth bowes, sword, and bil.
[340] And what the rufler spake the lowte tooke for a verdite,
For there the best was worst, the worst was best regarded.

For when men goe a madding, there still the viler part
Conspire together and wil have al the sway,
And be it well or yll they must have al the porte,
[345] As they wyl do, the rest must nedes obey,
They prattle and prate as doth the Popyngaye:
They crye and commaund the rest to kepe tharray,
Whiles they may range and robbe for spoyle and pray.

And when we had prepared every thyng,
[350] We went to Tawnton wyth al our prouision,
And there we slewe the prouost of Penryn,
For that on the subsidie he sat in commission:

He was not wyse, nor yet of great discrescion,
That durst approche his enemies in theyr rage,
When wyt nor reason could theyr yre asswage.   [355]

    From thens we went to Wels, where we were receiued
Of this lorde Awdeley as of our chiefe captayne,
And so had the name, but yet he was deceyved,
For I in dede did rule the clubbyshe trayne,
My cartly knyghtes true honour dyd disdayne: [360]
For like doth love his like, it will be none other,
A chorle wil love a chorle before he wyll his brother.

    Then from Wels to Wynchester, and so to Blackheth field,
And there we encamped looking for more ayde,
But when none came, we thought our selves begylde,   [365]
Such Cornyshemen as knewe they were betrayed,
From theyr fellowes by nyght away they strayed:
There myght we learne howe vayne it is to trust,
Our fayned frendes in quarels so vniust.

    But we the sturdy captaynes that thought our power was
        strong   [370]
Were bent to trie our Fortune what ever should betide
We were the bolder, for that the kyng so long
Deferred battayle: whych so increast our pryde,
That sure we thought the kyng him selfe dyd hide
Within the citie, therfore wyth courage hault,   [375]
We did determyne the citye to assault.

    But he workyng contrary to our expectacion,
Was fully minded to let vs runne our race,
Tyll we were from our domestical habitacion,
Where that of ayde or succour was no place,   [380]

[363] From Wels F.
[378] runne *is misprinted* ruune *in the text.*

415

And then to be plagued as it should please his grace,
But all doubtfull poyntes, howe ever they did sound,
To our best vayle we alway dyd expound.

[385] When that the kynge sawe tyme, wyth corage bolde
He sent a power to circumvent vs all:
Where we enclosed as simple shepe in folde,
Were slayne and murdred as beastes in Bochers stall,
The kyng him selfe, what ever chaunce myght fall,
Was strongly encamped wythin saynct Georges fyeld,
[390] And there abode tyl that he heard vs yelde.

Then downe we kneled, and cryed to save our lyfe,
It was to late our folly to bewayle,
There were we spoyled of armour, cote, and knyfe:
And we which thought wyth pride the citye to assayle,
[395] Were led in prysoners naked as my nayle,
But of vs two thousand they had slayne before,
And we of them thrée hundred and no more.

This my Lord and we the Captayns of the West,
Tooke our Inne at Newgate, fast in fetters tyde,
[400] Where after tryall we had but litle rest,
My Lorde thorowe London was drawen on a slyde,
To Tower Hil where wyth axe he dyed,
Clad in his cote armor paynted all in paper,
Al torne and reversed in spyte of his behaver.

[405] And I wyth Thomas Flamoke, and other of our bent,
As traytors at Tyborne our iudgement dyd obey:
The people looked I should my fault lament,
To whom I boldly spake that for my fond assaye,

[382] poyntes *is printed* playntes *but is corrected in Be.* plaints, C–F.
[387] in butchers stall, C–G.
[402] with an axe C–G.
[404] Torne and C–G.

I was sure of fame that never should decay:
Whereby ye may perceyve vayne glory doth enflame   [410]
As wel the meaner sorte as men of greater name.

But as the sickely pacient, sometyme hath desyre
To taste the thinges that Phisicke hath denyed,
And hath both payne and sorowe for his hire,
The same to me ryght wel myght be applyed,   [415]
Whych while I raught for fame on shame did slyde.
And seeking Fame, brought forth my bitter bane,
As he that fyred the Temple of Diane.

I tel thée Baldwyn, I muse right ofte, to sée
Howe every man for wealth and honour gapeth,   [420]
Howe every man would clymbe above the skye,
Howe every man thassured meane so hateth,
How froward Fortune ofte their purpose mateth:
And if they happe theyr purpose to obtayne,
Theyr wealth is woe, their honour care and payne.   [425]

We sée the servaunt more happy than his lord,
We sée him live when that his lord is dead,
He slepeth sound, is mery at his borde,
No sorowe in his hart doth vexe his head:
Happy then is he that povertye can wed,   [430]
What gaine the mightye conquerours when they be dead
By all the spoyle and bloud that they have shedde?

The terrible tower where honour hath his seate,
Is hye on rockes more slypper then the yse,
Where styll the whorling wynde doth roare and beate,   [435]
Where sodayne qualmes and peries styl aryse,

[412]   the fickle patient, CG.
[415]   well may be C–G.
[436]   periles G.

And is beset wyth many sundry vice,
So straunge to men when fyrst they come thereat,
They be amased, and do they wote not what.

[440]   He that prevayles and to the Tower can clyme,
With trouble and care must nedes abrydge his dayes,
And he that slydes may curse the hower and tyme,
He did attempt to geve so fond assayes,
And al his life to sorrowe and shame obayes.
[445]   Thus slyde he downe or to the top ascend,
Assure him selfe repentaunce is the ende.

Wherfore good Baldwine do thou record my name,
To be ensample to such as credite lyes,
Or thyrst to sucke the sugred cup of Fame,
[450]   Or do attempt agaynst theyr prynce to ryse,
And charge them all to kepe wythin theyr syse:
Who doth assay to wrest beyond his strength,
Let him be sure he shal repent at length.

And at my request admonishe thou all men,
[455]   To spend well the talent which God to them hath lent,
And he that hath but one, let him not toyle for ten,
For one is to much, onles it be wel spent:
I have had the proofe, therfore I nowe repent,
And happy are those men, and blyst and blist is he,
[460]   As can be wel content to serve in his degree.

[447]   Wherfore Baldwine *F.*

IT is pitie (quoth one) that the meter is no better seing the matter is [Prose 27]
so good: you maye doo verye well to helpe it, and a littell fylyng
would make it formall.

The Author him selfe (quoth I) could haue doen that, but he woulde
not, and hath desyred me that it maye passe in suche rude sorte as you [5]
haue heard it: for he obserueth therein a double *decorum* both of the
Smith, and of him selfe: for he thinketh it not mete for the Smyth to
speke, nor for himselfe to write in any exacte kynde of meter. Well
sayd an other: The matter is notable to teach all people as well offycers
as subiectes to consyder their estates and to lyue in loue and obedience [10]
to the hygheste powers, whatsoeuer they be, whom god eyther by
byrth, lawe, succession, or vniuersal eleccion, doth or shall aucthorise
in his owne roume to execute his lawes & iustice, amonge any people
or nacyon: For by all these meanes God placeth his deputies. And
in my iudgement there is no mean so good either for the common [15]
quyet of the people, or for gods free choyse, as the naturall ordre of
enheritauns by lineal dyscent: for so it is left in gods handes, to creat
in the wombe what prince he thinketh metest for his purposes: The
people also knowe their princes, & therfore the more gladly & willingly
receyue & obey them. And although some Realmes more carefull than [20]
wise, have entayled their crowne to the heire male thinking it not
meete for the feminine sexe to beare the royall office: yet if they consyder all circumstaunces, and the chiefest vses of a Prince in a realme,
they shall se howe they are deceiued: for princes are gods lieutenauntes
or deputies, to se gods lawes executed among theyr subiects, not to rule [25]
accordyng to their owne lustes or deuyses, but by the prescript of Gods
lawes: so that the chiefest poynt of a princes offyce consysteth in
obedience to god and to his ordynaunces, and what should let but that

[19]   therfore *is misprinted* theefore *in the text.*
[20]   thē [them] *is misprinted* thr *in the text.*
[21]   to th'eir male *C.* to their male *D–G.* [*Read* thire *G.*]
[24]   they *is omitted in the text but serves as the catchword on the page.*

419

a woman may be as obedyent vnto god as a man? The second poynt of
[30] a princes offyce is to prouyde for the impotent, nedy, and helples, as
wydowes orphanes, lame and decrepite persons: And seing women
are by nature tender harted, mylde, and pytefull, who maye better then
they discharge this dutie? Yea but a woman lacketh courage boldnes
and stomake to withstand the aduersarie, & so are her subiectes an open
[35] spoyle to their enemyes. *Debora, Iael, Iudith, Thomiris,* and other do
proue the contrarye. But graunte it were so: what harme were that,
seynge victorie consysteth not in wit or force, but in goddes good
pleasure. I am sure that whatsoeuer prynce doth his dutie in obeying
god, and causyng iustice to be mynistred according to gods lawes, shall
[40] not onelye lacke warre (be he man woman or chylde) But also be a
terror to al other princes. And if god suffer any at any tyme to be
assayled, it is for the destruccion of the assayler, whether he be rebel or
forreyn fooe, and to the honour and profit of the vertuous prince in
whose byhalfe rather than he shall myscary god him selfe will fyght with
[45] enfections & erthquakes from the lande and waters, and with stormes
and lyghtnynges from the ayer & skyes. Mo warres haue ben sought
through the wilful & hauty courages of kinges, and greater destruccions
happened to realmes thereby, than by any other meanes. And as for
wysedome and pollicie, seing it consisteth in folowing the counsayl of
[50] many godly, learned, & long experienced heades, it were better to have
a woman, who consideringe her owne weakenes and inabilitye, shoulde
be ruled thereby, than a man which presuming vpon his owne fond
brayne, wil heare no advise save his owne. You muse peradventure
wherefore I saye this. The frantyke heades whiche disable our Queene,
[55] because she is a woman, and our kynge because he is a straunger, to be
our princes and chiefe governours, hath caused me to saye thus much.
For whatsoever man, woman, or childe, is by the consente of the whole
realme established in the royall seat, so it have not bene iniuriously
procured by rigour of sword and open force, but quietlye by title,
[60] eyther of enherytaunce, succession, lawful bequest, common consent, or

[48]   realme *F.*

eleccion, is vndoubtedlye chosen by God to be his deputie: and whosoever resisteth anye such, resisteth agaynst God him selfe, and is a ranke
traytour and rebell, and shall be sure to prosper as wel as this blacke
Smith, and other such have done. All resist that wilfully breake any law,
not beinge agaynst Gods law, made by common consent for the wealth [65]
of the realme, and commaunded to be kept by the authoritye of the
prince: or that deny to paye such duties, as by consent of the hygh
courte of parliament, are appoynted to the Prince for the defence and
preservacion of the realme.

You have sayde verye truelye herein, (quoth I) and I trust this terrible [70]
example of the blacke Smith, wil put all men in minde of their duties
and teach them to be obedient to all good lawes, and lawful contributions. The Scriptures do forbyd vs to rebell, or forcibly to withstand
Princes, though they commaund vniust thinges: yet in any case we may
not do them, but receyve quietly at the princes hand whatsoever [75]
punishement God shall suffer to be layed vpon vs for our refusall: God
wyll suffer none of his to be tempted above their strength. But because
the night is cum, I will trouble you no longer, I have certayne rabets
here, but they are not wurth the readinge. I will cause these which you
have allowed, to be printed as soon as I may conueniently. This sayd we [80]
take leue eche of other, and so departed.

[63–64] as the Blacke Smith C–G.
[64]   wilful F.

[*For the collation of the passage beginning* But because *in l.* 77, *see Prose* 24
(C–F). *In the* 1587 *edition* (G), *the lines added after* strength *introduce a new
tragedy, that of Sir Nicholas Burdet. I have therefore printed the addition to this
prose link with the rest of the new material added in the* 1587 *edition. See below,*
p. 463.]

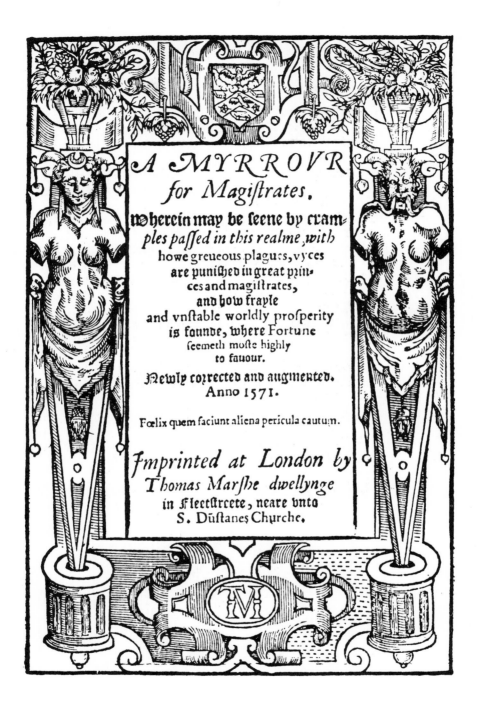

A MYRROVR
for Magiſtrates,
wherein may be ſeene by cram-
ples paſſed in this realme, with
howe greueous plagues, vyces
are puniſhed in great princes and magiſtrates,
and how frayle
and vnſtable worldly proſperity
is founde, where Fortune
ſeemeth moſte highly
to fauour.

Newly corrected and augmented.
Anno 1571.

Fœlix quem faciunt aliena pericula cautum.

Jmprinted at London by
Thomas Marſhe dwellynge
in Fleetſtreete, neare vnto
S. Dùſtanes Churche.

The table.

FINIS

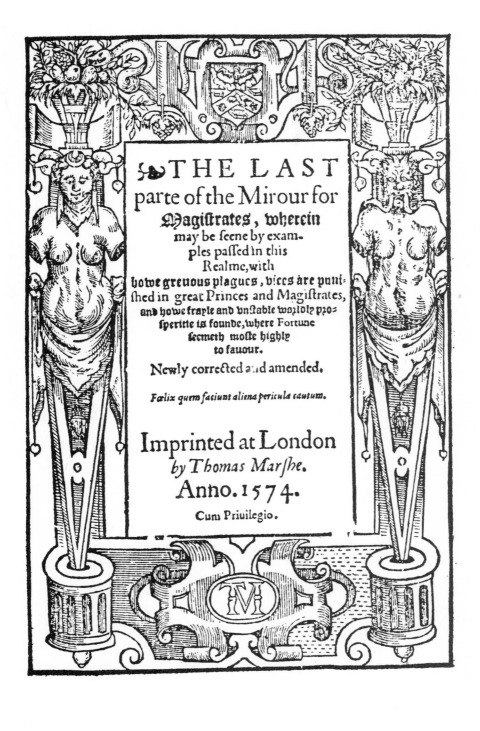

THE LAST
parte of the Mirour for
Magiſtrates, wherein
may be ſeene by exam-
ples paſſed in this
Realme, with
howe greuous plagues, vices are puniſhed in great Princes and Magiſtrates,
and howe frayle and vnſtable worldly proſperitie is founde, where Fortune
ſeemeth moſte highly
to fauour.

Newly corrected and amended.

Fœlix quem faciunt aliena pericula cautum.

Imprinted at London
by *Thomas Marſhe.*
Anno. 1574.

Cum Priuilegio.

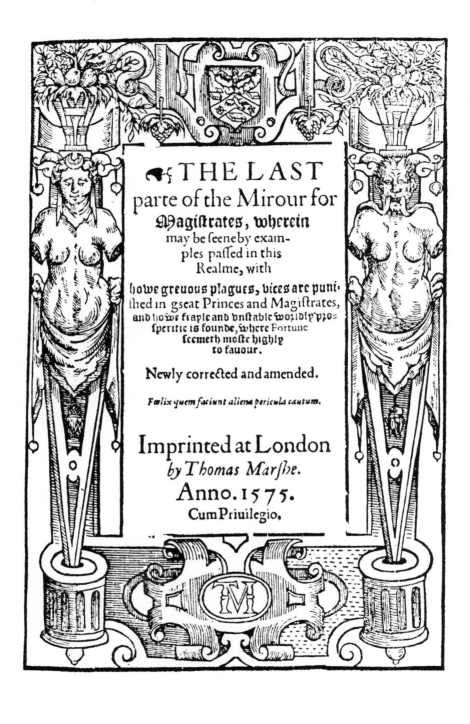

THE LAST
parte of the Mirour for
Magiſtrates, wherein
may be ſeene by exam-
ples paſſed in this
Realme, with

howe greuous plagues, vices are puniſhed in gseat Princes and Magiſtrates,
and howe frayle and vnſtable worldly proſperitie is founde, where Fortune
ſeemeth moſte highly
to fauour.

Newly correſted and amended.

Fælix quem faciunt aliena pericula cautum.

Imprinted at London
by *Thomas Marſhe.*
Anno. 1575.
Cum Priuilegio.

TRAGEDIES ADDED
IN
THE EDITION OF
1578

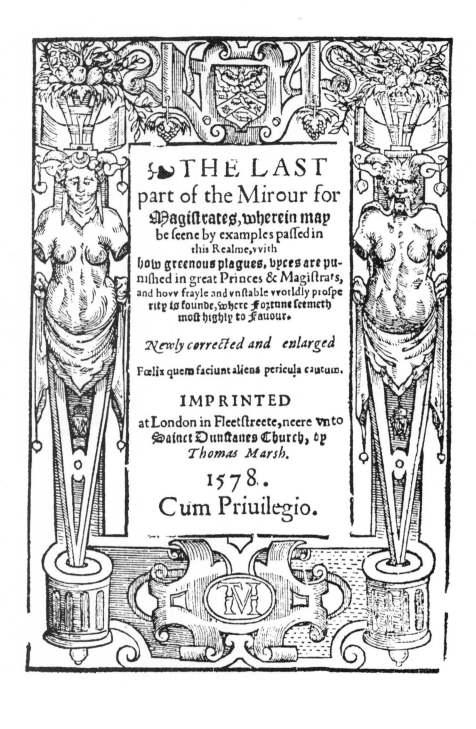

THE LAST

part of the Mirour for
Magiſtrates, wherein may
be ſeene by examples paſſed in
this Realme, vvith
how greenous plagues, vyces are puniſhed in great Princes & Magiſtrats,
and hovv frayle and vnſtable vvorldly proſpe
rity is founde, ſwhere Fortune ſeemeth
moſt highly to Fauour.

Newly corrected and enlarged

Fœlix quem faciunt aliens pericula cautum.

IMPRINTED

at London in Fleetſtreete, neere vnto
Sainct Dunſtanes Church, by
Thomas Marſh.

1578.

Cum Priuilegio.

Ere I had raygned fully fiftene yeare,
While time I lay at Pertho at my place,
With the Queene my wife and children me to cheare,
My murdring vncle with the double face,
That longed for my kingdome and my Mace.
To slaye me there suborned Robert Grame,
With whom his nephew Robert Stuart came.

And whan the tyme fit for their purpose found,
Into my priuy Chamber they astart,
Where with their swordes they gaue me many a wound,
And slue al such as stucke vnto my part:
There loe my wife did shew her louing hart,
Who to defend me felled one or twayne,
And was sore wounded ere I could be slayne.

See Baldwin, Baldwin, the vnhappy endes,
Of such as passe not of their lawful oth:
Of those that causeles leaue their fayth or frendes,
And murther kinsfolke through their foes vntroth,
Warne warne al Princes, al like sinnes to loth,
And chiefly such as in my realme be borne,
For God hates highly al that are forsworne.

FINIS

Han this was sayd, let king Iamy go said maister Ferrers, & returne we to our own storye, and see what broyles were amonge the Nobilitye in the kinges minoritye. Howe the
Cardi-

*H*nmfrey Plantagenet.

Cardinall Beaufozde maligneth the state of Duke Humfrey the kinges vncle and Protectoure of the Realme, and by what driftes he fyzst banisheth hys wyfe from him. And lastlye how the sayd Duke is murderously made awaye throughe conspiracye of Queene Margaret and other: both whose trage= dies I haue here ioyned together, for they be nota= ble. That wil do very wel (sayd another) but take heede ye stay not to long vppon them, I warrante you (quoth I)and therfoze I would that firste of al ye gecue eare, what the Duke him= selfe doth say, as foloweth.

How

Hen this was sayde (quod one
of the companye) let passe these
Scottish matters, and returne
we to our English storyes whi
che minister matter enoughe of
tragedy, without sekyng or tra
uaylinge to forreine countryes.
Therfore returne we to the rest of þ Tragical tro¬
bles and broyles which hapned in this realme du¬
ring the minority of king Henry the vi. & the sundry
falls and ouerthrowes of great princes & other no¬
ble persons happening therby. Wel sayd (qd M. fer.)
and as it happeneth, I haue here ready penned ii.
notable tragedies, the one of Humfrey Duke of
Glocestre, the other of the Duches Elienor his wife
which as (me semeth) be two of þ most memorable
matters fortuning in þ time But whether of the is
fyrst to be placed in the order of our boke, I some¬
what stande in doute. For albeit the sayde Dukes
death happened before the deceasse of the Duches,
yet was her fall first, which fynally was cause of o
uerthrow to both why shoulde you doubte then
(quod the rest of þ company) for seyng þ cause doth
alwaies go before theffect and sequel of any thing:
it is good reason you should begin w her first.
And therfore we pray you lette vs heare
fyrst what she hath to say, for al thys
whyle we haue not hard the
complaint of any Lady
or other woman.

Ꮤhe

The Verso of Fol. 39 introduced as a cancel into the 1578 Edition

WHen this was sayde (quod one of the companye) let passe [Cancel for
these Scottish matters, and returne we to our English Prose 10]
storyes whiche minister matter enoughe of tragedy,
without seking or trauaylinge to forreine countryes. Therfore returne
we to the rest of the Tragical troubles and broyles which hapned in this [5]
realme during the minority of king Henry the vi. & the sundry falls and
ouerthrowes of great princes & other noble persons happening therby.
Wel sayd (quoth M. Fer.) and as it happeneth, I haue here ready penned
ii. notable tragedies, the one of Humfrey Duke of Glocestre, the other
of the Duches Elienor his wife which as (me semeth) be two of the [10]
most memorable matters fortuning in that time But whether of them
is fyrst to be placed in the order of our boke, I somewhat stande in doute.
For albeit the sayde Dukes death happened before the deceasse of the
Duches, yet was her fall first, which fynally was cause of ouerthrow to
both. why shoulde you doubte then (quod the rest of the company) [15]
for seyng the cause doth alwaies go before theffect and sequel of any
thing: it is good reason you should begin with her first. And therfore
we pray you lette vs heare fyrst what she hath to say, for al thys whyle
we haue not hard the complaint of any Lady or other woman.

[1]   quoth one G.
[8]   (quod Maister *Ferrers*) as it G. have penned here G.
[12]   is to bee placed first in G.
[14-15] was cause of both. G.

> [*See the collation of Prose 10, above, for the prose link used in the original issue*
> *of the 1578 edition to introduce the tragedy of Humphrey Duke of Gloucester. This*
> *variant version of Prose 10 served to introduce the tragedy of Elianor Cobham in the*
> *cancel in the 1578 text. See Introduction, pp. 17–18.*]

[Tragedy 28]

HOW DAME ELIANOR COBHAM
Duchesse of Glocester
for practising of witchcraft and Sorcery, suffred open penance, and after was banished the realme into the yle of Man.

𝕴F a poore lady damned in exyle
Amongst princes may bee allowed place
Then gentle Baldwin stay thy pen awhyle
And of pure pitty ponder wel my case,

[5] How I a Duches, destitute of grace
Haue found by proofe, as many haue & shal
The prouerbe true, that pryde wil hauve a fall

A noble Prince extract of royal blood
Humfrey sometyme Protector of this land

[10] Of Glocester Duke, for vertu cald (the good)
When I but base beneath his state did stande
Vouchsafte with me to ioyne in wedlockes bande
Hauing in Court no name of high degree
But Elinor Cobham as parents left to mee

[15] And though by byrth of noble race I was,
Of Barons bloud, yet was I thought vnfitte,
So high to matche, yet so it came to passe,
Whyther by grace, good fortune, or by witte
Dame Venus lures so in myne eyes did sitte,

[20] As this great Prince with out respect of state
Did worthy me to be his wedded mate

432

His wyfe I was, and he my true husband
Though for a whyle he had the company
Of lady Iaquet the Duchesse of holland
Beyng an heyre of ample patrimony [25]
But that fel out, to be no matrimony
For after war, long sute in law and strife
She proued was the Duke of Brabants wife.

Thus of a Damsel a Duchesse I became,
My state and place aduanced next the Queene [30]
Wherby me thought I felt no ground, but swam
For in the Court myne equall was not seene
And so possest with pleasure of the splene
The sparkes of pride so kyndled in my brest
As I in court, would shyne aboue the rest [35]

Such gyftes of nature god in me hath graft
Of shape and stature, with other graces moo
That by the shot of Cupids fiery shafte
Which to the hart of this greate prince did goe
This mighty Duke, with loue was linked so [40]
As he abasyng the height of his degree,
Sette his hole harte, to loue and honour mee

Grudge who so would, to him I was most deere
Aboue all Ladyes aduanced in degree
(The Quene except) no Princesse was my peere [45]
But gaue me place, and lords with cap and knee
Dyd all honour and reuerence vnto me
Thus hoysted high vpon the rollinge wheele
I sate so sure, me thought I could not reele.

And weening least that fortune hath a turne, [50]
I lookt aloft, and would not looke alow,

[36] had graft G.
[40] was kindled so, G.

The brondes of pryde so in my breast did burne
As the hot sparkes, burst forth in open showe,
And more and more the fyre began to glowe,
[55] Without quenching, and dayly did encrease,
Til fortunes blastes with shame did make it ceasse.

For (as tis sayde) Pryde passeth on afore,
And shame followes, for iust rewarde & meede
Wold god ladyes, both now and euermore
[60] Of my hard hap, which shall the story reede
Wold beare in mynde, and trust it as their Crede:
That pryde of harte, is a most hateful vice,
And lowlines, a pearle of passing pryce.

Namely in Quenes, and Ladies of estate
[65] Within whose myndes, all mekenes should abound
Since high disdayne, doth alwayes purchace hate.
Beyng a vyce, that most part doth redound
To their reproch, in whom the same is found.
And seeldome gets good fauour or good fame
[70] But is at last, knit vp with worldly shame.

The proofe wherof I founde most true indede,
That pryde afore, hath shame to wayte behynde.
Let no man doubt, in whom this vice doth brede,
But shame for pryde by iustice is assynde,
[75] Which I wel founde, for truely in my mynde
Was neuer none, whom pryde did more enflame,
Nor neuer none, receiued greatter shame.

For not content to be a Duchesse greate,
I longed sore to beare the name of Queene
[80] Aspyring stil vnto an higher seate,
And with that hope my selfe did ouerweene

[60]   shall *is misprinted* shlal *in the text.*

434

Sins there was none, which that tyme was betweene
Henry the king, and my good Duke his Eame
Heyre to the crowne and kingdome of this Realme.

So neare to be, was cause of my vayn hope [85]
And long awayte when this fayre hap would fal.
My studies all were tending to that scope,
Alas, the whyle to councel I did call
Such as would seme, by skill coniectural
Of art Magicke and wicked Sorcery [90]
To deeme and dyuine the princes desteny

Among which sort of those that bare most fame
There was a Beldame called the wytch of Ey,
Old mother Madge her neyghbours did hir name
Which wrought wonders in countryes by heresaye [95]
Both feendes and fayries her charmyng would obay
And dead corpsis from graue she could vprere
Suche an Inchauntresse, as that tyme had no peere

Two pryestes also, the one hight Bolenbroke
The other Suthwell, great Clerkes in coniuration [100]
These twoo Chapleins, were they that vndertooke
To cast and calke, the kinges constellation
And then to iudge by depe dyuination.
Of thinges to come, and who should next succede
To Englandes crowne, al this was true in deede. [105]

And further sure they neuer did proceede
Though I confesse, that this attempt was ill,
But for my part, for any thing in dede
Wrought, or els thought, by any kynd of skill.
God is my iudge I neuer had the will [110]
By any Inchauntment sorcery or charme
Or other wyse, to worke my princes harme.

435

Yet netheles, when this case came to light,
By secrete spyes to Cayphas our Cardinal
[115] Who long in hart had borne a priuy spyght,
To my good Duke his nephew naturall
Glad of the chance, so fitly forth to fall
His long hid hate, with iustice to color
Used this case with most extream rigor.

[120] And caused me with my complyces all,
To be cyted by processe peremptory,
Before Iudges, in place Iudiciall
Whereas Cayphas, sytting in his glory
Would not allow my answer dilatory
[125] Ne Doctor or Proctor, to allege the lawes.
But forced me to pleade in myne owne cause.

The kynges councel were called to the case
My husband than shut out for the season
In whose absence I found but little grace
[130] For Lawiers turned our offence to treason
And so with rigor, without ruth or reason
Sentence was gyuen that I for the same
Should do penance, and suffer open shame.

Nay the lyke shame had neuer wight I weene
[135] Duchesse, Lady, ne Damsel of degree,
As I that was, a Princesse next the Quene,
Wyfe to a Prince, and none so great as hee,
A Kinges vncle, Protector of his countrey,
With Taper burning, shrouded in a sheete
[140] Three dayes a row, to passe the open streate.

Barelegd, and bare foote, to al the worldes wonder
Ye, and as though such shame did not suffise

[128]   *The text mistakenly prints) after* than.

With more despyte, then to part a sunder,
Me and my Duke, which Traytors did deuyse
By Statute law, in most vnlawful wise,   [145]
Fyrst sending me, with shame into exile.
Then murdryng him, by trechery and gyle.

   Ye and besydes, this cruel banishment
Far from al frendes, to comfort me in care
And husbandes death: there was by Parliment   [150]
Ordaynd for me, a messe of courser fare.
For they to bring me to beggers state most bare
By the same acte, from me did then withdraw.
Such right of dower, as widowes haue by law.

   Death (as tis sayd) doth set al thinges at rest,   [155]
Which fel not so in myne vnhappy case,
For sins my death, myne enmies made a Iest
In minstrels ryme myne honour to deface.
And then to bring my name in more disgrace
A song was made in manner of a laye   [160]
Which old wyues sing of me vnto this day.

   Yet with these spytes, theyr malice did not end
For shortly after, my sorrowes to renew
My Loyal Lord, which neuer did offende
Was cald in hast, the cause he little knew   [165]
To a Parliament, without Sommons due
Whereas his death, was cruelly contryued
And I his wyfe of earthly ioyes depryued.

[158] rymes, G.

For al the while my Duke had life & breath
[170] So long I stoode, in hope of my restore
But when I hard of his most causeles death
Then the best salue for my recureles sore
Was to dispayre of cure for euermore,
And as I could, my careful hart to cure.
[175] With pacience, most paynful to indure.

O Traitors fel, which in your hartes could fynde
Like feendes of hel, the guiltles to betraye
But ye chefely, his kinsemen moste vnkynde
Which gaue consent to make him so away,
[180] That vnto God, with al my hart I pray,
Vengeance may light on him that caused all,
Beaufort I meane, that cursed *Cardinall.*

Which Bastard preest of the house of Lancaster
Sonne to Duke John, surnamed John of Gaunt
[185] Was first create, Byshop of Winchester,
For no learning, wher of he myght wel vaunt
Ne for vertue, which he did neuer haunt
But for his gold & Summes that were not small
Payd to the pope, was made a Cardinall.

[190] Proude Lucifer, which from the heauens on hye
Downe to the pit of Hel below was cast,
And beyng ons an Aungell bright in sky
For his high pryde, in Hel is chayned fast
In depe darknes, that euermore shall last
[195] More hault of hart was not before his fal
Then was this proud and pompos Cardinall

Whose lyfe good Baldwine paint out in his pickle,
And blase this Baal & Belligod most blinde,
An Hipocryte, all faythles false and fickle,
[200] A wicked wretch, a kinseman most vnkynde,

438

A Deuil incarnate, all deuilishly enclynde
And to discharge my conscience all at ones
The Deuil him gnaw both body, blood and bones

    The spyteful Preest would needes make me a Witch,
As would to god I had bene for his sake,   [205]
I would haue clawd him where he did not itche,
I would haue played the Lady of the Lake
And as Merlin was, cloasde him in a Brake,
Ye a Meridian, to Lul him by daylight
And a night mare to ryde on him by night.   [210]

    The fiery feends with feuers hot and frenzye
The Ayery hegges with stench and carren sauours
And watry ghostes with gowtes, and with dropsie
The earthy Goblins, with Aches at all houres
Furyes & Fairies, with al infernal powers   [215]
I would haue stird from the darke dongeon
Of hell Centre, as depe as Demagorgon.

    Or had I now the skil of dame *Erichto*
Whose dreadful charmes, as Lucane doth expresse
All feendes did feare, so far forth as Prince Pluto   [220]
Was at her cal for dread of more distresse
Then would I send of helhounds more and lesse,
A legion at least, at him to crye and yel.
And with that chyrme, herrie him downe to hell

    Which neede not, for sure I thinke that hee   [225]
Who here in earth leades Epicurus lyfe,
As farre from god as possible may be
With whom all sinne and vices are most ryfe
Using at wil both widow mayd and wyfe
But that some Deuil his body doth possesse   [230]
His life is such, as men can iudge no lesse

[201]   deuilishly *is misprinted* deuishly G.

And god forgeue my wrath and wreakful mynde
Such is my hate to that most wicked wretch
Dye when he shal, in hart I could wel fynd

[235] Out of the graue his corps againe to fetch
And racke his lymmes as long as they would stretch
And take delyte to listen euery daye
How he could sing a masse of welawaye

The yle of Man was the appointed place
[240] To penance mee for euer in exile
Thither in hast they poasted me apace,
And doubtinge skape, they pind me in a Pyle
Close by my selfe in care, alas the whyle
There felt I fyrst pore prisoners hungry fare,
[245] Much want, thinges skant, and stone walls hard and bare

The change was strange, from silke and cloth of Gold
To rugged fryze my carcas for to cloathe,
From princes fare, and dayntyes hot and cold,
To rotten fish, and meates that one would loathe
[250] The dyet and dressing were mutch a lyke boath
Bedding and lodging were all alike fyne,
Such Down it was, as serued wel for swyne.

Neither do I myne owne case thus complayne
Which I confesse came partly by deserte
[255] The onely cause which doubleth al my payne
And which most nere goeth now vnto my harte.
Is that my fault, dyd finally reuerte
To him that was least gilty of the same
Whose death it was, though I abode the shame.

[260] Whose fatal fall, when I do call to mynde,
And how by me his mischiefe fyrst began
So oft I cry on fortune most vnkinde
And my mishap most bitterly do banne,

That euer I to such a noble man,
Who from my cryme was innocent and cleare, [265]
Shoulde be a cause to buy his loue so deare

Oh to my hart how greuous is the wounde
Calling to mynd this dismal deadly case
I would I had bene doluen vnder ground.
When he first saw, or loked on my face, [270]
Or tooke delight in any kynd of grace
Seming in mee, that him did stirre or moue
To fancy me, or set his hart to loue.

Farewel Grenewych my Palace of delyght,
Where I was wont to see the Cristal streames, [275]
Of royall Thames most pleasant to my syght
And farewel Kent, right famous in all realmes
A thousand tymes I mynd you in my dreames
And when I wake most grefe it is to me
That neuer more agayne I shall, see you [280]

In the night tyme when I should take my rest
I weepe, I wayle, I weat my bed with teares
And when dead sleape my spirites hath opprest
Troubled with dreames, I fantazy vayne feares
Myne husbands voyce then ringeth at myne eares [285]
Crying for help, O saue me from the death
These villaynes here do seeke to stop my breath.

Ye and somtymes me thinkes his drery ghost
Appeares in sight, and shewes me in what wyse,
Those fel tyrantes, with tormentes had emboost [290]
His wynd and breath, to abuse peoples eyes

[280]   shall you see. G.

441

So as no doubt or question should aryse
Amonges rude folke which little vnderstande,
But that his death came onely by gods hand

[295]   I playne in vayne, where eares be none to heare
But roaring Seas, & blustring of the wynd
And of redresse am near a whit the neere
But with wast woordes to feede my mournful mynde,
Wishing ful oft, the Parcas had vntwynde
[300]   My vital stringes, or Atropos with knife,
Had cut the lyne of my most wretched lyfe.

Oh that Neptune, and Eolus also,
Thone God of Seas, the other of weather
Ere myne Arriual, into that yle of woe
[305]   Had suncke the ship wherin I sayled thether
(The shipmen saued) so as I togeather
With my good Duke, mought haue bene dead afore
Fortune had wroken her wrath on vs so sore.

Or els that God when my first passage was
[310]   Into exile along Saynt Albanes towne
Had neuer let me further for to passe,
But in the Streat with death had strucke me downe
Then had I sped of my desyred bowne
That my pore corps mought there haue lien with his
[315]   Both in one graue, & so haue gone to blysse.

But I alas, the greatter is my greefe
Am past that hope to haue my sepulture
Nere vnto hym, which was to me most leefe
But in an yle, and country most obscure,
[320]   To pyne in payne, whilst my poore life will dure
And beyng dead, all honorles to lye
In simple graue, as other poore that dye.

[293]   Among G.

442

ELEANOR, DUCHESS OF GLOUCESTER

My tale is tolde, and tyme it is to ceasse
Of troubles past, al which haue had their ende
My graue I trust, shal purchasse me good peace   [325]
In such a world, where no wight doth contend
For highest place, whereto all flesh shal wend
And so I end, vsyng on word for all,
As I Began, that pryde wil haue a fall

[325]   mee such peace G.
[327]   For higher place, G.

[Prose 28] SVerly (sayd one of the companye) thys Lady hath don much to moue the hearers to pitye her, & hath very wel knyt vp the ende of her tragedy according to the beginning but I meruayle much where she learned al this Poetry touched in her tale, for in her dayes,

[5] learninge was not common, but a rare thinge, namely in women, yes (quod Maister Ferrers) that might she very wel learn of the Duke her Husbande, who was a Prince so excellently learned, as the like of his degree was no where to be founde, And not onelye so, but was also a Patron to Poetes & orators muche lyke as *Mecenas* was in the tyme of

[10] *Augustus Cesar* This Duke was foundor of the Diuinite Schole in Oxforde, whereas he caused *Aristotles* workes to be translated out of Greeke into Latin, and caused many other things to be done for aduauncement of lerning, hauing alwaies lerned men near about him no meruaile therfore though the Duchesse broughte som pece away. Me

[15] think (quod another) she passeth bounds of a Ladies modesty, to inuey so cruelly agaynst the Cardinall Beaufort. Not a whit (quod another) hauing such cause as she had, & somewhat ye must beare with womens passions. Therefore leaue we her to eternall rest, & lette vs heare what Maister Ferrers wil say for the Duke her husband whose case was the

[20] more lamentable, in that hee suffered without cause. And surely thoughe the Cardinal against nature was the Dukes mortall Foe, yet the chiefe causers of his confusyon, was the Quene, and William Delapoole Erle of Suffolke and afterwards Duke, whose counsel was chefely followed in the contryuing of this noble mans destruction, She through ambicion

[25] to haue soueraynty and rule and he through, flattery to purchace honour and promotion, which as he in shorte time obtayned: so in as short tyme he lost agayne, & his life withal by the iust iudgement of

[*This prose link is part of the cancel introduced into the 1578 edition. For the prose link which precedes the tragedy of Humphrey Duke of Gloucester in the uncancelled 1578 text, see pp. 429–30 and the collation of Prose 10, p. 161.*]

[2–3] knit vp her tragedy G.
[15]) *is misprinted* (*in the text.*

God, receiuing such measure as he before mette to this good Prince.
This drift of his turned to the vtter ouerthrow of the king himselfe, the
Quene his wife, & Edward their son a most goodly prince, & to the [30]
subuersion of the hole house of Lancaster, as you may see at large in the
Chronicles: but now let vs heare what the Duke will saye.

HOW HVMFREY PLANTAGENET [Tragedy 29]
Duke of Glocester
Protector of England, during the minoritie of his
Nephue kinge Henrye the sixt, (commonlye
called the good Duke) by practise of enemies
was brought to confusion.

As highest hilles with tempestes bene most touched
And tops of trees, most subiect vnto wynde,
And as great towers with stone strongly cowched,
Haue heauy falles when they be vnderminde,
Euen so by proofe, in worldly thinges we fynde, [5]
That such as clyme the top of high degree
From perril of falling neuer can be free.

To proue this true (good Baldwin) harken hyther,
See and behold me vnhappie Humfrey,
Englands Protector and Duke of Glocester [10]
Who in the time of the sixt king Henrie,
Ruled this Realme yeares mo then twentie:
Note wel the cause of my decay and fall,
And make a mirrour for Magistrates all.

[6] as *is misprinted* a *in the text.*

[15]   In their most weale, to beware of vnhap,
And not to sleepe in slombring sickernesse,
Whilst Fortune false doth lul them in her lap
Drowned in dreames of brittle blessednesse,
But then to feare her freakes and ficklenesse,
[20]   Accompting stil the higher they ascend:
More nigh to be to Daunger in the end.

     And that vayne trust in bloud or royall race.
Abuse them not with carelesse assuraunce
To trust Fortune, but waying wel my case,
[25]   When she most smyleth to haue in remembraunce
my soden fall, who in al apparaunce:
Hauing most stayes, which man in state mainteine,
Haue found the same vntrustie and most vayne.

     Better then I, none may the same affirme,
[30]   Who trusting all in height of high estate,
Led by the eares with false flatteries chyrme,
Which neuer Prince could banishe from his gate,
Did little thinke on such a sodein mate,
Not heeding, lesse dreeding, al vnaware,
[35]   By foes least feared, was trapt into a snare.

     If noble byrth or high authoritie
Nomber of Frendes, kindred, or alliaunce,
If wisedome, learning, or worldly pollicye
Mought haue beene stayers to Fortunes variaunce,
[40]   None stoode more strong, in worldly countenaunce,
For al these helpes had I to auayle mee,
And yet in fyne, al the same did fayle mee.

     Of King Henry the fourth, fourth sonne I was
Brother to Henry, the fyft of that name,
[45]   And vncle to Henry the sixt, but alas,

[35]   trapt in a G.

What cause had I to presume on the same?
Or for vayne glorye, aduauncing my fame
My selfe to cal in recordes, and wrytinges,
The sonne, brother, and vncle vnto kinges.

This was my boast, which lastly was my bane, [50]
Yet not this boast, was it that brought mee downe
The very cause, which made my weale to wane
So neere of Kin that I was to the Crowne,
That was the Rocke that made my Ship to drowne.
A rule there is not faylinge, but most sure [55]
Kingdome, no kyn doth know, ne can indure.

For after my Brother the fyft Henry
Wan by Conquest the Royall Realme of Fraunce,
And of two Kingdomes made one Monarchy
Before his death, for better obeysaunce. [60]
To his younge Sonne, not ripe to gouernaunce
Protector of England I was by Testament,
And Ihon my Brother, in Fraunce made Regent.

To whom if God had lent a longer life,
Our house to haue kept from stormes of inward strife [65]
Or it had beene the Lorde Almighties will
Plantagenettes name in State had standen still
But deadly discord which Kingdomes great doth spill
Bred by desire of high Dominacion,
Brought our whole house to playne desolation. [70]

It is for trowth in an History Founde
That Henry Plantagenet fyrst of our name
Who called was, Kinge Henry the seconde
Sonne of Dame Mawde, the Empresse of High Fame
Would oft report, that his Auncient Grandame [75]
Though seeminge in Shape, a Woman naturall,
Was a Feende of the Kinde that (*Succubae*) some call.

447

Which olde fable, so longe time tolde before
When this Kinges sonnes against him did rebell:
[80] Hee cald to minde, and beinge greeued sore.
Loe! now (quoth hee) I see and proue full well
The Story true, which folke of old did tell
That from the deuill descended all our race,
And now my children, do verefy the case.

[85] Whereof to leaue a longe memoriall,
In minde of man euermore to rest
A Picture hee made and hong it in his Hall,
Of a *Pellicane* sittinge on his Nest,
Wyth foure yonge Byrdes, three peckinge at his brest
[90] Wyth bloudy Beakes, and further did deuise
The yongest Byrde, to pecke the fathers eyes.

Meaninge hereby, his rebell children three
Henry, and Richard who bet him on the brest:
Ieffrey only, from that offence was free)
[95] Henry died of Englandes, Crowne possest:
Richard liued his father to molest,
Iohn the yongest peckt still his fathers eye
Whose deedes vnkinde, the sooner made hym dye.

This kinge (some wryte) in his sicknesse last
[100] Sayde, as it were by way of Prophecy
How that the Deuill, a Darnell grayne had cast
Amonge his Kin to encrease enmity,
Which should remayne in their Posterity,
Till mischiefe, and murder had spent them all
[105] Not leauinge one to pisse agaynst the wall.

And yet from him in order did succede
In England here, of crowned kinges fourtene
Of that surname, and of that lyne and seede,

[84] children verify G.

448

With Dukes and Earles, and many a noble Queene,
The number such as al the worid would weene   [110]
So many ympes could neuer so be spent,
But some heire Male, should be of that discent.

   Which to be true if any stand in doubt,
Because I meane not further to digresse,
Let him peruse the stories throughout   [115]
Of English kinges, whom practise did oppresse,
And he shal fynde the cause of their distresse
From first to last, vnkindly to beginne,
Always by those that next were of the kynne.

   Was not Richard, of whom I spake before,   [120]
A rebel playne vntil his father dyed,
And Iohn likewise an Enmie euermore
To Richard againe, and for a rebel tryed?
After whose death, it cannot be denyed,
Against all right this Iohn most cruellye   [125]
His brothers children caused for to dye.

   Arthur and Isabell (I meane) that were
Geffreyes children, then Duke of Britaine
Henries third sonne, by one degree more neere,
Then was this Iohn, as stories shew most playne,   [130]
Which two children were famisht or els slayne,
By Iohn their Eame cald *Saunzterre* by name,
Of whose fowle act, al countries speake great shame.

   Edward, and Richard, second both by name
Kinges of this land, fel downe by fatall fate   [135]
What was the cause, that princes of such fame,
Did leese at last their honour, life, and state?
Nothing at all, but discord and debate,
Which when it haps in kindred or in bloud,
Erynnis rage was neuer halfe so wood.   [140]

Be sure therfore ye kinges and princes all
That concorde in kingdomes is chiefe assuraunce,
And that your families do neuer fall,
But where discord doth leade the doubtful daunce
[145]   With busie brawles and turnes of variaunce,
Where mallice is Minstrel, the pype ill report,
The Maske mischiefe, and so endes the sport,

But now to come to my purpose againe,
Whilst I my charge applied in England,
[150]   My brother in Fraunce long time did remaine,
Cardinal Beauford tooke proudly in hand,
In causes publique against me to stand,
Who of great mallice so much as he might
Sought in al thinges to do mee dispight.

[155]   Which proude prelate to me was bastard Eame,
Sonne to Duke Iohn of Gaunt as they did fayne,
Who beeing made high Chauncellour of the Realme,
Not like a Priest, but like a prince did reigne,
Nothing wanting which might his pride mainteine,
[160]   Bishop besides of Winchester he was,
And Cardinall of Rome which Angels brought to passe.

Not Gods Aungels, but Angels of old Gold,
Lyft him aloft in whom no cause there was
By iust desert, so high to be extold,
[165]   (Ryches except) where by this Golden asse,
At home and abroade al matters brought to passe,
Namely at Rome, hauing no meane but that
To purchase there his crimzin Cardinal hat.

Which thing the king my father him forbad
[170]   Playnly saying, that he could not abide,
Within his realme a subiect to be had

[149]   my *is misprinted* imy *in the text.*

His Princes peere, yet such was this mans pride,
That he forthwith after my father dyed,
(The King then young) obteyned of the Pope,
That honour high, which erst he could not hope.　　　　[175]

　　Whose proude attemptes because that I withstoode,
My bounden dutie the better to acquite,
This holy father waxed welnere wood,
Of meere malice deuising day and night,
To worke to me dishonour and dispite,　　　　[180]
Whereby there fel betweene vs such a Iarre,
As in this land was like a ciuil warre.

　　My brother Iohn which lay this while in Fraunce,
Heard of this hurle, and past the seas in hast,
By whose traueil this troublesome distaunce,　　　　[185]
Ceassed a while, but nethelesse in wast:
For rooted hate wil hardly be displast
Out of hyghe hartes, and namely where debate,
Happeneth amongst great persons of estate.

　　For like as a match doth lye and smolder,　　　　[190]
Long time before it commeth to the trayne.
But yet when fyre hath caught in the poulder,
No arte is able, the flames to restrayne:
Euen so the sparkes of enuye and disdayne,
Out of the smoke burst foorth in such a flame,　　　　[195]
That Fraunce and England yet may rue the same.

　　So when of two realmes the regiment royal,
Betwene brothers was parted equallye,
One placed in Fraunce for affayres Martiall,
And I at home for ciuil pollicie:　　　　[200]
To serue the state, we both did so applie,
As honour and fame to both did encrease,
To him for the warre, to me for the peace.

[205]

Whence enuye sprang, and specially because
This proude prelate could not abyde a Peere,
Within the land to rule the state by lawes,
Wherfore sifting my lyfe and actes most neere,
He neuer ceast, vntil as you shal heare,
By practise foule of him and his allies,
My death was wrought in most vnworthy wise.

[210]

And fyrst he sought my doinges to defame,
By rumours false, which hee and his did sowe
Letters and bylles to my reproch and shame
He did deuise, and al about bestow,
Whereby my troth in doubt should dayly grow,
In England fyrst and afterward in Fraunce,
Mouing al meanes to bring me to mischaunce.

[215]

One quarel was, that where by common law
Murder and theft beene punisht all alike,
So as manslears, which bloudy blades do drawe,
Suffer no more, then he that doth but pike,
Me thought the same no order politike,
In setting paynes to make no difference,
Betweene the lesser and greater offence.

[220]

I beeing seene somwhat in ciuil law,
The rules thereof reputed muche better,
Wherfore to keepe, offenders more in awe,
Like as the fault was smaller or greater,
So set I paynes more easier or bitter,
Waying the qualitie of euerye offence,
And so according pronounced sentence.

[225]

[230]

Amongst my other *Delicta Iuuentutis,*
Whilst rage of youth my reason did subdue,
I must confesse as the very truth is,
Driuen by desire, fond fancies to ensue,

[235]

452

A thing I did, whereof great trouble grew,
Abusing one to my no small rebuke,
Which wife was than to Iohn of Brabant Duke.

Called she was Lady Iaquet the fayre,
Delightful in loue like Helene of Troye: [240]
To the Duke of Bauier sole daughter and heire,
Her did I marrye to my great annoy
Yet for a tyme, this dame I did enioye,
With her whole landes, witholding them by force,
Til Martin the Pope, betwene vs made diuorce.   [245]

Yet all these blastes not hable were to moue
The anchor strong, whereby my ship did stay,
Some other shift to seeke him did behoue,
Whereto ere long il fortune made the way,
Which fynally was cause of my decay   [250]
And cruel death, contriued by my foes,
Which fel out thus, as now I shal disclose.

Elianor my wife, my Dutches only deare,
I know not how but as the nature is
Of women al, aye curious to enquiere   [255]
Of thinges to come (though I confesse in this
Her fault not small) and that shee did amisse,
By wytches skill, which sorcery some call,
Would know of thinges which after should befall.

And for that cause made her selfe acquainted   [260]
With mother Madge, called the wytch of Eye,
And with a Clerke that after was attainted,
Bolenbroke he hight, that learned was that way,
With other moe, which famous were that daye,
Aswel in Science, called Mathematicall,   [265]
As also in magicke and skil supernatural

[254]   nature *is misprinted* n, ture *in the text.*

These cunning folkes she set on worke to know,
The time how long the king should liue and raigne,
Some by the Starres, and some by deuils below,
[270] Some by witchcraft sought knowledge to attayne,
With like fancies, friuolous fond and vayne,
Whereof though I knew least of any man,
Yet by that meane my mischiefe first began.

Yet besides this there was a greater thing,
[275] How she in waxe by counsel of the witch,
An Image made, crowned like a king,
With sword in hand, in shape and likenesse syche
As was the kinge, which dayly they did pytch
Against a fyre, that as the waxe did melt,
[280] So should his lyfe consume away vnfelt.

My Dutchesse thus, accused of this cryme,
As she that should such practise first beginne,
My part was then to yeld vnto the time,
Geeuing her leaue, to deale alone therein
[285] And since the cause concerned deadly synne,
Which to the clergie onely doth perteine,
To deale therein I plainly did refrayne.

And suffered them her person to ascite
Into their Courtes, to aunswere and appeare,
[290] Which to my hart was sure the greatest spight,
That could be wrought, and touched me most neare,
To see my wife, and lady leefe and deare,
To my reproche, and plaine before my face,
Entreated so, as one of sorte most base.

[295] The clergie then examining her cause,
Conuinced her, as guiltie in the same,
And sentence gaue according to their lawes,
That she and they whom I before did name

Should suffer death, or els some open shame:
Of which penaunce my wife by sentence had   [300]
To suffer shame of both the two, more bad.

   And fyrst she must by dayes together three,
Through London streetes passe al along in sight
Bare legde and barefoote, that al the world might see,
Bearing in hand a burning taper bright,   [305]
And not content, with this extreeme despight,
To worke mee wo, in al they may or can,
Exilde she was into the Ile of Man.

   This haynous crime and open worldly shame,
With such rigour shewed vnto my wife,   [310]
Was a fyne fetch further thinges to frame,
And nothing els, but a preparatiue
First from office, and fynally from lyfe,
Me to depriue, and so passing further,
What law could not, to execute by murther.   [315]

   Which by slye driftes, and wyndlaces aloofe,
They brought about, perswading first the Queene,
That in effect it was the kinges reproofe,
And hers also, to be exempted cleane,
From princely rule, or that it should be seene   [320]
A king of yeares, stil gouerned to bee
Lyke a Pupil, that nothing could forsee,

   The daunger more considering the king
Was without childe, I being his next heire,
To rule the realme, as Prince in euery thing   [325]
Without restraint, and al the sway to beare
With Peoples loue, whereby it was to feare
That my hault hart, vnbrideled in desire,
Time would preuent, and to the crowne aspire.

[303]   al *is misprinted* a, *in the text.*

[330] These with such like, were put into her head,
Who of her selfe, was thereto sone enclinde,
Other there were, that this il humour fed,
To neither part, which had good wil or minde,
[335] The Duke of Yorke, our cousin most vnkinde,
Who keeping close a tytle to the crowne,
Lancasters house did labour to pul downe.

The stay whereof he tooke to stand in mee,
Seeing the king of courage nothing stout,
Neither of wit great peril to foresee,
[340] So for purpose, if he could bring about
Mee to displace, then did he little doubt
To gayne the Goale, for which he droue the ball,
The crowne I meane to catch ere it should fall

This hope made him against me to conspyre
[345] With those which foes were to ech other late,
The Queene did weene, to win her whole desire
Which was to rule, the king and al the state
If I were ryd, whom therfore shee did hate:
Forecasting not, when that was brought to passe,
[350] How weake of frendes, the King her husband was.

The Dukes two, of Excester, and Buckingham,
With the Marquise Dorset therein did agree,
But namely the Marquise of Suffolke William,
Contriuer chiefe of this conspiracie,
[355] With other mo, that sate stil and did see,
Their mortal foes on me to whet their kniues,
Which turnde at last to losse of all their lyues.

But vayne desire of soueraintie and rule,
Which otherwise (Ambition) hath to name,
[360] So stirde the Queene that wilful as a Mule,
Headlong she runnes, from smoke into the flame,

Driuing a drift, which after did so frame,
As shee, the King, with all their lyne and race,
Depriued were of honour, lyfe, and place.

So for purpose she thought it very good,   [365]
With former foes, in frendship to confeder,
The Duke of Yorke, and other of his bloud,
With Neuils all, knyt were then together,
And Delapoole, frend afore to neither:
The Cardinal also, came within this list,   [370]
As Herode and Pylate, to iudge Iesu Christ.

This cursed league, to late discouered was
By Bayardes blinde, that lincked in the line,
The Queene and Cardinal brought it so to passe,
With Marquise Suffolke maister of this myne,   [375]
Whose il aduise, was counted very fyne,
With other moe which fynely could disguise,
With false visours my mischiefe to deuise.

Concluding thus they point without delay
Parliament to hold, in some vnhaunted place,   [380]
Far from London, out of the common way,
Where few or none should vnderstand the case,
But whom the Queene and Cardinal did embrace,
And so for place they chose Saint Edmondesburye
Synce when (some say) England was neuer merye.   [385]

Somens was sent, this companie to call,
Which made me muse, that in so great a case,
I should no whyt of counsel be at all,
Who yet had rule, and next the king in place,
Me thought nothing, my state could more disgrace,   [390]
Then to beare name, and in effect to bee,
A Cypher in Algrim, as al men mought see.

[368] then altogether, G.
[371] Ihesus Christ, G.

And though iust cause I had for to suspect,
The tyme and place appointed by my foes,
[395] And that my frendes most plainlye did detect,
The subtil traine, and practise of al those,
Which against mee, great treasons did suppose,
Yet trust of truth with a conscience cleare,
Gaue me good hart, in that place to appeare.

[400] Vpon which trust with more hast then good speede,
Forward I went to that vnluckye place,
Dutie to show, and no whit was in dreade
Of any trayne, but bold to shew my face,
As a true man yet so fel out the case,
[405] That after traueyle, seeking for repose,
An armed band, my lodging did enclose.

The Vicount Beaumount, who for the time supplied,
The office of high Conestable of the Land
Was with the Queene and Cardinall allied,
[410] By whose support, he stoutlye tooke in hand,
My lodginge to enter with an armed band
And for high treason, my person did arest,
And layed me that night, where him seemed best

Then shaking and quaking, for dread of a Dreame,
[415] Halfe waked al naked in bed as I lay,
What tyme strake the chime of mine hower extreame,,
Opprest was my rest with mortal affray,
My foes did vnclose, I know not which way
My chamber dores, and boldly they in brake,
[420] And had me fast before I could awake.

Thou lookest now, that of my secret murther,
I should at large the maner how declare,
I pray thee Baldwin, aske of me no further,
For speaking playne, it came so at vnware,

458

As I my selfe, which caught was in the snare,   [425]
Scarcely am able the circumstaunce to shew,
Which was kept close, and knowen but vnto few.

But be thou sure by violence it was,
And no whit bred by sickenesse or disease,
That felt it well before my life did passe,   [430]
For when these wolues, my bodie once did cease,
Vsed I was, but smally to myne ease:
With tormentes strong, which went so nere the quicke,
As made me dye before that I was sicke.

A Palsey (they sayd) my vital sprites opprest,   [435]
Bred by excesse of melancholie blacke,
This for excuse to lay, them seemed best,
Least my true frendes the cause might further racke,
And so perhaps discouer the whoole packe,
Of the conspyrers, whom they might wel suspect,   [440]
For causes great, which after tooke effect.

Dead was I found, by such as best did know,
The maner how the same was brought to passe.
And than my corps, was set out for a show,
By view whereof, nothing perceiued was: [445]
Whereby the world may see as in a glasse,
The vnsure state, of them that stand most hye,
Which than dread least, when daunger is most nye.

And also see, what daunger they lyue in,
Which next their king are to succede in place: [450]
Since kinges most parte, be Ielous of their kynne,
Whom I aduise, forewarned by my case,
To beare low sayle, and not to much embrace,
The peoples loue: for as *Senec* sayth trulye:
O quam funestus est fauor populi.   [455]

[449]   they are in, G.

[Prose 29] THe good Duke hauing ended his wofull tragedye, after much talke had concerning discention among those that be magistrates, good Lord (quoth one) what mischief and destruction doth priuye grudge and mallice, rayse among all sortes of people, both
[5] hye and low? but especiallye among Magistrates being the head and guyde of the Common wealth: for what mischiefe did the discention betweene these two persons (being both of high estate) bring afterward to both the realmes: yea and the vtter ruine of most part of them that were the chiefe workers of this Dukes death, you saye troth (quoth I)
[10] and now for that, if I may craue your pacience awhile, you shal heare what I haue noted in the Duke of Suffolkes doinges, one of the chiefe procurours of Duke Humfreyes destruction, who by the prouidence of God came shortly after in such hatred of the people, that the king himselfe could not saue him from a straunge and notable death. For beeing
[15] banisht the realme for the terme of fyue yeares, to appease the continual rumours and inward grudges, that not onely the commons, but most part of the nobilitie of England, bare towardes him for the death of the sayde Duke, he saylinge towardes Fraunce was met with a shippe of Deuonshire, and beheaded forthwith the fyrst day of Maye, Anno *1450*.
[20] And the dead corps throwen vp at Douer vpon the sandes, which may lament his death after this maner.

[7–8] after to both realmes: G.
[8]   most of them G.
[9]   were workers G.

[*For the collation of the closing lines which serve to introduce the tragedy of the Duke of Suffolk, see the collation of Prose 10, on p. 161.*]

TRAGEDIES ADDED IN
IN
THE EDITION OF
1587

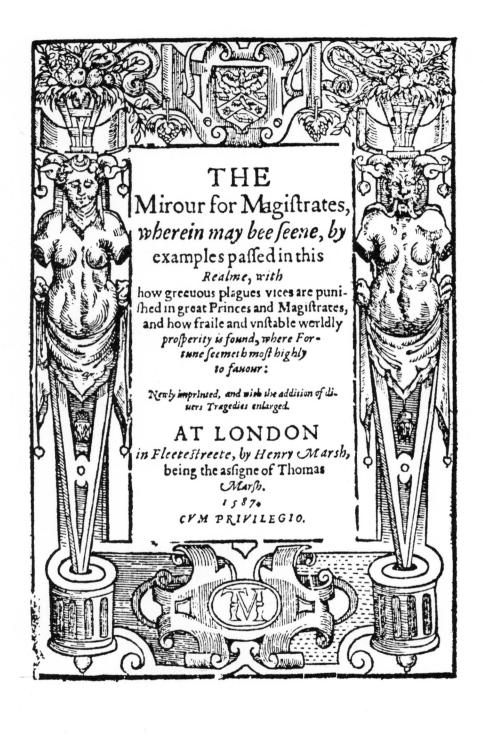

THE
Mirour for Magiſtrates,
wherein may bee ſeene, by
examples paſſed in this
Realme, with
how greeuous plagues vices are puniſhed in great Princes and Magiſtrates,
and how fraile and vnſtable werldly
proſperity is found, where For-
tune ſeemeth moſt highly
to fauour:

Newly imprinted, and with the addition of di-
uers Tragedies enlarged.

AT LONDON
in Fleeteſtreete, by Henry Marsh,
being the aſſigne of Thomas
Marſh.
1587.
CVM PRIVILEGIO.

This talke thus being ended: I was willed my maisters (quoth I) by [Continuation
Maister Holinshed, to bring Sir *Nicholas Burdet* vnto you. Were you? of Prose 27]
(quoth they.) On his word we will heare what he sayes. Read it I pray
you (quod one.) You must thinke then (quoth I) that you see him all
wounded as he was slaine at *Pontoise*, to say as foloweth.

[*In the* 1587 *edition this paragraph was substituted for the closing sentences of Prose* 27,
following the word strength *in line* 76. *See above, p.* 421.]

HOW THE VALIANT KNIGHT [Tragedy 30]
Sir Nicholas Burdet,
Chiefe Butler of Normandy, was slayne
at Pontoise, Anno 1441.

OF erst at Prince affayres wee counted were of truste,
To fight in waeged warres, as Captayne gainst the foes,
And might therefore aliue receiue the guerdon iuste,
Which ay his maiesty employde on those:
Why should wee so keepe silence now, and not disclose [5]
Our noble acts to those remayne aliue,
T'encourage them the like exployts t'achiue?

For if when as wee werde, for Prince and publique weale,
We might to ech for both haue time and place to speake,
Then why not now, yf wee to both appeale? [10]
Sith both well knowe our dealeings were not weake.
Wee clayme as ryghte, in trueth our myndes to breake,
The rather eke wee thinke to speake wee franchizde ar,
Because wee serude for peace and dyde in Prince his war.

463

[15]   Which graunted so, and held deserued due,
I may full well on stage supply the place a while,
Till I haue playnly layde before your vew
That I haue cause, as these, to playne of Fortunes guyle,
Which smirking though at first, she seeme to smoothe and smyle,
[20] (If Fortune bee) who deemde themselues in skyes to dwell,
She thirleth downe to dreade the gulfes of ghastly hell.

But here I let a while the Lady Fortune stay,
To tell what time I liu'd, & what our warres were then,
The great exployts wee did, and where our armies laye,
[25] Eke of the prayse of some right honourable men,
Which things with eyes I saw, calde now to minde agen.
What I performed present in the fight,
I will in order and my fall resite.

In youth I seru'd that royall *Henry* fifte the King,
[30] Whose prayse for martiall feats eternall fame retaynes,
When hee the *Normanes* stout did in subiection bring,
My selfe was vnder then his ensignes taking paynes.
With loyall hart I faught, pursude my Prince his gaines.
There dealt I so that time my fame to rayse,
[35] French wryters yet my name and manhoode prayse.

And erste as *Burdets* diuers warlike wights,
(In *Warwicke* shire theyr lands in *Arrow* ar)
Were for good seruice done made worthy Knights,
Whose noble acts be yet recounted far:
[40] Euen so my selfe well framde to peace or war,
Of these the heyre by due discent I came,
Sir Nicholas Burdet Knight, which had to name.

That time the noble *Iohn* of *Bedford* Duke bare sway,
And feared was in *Fraunce* for courage stout and fell,
[45] Hee lou'de mee for my fight and person, (though I say)
And with revenues mee rewarded yearely well.

I playde the faythfull subiects parte, the truth to tell,
And was accounted loyall, constant still,
Of stomake, worship great, and warlike scill.

But then (O greefe to tell) ere long this pearelesse King,   [50]
When hee restored had his right vnto the Crowne
The Duchye all of *Normandy*, eke subiect bring
The *Frenchemen* all, and set Lieutenants in eache towne
High Regent made of *Fraunce*, then Fortune gan to frowne,
Hee then departed life, too soone alas: [55]
Som men suppose his grace empoysonde was.

Thou Fortune slye, what meanste thou thus, these prancks to
    play?
False Fortune blereyde blinde, vnsteady startling still,
What meanste thou turning thus thy flattering face away,
Inconstant where thou bearest most good will?   [60]
Is it thy nature then? or iste thy wonted scill?
It cost thee naught, they say it commes by kinde,
As thou art bisme, so are thine actions blinde.

I nothing doubte then thou thy selfe shalt fall.
I trust to see the time when thou shalt bee forgot.   [65]
For why thy pride, and pompe and powre must vanish all,
Thy name shall dye for aye, and perish quite I wot.
And when thou shalt bee counted but a sot,
The noble wights which liude and dyde in worthy fame,
In heauen and earth shall finde an euerlasting name.   [70]

But words of course are these of Fortune had,
When vnto Princes haps chaunce good or ill.
God sends to euery sorte these tempests sad,
When from his worde they swarue and heauenly will.
Men must endeuour then to please his goodnesse still,   [75]
And then come life or death, come ioy, come smarte:
No Fortunes frowne can daunte the doughty harte.

The famous King so dead, his son but nyne months olde
Henry the sixt, of *England* was proclaymed King:
[80] And then the *Frenchmen* wexte more stoute and bolde,
His youth occasion gaue them to conspire the thing,
Which might them all from due subiection bring.
On which the Councell calde a Parliament:
Of *French* that might the treasons high preuent.

[85] Wherein the Duke of *Bedford* my good Lorde and frend
Was Regent made the Prince his deputy in *Fraunce*:
The Duke of *Glocester* Protectour was, to th'end
To rule in cases such at home might hap to chaunce:
They chose to garde the Prince, in honour to aduaunce
[90] *Henry Beuforde* Byshop of *Winchester*,
And *Thomas* the noble Duke of *Excester*.

But here before those things coulde well be setled sure,
(As great affayres of Kingdomes longer time do take)
The *Frenchmen* did by treason, force, and coyne procure
[95] Some townes which *English* were in *Fraunce* theyr fayth forsake.
A long discourse it were of all recitall make:
But of my chaunce that time, resite will I,
Which seru'd in warres my Prince in *Normandy*.

Before the Mount *S. Michaell* as in seige I lay,
[100] In confines of the *Normanes* and the *Bretons* land,
From townsemen famisht nigh we vitailes kept away,
And made them oft in daunger of dis-*Mounteing* stand:
But it being strong and also stoutly mand,
Euen by our losses they gate harte of grasse,
[105] And wee declineing saw what Fortune was.

Yet nathelesse wee thought by famine make them yeelde,
Eke they by fight or succours hoapt the seige to rayse,
T'accomplish which they rusht on sodayne out to feelde,
As bent to dy or win the wanted foode with prayse:

And wee as ready were for them at all assayes. [110]
These eager impes whome foodewant feazde to fight amayne,
Wee forc'd them dye, fall, fly, to take theyr forte agayne.

Where I in chase pursude them euen to the towne,
Tane prisner was, a while for ransom lay:
But then the worthy duke the Regent of renowne, [115]
Did for mee quite disburse the price requirde to pay.
The seige wee raysde, from thence wee went our way,
And I redeemed bare this blanke in minde,
Till of requite I might occasion finde.

Which thus ere long befell, to this a while giue eare: [120]
When Arthur Earle of *Richmond* to *S. Iaques* came
De Beuuron where my selfe and other captaynes were,
Which had repared well and fortefide the same,
Wee made him flye, to his immortall shame:
Euen thus to him and forty thousand moe, [125]
Fiue hundreth *English* gaue the ouerthroe.

Long while hee battery layde agaynst the wall,
Thereby to make a breatche for them to enter in.
But well perceiuing still his shot to profite small,
And that wee weyde not of his powre a pinne, [130]
On euery side afreshe hee did th'assault begin:
Yet wee so bare them off and beate them downe,
They durst not seaze or enter on the towne.

But wearied with the seige and sault they pausde a while,
Consulting what were best, and so did wee likewise: [135]
They founde the feate, they thought should surely vs beguile,
And in an euening came t'accomplish th'enterprise.
A sharp assaulte they gaue. Alarme my mates wee rise:
On both the sides they scalde, the forte to gayne.
But from the scales and walles wee flang them downe amayne. [140]

It was my charge that time to keepe a bulwarke bace,
Where *Bretons* came along to enter by a streit:
Twas in a botome lowe, a pond was by the place,
By which they needes must passe vp to a posterne gate.
[145] I meant to make them fishe the poole without a bayt,
Protesting ere they there should get the wall
Wee would as *English* dye, or gieue our foes the fall.

The trompets sound tan tara, tan tan tara right,
The guns were shot founce-founce-founce, fomp-fum, fow-
    powthow,
[150] The dromze went downe-dun downe, the fluits fyt-fyte-fyt,
    fyte,
The weapons clish-clash and the captaynes nowe-now nowe.
With billes wee beat them downe, with shafts wee shot them
    throw.
The gory ground did groane, the smoky shot and cryes
Dimd all the ayre, and thundred through the scyes.

[155]   S. *Denise* cryde the *French*, and *Bretons* glahe-lahee,
S. *George* the *English* cryde, fight-fight-fight, kill-kill-kill:
Fight-fight (quoth I) come on, they flee, they flee, they flee.
And there withall wee vsde a poynt of warlike scill,
Wee causde the men within to crye vnto vs still
[160] Fight *Suffolke* now, fight-fight and *Salsbury*:
Fight fight you noble Earles, the *Bretons* flee they flee.

With that amazed all the *Bretons* gan recoyle,
Some drowned in the pond, wherin they ran for feare,
And I pursude the flight, to wrecke my captiue foyle,
[165] Wee payde them in the chase disordred as they were,
Seuen hundred slew, tooke fifty prisners there,
Gaynde eyghteene standerds, and one banner more:
Yet I and mine not fully were fowrescore.

Of this exployt when th'Earle of *Richmond* herde,
Which gaue an hoate assault on th'other side the towne, [170]
No lesse was hee displeasde, amazed, than afferde,
To heare the names of those two Earles of high renowne,
His guilty courage quaylde, his heart was daunted downe,
Hee causde the trompets sounde retrayte away:
To scale our walles hee durst no longer stay. [175]

At midnight hee dislodgde, from seige hee made departe
The Constable of *Fraunce* (late Earle of *Richemond*) fled,
And coward *Fougiers* sped, with such as tooke his parte,
For haste perhaps with feare lest hee should lose his heade.
They left two hundred pypes of flowre and bisket bread, [180]
Greate gunnes foureteene, three hundred pypes of wine,
Two hundred frailes of figs and raysons fine.

Fiue hundred barels they of hering left beside,
Of pouder for our gunnes full forty barels more,
They fled without theyr tents, the dasterds durst not byde, [185]
For feare they could not stay, to take away theyr store.
Haue you oft hearde the like, of cowards such before?
Those forty thousand, *Bretons*, *Frenche*, and *Scots*,
Fowre score them foyled, made them flee like sots.

When this, that noble man, the Duke of *Bedford* hearde, [190]
How I did quite my selfe, and seru'd my Prince so well,
Hee mee procured of the King as great rewarde
As my deserts coulde wish, and more the truth to tell,
Chiefe butlership of *Normandy* vnto me fell,
Reuenues eke in *Normandy* of lands, [195]
A thousand crownes came yearely to my hands.

I after this was sent to make inroade
Upon the coaste of *Bretaine*, for to bate theyr pride,
A band of horsemen tooke without aboade,
The duke of *Somerset* made me theyr guide, [200]

To many townes about theyr bounds wee ride:
Set them on fire, or made them ransom pay,
Tooke store of prisners, wrought them much decay.

Retourned victours safe to *Normandy*,
[205] With good successe, for why the cause was good:
And of our Prince were guerdonde gratefully
With laude and gifts, as for our seruice stoode.
This makes the Captaynes venture life and bloode,
And souldiers serue with heart in what they may,
[210] Which are assurde of honour, prayse, and pay.

Yee worthy wights aliue, which loue your Countreys weale,
And for your Princes porte such warres doe vndertake,
Learne so for Countrey yours with forayne foes to deale,
See that of manhood good, so great accompts yee make.
[215] It nothing vayles in peace, to sweare, stur, face or crake:
In werres hee winnes the fame of noble wight
Who warlike deales, for Prince and publique right.

Yf you so poynted bee, to serue your Prince in war,
As erste was I, and muste before the muster take,
[220] Retayne such souldiers as well made, strong, seemely ar,
Brought vp to labour harde, of such accompt doe make:
These able are at neede to stand and keepe the stake,
When facing foysters fit for *Tiburne* frayes
Are foodesicke faynt, or hartsicke run theyr wayes.

[225] At home a man may finde a nomber euery day,
Which weare theyr weapons still, as all the worlde were war,
And keepe a coyle to beare the best of blades away,
With buclers braue at backs, to shew what men they are.
In peace at home they sweare, stare, foyste, royst, fight, and iar:
[230] But when abroade they feare of warres the smarte,
Some better souldiers yede from driueing cart.

In warres to serue (as wee) and weapons haue
When warlike stormes do rage, beseemes a warlike man:
In pleasaunt peace who sets him selfe to bandeing braue,
And faceing fares at home, abroade doe nothing can,   [235]
(Though nere so much hee boaste) fie on him cowerd than:
For not in gauntlet, sworde, targ, oathes, hayre, staring eyes:
But in the breast, good courage, vertue lyes.

But here perhaps (you say) I fall a noate too lowe,
Beneath the persons of these worthy Peeres and mee.   [240]
Tis true indeede, and yet such fruite hereof may growe:
As eke the Meane hereby, his iarring out may see.
Without good meane, the song can neuer sweetly gree.
Leaue out the meane, or let him keepe no tune:
And you shall sing when Easter falles in Iune.   [245]

Euen so, if meaner sorts doe iangle here and iar
To languish vnder *Mars*, but fill good peace with fight,
As discorde foule in musike, fit they for the war:
They neuer can atchiue the victory aright.
Leade such as square or feare, then farewell all, good night.   [250]
A sheepe is euen as good to starteing stand and beae:
As hee that iangles, wrangles, rangles, runnes aweae.

Then who so deales for warre, must wisely make his marte,
And choose such souldiers stout will stiffe in warfare stande.
Yf hee not recke what ruffian roysters take his parte,   [255]
Hee weeldes vnwisely then the mace of *Mars* in hande.
He must be able eke, to deeme for sea and lande
What men may serue, to best aduauntage make,
And them enstruct fine warlike poynts to take.

With scilfull knowledge fraight hee muste be voyde of feare, [260]
Of wisedom so discrete, so sober, graue and sage,
To deeme, perceiue, abyde, aduentures both to beare
As may in all exployts of fight with Fortune wage:

471

Hee must haue art in vre, and vse not rule by rage:
[265] Wise dealing sets the souldiers sure in ray,
Wilde ouer rashnesse casteth all away.

The cause, grounde, place and time, the order of theyr fights,
The valure of his foes, and what is theyr intent,
The weather fayre or foule, occasion of the nights,
[270] What witty wyles and pollicies may them preuent,
And how the time or store of th'enmies hath beene spent.
All these (I say) must well be weyde before,
By him that sets in warres of credit store.

In all which poynts that noble Duke his grace did passe,
[275] I meane the Regent good, for chuseing, vseing men,
By nature framde thereto, hee wonders scilfull was,
And frendly vsed all, instructing now and then
Not only Captaynes stout, that were his countrey men,
But also sondry souldiers as occasion came,
[280] And taught them how to warres themselues to frame.

His princely grace and gesture yet mee thinks I see,
And how hee bare himselfe, to deale for warre or peace:
In warre full *Mars*-like, hardy, sterne, and bolde was hee:
And meeke and prudent mercifull, when stormes of warres did
cease:
[285] Whom pity mou'd as much inflicted paynes to releace,
As euer wight in whom the broyles of war
Or force of fights, had entred in so far.

Which if agayne to rue the losse of such a frend,
In sight with playnts, of teares the fountaynes out might flow:
[290] So all lamenting *Muses* would mee waylings lend,
The dolours of my heart in sight agayne to show:
I would deplore his death, and *Englands* cause of woe,
With such sad mourning tunes, and such sobs, sighes, and teares
As were not seene for one, this ten times twenty yeares.

For why this noble Prince, when wee had needed moste,   [295]
To set the states of *Fraunce* and *England* in a stay,
That feared was of foes in euery forayne coaste,
To soone (alas) this Duke was taken hence away.
In *Fraunce* hee dyde helasse lament his losse wee may,
That Regent regall, rule of publique right.   [300]
Loe howe my hurtes afreshe beweepe this wanted wight.

"With that his woundes (mee thought) gan freshly bleede,
"And hee waxte faynt and fell, and my salte teares
"Ran downe my rufull cheekes, with trickling speede,
"(For who coulde chuse that such cause sees and heares.)   [305]
"O worthy Knight (quod I) whose loyall faith appeares:
"Cease wayles, rise vp, instruct my quiuering pen,
"To tell the rest of Fortunes dublings then.

I haue (quoth he) not Fortunes flatterie to accuse,
Nor Fate nor Destenie, nor any fancie fainde: [310]
I haue no cause t'affirme that these coulde ought misuse
This noble Prince, whose life & acts such fame and honour
        gaynde,
But our deserts, our sinnes, and our offences staynde
This noble Ile and vs, our sinnes (I say)
Offending God, hee tooke this Prince away.   [315]

Helasse how loath can I retourne, and leaue this pearle in *Roane*
My Lorde *Ihon* Duke of *Bedford*, there his corps yet lyes
Enclosde with costly tombe, wrought curiously of stone,
By North the altar high (delighting many Martiall eyes)
Within our Ladie churche, where fame him lifts to skies,   [320]
By dayly vew his name renoumbde exalted is,
And soule, I trust, full sweetly sweames in blisse.

Needes must I enterline my talke a while with this:
And then I will retourne to tell you how I sped.

[325] When once the *French* men sawe this noble Duke to misse,
Which *English* armyes all gaynste foes with fortunes led
They liude at large, rebeld against their soueraygne head,
Forsooke their oathes, alleageaunce all denyde,
And *English* men with all their force defyde.

[330]   While hee did liue, they durst not so to deale,
They durst not dare, with th'*English* oft to fraye,
They found it was not for theire owne or publique weale,
To rise againste theire Lorde the Regent in araye.
Soone after hee was deade, departed hence away,
[335] Both *French* and *Normanes* close to win did cloaze,
And wee deuided were, our rightes abroade to loaze.

The feende (I thinke) deuisde a way to make the breatche,
By enuye bred in breastes of two right noble Peeres,
Which mischiefe hatcht in *England*, then may teache
[340] All noble men that liue, hence many hundreth yeares,
Beware of Enuye blacke, how far shee deares.
Euen their examples tell, how true our Christe doth say:
Each realme, towne, house, in ciuile strife, shall desolate decay.

Perdie the Duke of *Yorke* was Regent made of *Fraunce*,
[345] At which the Duke of *Somerset* did much repine,
Hee thought they rather ought him so t'aduaunce
King *Henries* kin, for honour of his Princely lyne:
But marke the grape which grew on this vngracious vine,
I will not say it after stroyde their lynes and houses nye,
[350] But this I say, wee dayely sawe dishonour came thereby.

For though the hauty Duke were worthy it to haue,
As well for courage good, as vertues honour due:
Yet sith to'th Duke of *Yorke* th'election first it gaue,
And hee the sadle mist, what neded hee to rue?
[355] When tumultes great and sturres in *Fraunce* yet daylye grew,

Hee nilde the Regent hence dispatche in many dayes:
That losse might win him hurte, or long disprayse.

Wylde wengand on such ire, wherby the realme doth lose,
What gayne haue they, which heaue at honour soe?
At home disdayne and greefe, abroade they frend their foes.   [360]
I must bee playne in that which wrought my webs of woe,
My webs (quod I?) would God they had wrought no moe.
It was the cause of many a bleeding *English* breaste,
And to the *French*, their end of woefull warres addresse.

I dare aduouche yf they had firme in frendship boade,   [365]
And southly as beseemde ioynde frendly hand with hands,
They had not felt defame in any foraine roade,
Nor had not so beene sent, with losse from *Gallia* strands:
They might possession kept, still of their conquerde lands,
And able beene to tryde them selues so true,   [370]
As myght haue made their enmyes still to rue.

For while the Duke of *Somerset* made here so greate delayes,
That into *Fraunce* the succours smale and slackly came,
Not only *Paris* than was loste, within few dayes,
That famous flowre of *Fraunce*, of far renowmed fame,   [375]
The *Frenche* (I say) not only gate and kept the same,
But by this meanes, in *Fraunce* we dayly felt such smarte,
As might with pitie perst an adamantine harte.

O greate mishap, the noble Duke of *Bedford* once being dead,
Our welch went backe, by discords foule dispite wee loste   [380]
Not only townes in *Fraunce*, and captaines armyes led,
But many soldiers eke with labour, spence and cost:
And though full oft wee made the *Frenche* men smell of the rost,
Yet in the end wee gayne of fyght the fame,
And they by crafte and treason gate the game.   [385]

What resteth more, it were, perdie, to long to tell,
Of batayles great and broiles which happened dayly still,
The stories eke declare aduentures which befell:
Although (God wot) the writers wanted poyntes of scill,
[390] Of whom to speake a while, degresse agayne I will,
And partely shewe what one hee oughte to bee,
Which takes on him to write an Historie.

A chronicler should well in diuers tongues bee seene,
And eke in all the artes hee oughte to haue a sighte,
[395] Whereby hee myght the truth of diuers actions deeme,
And both supply the wantes, correct that is not righte:
Hee should haue eloquence, and full and fitly write,
Not mangle stories, snatching here and there:
Nor gloaze to make a volume greate appeare.

[400] Hee should bee of such countenaunce and wit,
As should giue witnes to the Histories hee writes,
Hee should bee able well his reasons so to knit,
As should continue well the matter hee resytes:
Hee should not prayse, disprayse, for fauour or dispytes,
[405] But should so place each thing in order due,
As myght approue the stories to bee true.

But this may haps the time may seeke at length redresse,
And then such stories nowe and noble acts as dye,
May come agayne to lighte (at least defaced lesse)
[410] Yf from the *Britaynes* first antiquities they try.
In greate defects yf they the trueth supply:
Then shall the readers fuller stories finde,
And haue wherby to recreate the minde.

But now retourne I must, and breifly heare declare
[415] Before my death, what sundry happes wee had.
In warres right variousely the states of Captaynes fare,
Now weale, now woe, now ioyfull, now right sad.

But who well ends, though all his haps were bad,
Let him earst sinke or swim, lose, wyn, bee slayne, die, fall,
Yf hee dye well, h'is thrise and fower tymes blest of all.　　　[420]

In *Fraunce* eyght leagues from *Paris*, *Pontoise* stands,
(Tweene that and *Roane*) which wee had wonne before:
And so wee held it *English* safely in our handes.
For to our Prince the men allegeaunce swore,
And they remaynd obedient euermore,　　　[425]
Tyll from their necks to reaue the *English* yoke,
They might finde meanes by whom to stricke the stroke.

When these sawe *Paris* loste, and cities moe beside,
And what in *Fraunce* and *Normandie* reuoltes had done,
They thought no longer subiect to abyde,　　　[430]
But sought occasion how they mighte by *Frenche* be won.
As of our losse reports did dayly to them run,
So with King *Charles* th'agreede when to betray the towne,
And force the *English* flee, or yeelde, or beate them downe.

For why, the powre of *Fraunce* coulde not with mighty hoste [435]
Performe to wyn by force from vs th'assaulted towne,
Them scaleing often from the walles wee toste,
On euery syde full fast wee flang the *French* men downe.
Our noble actes before had gotten such renowne,
And Fortune erste had past with vs so farre,　　　[440]
They had small hope to wyn our fortes by warre.

Wherefore King *Charles* assayde the secrete saute,
Not by his force of *French*, but by his golden fee,
Corrupting diuers Burgeses to make the faute,
Whereby an entry shoulde to his oppugning bee:　　　[445]
And they (as erste is sayde) were willing to agree,
Like periurde theeues conspirde by secrete fyne deuice,
Gaue *Pontoise* vp, and tooke the promiste price.

But in November next when it was sharpe and colde,
[450] And dayly froste had dryde and parched hard the grounde,
Wee were in hope agayne to get of *Pontoise* holde,
Which erste the Townesmen solde, for gayne of many a pound.
The snow fell fast, lay thick, and couered well the ground,
And ditches were so harde about the towne befrore,
[455] That on the Ise by euery syde wee safely might get ore.

The Lorde *Ihon Clifforde* was cheife captayne then,
Which with vs captaynes did this pollicie deuise,
That wee in clothing white and soldiers euery man,
Should in our armoure finelye vs disguyse.
[460] The nexte nyght so wee should to the assaute aryse,
And passe the frozen ditche vnto the wall,
With laders scale, and kill the watchmen all.

Wee so preparde our selues as time occasion gaue,
And drest in white coates trim, it ioyde our hartes to see
[465] How fine wee paste the ditch, what good successe we haue:
How on the walles we fynde the watch nigh frozen bee:
As noble *Greekes* on *Troie*, on *Pontoise* seasonde wee,
Wee slewe the watch, wee beate the soldiers downe,
Some prisners tooke, and tooke withall the Towne.

[470] Of stately captaynes *french*, was *Iohn de Villers* one
Within the taken towne, and *Narrabon* a Knight
Burgunion: yet they fled, away they gate them gone:
They durst not bide againste the blanched boyes to fight.
Wee paide the periurde knaues the Burgesses that night,
[475] And gate as much of honour and renowne
As they gate shame and losse, which bought and solde the towne.

Marke well the *frenchmens* foyles in all our worthy war
In these two regall *Henryes* times, and you shall see
How wee surpast the *french* in valure farre:

[471]   and *is misprinted* ans *in the text.*

478

And bend for Prince and realme so valiaunt for to bee: [480]
Which if yee shall, and deale in seruice as did wee,
I nothing doubt renowne and fame shall say,
That noble *England* beares for warres the palme away.

But when King *Charles* had heard how *Pontoise* men had sped,
His army strayght assembled hee therefore agayne,   [485]
Wherewith to win this towne afresh th'assaute hee led,
Hee pyners set to trenche and vnder mine amayne,
Made bastiles for defence, yet all this toyle was vayne.
For battery of our walles hee spent his pouder still,
Made freshly *frenche* assaults, but did no ill.   [490]

The noble Duke of *Yorke* discharged late before,
When now the Earle of *Warwicke* chaunst at *Roane* to dye,
Being Regent chosen once agayne of *Fraunce*, as yore,
(Th'Earle of *Warwicke* Regent was two yeares perdy)
Arryude in *Fraunce*, to rowse the *frenche* King he did hye,   [495]
(Which lay beseigeing *Pontoise*, as I sayde)
With him to fight, and eke to bring vs ayde.

The *frenche* King fled, for haste he left his store behinde:
When hee was once assurde the Duke of *Yorke* drue nere,
Hee durst not stay to bide the time or place assinde   [500]
To fight our Regent with, but fled away for feare.
By these assayes you see what men in *Fraunce* they were,
Discouradgde oft, slayne, put to flight and fall:
By sight, force, fight, and names of nombers small.

There when the Duke had fortefyde our *Pontoise* towne,   [505]
Then he pursude the *frenche* King erst that fled,
To *Poyssy*, where hee laye with Lords of *frenche* renowne.
Before which Towne, the Duke his noble army led:
The *frenche* King durste not out of *Poyssy* put his head:
And yet there came to skirmish out *frenche* gentilmen,   [510]
Of which some slayne, fowre tane, the reste retyrde agen.

The Duke to bid him batayle did pretend,
Yf hee coulde there encounter with him thoe:
But forth agayne hee durste not come nor send,
[515] For feare hee should receiue the foyle and ouerthroe.
On which the Duke dislodgde, departeing *Poyssy* froe,
To *Maunte*, and *Roane*, from thence his grace did hye,
T'appease the broyles of strife in *Normandy*.

But then the *frenche* King calling vnto mynde his losse,
[520] His charges in the seige, his bastiles trenches made,
How erste wee did them thence, sans bag and bagage tosse,
Eke how from seige hee durste not staye the store to lade,
And how their Fortunes ofte, in fighte went retrograde,
How neighboures ill to *Paris*, wee of *Pontoise* were:
[525] Hee cast asyde his *frenche* and faynteing feare.

The rather yet, for why, *Parisiens* ay did rayle,
They sayde hee wanted courage good, hee durst not fight,
Hee lackte no soldiers good, his feeble heart did fayle:
Le Roy (quoth they) *du France, les Anglois point ne nuit:*
[530] *Le Roy ne ose pas pour Pontoise faire poursuit:*
Le Roy est Lourd, sans cueur: car peu de gens,
Fait nostre Roy & pais faire grande dispens.

On this King *Charles* retournde with mighty hoste,
To vindicate this great reproche and shame:
[535] And vnto *Pontoise* gaue assaulte in poste
Full hotly, when wee feared leaste the same.
Whereon, to fight agaynst him all our force wee frame,
But number great at th'entry gote such hand,
Wee coulde not forth agayne their force aband.

[540] With trompets sounding, tan tan-tar'aloude
The larum bell wee rong, our selues to try dispose,
To make them pay the price of our distresse wee vowde,
Before wee would possession got, of *Pontoise* loze:

In euery street wee met the strength of all our foes,
And made them passe by deadly dint away, [545]
Which ventured first our *English* mates to slay.

Why now my frends, for *England* fighte, I cryde:
Yf euer *English* hearts your noble breasts posseste,
I promise you to make them flinche, yf I may byde:
Mates follow me. Amongst my foes I rusht before the rest: [550]
O here come on (quoth I) now fighte wee for the beste.
And therewithall I vsde such courage, force and myghte:
As made my foes to fall, and soldiers fitly fighte.

Yf we doe leese (quoth I) the *frenche* men shall not gayne:
So if wee wyn, tis worth the while to keepe arraye. [555]
Yf yee stand stiflye toet, wele make them peaze the paine,
And leade with losse of lyuely lymmes the lande awaye.
Although they fearcely fighte, in hope vs all to slaye:
Lo sixe to one they fall, and deade they lye:
Wee *English* men, in triomphe fight, and honour dye. [560]

With bloody broiles of war the haplesse towne did smoke,
The children sawe theire fathers deare, to bleede their last:
The wyues bewayled muche the fatall stroke,
Which forste their husbands bleede, fall, dye so fast:
Helas the weemen cryde, the woefull streets that past: [565]
(When soe they sawe the channels bloody streame)
What plague is this, that pesters so our Reame?

Is no remorce of lyfe, but kill, kill, kill? (helasse)
Kill, kill the *English* cry, and valiantly they fighte:
What hap had wee to see these mischiues com to passe? [570]
Helas le sang de nous amis, la mort helas:
The maydens cry, the widowes wayle, and aged mourne,
With wringing hands vplift, & wish them selues vnborne.

Of vs one thousand *Englishmen* within the Towne,
Sustaynde the force, the powre and puissaunce of their King: [575]

And of the *French* that faught, wee beate three thousand downe,
Wee slew no lesse, for all the nomber hee did bring.
Yf this vntrue shall seeme, discredite myne to ring,
A *french* Historian writeing for them selues shall say:
[580] Three thousand *Frenchmen* there, were slayne that day.

    Four hundreth *Englishmen* that tyme were slayne in fighte,
My selfe was one, with losse they wan the towne perdie:
But if I might haue liude t'aue tride our righte,
With one for euery seuen, by ods as wee did dye:
[585] I doubte not (so the rest, would done their partes as I.)
But that King *Charles*, his Lords, nor all his men,
Should scarce haue tane the towne of *Pontoise* then.

    What neade I more debate of these thinges here:
In *England* was the faulte, though we did feele the smarte.
[590] While they at home, at bate and strife for honours were,
They lost abroade of *Normandy* the greater parte.
To thinke on this torments agayne my wounded harte,
That Lords at home, should striue about the name,
And loose abroade their Countries weale and fame.

[595]   Let *English* Peeres abandon such contentious strife,
It hurtes the Publique weale, decayes the state:
It reaues the yeares too soone of longer lyfe:
It freates the breste with ruste of baend debate:
It giues the checke to him that giues the mate:
[600] Then thus I ende, that wight of all is bleste
Which liues in loue with God, his prince and country best.

    So *Higins* yf thou write, how this my fall befell;
Place it in *Baldwines Miroir* with the reste.
From crazed scull sith here my mynde I tell:
[605] Sith bleedeing hart these ruefull rymes expreste:
This mangled tale beseemes my person beste.
Do so (quoth hee) and let it passe euen thus:
Viuit (quoth I) *post funera virtus.*

482

THis Knight my maisters (quoth one) came somwhat to late in [Prose 30]
order. That is maruaile (quoth maister *Ferrers*) it seemes that
hee was forwarde enoughe in seruice. Yea (quoth another) hee
came the later home for that, and therefore wee must accept his cause.
How ere hee came (quoth M.H) hee sayes well, and like a noble gentle- [5]
man, as no doubt hee was. Hee should haue beene placed (quoth one)
after King *Iames* the first, King of *Scots*, of whome wee spake in the
yeare .1437. Now (quoth I) that you talke of King *Iames*, I haue King
Iames the fourth here, which was slayne at the batayle of *Brampton*, or
Floddon fielde, but hee is very rude. I like him (quoth one) the better: [10]
for if hee should bee otherwise, it would not well beseeme his person,
nor the place whence he comes. Reade it (quoth they) as it is. Thinke
then (quoth I) that you see him standing all wounded, with a shafte in
his body, and emongst other woundes, one geuen by a byll, both
deadly, to say in his rude and faithlesse maner as followeth. [15]

THE LAMENTATION OF KING IAMES [Tragedy 31]
the fourth, King of Scots,
slayne at Brampton, in the fiuthe yeare of
King Henry the eight, Anno Christi, 1513.

As I lay musing, my selfe alone,
In minde not stable, but wauering here & there,
Morpheus my frend espyed mee anone,
And as hee was wont, whistered in mine eare.
Shortly conuyede I was, I wist not where: [5]
Mine eyes were closed fast, I could not see.
I hearde a man crying sore, trembling for feare:
Miserere mei Deus et salua mee.

[Title]   *The closing period is misprinted as a comma.*

Miserere mei Deus, oft hee did reporte,
[10] With sorowfull sighes, as euer man herde.
For sorowe and pity, I gan nere to resorte:
His sore exclamations made mee afferde.
Mine eyes opened, I sawe his grim bearde:
I knewe not verely, who it should bee:
[15] Hee cryde, as hee had beene stickt with a swerde:
Miserere mei Deus & salua mee.

Of *Scotland* (hee sayde) late I was King,
With Crowne on my head, and scepter in hand:
In wealth and honour, I wanted nothing:
[20] In peaceable maner I ruled my land.
Full frendly and faythfull my subiects I fand.
Now am I exiled from life, land, and liberty:
King without realme, loe now where I stand:
Miserere mei Deus & salua mee.

[25] Thus for my folly, I feele I doe smart,
Both law, and nature doth me accuse
Of great vnkindnes: that I should take part
Against my brother, and his liege refuse.
I purposed war, yet I fayned truce.
[30] This did I, *frenche* King, for the loue of thee,
Inordinate affection so did mee abuse:
Miserere mei Deus & salua mee.

All this, King *Lewis*, I suffred for thy sake,
Wo be to the time that euer I thee knewe:
[35] For thee am I put in a sorowfull brake,
Thy wilfull appetite, doth mee sore rewe.
This worlde is not stable, it chaungeth a newe.
Now am I bond, some time I was free:
Exiled from liberty, I am kept in a mewe:
[40] *Miserere mei Deus & salua* mee.

Moreouer for thee, and thy realme of *Fraunce*,
(Contrary to mine othe solemnly made)
Vnto King *Henry* I made defiaunce,
To follow thine appetite was all the grace I hade.
In most cruell wise, I did his realme inuade: [45]
I troubled his subiects, by land and by sea:
My rewarde is no more, but the showle and spade:
Miserere mei Deus & salua mee.

For my wilfull periury, thus am I brought
From high degree, to the lowest of all.   [50]
Whom should I blame? I found that I sought,
By mine owne foly, I had a great fall.
Wherefore I feare mee, that now I shall
Haue payne long lasting, for mine iniquity:
Lord full of mercy yet to thee I call,   [55]
Miserere mei Deus & salua mee.

Vanquished in fielde I was to the rebuke
Of mee and all my realme: to our immortall shame.
There faught agaynst mee neyther King, nor Duke,
Prince, ne Marquise, ne many Lords of name.   [60]
One valiaunt Earle, our power ouercame:
Yet were wee in nomber, to his one, three:
Lord whom thou fauourest, winneth the game:
Miserere mei Deus & salua mee.

I was th'only author, of myne owne woe;   [65]
But yet I began it by wicked counsell,
Of my Lords spirituall and temporall also:
Which for their merits in fielde with mee fell.
I was curst (in deede) the truth for to tell,
And could not (by falshoode) eyther thriue or thie;   [70]
To assist my brothers foe I did not well,
Miserere mei Deus et salua mee.

Christes commaundements, I did all refuse:
The breatch of myne oathe, I did not regarde:

[75] Therfore I am domed as faythlesse as the Iewes.
Sore is the sentence, and cruell is the swerde:
Excepte thy mercy helpe, O Lord, I am marde:
Saue mee; for whom thou suffredst on a tree,
To thy mercye I appeale for my sauegarde:

[80] *Miserere mei Deus & salua* mee.

Herafter (by mee) my successours may beware,
An ensample take by my wretched ruyne:
Lest in lykewyse they bee taken with the snare,
As I am nowe: and pay the lyke fyne.

[85] Vanquished wee were, by power devyne:
For by mannes power it seemed not to bee.
Here now I ly, in an homely shrine,
Miserere mei Deus & salua mee.

I am a spectacle also in lyke case,

[90] To the *frenche* King, yf hee list to take heede,
I feare that hee cannot for lacke of grace,
The King and hee, bee not yet agreede.
Therefore let him looke, for a lyke speede,
As wee had that were of his leage and vnity,

[95] I trow hee doth neither God loue, nor dreede,
Miserere mei Deus & salua mee.

Who euer knew Christian King in such a case,
As I wretched creature that cannot haue
In Churche or in Churchyard any maner place,

[100] Emong Christen people to lye in a graue:
The earth mee abhorreth, all men mee depraue,
My frends forsake mee, and haue no pity,
The worlde taketh from mee all that hee mee gaue:
Miserere mei Deus & salua mee.

There is no more now, I must take my leaue,   [105]
In this wretched worlde I may no longer dwell:
But one thing there is doth mee sore greaue,
I not where to rest, in heauen or in hell,
None else thereof but only God can tell:
Adieu, this worlde is full of vanity,   [110]
I may no longer be with thee, farewell:
Miserere mei Deus & salua mee.

Farewell my Queene, sweete lady *Margaret*:
Farewell my Prince, with whom I vsde to play:
I wot not where wee shall together meete: [115]
Farewell my Lords, and Commons eke for aye:
Adieu, ye shall no ransom for mee pay:
Yet I beseeche you of your charity,
To the high lorde mercifull that yee pray:
Miserere mei Deus & salua mee.   [120]

[Prose 31] KIng *Iames* (quoth one) wil bee misliked for his *Miserere*. No (quod another) hee cryes *Peccaui*. It is to late (quoth he) there is no man that will like or beleeue him. Than (quod M.H.) he is still one and the same man: for in life he was neither well liked, beleeued,

[5] nor trusted. Why than (quoth one) if hee speake as hee was, let him passe as hee is; and if not, let him bee mended. Mended (quoth hee?) Nay hee is paste mending, hee is to olde: for it seemes by the copy, that it was pende aboue fifty yeares agone, or euen shortly after the death of the sayd King: for I found therewith, in an olde hand, the copyes of the

[10] sayd King *Iames* letters sent vnto King *Henry* at *Turwin*, and the Kings aunsweres & letters sent to him againe, with this lamentation ensuing them: and lastly the sayd batayle of *Floddon fielde*, in such verse described, with the order of the same, and the names of the noble men, Knights, and gentlemen, which serued at the same fielde. That would I

[15] faine heare (quoth one) it were pity that such particulers should bee lost. They would (quoth another) pleasure not only such as write our historyes, but also encourage our Countreymen well, to the like loyall seruice of their Prince, and especially those who should finde therein of their parents or auncestours to haue bene praysed for valure. I pray you

[20] (quoth hee) let vs haue them. There they are (quoth I) but I haue altered the verse, which we call *Intercalaris*, because the rest else would not haue beene well liked: but of the history I haue not chaunged one word.

The bataile of Brampton, or Floddon fielde,
faught in the yeare of our Redeemer 1513.
and in the fiuth yeare of the raygne of that
victorious prince, King Henry the eyght.

Rex regum in thy realme celestiall,
Glorified with ioyes of *Gabriells* company,
King *Iames* is dead, haue mercy on vs all:
For thou haste him prostrate so sodaynly,
Which was our noble Prince his enemy) [5]
That vs to withstand hee had no might:
So thy helpe O Lord preserude King *Henryes* right.

Into *England* this Prince prowdly did come,
With fourscore thousand in goodly aray:
And the Castle of *Norham* first hee had won, [10]
Prospering victoriously from day to day.
But agaynst him is gone the Earle of *Surrey*,
With him manfully for to fight,
By the helpe of God and in his Princes right.

This noble Earle full wisely hath wrought, [15]
And with thirty thousand forwarde is gone:
After wisedom and pollicy wondrously hee sought,
How by the *Scottish* ordinaunce hee might well come.
Thereto helped well *Basterd Heron*,
On the *Scots* hee did harme both day and night, [20]
So thy helpe O Lord preserude our Princes right.

Our Herald of Armes to King *Iemy* did say:
My Lord of *Surrey* greetes you well by mee,

[25]   Maruayling greatly of this your array,
And what you make here in this countrey.
Peace you haue broken, and olde amity:
Wherefore if yee abide hee will with you fight,
By the helpe of God and in his Princes right.

[30]   Abide? (hee sayde) els were it great dishonour hye,
That a King crowned an Earle durst not abide:
Yf *Surrey* bee so bolde to gieue battayle to mee,
I shall him tarry on *Floddon* hill side.
Open warre then soone was there cryde,
And our doughty men were redily dight,
[35]   By the helpe of God, and in theyr Princes right.

   S. Cutberds banner with the Byshops men bolde,
In the Vaunt garde forward fast did hye,
That royall relike more precious than golde,
And sir *William Bowmer* nere stoode it by.
[40]   *Adiuua pater* then fast did they cry,
Pray wee that God will graunt vs his might,
That wee may haue the powre to saue our Princes right.

   The Lord *Clifford* and the Lord *Latimer* also,
With the Lord *Couiers* of the North countrey,
[45]   And the Lord *Scrope* of *Vpsalle* forwarde did goe,
With the Lorde *Howarde* Admirall of the see,
Of noble hearte and courage good was hee,
As any went that time agaynst the *Scots* to fight,
By the helpe of God, and in theyr Princes right.

[50]   Sir *William Percy* and Lorde *Ogle* both same,
And Sir *William Gascoyne*, theyr cosin nere was hee:
The Shryue of *Yorkeshyre* Sir *Iohn Eueringame*,
And the Nobles at *Chesshyre* in theyr degree.
The Lord *Dacres*, and *Basterd Heyron* with heart free,
[55]   Which did harme the *Scots* by day and by night,
By the helpe of God, and in theyr Princes right.

Sir *Edmond Haward* of lusty franke courage
Boldly aduaunced himselfe eke in that stounde,
To the *Scots* our enemies he did greate hurte and domage,
Which were right greedy him and his bloud to confound: [60]
But theyr mischieuous intent on themselues did rebound,
And many a deadly stroke on them there did light,
So the helpe of God preserude our Princes right.

The Baron of *Killerton*, and both *Astones* were there,
With Sir *Iohn Bouthe*, and many Knightes moe: [65]
Sir *Iohn Gower* and Sir *Walter Griffin* drewe nere,
With Sir *Thomas Butler* and Maister *Warcoppe* also,
Sir *Christopher Warde*, & Sir *William Midylton* both two,
And Sir *William Maliuer*, all did manly fight,
By the helpe of God, and in theyr Princes right. [70]

In the mydle warde was the Earle of *Surrey*,
That noble man stoute, bolde, and hardy,
The father of wit wee call him may,
The Deputy of *England* most trusty was hee.
With him Lorde *Scrope* of *Bolton*, and Sir *George Darcye*, [75]
And Sir *Richard Maliuer* with Bucks heades bright,
By the helpe of God, and in theyr Princes right.

Sir *Phillip Tilney* was there ready and prest,
In the same warde, with all his mighty powre,
And Sir *Iohn Willowghby* as ready as the best, [80]
With Sir *Nicholas Aplyard* his helpe, ayde, and succour.
O what ioy was it to see that same howre,
How valiauntly our noble men with the *Scots* did fight,
By the helpe of God, and in theyr Princes right.

Yong Sir *William Gascoyne* was there indeede, [85]
With Sir *Richard Aldburgh*, and Sir *Christofer Danebe*,
Sir *William Scarkell*, and M. *Frosts* help at neede,
With Sir *Raphe Ellarkar* and M. *Thomas Lee*.

M. *Raphe Beeston*, and M. *Hopton* men might see
[90] Full well, perdy, they quite themselues in that fight,
By the helpe of God, and in theyr Princes right.

Sir *Edward Stanley* in the reare warde was hee,
A noble Knight both wise and hardy,
With many a noble man of the West countrey,
[95] And the whole powre of the Earle of *Darby*,
With a right retinue of the Byshop *Elye*,
And of *Lankeshyre* men manly did fight,
By the helpe of God, and in theyr Princes right.

Soone then the gunnes began a new play,
[100] And the Vaunt garde together are gone:
But our gunnes disseuered them out of aray,
And our bolde bilmen of them slewe many one.
So that of them scarce retourned none.
Thus were they punished by help of God almight:
[105] So thy helpe O Lord, preseru'd our Prince his right.

Then they sought embushments, but with small chere,
And in fowle maner brake theyr aray:
Yet some of our men by policy fled were,
That sawe King *Iemy* on the hill where he lay.
[110] They flee (hee sayes) folow fast I you pray.
But by that fit of flying wee wan the fight:
So the helpe of God preserude our Princes right.

To the Earle of *Surrey* King *Iemy* is gone,
With as comly company as euer man did see:
[115] Full boldly theyr big men agaynst vs did come
Downe the hill, with great myrth and melody:
And our men marked them to the *Trinity*,
Beseeching him there to shew his might,
In theyr whole defence, and in theyr Prince his right.

The red Lyon with his owne fathers bloud inclynate,   [120]
Came towards the white Lyon both meeke and mylde,
And there by the hand of God he was prostrate,
By the helpe of th'Eagle with her swadled chylde.
The Buckesheads also the *Scots* has beguilde,
And with theyr grey goose wings doulfully them dight,   [125]
By the helpe of God, and in our Prince his right.

The Moone that day did shine full bright,
And the Luce head that day was full bent:
The red Cressent did blinde the *Scots* sight,
And the Ship with her Ancre many *Scots* spent.   [130]
But (alas) the good white Griffin was felde on *Floddon* hil,
Yet escape hee did, not vanquisht in the fight:
So thy helpe O Lord, preserude our Prince his right.

The Treyfell was true, and that did well appeare,
And boldly the great Griffin vp the hill is gone: [135]
The Antlet did lace them with arrowes so nere,
That buffits the *Scots* bare, they lacked none.
The Cinquefoile also was stedfast as the stone,
And slewe of the *Scots* like a worthy wight:
So thy helpe O Lord, preserude our Prince his right.   [140]

The yong white Lyon was angry in that stounde,
And with his merry mariners the myrth him made,
His bells rang lay couched in the grounde,
Whereof the *Scots* were right sore affrayde.
And round about rydeing euermore he sayde   [145]
Go to my fellowes, all shalbe all or night,
By the helpe of God, wee saue our Prince his right.

The *Cornish* Choughe did picke them in the face,
And the Crab them blinded that they might not see:
They flewe and fell, they had none other grace,   [150]
With theyr new conquerour: but where now is hee,

Caryed in a cart, to his rebuke and his posterity,
And his Bullies so bonnye are put all to flight:
So thy helpe O Lord, preserude our Prince his right.

[155]   Of *Scots* lay slayne full xii. thousande,
And xi. Earles, the sooth for to say,
Xiii. Lords, and three Byshops as I vnderstande,
With two Abbots, which haue learnde a new play,
They should haue bene at home for peace to pray:
[160]   Wherefore they were thus wise punished by right:
So thy helpe O Lord preserude our Prince his right.

    Theyr ordinaunce is lost, and theyr royalty,
Wee haue theyr riches, God haue the prayseing:
What ech man would take, hee had his liberty.
[165]   Wherefore laude and honour to such a King,
From dolefull daunger vs so defending:
Hee has graunted vnto vs now his might,
And by his only ayde preserude our Princes right.

    O rex regum, ruler of vs all,
[170]   As thou for vs sufferedst thy passion,
Gieue the *Scots* grace, by King *Iemyes* fall,
For to eschue for euer like transgression,
Preserue the red rose, and be his protection.
Laude, honour, prayse be vnto God almight,
[175]   Who thus suppreste our foes, preserud our Princes right.

    O yee noble Lordes and Knights victorius,
I you beseech to haue mee excused,
Your noble acts no better that I discusse,
And that my simple saying be not refused.
[180]   Where in any thing I haue mee misused,
I mee submit to your charitable correction:
And in this maner shall be my conclusion.

494

AS *Baldwine* indeede being a Minister, had bene most fit to set [Prose 32]
forth the life of a Cardinall and Byshop (for causes belonging to
his knowledge and ministery) so to encourage a writer now
aliue to play the part of a Pasquill, and rather make his pen his plough,
than in a hard season, liue like a labourer, that doth seruice to many, and [5]
litle good to him selfe, I thought it necessary in a kinde of beneuolence
and curtesy of minde, to bestow some credit on that person that not
only hath preferred my tragedy to the Printer, (being of his owne
deuice and penning) but also hath enlarged, by playne and familier
verse, the matter the world desires to heare or read, and made things [10]
common among a multitude, that were secret and held priuat among a
fewe. Which study and paynes of his owne purpose, procures mee (as
one whom Fortune hath flattered and afflicted) to appeare vnto him, for
the hearing of my calamity, and for the setting out both of my rising vp
& falling downe. So, to the whole worlde, by his helpe and mine owne [15]
desire, I step out from the graue, where long I lay in forgetfulnes, and
declare in the voyce of a Cardinall, a curious discourse; yet sadly and
sorrowfully tolde, as well vnto *Churchyard* (the noter thereof) as to the
rest that pleaseth to heare any peece of my misfortune.

HOW THOMAS WOLSEY [Tragedy 33]
did arise vnto great authority and gouernment,
his maner of life, pompe, and dignity, and
how hee fell downe into great disgrace,
and was arested of high treason.

SHall I looke on, when states step on the stage,
And play theyr parts, before the peoples face?
Some men liue now, scarce four score yeares of age,
Who in time past, did know the Cardnalls grace.

495

[5] A gamesom worlde, when Byshops run at bace,
Yea, get a fall, in striuing for the gole,
And body loase, and hazarde seely sole.

 Ambitious minde, a world of wealth would haue,
So scrats and scrapes, for scorfe, and scoruy drosse:
[10] And till the flesh, and bones, be layde in graue,
Wit neuer rests, to grope for mucke and mosse.
Fye on prowde pompe, and gilted bridels bosse:
O glorious golde, the gaping after thee,
So blindes mens eyes, they can no daunger see.

[15] Now note my byrth, and marke how I began,
Beholde from whence, rose all this pryde of mine.
My father but, a playne poore honest man,
And I his son, of wit and iudgement fine,
Brought vp at schoole, and prou'd a good diuine:
[20] For which great gifts, degree of schoole I had,
And Batchler was, and I a litle lad.

 So, tasting some, of Fortunes sweete consayts,
I clapt the hoode, on shoulder, braue as Son,
And hopt at length, to bite at better bayts,
[25] And fill my mouth, ere banket halfe were don.
Thus holding on, the course I thought to ron:
By many a feast, my belly grue so big,
That *Wolsey* streight, became a wanton twig.

 Lo what it is, to feede on daynty meate,
[30] And pamper vp, the gorge, with suger plate:
Nay, see how lads, in hope of higher seate
Rise early vp, and study learning late.
But hee thriues best, that hath a blessed fate,
And hee speeds worst, that worlde will nere aduaunce,
[35] Nor neuer knowes, what meanes good lucke nor chaunce.

My chaunce was great, for from a poore mans son,
I rose aloft, and chopt and chaungde degree:
In *Oxford* first, my famous name begon,
Where many a day, the scholers honourd mee.
Then thought I how, I might a courtier bee: [40]
So came to Court, and fethred there my wing,
With *Henry* th'eight, who was a worthy King.

Hee did with words, assay mee once or twice,
To see what wit, and ready sprite I had:
And when hee saw, I was both graue and wice, [45]
For some good cause, the King was wondrous glad.
Than downe I lookt, with sober countnaunce sad,
But heart was vp, as high as hope could go,
That suttell fox, might win some fauour so.

Wee worke with wiles, the mindes of men like wax, [50]
The fawning whelp, gets many a peece of bred:
Wee follow Kings, with many coning knacks,
By searching out, how are theyr humours fed.
Hee haunts no Court, that hath a doltish hed:
For as in golde, the pretious stone is set, [55]
So finest wits, in Court the credit get.

I quickely learnde, to kneele and kysse the hand,
To waite at heele, and turne like top about,
To stretch out necke, and lyke an Image stand,
To taunt, to skoffe, and face the matter out, [60]
To preace in place, among the greatest rout:
Yet like a priest, my selfe did well behaue,
In fayre long gowne, and goodly garments graue.

Where *Wolsey* went, the world like Bees would swarme,
To heare my speach, and note my nature well. [65]
I coulde with tongue, vse such a kinde of charme,
That voyce full cleare, should sounde like siluer bell.

When head deuisde, a long discours to tell,
With stories straunge, my speach should spised bee,
[70]   To make the worlde, to muse the more on mee.

Each tale was sweete, each worde a sentence wayde,
Each eare I pleasde, each eye gaue mee the vewe,
Each Iudgment markt, and paysed what I sayde,
Each minde I fed, with matter rare and newe,
[75]   Each day and howre, my grace and credit grewe:
So that the King, in hearing of this newes,
Deuysed howe, hee might my seruice vse.

Hee made mee then, his Chaplayne, to say masse
Before his grace, yea twise or thrise a weeke:
[80]   Now had I time, to trym my selfe by glasse,
Now founde I meane, some liuing for to seeke,
Now I became, both humble, mylde, and meeke,
Now I applyde, my wyts and sences throwe,
To reape some corne, if God would speede the plowe.

[85]   Whom most I sawe, in fauour with the King,
I followde fast, to get some hap thereby:
But I obserude, a nother fyner thing,
That was, to keepe, mee styll in Princes eye.
As vnder wyng, the hawke in winde doth lye,
[90]   So for a pray, I prowlled here and there,
And tryed frendes, and Fortune euery where.

The King at length, sent mee beyonde the seas,
Embastour then, with message good and greate:
And in that time, I did the King so pleas,
[95]   By short dispatch, and wrought so fine a feate,
That did aduaunce my selfe to higher seate,
The deanrie then, of *Lincolne* hee mee gaue:
And bownty shewde, before I gan to craue.

His Amner to, hee made mee all in haste,
And threefolde gyftes, hee threwe vpon mee still: [100]
His counslour straight, listewise was *Wolsey* plaste,
Thus in shorte time, I had the world at will:
Which passed far, mans reason, wit, and skill.
O hap, thou haste, great secrets in thy might,
Which long lye hyd, from wily worldlyngs sight.   [105]

As shures of raine, fall quickly on the grasse,
That fading flowres, are soone refresht thereby:
Or as with Sun, the morning dewe doth passe,
And quiet calme, makes cleare a troubled skye:
So Princes powre, at twinkling of an eye   [110]
Sets vp a lofte, a favret on the wheele,
When giddy braynes, about the streetes doe reele.

They are but blinde, that wake where Fortune sleepes,
They worke in vayne, that striue with streame and tyde:
In double garde, they dwell, that destnye keepes,   [115]
In simple sorte, they liue that lacke a gyde:
They misse the marke, that shoote theyr arrowes wide,
They hit the pricke, that make theyr flight to glaunce
So nere the white, that shafte may light on chaunce.

Such was my lucke, I shot no shafte in vayne,   [120]
My bow stoode bent, and brased all the yeere:
I wayted harde, but neuer lost my payne:
Such wealth came in, to beare the charges cleere.
And in the end, I was the greatest peere
Among them all, for I so rulde the land,   [125]
By Kings consent, that all was in my hand.

Within on yeare, three Bishoprickes I had,
And in small space, a Cardnall I was made:
With long red robes, rich *Wolsey* then was clad,
I walkte in Sun, when others sate in shade: [130]

I went abroade, with such a trayne and trade,
With crosses borne, before mee where I past,
That man was thought, to bee some God at last.

With sonnes of Earles, and Lordes I serued was,
[135]   An hundreth chaynes, at leaste were in my trayne:
I dayly dranke, in gold, but not in glas,
My bread was made, of fynest flowre and grayne:
My daynty mouth, did common meates disdayne,
I fed like Prince, on fowles most deare and straunge,
[140]   And bankets made, of fine conceites for chaunge.

My hall was full, of Knightes, and Squires of name,
And gentlemen, two hundreth tolde by powle:
Tale yeomen to, did howrely serue the same,
Whose names each weeke, I saw within checke rowle.
[145]   All went to church, when seruis bell did knowle,
All dinde and supte, and slepte at Cardnalls charge,
And all would wayte, when *Wolsey* tooke his barge.

My householde stuffe, my wealth and siluer plate,
Mighte well suffice, a Monarke at this day:
[150]   I neuer fed, but vnder cloth of state,
Nor walkt abroade, till Vshars clearde the way.
In house I had, musitions for to play,
In open streete, my trompets lowde did sownde,
Which pearst the skies, and seemde to shake the grownde.

[155]   My men most braue, martcht two and two in ranke,
Who helde in length, much more then half a mile:
Not one of these, but gaue his maister thanke,
For some good turne, or pleasure got some while.
I did not feede, my seruantes with a smile,
[160]   Or glosing wordes, that neuer bring forth frute,
But gaue them golde, or els preferde theyr sute.

In surety so, whiles God was pleasde, I stoode,
I knewe I must, leaue all my wealth behinde:
I sawe they lou'd, mee not for byrth or bloode,
But serude a space, to try my noble minde.   [165]
The more men gieue, the more in deede they finde
Of loue, and troth, and seruice, euery way:
The more they spare, the more doth loue decay.

I ioyde to see, my seruantes thriue so well,
And go so gay, with little that they gote: [170]
For as I did, in honour still excell,
So would I oft, the wante of seruantes note:
Which made my men, on maister so to dote,
That when I sayde, let such a thing bee donne,
They woulde in deede, through fyre and water ronne.   [175]

I had in house, so many ofsars still,
Which were obayde, and honourde for their place,
That carelesse I, might sleepe or walke at will,
Saue that sometyme, I wayde a poore mans case,
And salude such sores, whose griefe might breede disgrace. [180]
Thus men did wayte, and wicked world did gaze,
On mee and them, that brought vs all in maze.

For worlde was whist, and durst not speake a woorde
Of that they sawe, my credite curbde them so:
I waded far, and passed ore the foorde,   [185]
And mynded not, for to returne I troe.
The worlde was wise, yet scarce it selfe did knoe,
When wonder made, of men that rose by hap:
For Fortune rare, falls not in each mans lap.

I climde the clouds, by knowledge and good wit,   [190]
My men sought chaunce, by seruice or good lucke:
The worlde walkte lowe, when I aboue did sit,
Or downe did come, to trample on this mucke:

And I did swim, as dainty as a ducke,
[195] When water serues, to keepe the body braue,
And to enioy, the gyftes that Fortune gaue.

And though my pompe, surpast all Prelates nowe,
And like a Prince, I liu'd and pleasure tooke:
That was not sure, so great a blur in browe,
[200] If on my workes, indiffrent eyes doe looke.
I thought great scorne, such liuings heare to brooke,
Except I built, some howses for the poore,
And order tooke, to gieue great almes at doore.

A Colledge fayre, in *Oxford* I did make,
[205] A sumptuous house, a stately worke in deede.
I gaue great lands, to that, for learning sake,
To bring vp youth, and succour scholers neede.
That charge of myne, full many a mouth did feede,
When I in Courte, was seeking some good turne,
[210] To mend my torch, or make my candell burne.

More houses gay, I builte, then thowsands do
That haue enough, yet will no goodnes shoe:
And where I built, I did mayntayne it to,
With such great cost, as few bestowes I troe.
[215] Of buildings large, I could reherse a roe,
That by mischaunce, this day haue lost my name,
Whereof I do, deserue the only fame.

And as for sutes, about the King was none
So apte as I, to speake and purchase grace.
[220] Though long before, some say *Shores* wife was one,
That oft kneelde downe, before the Princes face
For poore mens sutes, and holpe theire woefull case,
Yet shee had not, such credite as I gate,
Although a King, would heare the parret prate.

My wordes were graue, and bore an equall poyes,   [225]
In ballaunce iust, for many a weighty cause:
Shee pleasde a Prince, with pretty merry toyes,
And had no sight, in state, nor course of lawes.
I coulde perswade, and make a Prince to pawes,
And take a breath, before hee drew the sworde,   [230]
And spy the time, to rule him with a worde.

I will not say, but fancy may do much,
Yet worlde will graunt, that wisdom may do more:
To wanton gyrls, affection is not such,
That Princes wise, will bee abusde therefore: [235]
One sute of mine, was surely worth a score
Of hers indeede, for shee her time must watch,
And at all howres, I durst go draw the latch.

My voyce but heard, the dore was open streyght,
Shee might not come, till shee were calde or brought: [240]
I rulde the King, by custom, arte, and sleight,
And knew full well, the secrets of his thought.
Without my minde, all that was done was nought,
In wars or peace, my counsayle swayed all,
For still the King, would for the Cardnall call.   [245]

I kept a court, my selfe, as great as his,
(I not compare, vnto my maister heere)
But looke my Lords, what liuely worlde was this,
That one poore man, became so great a peere?
Yet though this tale, be very straunge to heere,   [250]
Wit wins a worlde: and who hath hap and wit,
With triumph long, in Princely throne may sit.

What man like mee, bare rule in any age,
I shone like Sun, more cleare then morning star:
Was neuer parte, so playde in open stage   [255]
As mine, nor fame, of man flewe halfe so far.

I sate on bench, when thowsands at the bar
Did pleade for right: for I in publique weale
Lorde Chaunclour was, and had the great broad seale,

[260] Now haue I tolde, how I did rise aloft,
And sate with pride, and pomp, in golden hall,
And set my feete, on costly carpets soft,
And playde at goale, with goodly golden ball:
But after, Lord, I must rehearse my fall.
[265] O trembling heart, thou canst not now for teares
Present that tale, vnto the hearers eares.

Best weepe it out, and sodayne silence keepe,
Till priuy pangs, make pinched heart complayne:
Or cast thy selfe, into some slumbring sleepe,
[270] Till wakened wits, remembraunce bring agayne.
When heauy tears, do hollow cheekes distayne,
The world will thinke, thy sprits are growne so weake,
The feeble tongue, hath sure no powre to speake.

A tale by signes, with sighes and sobs set out,
[275] Moues peoples mindes, to pity plaged men:
With howling voyce, do rather cry and showt,
And so by arte, shew forth thy sorrow then.
For if thou speake, some man will note with pen
What *Wolsey* sayde, and what thrue *Wolsey* downe,
[280] And vnder foote, flings *Wolseys* great renowne.

What force of that, my fall must needs be herd,
Before I fell, I had a time to rise:
As fatall chaunce, and Fortune mee preferd,
So mischiefe came, and did my state despise.
[285] Yf I might pleade, my case among the wise,
I could excuse, right much of mine offence:
But leaue a while, such matter in suspence.

The Pope, or pride, or peeuish parts of mine,
Made King to frowne, and take the seale from mee:
Now seru'd no words, nor plesaunt speeches fine,   [290]
Now *Wolsey*, lo, must needs disgraced bee.
Yet had I leaue (as dolefull prisner free)
To keepe a house (God wot) with heauy cheere,
Where that I founde, no wine, ne bread, nor beere.

My time was come, I coulde no longer liue,   [295]
What should I make, my sorrow further knowne?
Vpon some cause, that King that all did giue
Tooke all agayne, and so possest his owne.
My goods, my plate, and all was ouerthrowne,
And looke what I, had gathred many a day,   [300]
Within one howre, was cleanly swept away.

But harken now, how that my Fortune fell,
To *Yorke* I must, where I the Bishop was:
Where I by right, in grace a while did dwell,
And was in stawle, with honour great to pas.   [305]
The Priors then, and Abbots gan to smell,
Howe Cardnall must, bee honourd as hee ought,
And for that day, was great prouision brought.

At *Cawood* then, where I great buildings made,
And did through cause, exspect my stawling day,   [310]
The King deuisde, a secrete vnder shade,
Howe Cardnall shoulde, bee reste and brought away.
One *Wealsh* a Knight, came downe in good aray,
And seasned sure, because from Courte hee cam,
On *Wolsey* wolfe, that spoyled many a lam.   [315]

Then was I led, toward Courte, like dog in string,
And brought as biefe, that Butcherrowe must see:
But still I hoapt, to come before the King,
And that repayre, was not denyde to mee.

[320] But hee that kept, the Towre, my guide must bee.
Ah there I saw, what King thereby did meane,
And so I searcht, yf conscience now were cleane.

Some spots I founde, of pryde and popishe partes,
That might accuse, a better man then I:
[325] Now *Oxford* came, to minde, with all theire artes,
And *Cambridge* to, but all not worth a flye:
For schoolemen can, no fowle defects supplye.
My sauce was sowre, though meate before was sweete,
Nowe *Wolsey* lackte, both conning, wit, and spreete.

[330] A deepe conceyte, of that, possest my heade,
So fell I sicke, consumde as some did thinke.
So tooke in haste, my chamber and my bed,
On which deuise, perhaps the worlde might winke.
But in the heart, sharpe sorrow so did sinke,
[335] That gladnes sweete, (forsooke my senses all)
In those extremes, did yeelde vnto my fall.

O let mee curse, the popish Cardnall hat,
Those myters big, beset with pearle and stones,
And all the rest, of trash I know not what,
[340] The saints in shrine, theyr flesh and rotten bones,
The maske of Monkes, deuised for the nones,
And all the flocke, of Freers, what ere they are,
That brought mee vp, and left mee there so bare.

O cursed priestes, that prate for profits sake,
[345] And follow floud, and tyde, where ere it floes:
O marchaunts fine, that do aduauntage take
Of euery grayne, how euer market goes.
O fie on wolues, that march in masking cloes,
For to deuoure, the lambs, when shepperd sleepes,
[350] And woe to you, that promise neuer keepes.

You sayd I should, be reskude if I neede,
And you would curse, with candell, booke, and bell:
But when yee should, now serue my turne indeede,
Yee haue no house, I know not where yee dwell.
O Freers and Monkes, your harbour is in hell,   [355]
For in this world, yee haue no rightfull place,
Nor dare not once, in heauen shew your face.

Your fault not halfe, so great as was my pryde,
For which offence, fell *Lucifer* from skyes:
Although I would, that wilfull folly hyde,   [360]
The thing lyes playne, before the peoples eyes,
On which hye heart, a hatefull name doth ryes.
It hath beene sayde, of olde, and dayly will,
Pryde goes before, and shame comes after still.

Pryde is a thing, that God and man abores,   [365]
A swelling tode, that poysons euery place,
A stinking wounde, that breedeth many sores,
A priuy plague, found out in stately face,
A paynted byrd, that keepes a pecocks pace,
A lothsome lowt, that lookes like tinkers dog,   [370]
A hellish hownd, a swinish hatefull hog

That grunts and groanes, at euery thing it sees,
And holds vp snowt, like pig that coms from draffe.
Why should I make, of pride all these degrees,
That first tooke roote, from filthy drosse and chaffe,   [375]
And makes men stay, vpon a broken staffe?
No weakenes more, than thinke to stand vpright,
When stumbling blocke, makes men to fall downe right.

Hee needes must fall, that looks not where hee goes,
And on the starrs, walkes staring goezling like: [380]
On sodayne oft, a blostring tempest bloes,
Than downe great trees, are tumbled in the dike.

Who knowes the time, and howre when God will strike?
Then looke about, and marke what steps yee take,
Before you pace, the pilgrimage yee make.

[385]

Run not on head, as all the worlde were youres,
Nor thrust them backe, that cannot bide a shocke:
Who striues for place, his owne decay procures:
Who alway brawles, is sure to catch a knocke:
Who beards a King, his head is neere the blocke:
But who doth stand, in feare, and worldly dreede,
Ere mischiefe coms, had neede to take good heede.

[390]

I hauing hap, did make account of none,
But such as fed, my humour good or bad.
To fawning doggs, sometimes I gaue a bone,
And flong some scrapps, to such as nothing had:
But in my hands, still kept the golden gad,
That seru'd my turne, and laught the rest to skorne,
As for himselfe, was Cardnall *Wolsey* borne.

[395]

No, no, good men, wee liue not for our selues,
Though each one catch, as mutch as hee may get:
Wee ought to looke, to those that diggs and delues,
That alwayes dwell, and liue in endles det.
Yf in such sort, wee would our compas set,
Wee should haue loue, where now but hate wee finde,
And hedstrong will, with cruell hollow minde.

[400]

[405]

I thought nothing, of duty, loue, or feare,
I snatcht vp all, and alwayes sought to clime:
I punisht all, and would with no man beare,
I sought for all, and so could take the time.
I plide the Prince, whiles Fortune was in prime,
I fild the bags, and gold in hoorde I heapt,
Thought not on those, that thresht the corne I reapt.

[410]

So all I lost, and all I gat was nought,
And all by pride, and pompe lay in the dust: [415]
I aske you all, what man aliue had thought,
That in this world, had beene so litle trust?
Why, all thinges heare, with time decline they must.
Than all is vaine, so all not worth a flye,
Yf all shall thinke, that all are borne to dye.   [420]

Yf all bee bace, and of so small a count,
Why doe wee all, in folly so abound?
Why doe the meane, and mighty seeke to mount,
Beyonde all hope, where is no surety found,
And where the wheele, is alwayes turning round?   [425]
The case is plaine, if all bee vnderstood,
Wee are so vaine, wee knowe not what is good.

Yet some will say, when they haue heapes of golde,
With flocks of friends, and seruaunts at theyr call,
They liue like Gods, in pleasure treble folde,   [430]
And haue no cause, to finde no fault at all.
O blinde conceite, these gloryes are but small,
And as for friends, they change their mindes so mych,
They stay not long, with neither poore nor rich.

With hope of friends, our selues wee do deceaue,   [435]
With feare of foes, we threatned are in sleepe:
But friends speake fayre, yet men alone they leaue
To sinke or swim, to mourne, to laugh, or weepe.
Yet whan foe smiles, the snake begins to creepe,
As world falles out, these dayes in compasse iust,   [440]
Wee knowe not howe, the friend or foe to trust.

Both can betray, the truest man aliue,
Both are to doubt, in matters of greate weight,
Both will somtime, for goodes and honour striue,
Both seemeth playne, yet both can shewe great sleight,   [445]

Both stoups full lowe, yet both can looke on height,
And best of both, not worth a cracked crowne:
Yet least of both, may loase a walled towne.

[450]
Talke not of frends, the name thereof is nought,
Then trust no foes, if frendes theire credit loes:
If foes and frendes, of on bare earth were wrought,
Blame nere of both, though both one nature shoes,
Grace passeth kinde, where grace and vertue floes,
But where grace wantes, make foes and frends alike,
[455]
The on drawes sworde, the other sure will strike.

I prou'd that true, by tryall twenty times,
When *Wolsey* stoode, on top of Fortunes wheele:
But such as to, the height of ladder climes,
Knowe not what led, lies hanging on theire heele,
[460]
Tell mee my mates, that heauy Fortune feele,
Yf rising vp, breede not a gyddy brayne,
And faling downe, bee not a greuous payne.

He died of
a continu-
all flyxe in
the Abbey
of Leyce-
ster as
Stowe
writeth.
I tolde you how, from *Cawood* I was led,
And so fell sicke, when I arested was:
What needeth nowe, more wordes heere in bee sed?
I knewe full well, I must to pryson passe,
And sawe my state, as brittell as a glasse:
So gaue vp ghost, and bad the worlde farewell,
Where in, God wot, I could no longer dwell.

[470]
Thus vnto dust, and ashes I returnde,
When blase of life, and vitall breath went out,
Like glowing cole, that is to sinders burnde:
All fleshe and bloud, so ende, you neede not dout.
But when the bruite, of this was blowne aboute,
[475]
The worlde was glad, the Cardnall was in graue,
This is of worlde, lo all the hope wee haue.

Full many a yeare, the world lookt for my fall,
And whan I fell, I made as great a cracke,
As doth an oake, or mighty tottring wall,
That whirling winde, doth bring to ruin and wracke.   [480]
Now babling world, wil talke behinde my backe
A thousand things, to my reproache and shame:
So will it to, of others do the same.

But what of that? the best is wee are gone,
And worst of all, when wee our tales haue tolde,   [485]
Our open plagues, will warning bee to none,
Men are by hap, and courage made so bolde:
They thinke all is, theyr owne, they haue in holde.
Well, let them say, and thinke what thing they please,
This weltring world, both flowes and ebs like seas.   [490]

APPENDICES

Appendix A

Description of the Huntington Library Copies
of the *Mirror for Magistrates**

Title: ๑ *A MYRROVRE* / For Magistrates. / 𝔚𝔥𝔢𝔯𝔢𝔦𝔫 𝔪𝔞𝔭 𝔟𝔢 𝔰𝔢𝔢𝔫 𝔟𝔭 / 𝔢𝔵𝔞𝔪𝔭𝔩𝔢 𝔬𝔣 𝔬𝔱𝔥𝔢𝔯, 𝔴𝔦𝔱𝔥 𝔥𝔬𝔴𝔢 𝔤𝔯𝔢= / 𝔲𝔬𝔲𝔰 𝔭𝔩𝔞𝔤𝔢𝔰 𝔟𝔦𝔠𝔢𝔰 𝔞𝔯𝔢 𝔭𝔲𝔫𝔦𝔰𝔥𝔢𝔡 : 𝔞𝔫𝔡 / 𝔥𝔬𝔴𝔢 𝔣𝔯𝔞𝔭𝔩𝔢 𝔞𝔫𝔡 𝔟𝔫𝔰𝔱𝔞𝔟𝔩𝔢 𝔴𝔬𝔯𝔩𝔡𝔩𝔭 / 𝔭𝔯𝔬𝔰𝔭𝔢𝔯𝔦𝔱𝔦𝔢 𝔦𝔰 𝔣𝔬𝔲𝔫𝔡𝔢, 𝔢𝔟𝔢𝔫 𝔬𝔣 / 𝔱𝔥𝔬𝔰𝔢, 𝔴𝔥𝔬𝔪 𝔍𝔬𝔯𝔱𝔲𝔫𝔢 𝔰𝔢𝔢= / 𝔪𝔢𝔱𝔥 𝔪𝔬𝔰𝔱 𝔥𝔦𝔤𝔥𝔩𝔭 / 𝔱𝔬 𝔣𝔞𝔲𝔬𝔲𝔯.. / ★ / *Fœlix quem faciunt aliena pericula cautum.* / Anno . 1559. / [single rule] / LONDINI, / In ædibus Thomæ Marshe.†

Colophon: ℭ. 𝔍𝔪𝔭𝔯𝔦𝔫𝔱𝔢𝔡 𝔞𝔱 / 𝔏𝔬𝔫𝔡𝔬𝔫 𝔦𝔫 𝔍𝔩𝔢𝔱𝔢𝔰𝔱𝔯𝔢𝔱𝔢 𝔫𝔢𝔯𝔢 𝔱𝔬 / 𝔖𝔞𝔭𝔫𝔠𝔱 𝔇𝔲𝔫𝔰𝔱𝔬𝔫𝔢𝔰 ℭ𝔥𝔲𝔯𝔠𝔥 𝔟𝔭 / 𝔗𝔥𝔬𝔪𝔞𝔰 𝔐𝔞𝔯𝔰𝔥𝔢.

Collation: ℭ.⁴ (last leaf, probably blank, missing), A–M⁴, N², a–g⁴, the first three leaves of each gathering signed, except the title-page. Title, verso blank; dedication, signed "William Baldwin.", 2 leaves; ℭ. 𝔄 𝔅𝔯𝔦𝔢𝔣𝔢 𝔐𝔢𝔪𝔬𝔯𝔦𝔞𝔩 / 𝔬𝔣 𝔰𝔲𝔫𝔡𝔯𝔭𝔢 𝔘𝔫𝔣𝔬𝔯𝔱𝔲𝔫𝔞𝔱𝔢 / 𝔈𝔫𝔤𝔩𝔦𝔰𝔥𝔢 𝔪𝔢𝔫. / 𝔚𝔦𝔩𝔩𝔦𝔞𝔪 𝔅𝔞𝔩𝔡𝔴𝔦𝔫 𝔱𝔬 / 𝔱𝔥𝔢 𝔎𝔢𝔞𝔡𝔢𝔯. /, 2 leaves, last page blank; text,

---

* See facsimile title-pages for ornaments and borders.

† A different title-page is found in a second copy of this edition in the Bodleian Library. For the description of this title-page, I am indebted to Miss E. G. Parker:

¶ *A MYRROVR FOR* / Magistrates. / 𝔚𝔥𝔢𝔯𝔢𝔦𝔫 𝔪𝔞𝔭 𝔟𝔢 𝔰𝔢𝔢𝔫 𝔟𝔭 / 𝔢𝔵𝔞𝔪𝔭𝔩𝔢 𝔬𝔣 𝔬𝔱𝔥𝔢𝔯, 𝔴𝔦𝔱𝔥 𝔥𝔬𝔴𝔢 𝔤𝔯𝔢= / 𝔟𝔬𝔲𝔰 𝔭𝔩𝔞𝔤𝔢𝔰 𝔟𝔦𝔠𝔢 𝔞𝔯𝔢 𝔭𝔲𝔫𝔦𝔰𝔥𝔢𝔡, 𝔞𝔫𝔡 / 𝔥𝔬𝔴𝔢 𝔣𝔯𝔞𝔭𝔩𝔢 𝔞𝔫𝔡 𝔟𝔫𝔰𝔱𝔞𝔟𝔩𝔢 𝔴𝔬𝔯𝔡𝔩𝔭 / 𝔭𝔯𝔬𝔰𝔭𝔢𝔯𝔦𝔱𝔭 𝔦𝔰 𝔣𝔬𝔲𝔫𝔡𝔢 𝔢𝔟𝔢𝔫 𝔬𝔣 / 𝔱𝔥𝔬𝔰𝔢 𝔴𝔥𝔬𝔪 𝔣𝔬𝔯𝔱𝔲𝔫𝔢 𝔰𝔢𝔢= / 𝔪𝔢𝔱𝔥 𝔪𝔬𝔰𝔱 𝔥𝔦𝔤𝔥𝔩𝔭 / 𝔱𝔬 𝔣𝔞𝔟𝔬𝔲𝔯 / *Fœlix quem faciunt aliena pericula cautum.* / Anno 15[59] / ¶ *Imprinted at London in Flete strete* / *nere to Sayncte Dunstans Church* / *by* Thomas Marsh

Miss Parker notes: "The 59 supplied in MS.," and the "sheet of print of title, and border (separately), stuck on to the leaf. Probably a proof." The collation of the text is exactly that of the HN copy.

beginning on A. 3; ꝙ The Contentes and Table / of the booke., on g 3 verso; ℭ. ꝼautes escapeð in tꞕe printing. and colophon, on g 4.

Foliation: i–xlviii, lix–lxx, lxxxi–lxxxiiii, lxxv–lxxxv. The foliation begins on A 3 and ends on g 3.

Irregularities: B 2, E 3, F 3, K 3, a 3, e 3, f 3, g 3 are unsigned; B iii is misprinted A iii; lxxxiiii is mistakenly numbered lxxxiii.

Description: Sm. 4°, printed in black letter. Size of leaf, $7\frac{7}{16} \times 5\frac{3}{8}$ in. (18·9 × 13·7 cm.).

Title: ꝼ *A MYRROVR FOR* / Magistrates. / Wꞕerein maꝑe be seen bꝑ / example of otꞕer, witꞕ ꞕowe gre= / uous plages bices are punisꞕeð : anð / ꞕowe fraꝑle anð bnstable worlðlꝑ / prosperitꝑ is founðe, eben of / tꞕose wꞕom ꝼortune see= / metꞕ most ꞕigꞕlꝑ / to fauour. / ⸎ / *Fælix quem faciunt aliena pericula cautum.* / *Anno.* 1563. / ꝼ *Imprinted at London in Fletestrete* / *nere to Saynct Dunstans Churche* / *by Thomas Marshe.*

Colophon: None.

Collation: ℭ⁴, A⁴, B–N⁸, O–V⁴, X–Bb⁸, Cc⁴, the first three leaves of each gathering signed, except the title-page. Title, verso blank; dedication, signed "William Baldwin.", 3 leaves, last page blank; ℭ. ꝴ Briefe memoriall / *OF SVNDRYE VNFORTV-* / nate English-men. / ꝼ *Willyam Baldwin to* / *the Reader.* /, 2 leaves, last page blank; text, beginningon A. 3, Tꞕus enðetꞕ tꞕe / first parte., on L 1 [printed K. i.], verso blank; ℭ. Tꞕe seconðe / *PARTE OF THE* / Mirrour for Ma= / gistrates. / Wꝑlliam Balðwꝑn / to tꞕe Reaðer. /, 2 leaves; text, beginning on L 4, fol. lxxxviii; ꝼ *The contes and Table of the first* / *parte of this Booke,* on Cc 3 recto, and *The contentes of the* / *seconde parte.,* on the verso; *Faultes escaped in the Printing.,* on Cc 4.

Foliation: i–xlviii, lix–lxx, lxxxi–lxxxiiii, lxxv–cviii, cx–cxvii, cxvii–cxxxviii, cxxxviii, cxxxviii, cxliii, cliii–cli, cliiii–clxix, clxix, clxx, clxxii–clxxix, clx. The foliation begins on A 3 and ends on Cc 2.

Irregularities: B 2, C 2, E 2, F 2, H 2, I 2, L 2, O 3, R 3, S 3, T 3, U 3, Y 2, Z 2, Cc 3 are unsigned. C 4, I 4, K 4, Y 4, Aa 4 are signed. The following

signatures are mistakenly printed: L i [K i], N i [B i]. H 7 is signed
H iii. The foliation is chaotic, the following folios being erroneously
numbered: xiiii [xiii], xvi [xv], xx [xix], xxii [xxiii], xxvi [xxv],
xxvii [xviii], xxviii [xix], xxxii [xxxiii], xxxiii [xxii], xxxiv [xxv],
xxxvii [xxxv], xxxix [xlii], xli [xlii], xlv [xxxvi], xlvii [xlii], xlviii
[xlvii], lx [lxi], lxi [xliiii], lxvii [lxi], lxviii [lxi], lxxxii [lxiiii],
lxxxi [lxxxxi], lxxxv [xxxv], lxxxvii [lxxxxvi], lxxxix [lxxxxiii],
cxii [cxi], clix [clx], clxiii [clvi], clxiiii [clvi], clxxvii [clxxvi].

Description: Sm. 4°, printed in black letter. Size of leaf, $7\frac{1}{2} \times 5\frac{5}{16}$ in.
(19 × 13·5 cm.).

[The second copy of this edition substitutes *Mayster Sackuilles Induction.* for *The Induction.*, on fol. c xvi; *tree* for *blome*, in l. 7; and
Whil for *Whiles*, as the catchword on this page. It omits *FINIS.*
at the close of the index, on Cc 3 verso. The changes seem likely to
have been made while the type was standing.]

Title: A MYRROVR | *for Magistrates.* | 𝔚herein may be seene by
exam= | *ples passed in this realme, with* | howe greueous plagues, vyces |
are punished in great prin= | ces and magistrates, | and how frayle | and
vnstable worldly prosperity | is founde, where Fortune | seemeth
moste highly | to fauour. | Newly corrected and augmented. | Anno
1571. | Fœlix quem faciunt aliena pericula cautum. | *Imprinted at
London by* | *Thomas Marshe dwellynge* | in ff leetstreete, neare vnto |
S. Dūstanes Churche.

Colophon: IMPRINTED AT LON | *don by Thomas Marsh, dwelling* |
in ff leetstrete, neare vnto Sainte | Dunstanes Churche. | 1571.

Collation: ⋆4, A4, B–U8, X4, the second and third leaves of gathering ⋆,
the first two of A, and the first four of all other gatherings signed.
Title, verso blank; dedication, signed "W. B.", 2 leaves; *A TABLE* |
of the contentes of this booke. |, one leaf; *A BRIEFE MEMORI-* | *all of
Sundrie vnfortu-* | nate Englishmen. | [ornament] | *Willyam Baldwin
to* | the Reader. |, 2 leaves; text, beginning on A 3; colophon on X 4
verso.

Foliation: [1]–128, 140, 141, 141–168. The foliation begins on A3.

Irregularities: The following signatures are mistakenly printed: Eii [Dii], Siiii [Riiii]. Fols. 1 and 3 are unnumbered. The following foliations are mistakenly printed: 22 [20], 26 [19], 72 [64], 143 [145].

Description: Sm. 4°, printed in black letter. Size of leaf, $6\frac{15}{16} \times 4\frac{15}{16}$ in. (17·7 × 12·6 cm.).

[In the second copy of this edition, leaves D1, 2, 7, and 8 are from a different setting of type; *dart* is changed to *hart* on D1 [fol. 19], the catchword is omitted on this page, and there are numerous minor typographical changes. Fol. 26 is correctly numbered.]

Title: ❧ THE LAST / parte of the Mirour for / **Magistrates, wherein** / may be seene by exam- / ples passed in this / Realme, with / **howe greuous plagues, vices are puni-** / shed in great Princes and Magistrates, / **and howe frayle and vnstable worldly pro-** / **speritie is founde, where** Fortune / **seemeth moste highly** / **to fauour.** / Newly corrected and amended. / *Fœlix quem faciunt aliena pericula cautum.* / Imprinted at London / *by Thomas Marshe.* / Anno. 1574. / Cum Priuilegio.

Colophon: ❧ Imprinted at London by Thomas / **Marshe, dwelling in Fletestreete, neare** / vnto Saint Dunstones Churche. / Anno. 1574.

Collation: ⋆4, A4, B–X8, the second and third leaves of gathering ⋆, the first two of A, and the first four of all other gatherings signed. Title, verso blank; dedication, signed "W. B.", 2 leaves; A TABLE OF THE / contentes of this booke. /, 1 leaf; ❧ A BRIEFE MEMO- / riall of sondrie vnfortunate / **Englishmen.** / William Baldwin / **to the Reader.** /, 2 leaves; text, beginning on A3; colophon on X8.

Foliation: 1–[162]. The foliation begins on A3.

Irregularities: The following foliations are misnumbered: 72 [64], 76 [70], 119 [123], 155 [455], 156 [456]. Fol. 162 is not numbered, the number having been printed on 161 verso.

Description: Sm. 4°, printed in black letter. Size of leaf, $7\frac{1}{2} \times 5\frac{1}{2}$ in. (19·1 × 14 cm.).

Title: ❧ THE LAST / parte of the Mirour for / 𝕸𝖆𝖌𝖎𝖘𝖙𝖗𝖆𝖙𝖊𝖘, 𝖜𝖍𝖊𝖗𝖊𝖎𝖓 / may be seene by exam- / ples passed in this / Realme, with / 𝖍𝖔𝖜𝖊 𝖌𝖗𝖊𝖚𝖔𝖚𝖘 𝖕𝖑𝖆𝖌𝖚𝖊𝖘, 𝖛𝖎𝖈𝖊𝖘 𝖆𝖗𝖊 𝖕𝖚𝖓𝖎= / shed in gseat Princes and Magistrates, / 𝖆𝖓𝖉 𝖍𝖔𝖜𝖊 𝖋𝖗𝖆𝖞𝖑𝖊 𝖆𝖓𝖉 𝖚𝖓𝖘𝖙𝖆𝖇𝖑𝖊 𝖜𝖔𝖗𝖑𝖉𝖑𝖞 𝖕𝖗𝖔= / 𝖘𝖕𝖊𝖗𝖎𝖙𝖎𝖊 𝖎𝖘 𝖋𝖔𝖚𝖓𝖉𝖊, 𝖜𝖍𝖊𝖗𝖊 Fortune / 𝖘𝖊𝖊𝖒𝖊𝖙𝖍 𝖒𝖔𝖘𝖙𝖊 𝖍𝖎𝖌𝖍𝖑𝖞 / to fauour. / Newly corrected and amended. / *Fœlix quem faciunt aliena pericula cautum.* / Imprinted at London / *by Thomas Marshe.* / Anno. 1575. / Cum Priuilegio.

[This is a reissue of the 1574 edition, with a new setting of type for leaves *1–4, and with the colophon deleted from X 8 recto. It is bound with the second edition of the work of John Higgins, which had been first published in 1574. I transcribe the title-page for the sake of clarity: ❧ THE FIRST / parte of the Mirour for / 𝕸𝖆𝖌𝖎𝖘- 𝖙𝖗𝖆𝖙𝖊𝖘, 𝖈𝖔𝖓𝖙𝖆𝖞= / ning the falles of the first / infortunate Princes / of this lande: / *From the comming of Brute* / to the incarnation of our / 𝖘𝖆𝖚𝖎𝖔𝖚𝖗 𝖆𝖓𝖉 𝖗𝖊𝖉𝖊𝖒𝖊𝖗 / Iesu Christe. / *Ad Romanos. 13. 2.* / Quisquis se opponit potestati, Dei / ordinationi resistit. / Imprinted at London / *by Thomas Marshe.* / Anno. 1575. / Cum Priuilegio.]

Title: ❧ THE LAST / part of the Mirour for / 𝕸𝖆𝖌𝖎𝖘𝖙𝖗𝖆𝖙𝖊𝖘, 𝖜𝖍𝖊𝖗𝖊𝖎𝖓 𝖒𝖆𝖞 / be seene by examples passed in / this Realme, with / 𝖍𝖔𝖜 𝖌𝖗𝖊𝖊𝖓𝖔𝖚𝖘 𝖕𝖑𝖆𝖌𝖚𝖊𝖘, 𝖛𝖞𝖈𝖊𝖘 𝖆𝖗𝖊 𝖕𝖚- / nished in great Princes & Magistrats, / and how frayle and vnstable worldly prospe / 𝖗𝖎𝖙𝖞 𝖎𝖘 𝖋𝖔𝖚𝖓𝖉𝖊, 𝖜𝖍𝖊𝖗𝖊 𝕵𝖔𝖗𝖙𝖚𝖓𝖊 𝖘𝖊𝖊𝖒𝖊𝖙𝖍 / 𝖒𝖔𝖘𝖙 𝖍𝖎𝖌𝖍𝖑𝖞 𝖙𝖔 𝕵𝖆𝖚𝖔𝖚𝖗. / *Newly corrected and enlarged* / Fœlix quem faciunt aliena pericula cautum. / IMPRINTED / at London in Fleetstreete, neere vnto / 𝕾𝖆𝖎𝖓𝖈𝖙 𝕯𝖚𝖓𝖘𝖙𝖆𝖓𝖊𝖘 𝕮𝖍𝖚𝖗𝖈𝖍, 𝖇𝖞 / *Thomas Marsh.* / 1578. / Cum Priuilegio.

Colophon: None.

Collation: *4, A⁴, B–F⁸, G & H⁶, I–Z⁸, Aa⁴, the second and third leaves of gathering *, the first two of A, the first three of G & H and Aa, and the first four of all other gatherings signed. Title, verso blank; dedication, signed "W. B.", 2 leaves; A TABLE OF THE / Contentes of this Booke. /, 1 leaf; ❧ A BRIEFE MEMO- /

riall of sundry vnfortunate / Englishmen. / *WILLIAM BALDWIN* / *to the Reader* /, 2 leaves; text, beginning on A 3.

Foliation: 1–47, 47, 56–65, 65–68, 77–78, 78, 78–100, 100–105, 107–118, 120–123, 123–126, 128–129, 131–183, 183. The foliation begins on [A 3].

Irregularities: I 5, K 5, N 5, Q 5 are signed. L 4 is unsigned. D 1, E 2, E 4, O 1 are signed with Roman instead of Arabic numerals. Fol. 24 is unnumbered. Y 1, fol. 165, is missing in this copy. The following leaves are incorrectly numbered: 64 [71], 83 [84], 88 [89], 141 [142], 147 [137], 180 [18e], 182 [183].

Description: Sm. 4°, printed in black letter. Size of leaf, $7\frac{5}{16} \times 5\frac{1}{4}$ in. (18·6 × 13·4 cm.).

[This edition is generally found with a cancel. Fol. 39 [F 5] is cancelled and a new gathering of eight leaves substituted. This gathering is signed F¶. but is not foliated after the first leaf [39]. It contains the last three stanzas of the tragedy of King James the First, a new prose link to introduce the tragedy, "HOW DAME ELIANOR / Cobham Duchesse of Glocester. / for practising of witchcraft and Sorcery, suffred / open penance, and after was banished the / realme into the yle of Man.", the text of this tragedy, and a revised prose link to introduce the tragedy of Humphrey Duke of Gloucester.]

Title: THE / Mirour for Migistrates, / *wherein may bee seene, by* / examples passed in this / *Realme, with* / how greeuous plagues vices are puni- / shed in great Princes and Magistrates, / and how fraile and vnstable worldly / *prosperity is found, where For-* / *tune seemeth most highly* / *to fauour:* / *Newly imprinted, and with the addition of di-* / *uers Tragedies enlarged.* / AT LONDON / *in Fleetestreete, by Henry Marsh,* / being the assigne of Thomas / *Marsh.* / *1587.* / *CVM PRIVILEGIO.*

Colophon: IMPRINTED / *at London by Henry Marsh, being* / the assigne of Thomas Marsh, neare / *to Saint Dunstanes Churche* / in Fleetestreete. / 1587.

Collation: [ ]⁴, B–C⁴, A–Y⁸, Aa–Mm⁸; the first four leaves unsigned, the first leaf of B and C and the first four leaves of all other gatherings signed. First leaf, probably blank, missing; title, verso blank; dedication, signed "Iohn Higins.", 3 leaves; ⮞ A PREFACE TO / *the Reader.* /, signed "Iohn Higins.", 1 leaf; ⮞ THE CONTENTES / *of the booke.* /, 7 pages; Thomas Newton to the Reader, / *in the behalfe of this booke.* /, 1 page; *The authors induction.*, 2 leaves; text, A 1–O 4 recto; ⮞ A BRIEFE MEMO- / *riall of sondry vnfortu-* / nate Englishmen. / *WILLIAM BALDWINE* / to the reader. / ₓ*ₓ /, 3 pages; text, beginning on O 6; colophon on Mm 8 verso.

Foliation: 1–272. The foliation begins on A 1 [second series].

Irregularities: Signatures preceding D 3 use Roman numerals, but beginning with D 3, Arabic numerals, except E ii, E iii, and F ii. Aa 1 is signed A. The following foliations are mistakenly printed: 77 [67], 208 [20]. The title prints "Migistrates," but an "a" is inked-in over the first i.

Description: Sm. 4⁰. The dedication, signed "Iohn Higins.", the preface, "*WILLIAM BALDWINE* / to the reader.", and all links between the tragedies, are printed in roman type; "A PREFACE TO / *the Reader.*", by "Iohn Higins.", is printed in italics; and the tragedies are in black letter. Size of leaf, $7\frac{7}{16} \times 5\frac{1}{4}$ in. (18·9 × 13·3 cm.).

Appendix B

Indexes Showing the Titles and the Arrangement of the Tragedies in the Various Editions of the *Mirror for Magistrates**

The 1559 edition of the *Mirror* printed the following index of tragedies (the tragedy of "Good duke Humfrey murdered, and Elianor Cobham his wife banished" was not printed in the text):

⁊ The Contentes and Table of the booke.

The Epistle dedicatory.

¶ A prose to the Reader, continued betwene the tragedies from the beginning of the booke to the ende.

Tragedies beginning.

¶ Tresilian and his felowes hanged.	folio. i.
¶ Mortimer slayne.	folio. iiii.
¶ Thomas of Wodstocke murdered.	fol. viii.
¶ Mowbray lord Marshall banished.	fol. xii.
¶ King Richard the second murdered.	fol. xvi.
¶ Owen Glendour starved.	fol. xix.
¶ Percy earle of Northumberland beheaded.	fo. xxv.
¶ Richard earle of Cambridge beheaded.	fo. xxviii.
Thomas Montague earle of Salisbury slaine.	fo. xxx.
¶ King Iames the fyrst murdered.	fo. xxxvi.

* The variations of type in the titles indexed, and the line divisions in the titles, have been disregarded as irrelevant here. Contractions have been expanded as in the texts of the tragedies, and eccentricities in the printers' use of periods disregarded.

522

INDEXES

Finis.

The 1563 edition added to the index of the tragedies printed in 1559 an index of those printed in the 1563 edition for the first time. Save that it omitted all reference to the tragedy of "Good duke Humfrey", and indexed the tragedy of "William de la Poole" on fol. xl, and that of "Iacke Cade" on fol. xliiii, the index of "The contes and Table of the first parte of this Booke" followed the 1559 edition exactly in the arrangement and wording of the titles.

❡ The contentes of the second parte.

❡ A Prose to the Reader continued through the booke.

Complayntes beginning.

FINIS.

The 1571 edition rearranged the tragedies printed in the two earlier editions, rephrased their titles in the index, and added in the index the titles of two new tragedies (28 and 29) which did not appear in the text. (The editions of 1574 and 1575 followed this edition in their indexes, save that they omitted all mention of Tragedies 28 and 29.)

A TABLE
of the contentes of this booke.

INDEXES

FINIS.

The 1578 edition rephrased the titles of the tragedies in the index and restored Tragedy 11 to its original place in the index. This tragedy appears in the text for the first time. (See Introduction, pp. 17–18.)

A TABLE OF THE
Contentes of this Booke.

* Edward *is misprinted* Edware.

The 1587 edition printed in a common index the titles of the first and the last parts of the *Mirror*. The titles were all rephrased, and four new titles appeared to represent the tragedies added in this edition (70–72, 74). The tragedies of the original *Mirror* begin with 41.

THE CONTENTES
of the booke.

. . . .

INDEXES

F I N I S.

Appendix C

Collation of MS 364 in St John's College, Cambridge, with "The Induction" and "The complaynt of Henrye duke of Buckingham" (Tragedy 22) in the *Mirror for Magistrates**

The manuscript text for the induction and the tragedy is continuous, the general title being "*The Complaint of Henrie Duke of Buckinghame.*" In the induction the manuscript stanzas are not arranged as in the *Mirror* text, but appear in the following order: lines 1–231, 239–45, 337–43, 295–336, 232–38, 344–85, 246–94, 386–553. The *Mirror* text is regarded as the norm in this collation, and variations in the manuscript are noted.

[Title] *The Complaint of Henrie Duke of Buckinghame.*

    [9]   all bereved of
   [20]   me selfe
   [21]   the meades wheras
   [23]   the fair blew skies [*amended to* the azure skies]
   [24]   *Venus Hermes* in her message sped
   [29]   While *Scorpio* dreding *Sagittaries*
   [31]   *Ocean* aparte
   [33]   grislie fote with
   [37]   with glistening beames
   [41]   his ded hed [ded *deleted*]
   [42]   purper

* As elsewhere, I have expanded contractions. I have not considered problems arising from variations in the hand-writing.

[45] past Meridiem syx grees in my sight
[46] when that the stars fraught in the
[47] with flaming light [*amended to* with twinckeling light]
[54] thing is borne
[57] hevens beames
[58] stars beset in everie
[61] darke oppresse the daie
[62] sight resorted to
[63] chaunges here in
[65] that comes
[67] busie traunce presented
[68] suche falles of
[69] wisht their falles had bene descrive
[70] rest that fortune
[71] *left margin* *Sorowe apereth unto me.*
[71] with vneven pace [*amended to* with a doubled pace]
[72] night draw on
[74] wight that woe
[83] the stalke that [*amended to* the stone that]
[85] Her eien holow and drownd in teares aflote
[86] wherwith wyth lokes
[91] wight not half
[94] my heare vpstarted
[101] tel who thow
[111] and Lethes dedlie
[116] chaunce right woful
[121] thes wofull
[122] she shrekt
[127] stretcht me self
[133] and thus I then begoon.
[138] alas to comfort
[142] the stormes so
[143] never stram[ ] the [*amended to* never rore the]
[148] her terfull tale

[151]   men vnworthelie orethrowe

[152]   all arowe

[154]   thine eien shall

[158]   beating vpon

[167]   now bad me

[170]   gan worship her

[172]   thus pered vnto me [aper *written in and deleted before* thus]

[174]   I thus honnord her

[178]   and thow shalt   plaint thow make [thow *amended to* they]

[179]   swinge above the

[180]   but hugie is thunrest [*amended to* but grete is the unrest]

[182]   the place wher is this wofull plain [*amended to* hugie plain]

[185]   a hugie wood [*amended to* a mightie wood]

[196]   visite well hell [well *deleted*]

[200]   our traveles end

[201]   therwith I rose

[202]   astound we stalke [we *amended to* I] we proched nere

[203]   This dredfull

[204] *left margin* *The descripcion of hell. [The word "descripcion" is blotted in the MS.]*

[209]   a horrible

[212]   swelth that in thickend lumpes lies

[213]   such filthie vapours [*amended to* such stinking vapours]

[216]   we came whence

[217]   amid this dredfull

[218] *left margin* *Remorce of conscience.*

[231]   dethe but and yet [but *deleted*]

[232–38]   [*In the MS this stanza follows l. 336.*]

[232] *left margin* *Dreade.*

[233]   wyth fete vncerten

[234]   gastlie fear [*amended to* gastlie loke]

[239] *left margin* *Revenge.*

[241]   and sekes all meanes

[244]   flames as now determde is she

[245]   die the death or by deathe or by deathe venged to be [*the first* or by deathe *deleted*]

[*In the MS now follows the stanza, ll. 337–43, of the printed version.*]

[*In the MS now follow ll. 295–336.*]

[246]   Whan dethe had thus adrad vs with his dart

[247]   and shewed him self

[248]   lims softlie we gan depart

[252]   of povertie that

[253] *left margin* *Pouertie.*

[254]   consumd vnto the

[256]   on the same I thinke sure he had on

[257]   ten thousand patches [ten *amended to* a]

[260]   wild frute of

[266]   was povertie ybound

[271] *left margin* *Labour.*

[271]   of Busie labour brushing

[277]   night his misti

[279]   cesses he

[281] *left margin* *Sleape.*

[295] *left margin* *Olde age.*

[296]   his eien holowe

[307]   and syke

[308]   and still that he might live of Jove beseke [*amended to* and to be younge againe, of Jove beseke.]

[*In the MS here follows the stanza, ll. 316–22, deleted, but rewritten in its proper place.*]

[319]   to behold againe [*amended to* to enioie againe]

[322]   never in the

[325]   it did him

[328]   age liefe shold desire

[331]   and sometimes crept

[*In the MS here follows the misplaced stanza, ll. 232–38.*]

[*In the MS the stanza, ll. 337–43, follows l. 245.*]

535

[337] *left margin* *Maladie.*

[337] And nexte to her pale [*amended to* and fast by her pale]

[344] *left margin* *Famine.*

[351] gnawen in everie

[360] meanes ymay [y *deleted in* ymay]

[368] made the erth to

[372] *left margin* *Deathe.*

[377] ne rules ne realmes

[*After l.* 385 *there follow in the MS ll.* 246–94.]

[386] *left margin* *Warre*

[386] stode Mars warre [Mars *deleted*]

[395] fame *is deleted and* welthe ioy fame *are written in above the line,* welthe *and* ioy *being then also deleted.*

[397] til he their fame the welth their fame and al [fame the welth their fame *deleted,* riches welth their name *written in, and* riches *deleted*]

[400] *left margin* *Warres Targe and what was painted therin.*

[*In the MS l.* 404 *was written before l.* 403, *crossed out, and rewritten in the proper place.*]

[403] discord everie wher *is deleted and amended to* strief and wrath ech[ ] *which in turn is deleted.*

[405] *left margin* *Darius king of Percia whome Alexander conquerd.*

[407] in fight

[410] *left margin* *Hannibals victory conquest at Cannas.* ["*conquest*" *deleted*]

[414] *left margin* *The fight of at Trasimene and Trebie wher hanibal was victor in both.* ["*of*" *deleted*]

[417] *left margin* *The last battel betwen Scipio and Hanibal wher Scipio was victour.*

[419] Pompeie I saw and

[419] *left margin* *The Civile wars of pompei and Caesar.*

[423] *left margin* *The Crueltie of Scilla and Marius*

[426] *left margin* *Cirus slain by the quene Tomiris*

[428] *left margin* *Xerxes king of Percia put to flight in grece by.*

[432] *left margin* *Thebes raced by*

[433] *left margin* *Tirus sacked by Alexander*

[435] *left margin* *Troie destroied by the grecians.*

[450] force was now

[461] whurld to the ground [the *deleted*]

[463] *left margin* *Cassandra*

[466] *left margin* *Priam slain by Pirrhus.*

[470] descrive this dolful

[471] livelike fair ther did [*amended to* livelike fair did]

[477] Of from thes sightes as I cold scarce with drawe

[478] my terful eien [*line not completed*]

[480] *left margin* *Achaeron*

[481] and bubles swelth

[482] *left margin* *Charon*

[494] we stroke vp

[499] *left margin* *Cerberus*

[505] *left margin* *The hugie plaine wher al the princes weare. and al estates that died in aduersitie.*

[506] large kingdomes

[508] the wofull plain [*amended to* the hugie plain]

[509] shrekes the sundrie

[514] slain and here the lovers [*amended to* slain and lovers]

[533] *left margin* *Henrie duke of Buckingham apereth to sorow.*

[1] *left margin* *Buckinghams Complaint*

[10] and aien douncast

[11] this lief [*amended to* this live]

[12] fall that y shall tel belive [that *amended to* which]

[*The hand changes at l. 8. Lines 15–19 were written, deleted, and re-written in another hand. The MS continues in the other hand.*]

[21] tyme of nature

[22] harte so henrie [*amended to* harte to henrie]

[23] never him in weale ne woo

[25] his deathe he mekelie toke

[27] he proued

[29]   was eke my
[40]   fate algates wolde haue
[60]   our practises to [*amended to* secret driftes to]
[61]   me best seemd
[62]   Me selfe
[67]   but rather
[69]   To pull from
[85]   *left margin* Cirus end
[88]   his chief delyte
[99]   *left margin* Cambises end
[106] *left margin* Brutus and Cassius ende.
[107] iustlie was thy
[112] murder cryes out
[113] *left margin* Bessus end
[114] against the [*amended to* against his]

[*Between ll. 126 and 127 is inserted the stanza:*]

This worde murder so hidouslie soundes
And with soche poyson dothe infect the ayer
That oh alas I fele it how it woundes
My brest when it dothe in my mought repaire
And with soche dolor drounethe in despaire
My venomd harte that but for mercies might
I hyde my face before thalmighties sight.

[128] this foule faulte which [huge outrage *substituted for* foule
       faulte *and* huge *deleted*]
[129] dothe ofte befall
[134] *left margin* Alexanders dole for Clitus deth.
[142] spinnes in his
[153] in desert
[164] that with
[187] nephewes so deposd
[192] dounthrowing strait
[196] we, but who [*amended to* we, yet who]

[197]   blood that we
[208]   restles thoughtes so
[211] *left margin* *Valerius Maximus octauo Lib. ca.* 1°.
[220]   furtwith them to slepe them selves betake [*the first* them
       deleted]
[222]   such a heinous
[228]   but of the
[229]   till to
[231]   they lyve a
[246]   ill gain is
[259]   the resdew by
[264]   fortune do with
[267] *left margin* *Dionisius feare.*
[278]   dedlie feares beset
[280]   opprest by [*amended to* opprest with]
[281]   whos hate ne heapes
[283]   proud towers
[292] *left margin* *Phaereus crueltie*
[309] *left margin* *Pheraeus feare.*
[310]   trust ne proch
[315]   depe daungers that
[316]   and not
[321] *left margin* *Pheraeus end.*
[327]   the hatefull rout
[329]   beware er they do smert.
[336]   lo me self
[339]   but eke all
[343]   had nere so
[344]   I now once broke him in my
[346]   erst had yeld me to his hest [*amended to* erst we are his
      by sworne beheste]
[349]   then I thought alas
[350]   to me self thus weping wold
[354]   worldes disdain nor

[355] thos swete babes yet cold
[357] him but he wold reve them liefe
[359] rew nor wet
[362] hart endured to
[363] I rew in [*amended to* I wepe in]
[373] hart mine honnor

[*In the MS l. 377 was written before l. 376, crossed out, and rewritten in the proper place.*]

[378] gan more and more gan cast [*amended to* now more and more gan cast]
[379] I by secret [*amended to* I throughe secret]
[385] I me self
[386] feld amid his
[411] when I lest ferde
[414] a goodly [*amended to* a mighti]
[417] anenst that
[425] what doth bind
[428] *left margin* *Camillus exiled*
[432] not a horrible
[434] thow had lost
[439] cruell age vnthankfull
[440] fals vnconstancie
[442] *left margin* *Scipio exiled after he had overthrowen Hanibal the mortal fo of Rome.*
[442] mirrhour mai thow
[445] that recured the
[448] thow had so
[454] disdain saies evermore to
[455] *left margin* [*Th*]*e wordes that Scipio* [*w*]*rote on his graue.*
[455] vnth *is deleted at the beginning of the line.*
[459] of false
[463] *left margin* *Milciades cast in prison wher he died.*
[463] happie had thow

[468] and not cast the in depth of prison tho so [tho *deleted*]

[470] Oh how hard and steli hartes had thay [Oh *amended to* lo *and finally to* Alas   had *amended to* have *but restored to* had]

[471] contented thus to [*amended to* contented there to]

[474] that to thie corpse ay buriall do they denie [*amended to* that buriall to thie corpse eke they denie]

[476] thie guives on him to [*amended to* put on thie guives to]

[477] ^{left}_{margin} *Hanibal exiled after so maini conquestes.*

[477] hanniball so long

[478] and trustles fortune [trustles *amended to* brittell]

[479] his countries state

[480] that livd for

[483] of thie countrie art throwen

[486] the same [the *amended to* this]

[487] or is it crueltie her self that doth constrain [*amended to* or crueltie her self doth she constrain]

[490] but false faythe [*amended to* but fickell faythe]

[496] tried this trew [*amended to* tried it trew]

[497] an host ther

[499] to me self

[508] the groves with

[519] on that erst

[521] to gentries state

[523] of vearie trust

[530] thousand pound and

[533] strait bewraied

[540] with thos wordes

[542] he feld fell doun ded and [*amended to* he ded fell he doune and]

[543] amasd beheld him when he wold revart

[544] but greifes on greifes stil heapt about

[547] ^{left}_{margin} *The descripcion of midnight.*

[550] slept beside their

[560] partridge dremd not of the sparhaukes fate

541

[570] sodenlie sowned [*amended to* in sorte thus sowned]
[577] the rage that [*amended to* the wretche that]
[580] out sightes and
[588] Ragethe aienst him that erst betrayd
[594] and ayenst the
[596] of sightes sometymes
[604] that him dyd strayne
[610] as still as
[612] that downe ayen fell
[613] lookes cast vp and [*amended to* lookes vp cast and]
[616] abraied theise
[618] the welkyn wrapte
[620] the panges playntes that [panges *deleted*]
[622] let my yelde
[623] ye ye I
[625] snakie hed heare [hed *deleted*]
[628] afreshe the venomde
[633] That wreckedst [*the* d *deleted*] wronges and geves the
[649] soonne the moone and sters [and *amended to* the]
[651] the [?] the ayer [*amended to* the erthe the ayer]
[653] kindnes hath [hath *amended to* hast]
[654] truethe ne trust
[655] move ne thy
[657] in twayne [*amended to* in tway]
[661] of thyne vndoubted
[665] curse ayenst the
[671] and foule reproche
[673] let that be
[676] and sightes canne
[678] woorthie of sorowes
[679] oughtes yet to
[680] *left margin* here he curseth Banaster wishing him such plages as befel to him in dede.
[704] selfe maye see

[706] she which erst

[707] now moughtes lothe

[718] that fayne wolde dye [dye *amended to* deye]

[729] aye where am I what thing or what is this [what is this *amended to* whence is this]

[731] my sprite agasted [sprite *amended to* thought]

[735] and being ayen retourned thus he sayed [*amended to* when to him self returned, thus he saied.]

[*Between ll.* 739 *and* 740 *two lines are written and so deleted as to be indecipherable in the photostat. L.* 740 *has been amended to read as it does in the* Mirror, *but the original reading and the first emendation are also so deleted as to be indecipherable.*]

[743] as fates and fortune wold the same [*amended to* as fortune wold permit the same]

[*Between ll.* 745 *and* 746 *are written two lines which are deleted:*
but when the stormy waves of mine vnrest [hugie *substituted for* stormy *and deleted*]
with stormie thretes begin to have [?]rest

[746] in that of [in *deleted*]

[*Between ll.* 746 *and* 747 *is written and deleted the line:*
and I alas of lief and all bereft

[*Between ll.* 747 *and* 748 *is written and deleted:*
hath turnd the whele th

[748] hath turnd the whele & with vnfrendly frown [with vnfrendly frown *amended to* with a dolfull fall]

[756] *lower margin* so felle Iulius
so fell Nero
and so furth.
inveigh against fortune

[757] that happen vnto

[758] never felt no

[763] their hart more

[765] first born an erle then duke by true discent [*various phrases
have been substituted and deleted:* a furst   a lord   a lord,
an erle   then and. *Finally amended to* furst lord, then
erle, last duke by true discent]

[771] my mishap

[773] in welth in wo how fortune wold me

[775] kesars bid al

[777] rewles to right [to *deleted*]

[At the close of Buckingham's complaint there is written "*Finis.*" Four
additional pages of the manuscript contain, however, additional stanzas,
parts of stanzas, and suggestions which seem to relate to Sackville's
work on the *Mirror*. These pages are written in the Italian hand, with
occasional reversion to the secretary hand. I transcribe them here,
omitting, however, the deleted and discarded phrases. As heretofore,
I expand all contractions.]

Be this phaeton whirled within his cart
made all the Orient blushe at his vprise
and with a lashe that gave a fieri smart
whipt furth his stedes which now so fast them hies
that from their nostrelles sparkes of flame outflies
the faier and hevenlie light vnfolding then
with thousand cares to selie mortal men

Not maro with his meters maiestie
his loftie vers nor yet his wailful stile
wherwith he wrote the dolful tragedy
of Didoes deth by false Eneas wile
nor old ovid in his vnkind exile
his weping pen that wrott his plaintes with teares
could not set furth my sorowes nor my feares.

Not Chaucer cheif that wrot in english vers
above the best that ever brittain bred
not his most pitous plaint that sure wold perce

544

the hardest hart that can be thought or sed
of the black knight for dolour welny ded
nor yet the pen wherwith he wrote the pain
of woful mary woful magdalain

no not the hand that did endite complaint
of faithful Troilus in all his woe
nor when Chresed did make so ruful plain[t]
beknowing him whom she disceved so
although so conningli ful wel I know
was never boke that is or shalbe writ
what though this sorow far surpassed it.

 [*In l.* 4 forsaked *is written in as an alternative to* disceved.]

not worthy wiat worthiest of them all
whom Brittain hath in later yeres furthbrought
his sacred psalmes wherin he singes the fall
of David dolling for the guilt he wrought
and Vries deth which he so dereli bought
not his hault vers that tainted hath the skie
for mortall domes to hevenlie and to hie

Not surrea he that hiest sittes in chair
of glistering fame for ay to live and raighn
not his proud ryme that thunders in the aier
nor al the plaintes wherin he wrote his pain
when he lay fetterd in the fyry chain
of cruell love. they cold no whit suffyse
texpresse thes plaints in ful suffys my wyse

And lest of all I that haue les then lest
may once attempt to pen the smallest part
of those houge dolours boiling in the brest
of Buckingham or sorowes endles smart
a drery sight to hevie for my hart
I want the stede wherof thei haue the store
I rather crave pardon then praise herefore.

545

For in my stile no sugred sawes are fownd
my songes ar not of solace or delight
of sobbes and sighes they rather yeld the sownd
and wofull dities all with dolour dight
black teares alas is that wherwith I write
my mirth is mone and all my plesure pain
my swetest ioy to sorow and to plain.

my hed is heapt with paines and pensiefnes
my hart doth harbour nothing but vnrest
my hand hath nought but wo and hevines
huge heapes of harmes wherwith I am distrest
sighes vpon sighes smoke furth out of mi brest
streames floods and seas out of mine eies furth flow
I can not I depaint my smallest wo.

and well lo sittes me al this drerines
for in mi birth (ay me) I wot not why
but all was set to wo and hevines
[*Above* to wo and hevines *is written as an alternative* pight on
   woe and hevines]
saturne et?

Loke in the prolouge of Bochas fol. lxiiii.
I never lened to Helicon. so mayni floods as part Brittain part
   me from it.
I never drank of pernasus spring
save that a drop I wot not how pardi
was in my mouth let fal by mercurie
and that made me to haue a desire. but strait mercury departed
   from me
mine eloquence is rudenes.

I have no fresh licour out of the conduictes of Calliope.
I haue no flowers of rethoricke through Clio.

note the ix muses dwel with Citherea on parnaso.

of such as live ill yf thow
wilt nedes live their evell lief remembre withall their miserable
   deth.
I am to rude to boistous is my stile
vnsmoth and ragged more rougher then the file.

his golden raies oreguilt the hilles anone
and with his warme and gladsome leames gan drie
the erth that erst as cold as any stone
in teares bedewed all the night did lie
wailing the absence of the worldes eie.

remember Mr Burdens promise for the
showing of Senecas [   ] touching the
captation of auram popularem.
[*Miss Hearsey reads* chore *for the word I cannot read.*]

Appendix D

Collation of "The Lamentation of the kyng of Scotts" and "The batayle of Brampton or Flod-don feild", in Harleian MS 2252, now in the British Museum, with "The Lamen-tation of King Iames the fourth" and "The bataile of Brampton, or Flod-don fielde" (Tragedies 31 and 32) in the *Mirror for Magistrates*★

[The manuscript fulfils the description given in Prose 31. The marginal notes are in a different, and apparently a later, hand (or hands). The collation makes it apparent that the emendations were those used in the *Mirror* text.]

[Title] of the kyng of Scotts [*The title ends with* Scotts]
 [7] man crye sore
 [11] I began to
 [12] me sore aferde
 [13] sawe hee had a berd
 [15] byn steked
 [18] crowne on hed
 [19] I lackyd nothyng.
 [21] order my realme I cowde with a whyte wand
 [22] from lande

★ I have transcribed "ff" as it appears in the text, instead of as "F." Contractions are expanded.

[29] I purposyd

[34] be the

[35] yn sorowffull

[37] chaungeth aye me [*A marginal note reads* a newe *for* aye me]

[38] I bownde sometyme

[39] yn mewe

[42] to my oythe

[43] kyng herry

[44] ffolow your apetyte I dyde as ye me badde

[47] but showyll [*A marginal note would substitute* hence for to fade *for* showyll & spade]

[52] yn my awen torne I

[54] payn eternall for my Inequyte

[58] me & my   owr shame [*A marginal note would insert before* to *the words* & ek]

[63] ffaveryst he wynneth

[65] was only   of my woo

[66] but began by

[69] curssyd with candyll boke & bell

[70] I cowde not achyve yn no maner a degre

[71] assyste a sysmatyke we dyde not well [*A marginal note substitutes* an enemye *for* a sysmatyke]

[73] Crysts awtoryte I dyde refuse [*A marginal note substitutes* commademetes *for* awtoryte, *and* all *is inserted before* refuse]

[74] the sensurys of the chyrche [*A marginal note substitutes* breatche of myne othe *for* sensurys of the chyrche]

[75] am dammed by ryghtfull Justyce [*A marginal note substitutes* domed *for* dammed]

[76] is hys sentens and cruell swerde

[77] mercy lord

[78] thowe soffryd

[82] and exsampyll

[83] be take yn the

[84] pay a lyek

[85]   were with power

[91]   ffere & he   [*A marginal note substitutes* that *for* &]

[92]   The chyrche and   [*A marginal note substitutes* king *for* chyrche]

[95]   doth god neythyre love

[97]   Chrystyn man yn worse case

[98]   then I wrechyd caytyfe that

[99]   or chyrche yerd   maner of place

[101]   erthe abborryth me / all men doyth me   [doyth *marked for deletion*]

[102]   ffrends forsakyth me & hathe no   [*A marginal note substitutes* haue *for* hathe]

[107]   is that dothe

[116]   commons for

[119]   highe mercyffull lord for me pray

[*After the signature is added, in a later hand,* he was slayne at Bramstones hill the yeare of our Lorde 1513]

[*Immediately following the note concerning King James's death, there is written, in the later hand, the title which is used for the new tragedy in the* Mirror.]

[Title]   of Branston   our lorde 1513
[*At the top of the next page, on which the description of the battle is given, there is written* so thy helpe o lorde preservde our princes ryghte.]

[2]   with gawdes of [gawdes *crossed out and* joyes *written in*]

[3]   have mercy on kyng Jemys sowle   [*A marginal note substitutes for this line* K. J. is deade haue mercye on us all]

[4]   thy pete on him Lord thow magnyfye [thow *is crossed out and* do *written in. This line is* l. 4 *in the MS,* l. 4 *of the text is* l. 5 *of the MS,* l. 5 *of the text is omitted in the MS. A marginal note substitutes* power in us *for* pete on hym]

[7]   By the helpe of Saynte George owr Ladyes knyghte [*A marginal note inserts* so *at the beginning of the line. Another note substitutes*

o lorde preserved our Henryes ryght *for* of Saynte George owr Ladyes knyghte. *Part of the emendation has been corrected so that its original wording is indecipherable.*]

[10]	he has won
[14]	of S george owr ladyes knyghte
[17]	wonderly
[21]	By the helpe of S. george owr ladys knyghte
[23]	gretythe
[25]	whate ye make
[26]	peax ye haue
[28]	of S. george owr ladys knyghte
[29]	Abyde he sayd. Els were hyt grete dyshoneste [*A marginal note substitutes* trecherye *for* dyshoneste]
[31]	[*An insertion above the line substitutes* as batayle geve *for* to geve batell]
[33]	was cryed.
[34]	men ar redely
[35]	of Saynte george owr ladyes knyght
[37]	Vaunte Warde /
[41]	Pray you
[42]	By the helpe of Sente george our ladyes knyght
[44]	Conyes
[47–48]	ffor hym pray all England for hee Was the nobyleste man yn that ffyghte
[49]	of S. georg our ladys knyght
[50]	and the Lord
[53]	nobylls of
[55]	day & nyght
[56]	of S. George our ladys knyght
[57]	lusty & ffrank
[58]	hym selff as yn
[62]	them ther
[63]	By the helpe of S. george our ladys knyghte
[68]	bothe too

[70]   of S. george owr ladys knyghte
[72]   Ever more blessyd mote thowe be
[73]   wyte /. Well call hym we may
[74]   debyte most trusty of England was
[77]   of S george owr ladys knyght
[80]   as delygente as
[81]   Applyard ded helpe
[82]   Joye it was to see at the same
[84]   of S. george our ladyes knyght
[90]   well they   them yn
[91]   of S. George our Ladyes Knyght.
[94]   a Royall man
[96]   a royale   beshope of Elye
[97]   men which manly
[98]   of S. Georg owr ladyes knyght
[99]   then dyd the goonnes / begyn a
[100] vayntward
[102] many a on
[103] Whoo drust abyde strokks neuer agayn returned on
[104] by power of
[105] And by the helpe of S. George owr ladys knyght.
[106] They devyded them yn embushements with
[107] yn thys maner
[108] men that tyme ffled for ffere
[109] that seyng Kyng
[111] that gracyous ffleyng
[112] By the helpe of S. George owr ladys knyght.
[114] With the comlyeste company yn crystentte
[117] the holy Trenyte
[118] hym to showe there hys
[119] By the helpe of Sent Georg our ladyes knyght
[122] thands
[126] of S george owr Ladys Knight
[130] Ancre / the scotts dyd myche tene

[132] yet escapett he dyd by grace of god almyght [*A marginal note substitutes* not vanquisht in the fyght *for* by grace of god almyght]

[133] By the help of S. george our ladys knyght.

[136] Anlett

[138] as stone

[139] slewe vpe the Scotts by power of god almyght [*A marginal note substitutes* lyke a worthy wyght *for* by power of god almyght]

[140] By the helpe of S. George owr ladyes knyght

[143] bells dyd Ryng that lay

[144] scotts they were

[145] euermore there he

[146] Go we to hyt good ffellows / All shalbe owrs by the grace of gods myght [*A marginal note substitutes* or night *for* by the grace of gods myght]

[147] of S. Georg our ladyes knyght [*misspelled* lades knght]

[150] To ffle and ffal they non other grace [*In the later hand* had *is inserted after* they]

[151] ys shee

[152] to the grete rebuke to hym & hys posteritie [*The later hand amends it to the reading of the* Mirror *text.*]

[153] all vnto flyghte

[154] By the helpe of S. George owr ladys knyghte

[155] lythe slayne

[159] peax

[160] thys wyse

[161] By the helpe of S. george owr ladys knyghte

[163] the lovyng

[164] Whate euery man   had lyberte

[165] honor be to

[167] From danger dolefull us defendyng

[168] By the helpe of S. george owr ladys knyghte

[169] and ruler   of all

[170] vs suffryd

[171] Haue mercye on kyng jemys sowle
[172] Indulgens graunte hym for hys transgressyon
[174] And lawde honor & prayse be to the our lord almyghty
[175] for the redde lyon ys confusyd & the whyte hathe vyctory
[179] sayngs
[182] yn thus maner

> [*At the close of the poem is written, in the same hand:*
>
> Explycit Bellum de Brampton
> Per FFraunces Dyngley de manston.
>
> *The* B *in* Bellum *is apparently written as an L by a mistake of the scribe.*]